An Introduction To
Old
Testament
Study

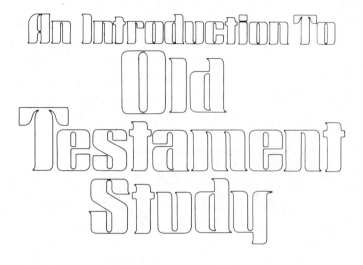

An Introduction To Old Testament Study

John H. Hayes

Abingdon Press • Nashville

AN INTRODUCTION TO OLD TESTAMENT STUDY

Copyright © 1979 by Abingdon

This book is printed on recycled, acid-free paper.

Library of Congress Cataloging-in-Publication Data

HAYES, JOHN HARALSON, 1934—
  An introduction to Old Testament study.
  Bibliography: p.
  Includes indexes.
  ISBN 0-687-01363-1
  1. Bible. O.T.—Criticism, interpretation, etc.—History.
  2. Bible. O.T.—Introductions. I. Title.
BS1160.H38
221.6   78-20993

94 95 96 97 98 99 00 01 02 03—15 14 13 12 11 10

MANUFACTURED IN THE UNITED STATES OF AMERICA

For

MEGAN ELIZABETH

my

בת זקנים

CONTENTS

ABBREVIATIONS

ANET   *Ancient Near Eastern Texts*, ed. J. B. Pritchard, Princeton: Princeton University Press, ³1969.

ASR   *American Sociological Review.*

BASOR   *Bulletin of the American Schools of Oriental Research.*

BJRUL   *Bulletin of the John Rylands University Library.*

CA   *Canon and Authority*, ed. G. W. Coats and B. O. Long, Philadelphia: Fortress Press, 1977.

CBQ   *Catholic Biblical Quarterly.*

CHB   *Cambridge History of the Bible* I–III, London: Cambridge University Press, 1963–70.

CJT   *Canadian Journal of Theology.*

CMHB   *The Canon and Masorah of the Hebrew Bible*, ed. S. Z. Leiman, New York: KTAV, 1974.

COTS   R. E. Clements, *A Century of Old Testament Study*, London: Lutterworth Press = *One Hundred Years of Old Testament Interpretation*, Philadelphia: Westminster Press, 1976.

CP   *Classical Philology.*

CTM	*Concordia Theological Monthly.*
EJ	*Encyclopedia Judaica.*
GOBT	K. Koch, *The Growth of the Biblical Tradition: The Form-Critical Method,* London/New York: A. & C. Black/ Charles Scribner's Sons, 1969.
HDB	*Hastings' Dictionary of the Bible.*
HTR	*Harvard Theological Review.*
HUCA	*Hebrew Union College Annual.*
IDB	*Interpreter's Dictionary of the Bible.*
IDBS	*Interpreter's Dictionary of the Bible Supplementary Volume.*
IEJ	*Israel Exploration Journal.*
IJH	*Israelite and Judaean History,* ed. J. H. Hayes and J. M. Miller, London/Philadelphia: SCM Press/Westminster Press, 1977.
Int	*Interpretation.*
IOS	*Israel Oriental Studies.*
JAAR	*Journal of American Academy of Religion.*
JBL	*Journal of Biblical Literature.*
JBR	*Journal of Bible and Religion.*
JQR	*Jewish Quarterly Review.*
JR	*Journal of Religion.*
JSS	*Journal of Semitic Studies.*
JSOT	*Journal for the Study of the Old Testament.*
JTS	*Journal of Theological Studies.*
LTQ	*Lutheran Theological Quarterly.*
MD	*Magnalia Dei: The Mighty Acts of God,* ed. F. M. Cross, W. E. Lemke, and P. D. Miller, Jr., Garden City: Doubleday, 1976.
MQ	*McCormick Quarterly.*
OTFC	*Old Testament Form Criticism,* ed. J. H. Hayes, San Antonio: Trinity University Press, 1974.

OTMS	*Old Testament and Modern Study*, ed. H. H. Rowley, London: Oxford University Press, 1951.
OTS	*Oudtestamentische Studiën.*
PAAJR	*Proceedings of the American Academy for Jewish Research.*
QHBT	*Qumran and the History of the Biblical Text*, ed. F. M. Cross and S. Talmon, Cambridge: Harvard University Press, 1975.
RB	*Revue biblique.*
RTI	D. A. Knight, *Rediscovering the Traditions of Israel*, Missoula: Scholars Press, 1975.
SAIW	*Studies in Ancient Israelite Wisdom*, ed. J. L. Crenshaw, New York: KTAV, 1976.
SBLSP	*Society of Biblical Literature Seminar Papers.*
SP	*Studia Patristica.*
TB	*Tyndale Bulletin.*
TDNT	*Theological Dictionary of the New Testament.*
VT	*Vetus Testamentum.*
VTS	*Vetus Testamentum Supplements.*
WHJP	*World History of the Jewish People, First Series: Ancient Times.*
ZAW	*Zeitschrift für die alttestamentliche Wissenschaft.*

PREFACE

This volume seeks to introduce the reader to the issues and approaches involved in contemporary Old Testament study. In a limited way, it also focuses on the history of Old Testament study. It does not pretend to be a full introduction to the Old Testament itself.

Since the work is intended for an English reading audience, only items written in English or available in translation are noted in the bibliographies. No attempt has been made to present full bibliographical data. Those works have been noted which are of special importance or which provide the reader with summaries of research or additional bibliographical information.

A word of thanks is due to two Candler students, Dr. Lyle Linder and Sammy Davis, who have read the manuscript and made suggestions about content and style as well as assisted with preparation of the indexes. Joyce Ann Baird is due a special note of appreciation for typing the manuscript with her usual skill and competence.

John H. Hayes
Candler School of Theology

CHAPTER 1

THE CANON
OF THE
OLD TESTAMENT

H. F. von Campenhausen, *The Formation of the Christian Bible* (Philadelphia: Fortress Press, 1972); S. Z. Leiman, *The Canonization of Hebrew Scripture: The Talmudic and Midrashic Evidence* (Hamden, CT: Anchon Books, 1976); J. P. Lewis, "What Do We mean by Jabneh?" *JBR* XXXII (1964) 125-32 = *CHMB*, 254-61; R. Meyer, "The Canon and Apocrypha in Judaism," *TDNT* III (1966) 978-87; A. Momigliano, "The Second Book of Maccabees," *CP* LXX (1975) 81-91; A. Oepke, *"Biblio apokryphoi* in Christianity," *TDNT* III (1966) 987-1000; H. M. Orlinsky, "The Canonization of the Hebrew Bible and the Exclusion of the Apocrypha," in his *Essays in Biblical Culture and Bible Translation* (New York: KTAV, 1974) 257-86; *idem*, "The Septuagint as Holy Writ and the Philosophy of the Translators," *HUCA* XLVI (1975) 89-114; J. D. Purvis, *The Samaritan Pentateuch and the Origin of the Samaritan Sect* (Cambridge: Harvard University Press, 1968); J. A. Sanders, "Cave 11 Surprises and the Question of Canon," *MQ* XXI (1968) 284-98 = *CMHB* 37-51; *idem*, *Torah and Canon* (Philadelphia: Fortress Press, 1972); *idem*, "Adaptable for Life: The Nature and Function of Canon," *MD*, 531-60; A. C. Sundberg, Jr., "The Old Testament in the Early Church: A Study in Canon," *HTR* LI (1958) 205-26; *idem*, *The Old Testament of the Early Church* (Cambridge: Harvard University Press, 1964); *idem*, "The Protestant Old Testament Canon: Should It Be Re-examined?" *CBQ* XXVIII (1966) 194-203; *idem*, "The 'Old Testament': A Christian Canon," *CBQ* XXX (1968) 143-55 = *CMHB*, 99-111; *idem*, "The Bible Canon and the Christian Doctrine of Inspiration," *Int* XXIX (1975) 352-71; G. Vermes, *The Dead Sea Scrolls in English* (Hammondsworth/Baltimore: Penguin Books, 1962, ²1975); B. Z. Wacholder, *Eupolemus: A Study of Judaeo-Greek Literature* (Cincinnati: Hebrew Union College, 1974); S. Zeitlin, "An Historical Study of the Canonization of the Hebrew Scriptures," *PAAJR* III (1931-32) 121-58 = *CMHB*, 164-201.

The Old Testament or Hebrew Bible, considered sacred by Jews and Christians, exists in three major canonical forms. These are the Jewish, Roman Catholic (and Orthodox), and Protestant canons. The Roman Catholic Church accepts forty-six books as the canonical Old Testament. Protestantism possesses a canon of thirty-nine books. The Jewish canon consists of twenty-four books, which are identical with the thirty-nine of Protestants although in a different enumeration and arrangement.

The Jewish canon contains the following books separated into three divisions:

I. Torah (Pentateuch)
1. Genesis (Bereshith)
2. Exodus (Shemoth)
3. Leviticus (Wayiqra)
4. Numbers (Bemidbar)
5. Deuteronomy (Debarim)

II. Nebiim (Prophets)
Former
6. Joshua (Yehoshua)
7. Judges (Shofetim)
8. Samuel (Shemuel)
9. Kings (Melakim)
Latter
10. Isaiah (Yeshayahu)
11. Jeremiah (Yirmeyahu)
12. Ezekiel (Yehezqel)
13. Book of the Twelve
      (Tere Asar)

III. Kethubim (Writings)
14. Psalms (Tehillim)
15. Job (Iyyob)
16. Proverbs (Mishle)
17. Ruth
18. Song of Songs (Shir Hashirim)
19. Ecclesiastes (Qoheleth)
20. Lamentations (Ekah)
21. Esther
22. Daniel
23. Ezra-Nehemiah (Ezra-Nehemyah)
24. Chronicles (Dibre Hayamim)

The books in the Roman Catholic canon which are not found in the Jewish Bible and Protestant Old Testament are Tobit, Judith, Wisdom of Solomon, Ecclesiasticus (or Wisdom of Ben Sirach), Baruch (including the so-called "Epistle of Jeremiah"), I Maccabees, and II Maccabees. In addition, Esther and Daniel in the Catholic canon contain material not found in the Protestant and Jewish canons. Six additions, comprising 107 verses, appear in the larger version of the book of Esther. The longer form of Daniel incorporates the Prayer of Azariah and the song of the

Three Young men (68 verses), the Story of Susanna (64 verses), and the Story of Bel and the Dragon (42 verses). The Greek Orthodox canon is identical with that of Roman Catholicism except for the book of Baruch, which is excluded from the Orthodox canon.

Some of the twenty-four books of the Jewish canon are divided in the following way to produce the thirty-nine books in the Protestant canon: Samuel, Kings, Chronicles, and Ezra-Nehemiah are divided into eight books; and the Book of the Twelve is divided into twelve separate works (the prophets from Hosea to Malachi). In the Christian canons, many of the works found in the third section of the Jewish canon have been distributed to fit into a fourfold pattern of law, historical books, poetry and wisdom, and prophetical writings. Ruth, Chronicles, Ezra-Nehemiah, and Esther are placed with the historical works. Lamentations and Daniel are placed with the prophets. In addition, several of the poetical and wisdom books appear in the Christian canons in a slightly different order than in the Jewish canon. In the Catholic canon, Tobit and Judith follow Nehemiah, Wisdom of Solomon and Ecclesiasticus follow the Song of Solomon, Baruch follows Lamentations, and I and II Maccabees come after Malachi.

How did these different canons of the Hebrew scriptures or the Old Testament develop? Why are they so different? Is it possible to determine when and how the ancient Jewish and Christian communities established and recognized a sacred collection of canonical Old Testament writings? What was the relationship between the early Jewish and Christian canons of the Old Testament? Throughout history, these questions have been matters of discussion and debate. In recent years, new interest in canonical studies and new approaches to the problems involved in the history of the canon have developed and become a central concern in biblical studies (see especially Sanders and Sundberg).

Before discussing the origin and nature of the three Old

Testament canons, a few preliminary factors should be noted. (1) The term "canon," which derives from a Semitic word meaning "reed" and then "rod," "rule," and "norm," was first applied to a collection of sacred writings by church fathers in the fourth century CE. Prior to this time, the biblical materials were referred to as "scripture(s)," "sacred scriptures," or books that "defile the hands." The last expression meant that the writings were so holy that the holiness must be washed away from the hands after handling them. (2) The concept of canon implies the existence of a collection of writings which are accepted as authoritative, as unchangeable, and as normative for religious faith and practice. Thus a canon of scripture has both positive and negative connotations. Positively, a canon denotes certain works that are included in the category of sacred and authoritative. Negatively, a canon excludes certain works which are not accepted as authoritative. A canon exists only when both the exclusive and inclusive factors are consciously functioning in the concerns of the religious community. (3) The creation of biblical canons in both Judaism and Christianity was a final stage in a long process. The Bible certainly does not represent all the literature produced in ancient Israel. The scriptures themselves refer to extinct writings such as the "book of the wars of Yahweh" (Num 21:14), the "book of Jashar" (Josh 10:13; II Sam 1:18), and the "book of the acts of Solomon" (I Kings 11:41) and so on. In the course of Israel's history many such works were lost, destroyed, or perhaps partially incorporated into biblical works. In addition to now lost works, numerous writings which have survived never possessed or were gradually excluded from any widespread usage in the process which produced closed canons of scripture. Behind the works which became canonical lies a long process in which their contents were shaped and fashioned. The study of this process has been called "canonical criticism" (see Sanders, especially 1976). Both internal and external concerns contributed to this shaping and fashioning process. The community or parts thereof responded to new crises and new modes of life so as to preserve its identity while adapting to new conditions. In this chapter, we are concerned primarily with the final phases of the process, that is, with the inclusion-exclusion operation.

A. Early References to a Developing Canon

The first available evidence suggesting the existence of sacred and authoritative writings identical to portions of the Old Testament comes from the second century BCE. In his hymn praising famous men, Jesus ben Sirach provides a roll call of the heroes of the faith (see Ecclesiasticus 44-49). References to these men follow the order in which they appear in the Hebrew scriptures. The names included are drawn from the Torah (Enoch, Noah, Abraham, Isaac, Jacob, Moses, Aaron, Phinehas), the Prophets (Joshua, Caleb, Samuel, Nathan, David, Solomon, Rehoboam, Jeroboam, Elijah, Elisha, Hezekiah, Isaiah, Josiah, Jeremiah, Ezekiel, the Twelve Prophets), and perhaps the Writings (Zerubbabel, Joshua, the high priest Nehemiah). References to Zerubbabel and Joshua could have been influenced by the prophetical books of Haggai and Zechariah. Written in Hebrew about 180 BCE, this work demonstrates that Jesus ben Sirach possessed knowledge of the main figures in the scriptures. This implies some collection of writings or at least a standardized version of history. If Ben Sirach's list of Israelite heroes follows a collection of texts, then it reflects the following order: the Torah, followed by Joshua, Judges, Samuel, Kings, Isaiah, Jeremiah, Ezekiel, and the Twelve. In addition, Ben Sirach seems to have been familiar with and used other works which later became part of the canon. His writing does not reflect the use of Ruth, Song of Songs, Esther, Daniel, and perhaps Job (see Leiman, 29).

When Ben Sirach's grandson translated his grandfather's Hebrew work into Greek sometime after 132 BCE, he provided the translation with a short explanatory prologue. In this foreword to the work, the grandson comments on his ancestor's reasons for writing:

Whereas many great teachings have been given to us through the law and the prophets and the others that followed them, on account of which we should praise Israel for instruction and wisdom; and since it is necessary not only that the readers themselves should acquire understanding but also that those who love learning should be able to help the outsiders by both speaking and writing, my grandfather Jesus, after devoting himself especially to the reading of the law and the prophets and the other books of our fathers, and after acquiring considerable proficiency in them, was himself also led to write something pertaining to instruction and wisdom, in order that, by becoming conversant with this also, those who love learning should make even greater progress in living according to the law.

You are urged therefore to read with good will and attention, and to be indulgent in cases where, despite our diligent labor in translating, we may seem to have rendered some phrases imperfectly. For what was originally expressed in Hebrew does not have exactly the same sense when translated into another language. Not only this work, but even the law itself, the prophecies, and the rest of the books differ not a little as originally expressed.

A number of elements in this passage are significant for an understanding of this historical development of the canon. (1) The grandson of Ben Sirach refers in three places to what appears to be two clearly defined collections of sacred writings: the Law *(Torah)* and the Prophets *(Nebiim)*. (2) A third group of texts is noted and designated "the others that followed them," "the other books of the fathers," and "the rest of the books." (3) No single term or descriptive phrase is used to refer to this third body of writings. (4) The grandson makes claims for Ben Sirach's work which seem to place it on a level with the other books and he describes his grandfather's work as a *biblion*, a term he used in denoting the non-Torah and non-prophetic works. (5) Reference is made to the existence of Greek translations of the law, the prophecies, and the rest of the books.

The evidence of Ben Sirach's work and his grandson's prologue leads to the following conclusions about the development of a sacred collection of texts which would eventually constitute an authoritative canon: (1) During the second century BCE, certain circles in Judaism possessed and utilized two collections of texts, the Law and the Prophets (see also II Macc 15:9). (2) The extent of these collections may have coincided with the later first two parts of the Jewish canon, the Torah and the Nebiim, although this is an inference drawn from Ben Sirach's enumeration of famous men rather than from any list of works. (3) Other works were utilized in these communities, probably in the sense of scripture or edifying literature, but the exact number and content of these writings cannot be determined. (4) No concept of a canon as a closed, unalterable collection is directly referred to or indirectly alluded to.

Further texts relevant to the development of a canon are found in the books of Maccabees, which were probably written late in the second century BCE. II Maccabees opens with two letters; the second in 1:10–2:15 purports to have been written during the days of Judas Maccabeus. Quite likely, however, II Macc 1:18–2:15 was written by the composer of the book who was summarizing a five-volume history written by an otherwise unknown Jason of Cyrene (see Momigliano). This section contains a number of legends about Nehemiah and Jeremiah which are not attested in the Old Testament although reference is made to works where these are reported (see II Macc 2:1,4,13). These writings (*graphē*) or records (*apographais*) probably refer to such works as those of the Jewish historian Eupolemus (see I Macc 8:17; II Mac 4:11), who wrote sometime after the Maccabean revolt and reported some of these apocryphal tales (see Wacholder, 38-40, 237-42). Further, Nehemiah is said to have "founded a library and collected books about the kings and prophets, and the writings of David, and letters of kings about votive offerings" (II Macc 2:13). This text seems to be arguing that Nehemiah was responsible for the establishment of a Jerusalem library and for collecting a major portion of the sacred writings. "Books about the kings and prophets" probably refers to those works now found in the second section of the Hebrew canon, i.e., Joshua to II Kings and Isaiah to Malachi, although this and the subsequent references to the various books could refer totally to nonbiblical works. Chronicles, of course, could be classified as a book about the kings and may also have been included in this reference. "The writings of David" may refer to the book of Psalms. "Letters of kings about votive offerings" could denote the material in or the book of Ezra, which contains the edicts of Persian kings concerning Jewish worship and the return from exile. Several conclusions may be drawn from these statements about Nehemiah. (1) The statements reflect the beliefs of the author about how some of the sacred books were collected; that is, it reflects a current opinion from the late second century and not necessarily the way things actually happened. (2) The writer probably assumes, although he does not mention, the supposition that Ezra brought back the Torah from Babylon (see II Macc 2:2). Thus Ezra and Nehemiah were considered responsible for collecting, authenticating, and making available the Law and the Prophets. (3) Additional books—"the writings of David and letters of kings about votive offerings"—were in existence and were held in high esteem. (4) These additional works do not yet include all of the books which later went to make up the third section of the Hebrew canon. (5) The library assembled in Jerusalem, at least in the author's own day, may have possessed such works as those designated records or writings in II Macc 2:1,4,13.

After describing the activity of Nehemiah, II Maccabees

proceeds to attribute a similar endeavor to Judas Maccabeus: "In the same way Judas also collected all the books that had been lost on account of the war which had come upon us, and they are in our possession. So if you have need of them, send people to get them for you" (II Macc 2:14-15). This text does not specify what books Judas collected but it does imply his establishment of some type of library. The book of I Maccabees notes that Judas and his followers rescued the Law from the hands of the Gentiles (I Macc 1:56; 2:48). Leiman (29-30) has suggested that the Maccabeans, shortly after the death of Antiochus IV in 164 BCE, completed the Jewish canon by closing the third section, the Writings (Ketubim), as a response to the Seleucid attempt to destroy the scriptures.

There is no evidence that the Maccabeans closed the Jewish canon. II Maccabees only presents Judas and his followers as rescuing the Law from the Gentiles. However, there is internal evidence in the Hebrew scriptures that suggests that a rather extensive revision was made in the chronological references of the Torah and the Former Prophets (Joshua-II Kings) during the early Maccabean period. As is well known, different chronologies are found in the Hebrew, Greek, and Samaritan versions of the genealogies in Gen 5 and 11:10-32 and in such passages as Ex 12:40 (on the versions, see below, pp. 57-67). Also the Greek and Hebrew texts often differ in the chronological references in the books of Kings. The following dates, calculated in years from creation, illustrate the differences:

	Hebrew	Greek	Samaritan
Birth of Abraham	1946	3312	2247
Jacob's Descent into Egypt	2236	3602	2537
Date of the Exodus	2666	3817	2752

According to the chronological reference in the Hebrew of I Kings 6:1, Solomon began work on the temple in his fourth year, which was 480 years after the exodus (the

Greek reads 440 years). The figure clashes with other references found in Judges-II Samuel. Chronological data for the period of the judges totals 490 years. To this must be added the 40 years in the wilderness; the time for the careers of Joshua, Samuel, and Saul; and the first four years of Solomon. Nonetheless, according to the Hebrew reference in I Kings 6:1, the construction of the temple would have begun in the year 3146 after creation. The total years for the reigns of Judean kings from the beginning of temple construction to the exile number 430, which gives a date of 3576 for the end of the Jerusalem temple. Calculating 50 years for the exile, the new altar in Jerusalem was dedicated 480 years after construction began on the first temple (see II Chron 36:22) or in the year 3626. The Maccabean rededication of the temple in Jerusalem (I Macc 4:36-59) took place in about 164 BCE or 374 years later. The Maccabean rededication of the temple took place in the year 4000 after creation.

The above chronological issues strongly suggest that the Hebrew text of the Torah and Former Prophets was edited during the early Maccabean period as propaganda on behalf of the Maccabeans and their work in rededicating the temple. A date for this event in the year 4000 after creation, in light of the Greek and Samaritan divergencies, is too coincidental to be accidental. Although II Macc 2:14 only suggests that Judas collected the books that were endangered during his days, it also seems that editorial revision, especially in chronological references, also took place. If the text of the Law and the Former Prophets was revised by the early Maccabeans, this would not mean that these works did not possess authoritative status. Such a revision would simply suggest that the text had not acquired a status which prohibited any alteration.

Sometime during the second century and probably no later than 150 BCE, a new sect developed in Judaism. Part of this group settled at Qumran on the western shores of the Dead Sea. Discoveries of texts and scriptures of this community have been made in caves in the Qumran region, beginning in 1947. The Qumran community seems to have accepted the Law and the Prophets as sacred scripture. In at least two passages, the Dead Sea Scrolls refer to the Torah and the Prophets as the Books of the Law and the Books of the Prophets (for the references, see Vermes, 86, 104). In addition to this, other writings were used by the community and no doubt were considered authoritative. In this second category—the non-Torah and non-prophetic books—belong not only the remaining works that made their way into the Hebrew canon with the exception of Esther but also works such as Ecclesiasticus and Tobit, numerous writings from the so-called Pseudepigrapha, and sacred writings unique to the community (see Vermes). The evidence from Qumran would suggest that the writings which now comprise the first two divisions of the Jewish canon probably had achieved an authoritative status (as in the prologue to Ecclesiasticus) but that in addition to these two divisions, a wide range of writings functioned as "scriptures." The evidence also suggests that certain works which became a part of the third division had not yet acquired a set and uniform content. This is best illustrated by the book of Psalms (see Sanders, 1968). Numerous fragmentary copies of the Psalter have been found at Qumran. The most famous of these is the major psalms scroll from cave eleven which contains parts or all of forty-one biblical psalms in addition to eight texts not now found in the biblical version of this book. The forty-one psalms, however, do not appear in the order of the biblical Psalter and at places vary considerably from the biblical text. This suggests that the Psalter had not yet reached a final form or a defined content when the Qumran community split off from the Jerusalem community.

Two versions of the Torah—the Samaritan and the Greek—were in existence by the second century BCE and demonstrate that at least the Torah had what might be called canonical authority for a variety of Jewish communities. The Samaritans accepted only the Pentateuch as authoritative and copied this in an archaic script. When the Samaritan Pentateuch came into being and when this Jewish group finally broke with the Jerusalem community are disputed matters. No doubt both of these had occurred by the end of the second century BCE (see Purvis). When the first Greek translation of the Torah was made can no longer be determined. *The Letter of Aristeas*, probably written in the second century BCE, claims divine authority and inspiration for a Greek translation of the Torah (the so-called Septuagint) which was supposed to have been an official translation produced in Egypt (see Orlinsky, 1975). At the moment, the historical character of the letter's contents are not of concern. The point is that the letter demonstrates the authoritative status of the Torah (even in Greek translation!) in Egypt in the second century BCE.

In summary, what may be said about the second century BCE developments leading toward a canon of sacred scripture? (1) No concept of a canon which implied a list of included books over against excluded books existed. (2) The Torah was accepted as authoritative, sacred, and inspired by Judaism as a whole. (3) The existence of two authoritative collections (Torah and Nebiim) is attested in Ecclesiasticus and the Dead Sea Scrolls, but it is impossible to determine the works in the second collection except indirectly (see Eccl 44-49). (4) Other writings were in circulation and utilized as "sacred scripture." These writings, however, were not equivalent to what became the third division of the Hebrew canon. (5) Some works which later became part of the canon had not yet reached their final form. This is most clearly illustrated by the book of Psalms at Qumran.

B. The Close of the Jewish Canon

The next references which illuminate the history and development of a canon come from the first century CE.

Philo Judaeus (about 20 BCE–50 CE) of Alexandria was a prolific writer on a variety of subjects. Unfortunately he offers no discussion of the books which the Jewish community of his day accepted as authoritative. In discussing the Jewish sect known as the Therapeutae (in his *De Vita Contemplativa* 25), he refers to its use of "laws and oracles delivered through the mouth of prophets, and psalms and other books by which knowledge and piety may be increased and perfected." This statement suggests that he was not familiar with a tripartite division of the sacred writings or with any concept of a closed canon. This same situation is reflected in the New Testament where references to the "law and prophets" or "Moses and the prophets" occur (Matt 22:40; Luke 16:16; 24:27; Acts 13:15). The only New Testament reference to a tripartite division of texts is found in Luke 24:44, which speaks of the "law of Moses, and the prophets, and the psalms"; but such a reference cannot denote the later Jewish canon.

The fullest statement from the first century CE on the canon is that by Josephus (about 37-100 CE) written about 90-95 CE. In comparing the sacred Jewish writings with those of the Greeks, he wrote:

It therefore naturally, or rather necessarily, follows (seeing that with us it is not open to everyone to write the records, and that there is no discrepancy in what is written; seeing that, on the contrary, the prophets alone had this privilege, obtaining their knowledge of the most remote and ancient history through the inspiration which they owed to God, and committing to writing a clear account of the events of their time just as they occurred)— it follows, I say, that we do not possess myriads of inconsistent books, conflicting with each other. Our books, those which are justly accredited, are but two and twenty, and contain the record of all time.

Of these, five are the books of Moses, comprising the laws and the traditional history from the birth of man down to the death of the lawgiver. This period falls only a little short of three thousand years. From the death of Moses until Artaxerxes, who succeeded Xerxes as king of Persia, the prophets subsequent to

Moses wrote the history of the events of their own times in thirteen books. The remaining four books contain hymns to God and precepts for the conduct of human life.

From Artaxerxes to our own time the complete history has been written, but has not been deemed worthy of equal credit with the earlier records, because of the failure of the exact succession of the prophets.

We have given practical proof of our reverence for our own Scriptures. For, although such long ages have now passed, no one has ventured either to add, or to remove, or to alter a syllable; and it is an instinct with every Jew, from the day of his birth, to regard them as the decrees of God, to abide by them, and, if need be, cheerfully to die for them. Time and again ere now the sight has been witnessed of prisoners enduring tortures and death in every form in the theatres, rather than utter a single word against the laws and the allied documents. (*Contra Apionem* I 37-43)

Josephus' statement contains a number of important considerations concerning the canon. (1) The sacred writings were believed to have been composed by inspired men and cover history from the creation to the time of Artaxerxes. (2) Works describing the history after Artaxerxes exist but do not possess an inspired character since the succession of the prophets ended in the Persian period. (3) The sacred books are limited in number; namely, twenty-two. (4) The contents of the books are consistent and without discrepancies. (5) The scriptures are the object of great reverence and their wording and contents are sacrosanct. (6) The scriptures are separated into three divisions.

This quote from Josephus also raises a number of problems. (1) His division of the books (five books of Moses, thirteen books in the prophets, and four remaining books) parallels no known ancient collection of the Hebrew scriptures. Is Josephus here merely giving his own preferential ordering of the books which reflects his strong historical interests? Or is he drawing upon some arrangement and tradition whose origin and location can no longer be determined? Josephus had contacts with practically all elements in Palestinian Judaism; he claims to have received from the Romans the sacred writings from the temple (*Life* 418) and he was associated with both Alexandria and Rome. Was his ordering of the books derived from the tradition of one of these centers or does it perhaps reflect the priestly tradition from the Jerusalem temple? This cannot be determined, but Josephus' testimony suggests that the ordering of the material which was to become the second and third parts of the Jewish canon was still fluid in his day.

(2) Josephus reports that "our books, those which are justly accredited, are but two and twenty." Does this imply that at the time of his writing, even the exact contents of the second and third divisions of sacred scripture were still uncertain? Many scholars have assumed that Josephus' twenty-two are actually equivalent to the later twenty-four books (see Leiman, 32-34 and references cited there). This position argues that Josephus counted Ruth as part of Judges and Lamentations as part of Jeremiah. Evidence to support such a view is the following: (a) In the Talmud, Judges and Ruth are ascribed to a common author (Samuel) and Jeremiah is considered the author of Lamentations (see the Talmudic statement, below p. 87). (b) A number of later Christian writers (but never Jewish) refer to the twenty-two books which make up the Hebrew canon and in some cases Ruth-Judges and Jeremiah-Lamentations are explicitly treated as units (for the references, see Leiman, 37-50). A minority of scholars assume that when Josephus referred to twenty-two books his total was lacking two books which ultimately came to be included in the third division of the canon (see Zeitlin, 172-78; Orlinsky, 1974, 272-77). Evidence to support such a view is the following: (a) Josephus' statement is quite clear and should be taken literally. (b) Evidence from later Judaism suggests that some works—perhaps Ecclesiastes and Esther—were included in the third divison after the time of Josephus. The Mishnah reports

that there was discussion near the end of the first century CE about the sacredness of some works:

> All the holy writings defile the hands [are sacred]. Song of Songs and Ecclesiastes defile the hands. Rabbi Judah said, "Song of Songs defiles the hands, but Ecclesiastes was in dispute." . . . But Rabbi Akiba said, "God forbid! No one in Israel disputed the fact that Song of Songs defiles the hands, for the entire world does not compare with the day that Song of Songs was given to Israel. All the writings are holy, but Song of Songs is holiest of all. If there was a dispute, it was only about Ecclesiastes." (*Yadaim* 3:5)

This text suggests that the inclusion of Ecclesiastes was probably a debatable issue no doubt because of the radical skepticism of the work. In addition to Song of Songs and Ecclesiastes, the book of Esther was also a debated inclusion (see Zeitlin, 175-78). The evidence that Esther was included late is as follows: (a) The festival of Purim, which is advocated in Esther, is given as a semi-holiday by the *Megillat Taanit,* which lists the days when fasting is prohibited but which are not noted in the biblical text. This suggests that Esther was not yet accepted as scripture when Megillat Taanit was drawn up (late first century CE?) otherwise there would have been no reason to mention Purim. (b) Later rabbis appealed to *Megillat Taanit* to support the celebration of Purim rather than the book of Esther. (c) The Talmud notes that "Esther does not defile the hands" (Rabbi Samuel, 3rd century), that the book "was composed by divine inspiration to be read but not to be written down," and that "Esther petitioned the sage 'Record me for posterity.' " (*Megillah 7a*). (d) Several Christian writers, of whom the most important witness is Melito, bishop of Sardis (about 170 CE), did not list Esther among the works that the Jewish community considered canonical.

The above considerations suggest that at the time of Josephus the status of Ecclesiastes and Esther was unsettled. Esther was probably not accepted as a "writing which defiles the hands" until the second century CE and then due to the pressure of public opinion and the influence of its use in Purim (so Zeitlin, 176).

The oldest reference to a Jewish canon composed of twenty-four books is found in II Esdras 14, a work whose first edition probably appeared during the first half of the second century CE. In this account, Ezra is divinely commanded to take five scribes and writing materials, to go apart into a field, to drink a liquid that looked like water with the color of fire, and to dictate to the scribes who would write without knowledge of the characters they were recording.

So during the forty days ninety-four books were written. And when the forty days were ended, the Most High spoke to me, saying, "Make public the twenty-four books that you wrote first and let the worthy and the unworthy read them; but keep the seventy that were written last, in order to give them to the wise among your people. For in them is the spring of understanding, the fountain of wisdom, and the river of knowledge." And I did so. (II Esdras 14:44-48)

This text clearly assumes a twenty-four book canon. However, to stress this point is not the central emphasis of the passage. (1) The text is really arguing for the continued use of the books—the "seventy"—which did not make it into the canon. (2) An inspiration and divine dictation are claimed for these as for the twenty-four. (3) The text advocates the use of these books by the wise who can understand their great wisdom while the canonical works are to be available to and used by all. The question of the use of these noncanonical books was debated as the following statement from the Mishnah illustrates:

The following have no share in the world to come: he who maintains that the resurrection is not intimated in the Torah, or that the Torah was not divinely revealed, and an Epicurean [a byword for one of deviant belief]. Rabbi Akiba [died in 135 CE] adds: one who reads the outside books [the noncanonical works]. . . . (Sanhedrin 10:1)

The use of the "outside books" continued to be a topic of discussion within Judaism for sometime and such works as Ecclesiasticus continued to be widely quoted (see Leiman, 86-102).

In summary, what can be said about the final stages of the canonization process in Judaism? (1) In the second century BCE, the Torah was accorded an authoritative and sacred status even in its Greek translation. (2) The Prophets were no doubt considered as inspired writings, but the exact titles and number of the books in this group cannot be determined. (3) The third division of the Hebrew canon or what was to comprise this group was very fluid during the last century BCE and the first century CE. Various sacred writings were utilized as venerated texts perhaps varying from group to group in Judaism. (4) By the time of Josephus' writing (about 90 CE), Judaism had moved toward a canon that provided a list of authoritative works. (5) The development of a final, closed canon of scripture was the work of Pharisaic and rabbinical Judaism which came to prominence after the fall of Jerusalem in 70 CE. (6) Various criteria were used to determine canonicity (most already reflected in Josephus): (a) books had to be written during the age of prophecy which ended during the Persian period; (b) the books were inspired by God and were written by prophets; and (c) the books could not be inconsistent. The criterion of widespread acceptance no doubt was important even if unstated. (7) Works were excluded when they failed to meet the above criteria or where their contents or legal practices openly contradicted Jewish faith and practices as understood in Pharisaic Judaism (see Orlinsky, 1974, 277-86). (8) The period from 70 (the date of the temple's destruction) until about 100 CE was a decisive stage in canonical development. The exact manner in which developments took place during the period, however, cannot be determined and one should avoid speaking of the authoritative actions of councils such as has been assumed for the so-called Council of Jamnia/Jabneh in 90 CE (see Lewis). (9) The final tripartite Jewish canon, including Esther and with the Talmudic distribution of the works among the three divisions, was a product of the second century CE.

C. The Old Testament in the Early Church

When we turn to the Old Testment canon in the Christian church, several general factors should be kept in mind. (1) The early church did not inherit a closed canon of normative scriptures from Judaism. (2) The church did receive from Judaism the Law (the five books of Moses) as authoritative and normative and probably also those works which Judaism designated the Prophets. In addition to these, Christianity was heir to numerous other sacred writings, many of revered and widespread usage. (3) The early church, due to its rapid orientation to the Greco-Roman world, utilized the scriptures in Greek translations as had some Jewish communities for some time. (4) The early church developed its own Old Testament, which was more inclusive than the Hebrew canon and was characterized by a different order for many of the writings.

The early church utilized and quoted as scripture a larger group of writings than that which came to be accepted as canonical in Judaism. Quotations from and reliance upon various extracanonical works have been seen in the New Testament. The extent of these will vary from scholar to scholar since none of these works are quoted by name (compare Sundberg, 1964, 54-55; Oepke, 988-92; Leiman, 40-41). The clearest use of extracanonical works by a New Testament writer is found in the book of Jude. The author of this work alludes to an episode (v. 9) known from the *Assumption of Moses* and refers to a prophecy by Enoch (vv. 14-15; from 1 *Enoch* 1:9).

The fact that Christianity went its own way apart from,

but not completely out of touch with, Judaism in regard to the canon is supported by a number of considerations. (1) Many Christians were aware that the collection of scriptures which they used differed from the Jewish canon. Melito, bishop of Sardis (about 170 CE), wrote to his brother Onesimus providing him with a list of books in the Hebrew canon. Onesimus desired "to know the accurate facts about the ancient writings, how many they are in number, and what is their order. . . . " According to Eusebius' account (*Church History* IV. xxvi. 13), Melito claimed to have traveled to the East and explored the issue. His list of twenty-two books, which omits Esther and Lamentations, the latter probably assumed to be part of Jeremiah, and Onesimus' inquiry indicate "the unsettled state of the Old Testament canon of the Christian church in the second century C.E." (Leiman, 48). Over thirty such lists as Melito provides are known prior to the sixth century and tend to vary in content and sequence of books.

Origen, early in the third century, shows quite clearly that he recognized the differences between Christian and Jewish scriptures by referring to "their scriptures" and "our scriptures." He notes that Jews did not use Tobit and Judith although the churches did (*Ad Africanum* XIII). Origen also knew that the Greek translation often contained textual readings not found in the Hebrew and vice versa.

And I make it my endeavor not to be ignorant of their various readings, lest in my controversies with the Jews I should quote them what is not found in their copies and that I may make some use of what is found there, even though it should not be in our scriptures. (*Ad Africanum* V)

He even accused the Jewish leaders of taking "away from the people every passage which might bring discredit among the people" (i.e., some passages and terms in the Greek text that were interpreted in a Christian sense were not found in the Hebrew text; see *Ad Africanum* IX). Origen carried on correspondence with Africanus concerning the validity and authenticity of some of the additions to Daniel found in the Greek (see below, pp. 90-91), a further sign of the knowledge that Jewish and Christian collections differed.

(2) Christian writers quoted as scripture many of the writings which were not included in the Hebrew canon. Tobit, Sirach, Wisdom of Solomon, and other works are quoted by the church fathers and introduced by phrases as "it is written" and "scripture says."

(3) Some texts which never became part of the Christian Old Testament were sometimes quoted as scripture. This is best illustrated by the book of Enoch. Tertullian (about 160-220 CE) defended the authoritative status of the work and wrote:

I am aware that the Scripture of Enoch . . . is not received by some, because it is not admitted into the Jewish canon either. I suppose they did not think that, having been published before the deluge, it could have safely survived that worldwide calamity, the abolisher of all things. If that is the reason (for rejecting it,) let them recall to their memory that Noah, the survivor of the deluge, was the grandson of Enoch himself. If he had not this (conservative power) by so short a route, there would still be this (consideration) to warrant our assertion of (the genuineness of) this Scripture: he could equally have received it, under the Spirit's inspiration, after it had been destroyed by the violence of the deluge, as, after the destruction of Jerusalem by the Babylonian storming of it, every document of the Jewish literature is generally agreed to have been restored through Ezra.

But since Enoch in the same Scripture has preached likewise concerning the Lord, nothing at all must be rejected by us which pertains to us. . . . By the Jews it may now seem to have been rejected for that (very) reason, just like all the other (portions) which tell of Christ. . . . To these considerations is added the fact that Enoch possessed a testimony in the Apostle Jude. (*On Apparel of Women* I 3; quoted from Sundberg, 1964, 164-65)

Tertullian here advances four arguments to support the acceptance of Enoch as scripture: (a) its great antiquity, (b) its possible renewal by divine inspiration, (c) its prophecies concerning Christ, and (d) its utilization by the apostle Jude.

Origen wrote that "the books which bear the name Enoch do not at all circulate in the churches as divine" (*Contra Celsum* V 54) although in *De Principiis* IV 35, he refers to Enoch as a prophet and quotes two passages from *I Enoch* 17 as grounds out of scripture for understanding a particular subject.

The use of Enoch materials as scripture, although infrequent in the early church, suggests that early Christians did not work with a closed canon.

(4) The great Christian uncial manuscripts from the fourth century testify to the generally unsettled state of the Old Testament in the early church (see the charts in Sundberg, 1964, 58-59). Among the Old Testament writings, Codex Vaticanus contains Wisdom of Solomon, Sirach, Judith, Tobit, Baruch, and the Epistle of Jeremiah. Codex Sinaiticus contains Tobit, Judith, I-II Maccabees, Wisdom of Solomon, and Sirach. Codex Alexandrinus, which dates perhaps from the next century, contains Baruch, Epistle of Jeremiah, Tobit, Judith, I-IV Maccabees, Wisdom of Solomon, Sirach, and Psalms of Solomon. This manuscript evidence demonstrates the fluidity in both contents and the sequential arrangement of books in the early church's Old Testament.

During the latter half of the fourth century and the first quarter of the fifth century, the early church moved toward the establishment of a specific Old Testament canon although not without differences of opinion and controversy. Scholars and the church in the East tended to support an Old Testament limited by the Jewish canon while the church and theologians in the West tended to support a more inclusive collection.

In the East, the Council of Laodicea (about 360 CE?) opposed the use of noncanonical books in the church and spelled out the contents of the Old Testament. The list of the canonical books given by the council followed "the

Jewish canon but according to the Greek recension, Jeremiah including Lamentations, Baruch, and the Epistle of Jeremy, two books of Ezra, and we should probably understand Daniel and Esther in their expanded forms" (Sundberg, 1964, 148).

Athanasius (295-373), bishop of Alexandria, was strongly influenced by the Jewish tradition in his enumeration of the canonical books of the Old Testament although he places the Writings before the Prophets; includes II Esdras, combines Baruch, Lamentations, and the Epistle of Jeremiah (Jeremy) with the book of Jeremiah; and omits Esther (see his *Letters on the Paschal Festival* XXXIX). He enumerates the books which he places in the category of noncanonical or apocryphal writings: Wisdom of Solomon, Sirach, Esther(!), Judith, and Tobit.

Jerome (about 347-419), after his settlement in Bethlehem, was a strong supporter of the Hebrew canon and among the early Christian scholars had the closest contact with the Jews of his day. He was familiar with the tripartite division of the Jewish canon: Torah (Genesis, Exodus, Leviticus, Numbers, and Deuteronomy), Prophets (Joshua, Judges with Ruth, Samuel, Kings, Isaiah, Jeremiah with Lamentations, Ezekiel, and the Book of the Twelve); and the Writings (Job, Psalms, Proverbs, Ecclesiastes, Song of Songs, Daniel, Chronicles, Ezra with Nehemiah, and Esther). He was also aware of a division in which Ruth and Lamentations were placed among the Writings (see his *Preface to the Books of Samuel and Kings*, quoted in Leiman, 45-47). Jerome concluded his discussion of the contents of the canon by saying:

This preface to the Scriptures may serve as a "helmeted" introduction to all the books which we turn from Hebrew into Latin, so that we may be assured that what is not found in our list must be placed among the apocrypha. Wisdom, therefore, which generally bears the name of Solomon, and the book of Jesus, the Son of Sirach, and Judith, and Tobit . . . are not in the canon.

The first book of Maccabees I have found to be in Hebrew, the second is Greek, as can be proved from the very style.

Jerome argued that while the uncanonical books might be read in the churches they should be used solely "for edifying the people, not for the corroboration of ecclesiastical doctrines" *(Preface to Solomon's Books)*. For Jerome, the writings of the Hebrew canon constituted the works used and quoted by Jesus and the early church and thus whose usage had an apostolic authority.

Not all the fathers in the East agreed with Athanasius and Jerome and even the latter two scholars frequently quoted from the works they had designated "apocrypha" as if they were scripture (see Sundberg, 1964, 58, 138-42).

In the western church, the view espoused by Augustine, among others, came to prevail. Augustine (354-430) argued for an inclusive canon of forty-four books (i.e., the books contained in the Hebrew canon, combining Ruth with Judges and Lamentations with Jeremiah, plus Tobit, Judith, I-II Maccabees, I-II Esdras, Wisdom of Solomon, and Ecclesiasticus; *On Chrisian Doctrine* II.viii.13). He appealed to the tradition and practice of the church as authority for his position.

In order to know what are the canonical Scriptures, you must follow the authority of the greatest possible number of catholic churches, especially of those which were founded by apostles and merited receiving epistles. Those received by all the churches will, therefore, be preferred to those received only by some. Of these latter, those will be preferred which are received by the greatest number and by the most important churches, to those which are received only by the fewest and smallest churches. If we were to find some held by the majority while others were held by the most important, although it would not be possible to decide easily, however, I would reckon them as having equal authority. *(On Christian Doctrine* II.viii.12)

Augustine offered arguments for the exclusion of some works from the canon although these had circulated in the church.

If I may recall far more ancient times, our patriarch Noah was certainly even before that great deluge, and I might not undeservedly call him a prophet, forasmuch as the ark he made, in which he escaped with his family, was itself a prophecy of our times. What of Enoch, the seventh from Adam? Does not the canonical epistle of the Apostle Jude declare that he prohesied? But the writings of these men could not be held as authoritative either among the Jews or us, on account of their too great antiquity, which made it seem needful to regard them with suspicion, lest false things should be set forth instead of truth. For some writings which are said to be theirs are quoted by those who, according to their own humor, loosely believe what they please. But the purity of the canon has not admitted these writings, not because the authority of these men who pleased God is rejected, but because they are not believed to be theirs. Nor ought it to appear strange if writings for which so great antiquity is claimed are held in suspicion, seeing that in the very history of the kings of Judah and Israel containing their acts, which we believe to belong to the canonical Scripture, very many things are mentioned which are not explained there, but are said to be found in other books which the prophets wrote, the very names of these prophets being sometimes given, and yet they are not found in the canon which the people of God received. Now I confess the reason for this is hidden from me; only I think that even those men, to whom certainly the Holy Spirit revealed those things which ought to be held as of religious authority, might write some things as men by historical diligence, and others as prophets by divine inspiration; and these things were so distinct, that it was judged that the former should be ascribed to themselves, but the latter to God speaking through them: and so one pertained to the abundance of knowledge, the other to the authority of religion. In that authority the canon is guarded. So that, if any writings outside of it are now brought forward under the name of ancient prophets, they cannot serve even as an aid to knowledge, because it is uncertain whether they are genuine; and on this account they are not trusted, especially those of them in which some things are found that are even contrary to the truth of the canonical books, so that it is quite apparent they do not belong to them. (City of God XVIII 38)

For Augustine, the appropriate and inspired version of the Old Testament for the church was that based on the Greek version. However, he claimed that the Hebrew text had been given through inspiration and did not accuse the Jews of having altered the text. Augustine argued that the persons who had produced the writings and translations found in the Greek version of the Septuagint were as equally inspired as the original prophets.

If anything is in the Hebrew copies and not in the version of the Septuagint, the Spirit of God did not choose to say it through them [i.e., the Septuagint writers and translators], but only through the prophets. But whatever is in the Septuagint and not in the Hebrew copies, the same Spirit chose rather to say through the latter, thus showing that both were prophets. (*City of God* XVIII 43)

The inclusive canon of the Old Testament, supported by arguments such as those of Augustine, was accepted and espoused by local church councils in the late fourth and early fifth centuries; Hippo in 393 and Carthage in 397 and 419.

D. Protestants and the Hebrew Canon

The acceptance and usage of the inclusive canon of the Old Testament were almost universal in the medieval church. Jerome's position, which argued for an Old Testament canon limited to the books in the Hebrew Bible, however, continued to have limited influence. Jerome's view was adopted in the Wycliffe Bible in the early fourteenth century. The revival of Christian interest in the study of Hebrew in the fifteenth century made the church more aware of the difference between the Hebrew and Christian canons. Johannes Reuchlin (1455-1522), a Catholic German humanist, was very competent in Hebrew and advocated that only those scriptures found in the Hebrew canon should be considered as the Old Testament of the church.

The issue of the canon became a matter of great controversy as a result of the Protestant Reformation. Martin Luther and his followers, especially Andreas Bodenstein of Karlstadt, argued that the text of the Bible was to be accepted over the authority of the church and its traditions. In his debates with Johann Maier of Eck, held at Leipzig in June and July of 1519, Luther opposed the doctrine of purgatory. Eck argued that such a doctrine was biblical and confronted Luther with the teaching of II Macc 12:46. Luther then advocated that the canon of the Old Testament should be limited to those works found in the Hebrew scriptures and appealed to Jerome's authority and the latter's argument that the Jewish canon was the scripture used by Jesus and the early church. In Luther's first complete German translation of the Bible in 1534, he included Judith, Wisdom of Solomon, Tobit, Ecclesiasticus, Baruch, Epistle of Jeremiah, I-II Maccabees, the Additions to Daniel and Esther, and the Prayer of Manasseh at the end of the translation with the heading: "Apocrypha, that is books which are not held to be equal to holy scripture and yet are profitable and good to read."

Protestantism, as a rule, followed the example of Luther and relegated those books not found in the Hebrew canon to separate appendices in editions of the Bible or else dropped them entirely. In both cases they were no longer assigned any authoritative status. The Church of England, in article six of the Thirty-nine Articles (1562), followed Jerome and said of the "apocryphal" works that "the church doth read them for example of life and instructions of manners; but yet it doth not apply them to establish any doctrine." The Westminster Confession of 1648 went much further: "The books commonly called Apocrypha, not being of divine inspiration, are no part of the canon of Scripture; and therefore of no authority to the church of God, nor to be otherwise approved, or made use of, than any other human writings" (I 3).

The Catholic church, in reaction to the Protestant Reformation and Luther's position on these writings, engaged in serious discussion over the content of the Old Testament canon. Even at the Council of Trent in March, 1546, various options were debated. The council finally decided to declare all the works in the Latin Vulgate (the inclusive canon) as canonical, authoritative, and inspired although I and II Esdras and the Prayer of Manasseh were placed in an appendix following the New Testament. The Eastern Orthodox Church established its canon at the Synod of Jerusalem in 1672.

E. The Canon and Contemporary Studies

Subsequent reflection and scholarly research on the origin of the canon have led to a number of positions and practices within the church and scholarship in general.

(1) Catholic scholars and writers tend to refer to canonical and deutero-canonical books. The former designates those works contained in the Hebrew canon and about which there has never been any major controversy in the church. The latter term refers to those works which Protestants designate the Apocrypha.

(2) The view, advocated in rabbinic Judaism and adopted in most of Protestantism, that the Hebrew canon was closed in the time of Ezra has been generally abandoned. The recognition that some works, such as Daniel, were produced after the time of Ezra raised insurmountable obstacles for this view.

(3) The belief that the Septuagint, or Greek version of the Old Testament, represented the canon of Alexandrian Judaism while the Hebrew canon represented the canon of Palestinian Judaism can no longer be substantiated (see Sundberg, 1964). No normative Alexandrian canon ever existed in Judaism.

(4) The Septuagint, or inclusive Old Testament canon, was the creation of the early church. The church did not inherit a closed canon of scripture from Judaism.

(5) A renewed interest in the apocryphal or deutero-

43

canonical writings has become characteristic of Protestantism. Many modern editions of the Bible have restored these works. The latest edition of the *Oxford Annotated Bible*, for example, contains not only the deutero-canonical books but also III and IV Maccabees.

(6) Some Protestant scholars are calling for a reconsideration of the church's attitude toward the Aprocrypha. The fact that the apocryphal writings were considered as scripture by much of the church for centuries raises the question of what does constitute the Christian canon. Sundberg, for example, has written:

Any Protestant doctrine of canonization that takes seriously the question of Christian usage and historical and spiritual heritage will lead ultimately to the Christian OT as defined in the Western Church at the end of the fourth and the beginning of the fifth centuries. . . . it is evident that both in content and doctrine, Protestantism, in its view of OT canon, has broken away from its historical heritage. The basis for this rupture has mistakenly been thought to be that the earliest Christian OT usages, that of Jesus, the apostles, and the NT writers, paralleled the Jewish canon. Since that basis no longer obtains, it remains for Protestant Christians either to return to the historical heritage from which Protestantism sprang or to develop a new apologetic for its OT canon. (1966, 202-3)

CHAPTER 2

THE TEXTUAL CRITICISM OF THE OLD TESTAMENT

W. F. Albright, "New Light on Early Recensions of the Hebrew Bible," *BASOR* CXL(1955)27-33 = *QHBT*, 140-46; D. R. Ap-Thomas, *A Primer of Old Testament Text Criticism* (Oxford: Blackwell, ²1965); J. Barr, *Comparative Philology and the Text of the Old Testament* (Oxford: Clarendon Press, 1968); D. Barthélemy, "Text, Hebrew, History of," *IDBS*, 878-84; L. Blau, "Massoretic Studies," *JQR* VIII (1896)343-59; IX(1897)122-44, 471-90 = *CMHB*, 606-65; F. M. Cross, "The History of the Biblical Text in the Light of Discoveries in the Judaean Desert," *HTR*, LVII(1964)281-99 = *QHBT*, 177-95; idem, "The Contribution of the Qumran Discoveries to the Study of the Biblical Text," *IEJ* XVI(1966)81-95 = *QHBT*, 278-92; idem, "The Evolution of a Theory of Local Texts," *QHBT*, 306-20; J. A. Fitzmyer, *The Dead Sea Scrolls: Major Publications and Tools for Study* (Missoula: Scholars Press for SBL, 1975); C. D. Ginsburg, *Introduction to the Massoretico-Critical Edition of the Hebrew Bible* (London: Trinitarian Bible Society, 1897; reissued, New York: KTAV, 1966); M. Hadas, *Aristeas to Philocrates (Letter of Aristeas)* (New York: Harper for Dropsie College, 1951); S. Jellicoe, *The Septuagint and Modern Study* (Oxford: Clarendon Press, 1968); idem, ed., *Studies in the Septuagint: Origins, Recensions, and Interpretations* (New York: KTAV, 1974); R. W. Klein, *Textual Criticism of the Old Testament: The Septuagint after Qumran* (Philadelphia: Fortress Press, 1974); R. A. Kraft, "Earliest Greek Versions ('Old Greek')," *IDBS*, 811-15; W. McKane, "Observations on the tiḳḳûnê sôpᵉrîm," *On Language, Culture, and Religion: In Honor of Eugene A. Nida*, ed. M. Black and W. A. Smalley (The Hague/Paris: Mouton, 1974)53-77; B. M. Metzger, "Versions, Ancient," *IDB* IV 749-60; H. M. Orlinsky, "Prolegomenon: The Masoretic Text: A Critical Evaluation," in reissue of Ginsburg, I-XLV = *CMHB*, 833-77; J. D. Purvis, *The Samaritan Pentateuch and the Origin of the Samaritan Sect* (Cambridge: Harvard University Press, 1968); idem, "Samaritan Pentateuch," *IDBS*, 772-77; B. J. Roberts, *The Old*

Testament Text and Versions: The Hebrew Text in
Transmission and the History of the Ancient Versions
(Cardiff: University of Wales, 1951); S. Talmon, "The
Three Scrolls of the Law that were Found in the Temple
Court," Textus II(1962)14-27 = CMHB, 455-68; idem,
"Aspects of the Textual Transmission of the Bible in the
Light of Qumran Manuscripts," Textus IV(1964)95-132 =
QHBT, 226-63; idem, "The Old Testament Text," CHB
I(1970)159-99 = QHBT, 1-41; idem, "Conflate Readings
(OT)," IDBS, 170-73; idem, "The Textual Study of the
Bible—A New Outlook," QHBT, 321-400; J. A. Thomp-
son, "Textual Criticism, OT," IDBS, 886-91; E. Tov,
"Septuagint," IDBS, 807-11; G. Vermes, "Dead Sea
Scrolls," IDBS, 210-19; idem, "Manuscripts from the
Judean Desert," IDBS, 563-66; G. E. Weil, "Qere-kethib,"
IDBS, 716-23; E. Würthwein, The Text of the Old
Testament: An Introduction to Kittel-Kahle's Biblia
Hebraica (Oxford/New York: Blackwell/Macmillan,
1957).

The goals of Old Testament textual criticism are
twofold: (1) an understanding of the transmission of the
text in its various forms throughout history and (2) the
reconstruction of the text in its most authentic and
original form. These perhaps unattainable goals are, of
course, not unique to the study of the biblical text.
They are characteristic of any criticism which must work
with texts which have undergone a long period of
transmission.

Three basic factors characterize the issues and problems associated with the textual criticism of the Hebrew
Bible. Talmon has summarized these in the following
manner:

[1] Not one single verse of this ancient literature has come to us
in an original manuscript, written by a biblical author or by a
contemporary of his or even by a scribe who lived
immediately after the time of the author. Even the very
earliest manuscripts at our disposal, in Hebrew or in any

translation language, are removed by hundreds of years from the date of origin of the literature recorded in them.

[2] There is probably no other extant text, ancient or modern, which is witnessed to by so many diverse types of sources, and the history of which is so difficult to elucidate as that of the text of the Old Testament.

[3] The further back the textual tradition of the Old Testament is followed, i.e. the older the biblical manuscripts perused, and the more ancient the records which come to the knowledge of scholars, the wider is the over-all range of textual divergence between them. . . . In other words, the later the witnesses which are reviewed, the more pronounced their conformity, and the fewer their divergences, both in number and type. (*QHBT*, 3-5)

A. Hebrew Manuscripts and Texts

The primary witnesses for the text of the Old Testament fall into two general categories: Hebrew manuscripts of the Bible and translations made from Hebrew manuscripts. First of all, we shall examine the Hebrew manuscript evidence.

In the eighteenth century, two eminent textual critics, B. F. Kennicott and J. B. de Rossi, compiled huge volumes detailing the different readings found in numerous Hebrew copies of the Old Testament. Kennicott examined 615 manuscripts and 52 printed editions while de Rossi's work included 731 manuscripts and 300 other editions. "As a result of their examinations they concluded that . . . the differences were so incidental and unimportant that they could be virtually discounted, and that every manuscript and printed edition presupposed, ultimately, one single archetype which was standard and universally recognized and acknowledged" (Roberts, 24). Most of the manuscripts examined date from after the twelfth century and illustrate Talmon's principle that the later the witnesses reviewed, the more pronounced their conformity.

Medieval manuscripts of the Hebrew Bible, such as

those examined by Kennicott and de Rossi, thus reflect one textual tradition which scholars refer to as the *textus receptus*. Several early medieval manuscripts are known and all reflect, with minor variations, this *textus receptus*. The oldest of these manuscripts is a copy of the prophetical books from the Karaite synagogue in Cairo which was made in 896 CE. A Babylonian codex of the Prophets (sometimes called the St. Petersburg Codex) dates from 916 CE. The British Museum possesses a tenth-century copy of most of the Pentateuch. The two most valuable manuscripts are the Leningrad Codex and the Aleppo Codex. The former, which dates from the eleventh century (1008 CE) and contains the entire Bible, was employed as the text for the most widely used critical edition of the Old Testament. This is the *Biblia Hebraica*, edited by Rudolf Kittel (1937). The "Kittel text" has been reedited as the *Biblia Hebraica Stuttgartensia*. The latter, an incomplete codex, which dates from about 930 CE, received its name from the Syrian city of Aleppo, where it was kept in a Sephardic synagogue. Although it was once feared that the Aleppo Codex had been destroyed, this manuscript has recently become available to scholars and is the basis of an edition of the Hebrew scriptures being produced by the Hebrew University Bible Project. This codex was presumably prepared by Aaron ben Moshe of the famous ben Asher family and the textual products of this family were declared the normative form of the Old Testament by the famous Jewish philosopher Maimonides (d. 1204).

Medieval Hebrew manuscripts contain a number of features which were added to the text as scholarly aids to the correct reading and writing of the text. To add such material to scrolls read in the synagogue was strictly forbidden and thus these additions were made to texts produced in book form or as a codex intended for scholarly work and as aids to be memorized by synagogue readers but not for liturgical usage. These features were added by the so-called Masoretes (from the Hebrew word masora = "tradition"), who were scribes that handed down such learned information. The masora was written at the top or bottom of a page of text (the masora magna) or else at the sides of the text or between columns of texts (the masora parva). These notes reported such things as how often a word or a certain form of a word appears in the Bible, drew attention to unusual spellings, noted where a word is written or spelled in one way but should be read in another way, and marked such items as the beginning and end of verses and units.

In addition to the masora, texts were supplied with certain marks or signs indicating how readings were to be accentuated and how the words were to be pronounced in reading. The most important of these signs are the so-called vowel points. The text itself contained only the consonants of the words although a few of the consonants (the matres lectionis) could be and were occasionally used to indicate vowel sounds. Different vowels with the same consonants could change the meaning of a word and the sense of a passage. For example, if the practice of writing only the consonants prevailed in English, the letters bd could be read as bad, bed, bid, bud, abide, abode, and so on although the context generally would provide the necessary clues. The Babylonian Talmud (Baba Bathra 21a-b) reports, for example, a rabbinical discussion about the correct reading of zkr in Deut 25:19. If the expression is read zĕkar, it means every male; if read zēker, it means remembrance. The question was: Should the word be vocalized so that the passage stipulates that all Amalekites should be blotted out or only the males?

Various systems for adding the vowel signs and other marks were employed by the Masoretes during the Middle Ages (see Roberts, 40-63). Three major systems have been preserved in manuscripts and have been designated by scholars as the Babylonian, the Palestinian, and the Tiberian. The first two probably reflect the early rabbinical tradition of pronunciation in Babylonia and Palestine while "there are good reasons for believing that the Tiberian system was invented by the Masoretes and grammarians of Tiberias" (Barthélemy, 883). The Tiberian system, which uses a number of dots and dashes written above and below the consonants to represent the vowels, came to predominance after the tenth century although the other forms have been preserved in scattered places. Yemenite Jews, for example, continue to use a Babylonian vocalic notation.

A text provided with such *masora*, vowel signs, and accent marks by the Masoretes is known as a Masoretic Text. It is doubtful if one should speak of *the* Masoretic Text as if only one form of such texts existed (see Orlinsky). In spite of the differences in *masora* and vocalization, the various forms of such texts do not vary greatly insofar as the consonantal text is concerned. It should not be assumed that the Masoretes invented the vocalization of the consonantal text. What they devised or invented was merely the system or systems to mark how the consonantal text was or should be vocalized. For centuries before the Masoretes, the biblical text was read aloud in synagogues week after week and year after year. The way in which the text was read was passed on orally and by learned scribes and lectors, although one should assume some developments and differences in pronunciation based on historical changes and dialectical and regional peculiarities. The vocalization, of course, preserves the way in which the text was understood at the time which may contain some misreading and misunderstanding of the consonantal text. However, one should assume that the vocalization has preserved an understanding of the text which is neither arbitrary nor chaotic but "which goes back to origins long before the graphic marking of the vocalization by the Massoretes began" (Barr, 221; see his chapter on "The Massoretes, Vocalization and Emendation," 188-222).

The traditional Hebrew text of the Old Testament, which was the subject of Masoretic transmission and editing from the sixth to the tenth century, was also edited by textual scribes in the centuries preceding. Such editorial activity of the scribes (the *sopherim*) does not constitute anything approaching a full-blown *masora*. In some cases, this editorial activity has left traces in the consonantal text, but in other cases, the nature of this activity is known only from rabbinic or Masoretic references.

One such activity of these scribes who copied and transmitted the manuscripts was the counting of words and letters in the various books of the Bible. The Talmud describes this activity in the following terms:

The ancients were called *sopherim* because they reckoned every letter in the Torah. They said that the *w* in *ghwn* [Lev 11:42] is the middle consonant in the Torah, *drsh drsh* [Lev 10:16] the middle word, and *whtglh* [Lev 13:13] the middle verse. Further, the ᶜ of *yᶜyr* [Ps 78:38] is the middle of the Psalter. (*Kiddushin* 30a)

The purpose of such calculation was of course the desire to make it possible for copyists to make accurate reproductions of manuscripts of the text.

Another scribal activity was the division of the text into sections and verses. A section (*parasha*) was a sense unit separated according to its content. The verse (*pesuq*) was a smaller sense unit. Various rabbinic references support the idea that the text was divided into verses quite early (see Blau). With regard to the reading and interpretation of the text in the synagogue, the Mishnah states the following rule: "No more than one verse [from the Torah] at a time is read to the interpreter, but three verses [may be read at a time] from the prophets" (*Megillah* 4:4). There was, of course, no numeration of the verses. The *parashas* were divided into "open" and "closed." The open *parashas* began on a new line; if the preceding line was full, a line was skipped. The closed *parashas* began with an indentation or after a blank space. (The present chapter divisions of the Hebrew Bible were introduced in the Middle Ages, following the Vulgate.)

The following quote from the Babylonian Talmud contains a reference to additional work of the scribes. "Rab Isaac said: 'The pronunciation fixed by the sopherim, the omissions of the scribes, words read which are not written in the text, and words written in the text which are cancelled in reading, are a law of Moses of Sinai' " (Nedarim 37b). Rabbi Isaac is here claiming that such activity by the scribes had Mosaic authority just as many later Jewish and Christian scholars argued that the vowel pointing was revealed to Moses on Sinai and was therefore infallible.

The "pronunciation of the sopherim" (miqra' sopherim) concerned, as references in the Talmud suggest, the pronunciations of certain words at a stage prior to the development of vowel pointing. This concern with the reading of the text before the fixation of vocalization in writing reflects editorial tradition transmitted at the oral stage. The "omissions of the scribes" (ᶜiṭṭure sopherim) refers to places in the text where something should be omitted. The examples offered are very few and deal primarily with places where the conjunction "and" was not to be read (for example, in Gen 18:5, 24:55; Num 31:2; Ps 36:7; 68:26).

"Words read which are not written in the text" refers to certain words which had to be supplied for the consonantal text to make sense. Rabbi Isaac only gave seven examples of these which include "Euphrates" in II Sam 8:3 and "man" in II Sam 16:23. "Words written in the text which are cancelled in reading" is illustrated by only a few examples which are primarily the product of scribal errors: the duplication of "bend" in Jer 51:3 and "five" in Ez 48:16; however the reference to omit "please" in II Kings 5:18 is different from the first two examples and does not seem to be an effort to eliminate a scribal mistake.

References to not reading words written and to reading words not written parallel the latter Masoretic qere-kethib ("what is read; what is written") notations in the masora. Several systems were used by the Masoretes to note where one reading appears in the consonantal text but something else is to be read. Manuscript evidence and scholarly calculations vary as to how many cases of qere-kethib are found in the marginal readings. The number varies from 848 to 1566. The qere reading sometimes marks no great difference from the kethib whereas on other occasions it suggests an entirely different word or radically alters the meaning by the change in vocalization. The qere generally, but not always, seems to provide a more sensible reading. For example, the kethib in Amos 8:8 reads "the land . . . will be watered" while the qere reads "the land . . . will sink." Or in II Sam. 23:20, the qere reads "son of a man of valor" while the kethib reads "son of a living man." Sometimes the kethib seems to make more sense: in Job 9:30, the kethib reads "with snow" while the qere reads "with waters of snow."

Quite early in the history of the text's transmission, the sacred name of God was not pronounced in the reading of the text. This name, whose consonants are YHWH, was pronounced as Yahweh according to the testimony of some of the church fathers. In reading the text, adonai ("Lord") was read instead, a practice preserved in the RSV. Thus the kethib was not read. The reading of "Lord" was thus considered a qere perpetuum and the Masoretes pointed the consonantal text with the vowels for adonai or those of the Aramaic term shĕma', which means "the name." Our term Jehovah is a composite representing the consonants of YHWH read with the vowels of adonai.

The pre-Masoretic scribal activity on the text which we just examined was primarily carried out to preserve the purity of the text, to guard against erroneous readings, and to avoid blasphemy in the use of the name of God. That the qere-kethib system was used on occasion to preserve double readings is quite possible, i.e., the scribes may have been familiar with variants among texts and chose to preserve two, one as the kethib and the other as the qere (see the summary of the issues in Weil).

Rabbinical references provide evidence that the pre-Masoretic scribes not only guarded and preserved the text but at times also went so far as to alter the text itself. Statements as to the exact number of these changes or emendations of the scribes (tiqqune sopherim) vary. The total number of changes attested in the various lists is twenty-three although the dominant Masoretic tradition speaks of eighteen (see McKane). The eighteen passages involved are: Gen 18:22; Num 11:15; 12:12; I Sam 3:13; II Sam 16:12; 20:1; I Kings 12:16; II Chron 10:16; Jer 2:11; Ez 8:17; Hosea 4:7; Hab 1:12; Zech 2:8; Mal 1:12; Ps 106:20; Job 7:20; 32:3; Lam 3:20. Many of the changes assumed seem to have the purpose of making the text more theologically acceptable by changing expressions which seemed to lack proper reverence. Some examples will suffice: Gen 18:22 originally read "YHWH still stood before Abraham" rather than "Abraham still stood before YHWH"; II Sam 20:1 read "to his gods" rather than "to his tents"; Ez 8:17 read "my God's nose" rather than "their nose"; and Job 32:3 read "they condemned God" rather than "they condemned Job." Some points should be noted about such emandations. (1) As a rule they are rather minimal changes and do not drastically alter the text, especially when considered in light of the passages' contexts. (2) The tiqqune sopherim do provide admitted evidence that scribal activity could and did go so far as to produce alterations in the text.

In summarizing the discussion of the main features of what can be known about the history of the Hebrew text in light of early rabbinic scribal activity, the following points are noteworthy. (1) The scribes seemed to have worked with a rather standardized text and not with texts of widely varied character. (2) Manuscripts no doubt varied in lesser and greater degree from each other. The qere-kethib references perhaps occasionally preserve some of the variants. Rabbinical exegesis and homily, which have not been discussed, sometimes made references to such variants(see Talmon, *QHBT*, 256-63). A rabbinic tradition preserved in four different sources claims that three scrolls of law were kept in the temple (see Talmon, *CMHB*, 455-68). When a question arose about the accuracy of a reading, the scrolls were compared and where two texts agreed against the third, the reading of the two was adopted. Whether this tradition is historical or not, it testifies to the rabbinic recognition of variant readings among manuscripts. Texts with obvious errors in them were to be corrected within thirty days after discovery or destroyed (see Babylonian Talmud, *Kethuboth* 106a and *Pesahim* 112a). (3) Enormous effort was expended to preserve a stable textual tradition. (4) The scribes concluded that the text had suffered occasional mistakes in transmission and sometimes needed correction. Again this is illustrated in the *qere-kethib* readings. (5) The scribes testified to the fact that the text had in places undergone scribal alteration and noted some of them *(tiqqune sopherim)*. (6) The concept and existence of a standard *textus receptus* must have already characterized pre-Masoretic rabbinic Judaism in the second to sixth centuries CE.

Until quite recently, no major Hebrew manuscript evidence of the Bible existed which could elucidate the history of the text prior to the Masoretic period. Since 1947, major mauscript evidence has come to light as the result of textual discoveries in caves along the Dead Sea and in caves and ruins in the Judean Desert. Much of this manuscript evidence exists in very fragmentary form—literally thousands of fragments—and unfortunately large quantities have not yet been published even though discovered over two decades ago. Four basic find spots are involved: caves in the Wadi Murabbaᶜat (halfway between Jericho and Ein Gedi), caves in Nahal Hever and Nahal Se'elim (between Ein Gedi and Masada), the ruins of the Herodian fortress on Masada, and caves in the area of Wadi Qumran (the location of the finds of the so-called Dead Sea Scrolls).

The finds at Murabbaᶜat contain passages from Genesis, Exodus, Numbers, Deuteronomy, Isaiah, and the Minor Prophets (for a convenient list, see Fitzmyer, 41-45). The documents from Murabbaᶜat date from the time of the second revolt against Rome (132-135 CE). In practically all matters they are identical with the later consonantal Masoretic texts. "They attest, not only a masoretic consonantal text, but also the same interval divisions of the text into sections, the same type of script, and the same format and arrangement of the writing on a leather scroll" (Vermes, 564). The Hebrew textual fragments from Nahal Hever and Nahal Se'elim represent a few passages from Exodus, Numbers, and Psalms (see Fitzmyer, 46-50) and do not differ substantially from the later Masoretic texts.

The finds from Masada, which was destroyed by the Romans in 74 CE, include fragments from Genesis, Leviticus, and Ps 81:3-85:10 as well as a large section from the Hebrew text of Sirach (39:37-44:20). Except for Sirach, the texts have not yet been published but preliminary reports suggest that the Gen 46:7-11 fragment may contain variants from the traditional text; however, the Lev 4:3-9 and Psalms fragments are in general agreement with the traditional text.

The evidence from these three sites—and especially the finds from Murabbᶜat—suggests that the traditional or normative Hebrew text of the Old Testament had become standardized by the early decades of the second century CE. This development parallels the final closing of the Hebrew canon. This evidence and inferences suggest that one can speak of the second century text as proto-Masoretic.

The textual evidence from Qumran presents a totally different picture. Among the Dead Sea, or Qumran, Scrolls, which were discovered in eleven caves in the area, are hundreds of fragments of every book in the Hebrew Bible with the exception of Esther. Scholars date the different scrolls and fragments from the third century

BCE to the first century CE. The community which utilized and no doubt produced the copies of many of the works was settled at Qumran from about the middle of the second century BCE until the time of the first revolt (66-74 CE). The texts thus constitute manuscript evidence older by a thousand years or more than the early medieval Masoretic texts. The Dead Sea Scrolls presented scholars with an unexpected variety of textual traditions. Vermes has summarized this phenomenon in the following way:

Perhaps the most crucial feature of the biblical Dead Sea Scrolls from the point of view of Jewish history is that they represent not one but several recensional traditions. Some MSS testify to the "received text" of the later Masoretes; others echo for the first time the Hebrew underlying the Greek translations of the Bible; still others correspond to the Samaritan version. (212).

In addition to their correspondence to various textual traditions, the Qumran texts frequently present readings that reflect exclusive textual uniqueness and are without parallel in any previously known tradition. The Qumran evidence thus illustrates the principle "that the further back the textual tradition of the Old Testament is followed, i.e. the older the biblical manuscripts perused, and the more ancient the records which come to the knowledge of scholars, the wider is the over-all range of textual divergence between them" (Talmon).

Before discussing the evidence of the Dead Sea Scrolls further with regard to the history and authenticity of the text, it is necessary to comment briefly on the two oldest non-Masoretic versions of the Old Testament—the Samaritan and Greek.

B. The Samaritan and Greek Texts

The Samaritan version of the Hebrew Pentateuch— whose existence was occasionally noted in the Talmud and by some of the early church fathers—was introduced to western scholars after the Italian explorer Pietro della Valle secured a copy in Damascus in 1616. When multilanguage texts of the Bible (called polyglots) were published, the Samaritan version was included, first in the Paris Polyglot (in 1632) and subsequently in the London Polyglot (1657).

The Samaritan Pentateuch is actually not a translation of the Hebrew Torah but an edition written in Hebrew. In fact, the Samaritan text is written in a modified form of a script which the Hebrews shared for centuries with the Phoenicians, Aramaeans, Moabites, and others. The Jewish community centered around Jerusalem shifted to a square script (also called "Assyrian" script) sometime between the fourth and second centuries although the old script continued to be used sporadically, i.e. on coins. The Samaritans preserved the use of the older or paleo-Hebrew script.

The Samaritans were a sect of Judaism and still survive as a small community. For the Samaritans, who shared the Pentateuch with their southern Jewish brothers, the sacred mountain which God had chosen was not Mt. Zion in Jerusalem but Mt. Gerizim near Shechem (see John 4:20). They claimed to represent the true descendants of Mosaic religion.

One of the oldest manuscripts of the Samaritan Pentateuch is the Abisha text, parts of which probably date from the eleventh century although the Samaritans claim the text was written down by Abisha, the son of Phinehas, thirteen years after the original conquest of Palestine.

The Samaritan Pentateuch varies from Masoretic texts in several thousand instances (the generally used figure is 6000). Many of these are very minor and of no consequence, frequently consisting of differences in orthography especially in the use of *matres lectionis*. Some of the differences from the traditional Hebrew text, however, are quite significant. The following are the most noteworthy:

(1) Following Gen 30:36 is material which reports a visit to Jacob by the angel of God paralleling Gen 31:11-13.

(2) The story of Moses' encounter with the pharaoh (Ex 7-11) has Moses repeat the speeches Moses receives from God to be delivered to the pharaoh as well as other minor material.

(3) Several variations appear in the Decalogue. (a) Following Ex 20:17 and Deut 5:18 material is included which parallels Deut 27:2-3a,4-7, and 11:30. These stress Mt. Gerizim as the chosen place. (b) In the Samaritan version, the material in Ex 20:19 includes the material parallel to Deut 5:24-27 and notes the response of the people. (c) Following Ex 20:21 is material paralleling Deut 5:28-31 and 18:18-22.

(4) Material paralleling Deut 1-3 occurs in various places throughout the book of Numbers and also material paralleling Num 20:17-18; 33:31-38a appears following Deut 2:8 and 10:6-7.

(5) More minor but significant differences are the reading of "Gerizim" instead of "Ebal" in Deut 27:4; the reading of "in front of Shechem" not found in the traditional text of Deut 11:30; and the twenty-one instances in the text of Deuteronomy where the Samaritan reads "the place which YHWH your God has chosen" rather than "the place which YHWH your God will choose" of the traditional text.

(6) The differences in chronological references in Gen 5 and 11 have already been noted (see above, pp. 24-25).

There are a number of uncertain factors about both the Samaritans and the Samaritan Pentateuch which raise questions about the value of this edition of the Hebrew Torah as a witness to the prestandardized text of the Pentateuch. (1) The date of the final separation of the Samaritans from the Judeans cannot be determined (see

Purvis). The Samaritans placed the rift as far back as the period of the Judges while later Judaism saw it as the result of the settlement of foreigners in the area after the fall of Samaria. As a rule, scholars place the final schism in the time of Ezra and Nehemiah (fifth and early fourth centuries BCE) or at a time of conflict between the Hasmoneans and the Samaritans late in the second century BCE. The latter view is becoming widely accepted. The determination of the date of the schism would give some suggestions as to when the Samaritan Pentateuch went its own way apart from other streams in Judaism. Unfortunately, certainty in this ara is impossible. (2) The Samaritans seemed to have made alterations and additions to the text in favor of their particular theological bias. This is probably the case in items 3 and 5 above where emphasis is placed on Shechem and Mt. Gerizim. However, in some of these cases, it may have been the southern Judean community which made changes in the text to eliminate references to Shechem and Gerizim (see especialy Deut 27:4).

References to the translation of Old Testament material into Greek are contained in the prologue to Ecclesiasticus and the *Letter of Aristeas*. Both of these works probably derive from the second century BCE. Thus they provide evidence that Hebrew texts were translated into Greek at an early date and prior to the major standardization of the Hebrew text at the end of the first and beginning of the second century CE.

The prologue to Ecclesiasticus notes: "What was originally expressed in Hebrew does not have exactly the same sense when translated into another language. Not only this work, but even the law itself, the prophecies, and the rest of the book differ not a little as originally expressed." This reference, written about 130 BCE, implies that most of the writings which came to compose the Hebrew canon already existed in Greek translation in the second century BCE.

The *Letter of Aristeas* purports to explain how the

Hebrew Torah was translated into Greek in Egypt about the middle of the third century BCE (for the text and a translation, see Hadas). This work claims to provide an eyewitness acount of how the translation was made in Alexandria by seventy-two scribes, six from each of the twelve tribes, sent from Jerusalem by the high priest Eleazar during the reign of Ptolemy Philadelphus (285-247) BCE) and at the latter's initiative. There are numerous problems associated with the historical value of the letter (on these, see Jellicoe, 1968, 29-58; and the essays in Jellicoe, 1974, 158-225). The following are general conclusions with which most scholarly opinion agrees:

(1) The document cannot be accepted at face value as an historical eyewitness account written by a Greek courtier in the court of Philadelphus.

(2) The work was written by a Jew as an apology for Judaism and its way of life based on the law and as support for a Greek translation as an inspired and authoritative version of the law equal to that of the Hebrew.

(3) The work testifies to the existence of an early translation of the Torah into Greek in Egypt.

(4) The letter provides the basis for the later legends which told of how the translators worked independently and produced identical translations (see, for example, Augustine, *City of God* XVIII 42).

(5) The practice, first attested in the second century CE, of referring to the Christian collection of Jewish scriptures in Greek translation as the Septuagint (from the Latin word for seventy) is based on the account of Aristeas.

(6) The letter refers to only the translation of the Pentateuch into Greek and not the entire Old Testament as later claimed or assumed by Christians.

Because of the various problems associated with the testimony of Aristeas and the diversity of known Greek texts, two main theories have evolved concerning the origin of the oldest Greek translation. (1) One theory argues that the various forms of the Greek Old Testament go back to one early Greek translation from which various textual forms developed. This approach seeks, therefore, to go behind the various recensions of the Greek text and thereby to establish the original form of the translation. Paul de Lagarde (1827-1891), a German textual critic, was a vociferous exponent of this view which is generally designated by his name. (2) A second view, associated with the name of Paul Kahle (1875-1964), argues that several Greek translations were produced in pre-Christian times and that these were made to meet the needs of Jewish congregations in the diaspora where Hebrew was no longer used as an everyday language. The letter written by Aristeas was composed as propaganda for a revision of one of the translations made late in the second century BCE. For Kahle, the so-called Septuagint was the result of the early church's desire to produce a standardized Greek version of the Old Testament. These two views, which stand at the opposite poles of the debate, are shared, opposed, and/or modified in scholarly research on the origin of early Greek translations and the Septuagint (see the essays in Jellicoe, 1974, 1-157).

Including all the various forms, over 2000 manuscripts or fragments of Greek texts of the Old Testament dating from the sixteenth century or earlier are known. The vast majority of these contain only sections or individual books from the Old Testament. When one recalls that the practice of combining all the books into a single volume called a codex as opposed to individual "books" on a scroll did not exist until the fourth century, this plurality of partial materials is what one would expect. Differences in readings exist among these texts, and in places they do not seem to reflect the reading of the traditional Hebrew text.

In order to understand the complex nature of the Old Greek translations and their importance as witnesses to the text of the Old Testament, several general considerations should be noted.ʌ(1) The Greek text which was known in the early church as the Septuagint (LXX) was subjected to several revisions in antiquity to produce editions referred to as "recensions" (see Jellicoe, 1968, 134-71). In his prologue to the book of Chronicles, Jerome (342-420) noted that three different editions of the LXX were in use in the eastern church. These were the Hexaplaric (or Origenian), the Hesychian, and the Lucianic recensions. Jerome's comment is as follows:

Alexandria and Egypt attribute the authorship of their Greek Old Testament to Hesychius. From Constantinople as far as to Antioch the rendering of Lucian the Martyr holds the field; while the Palestinian provinces in between these adopt those codices which, themselves the production of Origen, were promulgated by Eusebius and Pamphilas. And so the whole world is in conflict with itself over this threefold variety of text.

The Hexaplaric goes back to the textual work of Origen (186-254), who was aware of the differences among Greek translations and between the Greek and Hebrew texts. What Origen did was to produce a six-column Bible containing the Hebrew text, the Hebrew text transliterated into Greek, and four columns from four editions of the Greek. The fifth column of his Hexapla contained what was then known as the LXX. Whenever this text differed from the Hebrew text he was using, Origen noted this with a number of signs. Where a reading appeared in the LXX that was not in the Hebrew he noted this by placing an obelus ($\div$) at the beginning and a metobelus (:) at the end. When the Hebrew contained material not in the LXX, Origen added this to his text apparently marking this with an asterisk (*) at the beginning and a metobelus at the end. What Origen therefore did was to produce a revised version of the LXX by making additions from the Hebrew text, probably dependent on the Greek translations in his columns three, four, and six. Origen's manuscript, of almost 6500 pages, was apparently never copied. What was copied, as a rule, was his fifth column, but frequently without his critical symbols. Without the signs one could not tell where the Hebrew and Greek texts of his day differed. Origen's fifth column was translated into Syriac in the seventh century and some of his signs preserved. The fragments which survive of this translation make it possible to reconstruct at least some of Origen's text and the LXX text of his day. Since Origen worked in Palestine, his recension is often referred to as the Palestinian.

A second revision of the LXX was carried out in Egypt by bishop Hesychius, who died in 311. Little, for certain, is known about either Hesychius or his revision. Some scholars assume that the fourth–century Codex Vaticanus has preserved much of the Hesychian recension.

A third revision of the LXX was made by Lucian of Antioch in Syria, who was martyred in 312. It is generally assumed that Lucian did not work, like Origen, from the Hebrew text. Most scholars assume that Lucian revised a textual tradition in light of Origen's Hexaplaric text primarily by making additions. Many of the readings which are considered distinctively "Lucianic," based on quotations from the Syrian fathers, are also present in Josephus and other writers decades before Lucian. Thus scholars speak of proto-Lucianic readings.

(2) Origen included in his Hexapla three additional Greek translations. These were the translations of Aquila, Symmachus, and Theodotion (see Jellicoe, 1968, 74-99). Aquila, a Jewish proselyte from Pontus, produced a very literal translation of the Hebrew Bible based on rabbinic interpretation. Many passages in the Greek texts used by Christians had no counterpart in the current Hebrew text but were used as apologetic weapons by Christians. Aquila's translation was intended to provide an adequate translation for Jewish readers which would render the Hebrew literally. His translation was produced early in the second century but continued in use for centuries.

A second Jewish translation was that of Symmachus, prepared near the end of the second century. This work strove for literary excellence rather than for a literal rendering or, according to Jerome, the aim was to express the spirit of the text rather than the letter.

A third translation was that of Theodotion, also produced by a Jew, which was made near the end of the second century. This translation was widely used even among Christians. Theodotion stands midway between Aquila and Symmachus with regard to the literalness of the translation. Frequently the edition transliterates rather than translates Hebrew terms. The Theodotion text of the book of Daniel replaced the "LXX" version. Just as Lucianic readings appear before Lucianic, so Theodotionic readings appear before Theodotion.

(3) Quotations from the Greek Old Testament found in writers such as Philo, the New Testament, Josephus, and the early church fathers reflect a great textual variety sometimes agreeing with later recensions. For example, the book of Revelation quotes Daniel in its "Theodotion" form and many "Lucianic" readings are found in Josephus.

(4) Fragments of the Greek text of the Old Testament have been discovered at Qumran and in the Judean desert. These include a scroll of the Minor Prophets, consisting of twenty-four fragmentary columns of Jonah 1:14–Zech 9:4, and portions of Leviticus, Numbers, and Deuteronomy. The text of the minor prophets is not that of the standard LXX. These texts provide evidence that Greek translation texts were used and perhaps produced in Palestine in pre-Christian times. The tendency to see Alexandria and Egypt as the source of all early forms of the Greek text is thus called into question.

(5) The desire to utilize Greek translations to reconstruct the original form of the Hebrew text is complicated by the fact that it is sometimes difficult to know the exact Hebrew text which lay behind the Greek translation. An apparent difference may be due to a misunderstanding of

the original text by the translator and thus represent only a guess about the meaning of the text or it may be due to the fact that the translator was attempting to provide a literary expression of the meaning—perhaps a paraphrase—rather than a literal translation.

(6) The amount of diversity between Greek manuscripts varies. Some portions of the scriptures are fairly homogeneous in all the texts whereas other portions vary greatly.

The extant witnesses to several OG [Old Greek] sections attest a relatively small range of textual variation, which suggests that a single OG translation may underlie each (unless evidence of ancient alternative translation has disappeared, as almost happened in Daniel): the Pentateuch (with some special problems in Exodus and Deuteronomy), Joshua, Ruth, Isaiah, Job (later supplemented from Theodotion), Psalms, Proverbs, Koheleth (probably in Aquila's version), Chronicles, I Maccabees. A few other books have a relatively narrow base because they were probably written originally in Greek: II-IV Maccabees, Wisdom of Solomon. (Kraft, 813)

Outside of these sections noted by Kraft, Greek translations show a rather wide diversity.

At this point, a summary of the first two sections of this chapter would seem to be in order. Textual criticism of the Old Testament is necessary (1) because the Old Testament has gone through a long process of transmission during which the text could have developed, been changed, or corrupted and (2) because we possess various witnesses to that text which differ to lesser or greater degrees from one another. Behind the standardized text of the second century CE which formed the *textus receptus* of the Masoretes lies a diversity of textual forms now attested from the finds at Qumran. In addition to the Masoretic and Qumran forms of the Hebrew text, there exist the Samaritan version of the Hebrew Pentateuch and a variety of witnesses to the translation of the Old Testament Greek. In the case of the Samaritan Pentateuch, one is dealing with a textual tradition which developed within a rather closed and geographically limited community, although even here there are some differences among different manuscripts of the text. In the case of the Greek witnesses, one is confronted with an enormous variety of texts, recensions, and editions. Even if one does not take into consideration the three major recensions noted by Jerome (Hexaplaric, Hesychian, and Lucianic) and the three Jewish translations by Aquila, Symmachus, and Theodotion, there still exists a wide variety of Greek witnesses. It is difficult, if not impossible, to assume that all of these are simply variations or modifications of one original translation.

In the next section, some variant readings among the Masoretic tradition, Qumran texts, the Samaritan Pentateuch, and Greek translations will be examined to give some idea of the specific problems confronted in textual criticism. (Other ancient versions of the Old Testament besides the Samaritan and Greek exist, of course, but these two are the most valuable in textual criticism. On these other versions, see Roberts and Metzger.)

C. Differences Among the Texts

The most glaring examples of textual variations in the Old Testament are the so-called additions found in the Greek versions of the books of Daniel and Esther (see above, pp. 17-18). Practically all scholars agree that these passages never formed a part of the Hebrew text of these books since there is no textual evidence for such. They were added either at the time of translation or later and illustrate the manner in which the text could be expanded through the addition of pious legends or theological notations—the type of material utilized in the religious communities in understanding, clarifying, and expounding the text.

The second most significant set of variations among

ancient texts is found in the books of Job and Jeremiah. About one-sixth of the Hebrew book of Job is lacking in Greek texts. At the time of Origen, the current Greek text was about four hundred lines shorter than the Hebrew. These Origen supplied, marking them as additions. The Greek text of the book of Jeremiah is about one-eighth, or 2700 words, shorter than the Hebrew text. In addition, the so-called oracles against the nations which appear in Hebrew as Jer 46-51 appear in the Greek text following Jer 25:13 and also have a slightly different order in which the nations are treated. These differences in the texts of Job and Jeremiah may be explained in one of three ways:

(1) The Greek translators shortened the text and in the case of Jeremiah rearranged the text for what was considered a better order. Supporting this theory are: (a) many of the omissions in Jeremiah consist of material which is duplicated elsewhere in the book; (b) the reorganization of the material makes the book follow the pattern of Isaiah and Ezekiel in which speeches of judgment against Israel and Judah are followed by oracles against the nations, and the books conclude with oracles of promise about the future; and (c) the passages omitted in Job may have been omitted because of difficulties encountered in translating the material. This view assumes that the longer Hebrew form of the text was the more original and authentic.

(2) It may be assumed that the Greek form of Job and Jeremiah reflects an accurate translation of the text at the time the translation was made. That is, the Greek translation was based on a Hebrew source (called a *Vorlage* in German) different from the later form of the Hebrew text which must have been expanded subsequently. This view assumes that the shorter Greek form represents an earlier and more genuine form of the text.

(3) It is possible that the books of the Old Testament

69

circulated in different traditions and with varied texts within Judaism and that no effort was made to produce a standard text until later. The Greek would represent a translation of one of these traditions and the standardized Hebrew text would have preserved another. In the case of Jeremiah, this position seems to have support from the Qumran scrolls. Two different Hebrew traditions of the book were found in cave 4, one reflecting the shorter and another the longer text form. The shorter tradition is contained in a Hebrew fragment of Jer 10:4-11. This text omits verses 6-8 and 10 as does the Greek. These two fragments of Jeremiah were found in the same cave, were parts of different text forms in use by the same community, and were apparently used without any effort to produce a "standard" or "correct" form of the text.

Of these alternatives, number three appears to reflect the best interpretation. "In other words, the extant evidence imposes on us the conclusion that from the very first stage of its manuscript transmission, the Old Testament text was known in a variety of traditions which differed from each other to a greater or lesser degree" (Talmon, 40).

The following translations of Ex 1:1-5 illustrate the diversity of readings and agreements which sometimes exist among the Masoretic tradition (= MT), the Greek (= LXX), Qumran texts, partially restored (= Q), and the Samaritan (= Sam). Material in brackets is restored or added.

MT: And these are the names of the sons of Israel which came to Egypt with Jacob—each and his household came: Reuben, Simeon, Levi and Judah, Issachar, Zebulun and Benjamin, Dan and Naphtali, Gad and Asher. And it was that all the persons coming out of the loins of Jacob [were] seventy persons. And Joseph was in Egypt.

LXX: These are the names of the sons of Israel who

came to Egypt with Jacob, their father—each came with his household: Reuben, Simeon, Levi, Judah, Issachar, Zebulun, and Benjamin, Dan and Naphtali, Gad and Asher. And Joseph was in Egypt. And all the persons of Jacob were seventy-five.

Q: [And these are the names of the sons of Israel which came to Egypt] with Jacob, their father— each [and his household came: Reuben, Simeon, Levi and Judah,] Issachar, Zebulun, Joseph and Benjamin, [Dan and Naphtali, Gad and Asher. And it was that all the persons of Jacob were] seventy-five persons.

Sam: And these are the names of the sons of Israel which came to Egypt with Jacob—each and his household came: Reuben and Simeon and Levi and Judah and Issachar and Zebulun and Benjamin, Dan and Naphtali, Gad and Asher. And they were, all the persons coming out of the loins of Jacob, seventy persons. And Joseph was in Egypt.

The differences from the MT are as follows:

(1) Q lists Joseph as one of the sons going into Egypt and thus omits the statement that "Joseph was in Egypt."

(2) Sam adds the conjunction "and" between several of the names of the sons.

(3) LXX omits the conjunction "and" at the beginning.

(4) LXX notes that Joseph was in Egypt before giving the number of persons while MT notes this after giving the number of persons. Q of course has no reference to Joseph's being in Egypt.

(5) LXX and Q add "their father" after Jacob.

(6) LXX and probably Q read "And all the persons of Jacob" rather than "And all the persons coming out of the loins of Jacob."

(7) LXX and Q read "seventy-five" rather than "seventy."

71

(8) LXX and Sam read a plural verb "they were" rather than the singular "it was."

All forms of this text differ from one another in significant ways although MT and Sam show the greatest amount of agreement and are no doubt dependent upon the same textual tradition. The LXX and the Q fragment agree in a number of surprising ways but do not appear to be based on identical textual traditions unless a fair amount of freedom was taken with the text. The Q fragment with its variations from the MT and its agreements with the LXX suggest that the LXX was probably based on a Hebrew text which differed from the MT; that is, there are several Hebrew textual traditions of which the LXX translation reflects one, the Q fragment another, and the Sam and MT a third.

Frequently, variant readings among the versions suggest that errors in transmission have occurred in the MT. In Gen 4:8, the MT reads "and Cain said to Abel his brother, and when they were in the field. . . . " LXX and Sam read: "And Cain said to Abel his brother, 'Let us go out into the field' and when they were in the field. . . . " In this case, it seems clear that a phrase was accidentally omitted in copying due to the fact that the copyist's eye jumped from the first occurrence of "field" to its second occurrence and omitted the words in between.

There are a number of cases in the books of Samuel where omissions by the copyist, as in Gen 4:8, seem to have taken place. (Scholars have long noted difficulties in the text of Samuel and frequently used the LXX to "improve" the text.) The following is a translation of I Sam 14:41 with the material in italics found in the Greek but not in the Hebrew text:

MT: And Saul said to YHWH God of Israel, "Give a perfect [judgment? lot?]."

LXX: And Saul said, "O Lord, God of Israel, *why did you not answer your servant today? Is the blame in me or in Jonathan my son? O Lord, God of*

> *Israel, give clear [evidence], and if it should declare this, give holiness.*

Here neither the Hebrew nor the Greek makes very good sense. The context suggests that the passage talked about lots being cast to determine the guilty party. In the casting of the lots, the lots could give "Thummim" or "Urim" (see Deut 33:8). The Greek translator apparently did not understand the procedure and tried to give Greek translations for the technical Hebrew terms. When the section was omitted from the Hebrew, the Masoretes pointed the word to read the Hebrew term "perfect" (reading *tamim* rather than *thummim*, both of which have identical consonants). One must assume a Hebrew scribal omission and an inability of the Greek translator to understand the full text before him and then reconstruct the text (for an example, see RSV, which is based on the Vulgate and the Greek).

The Greek of I Sam 10:1 is much longer than the Hebrew text as shown in the following italicized words not found in the Hebrew:

> Then Samuel took a vial of oil and poured it on his head, and kissed him and said, "Has not YHWH anointed you *over his people, over Israel? And you shall reign over the people of the Lord and will save them out of the hands of their enemies roundabout. And this shall be a sign to you that the Lord has anointed you* to be prince over his heritage?"

Here it seems quite clear that the Hebrew text has suffered in transmission and that the scribe copying the text jumped from the first "YHWH has anointed you" to the second occurrence of the same phrase, omitting the words in between. Even without the omitted material, the text makes good sense and would have been clearly understandable. The Greek text in this case probably preserves a better reading than the Hebrew.

73

A final example of variant textual readings will demonstrate how theological concerns may have produced variant readings. The Hebrew of Deut 32:8-9 reads:

> When the Most High (Elyon) gave to the nations
>   their inheritance,
>   when he separated the sons of men,
> he fixed the boundaries of the peoples
>   according to the number of the sons of Israel.
> For YHWH's portion in his people,
>   Jacob his alloted heritage.

For the phrase "sons of Israel," the Greek reads "angels of God." A Hebrew fragment of this passage has turned up at Qumran which reads either "sons of God" or "sons of gods." How can this textual evidence be explained? (1) The Qumran text seems to preserve the most original text here. (2) The traditional Hebrew text may have been changed by the scribes since the passage seems to imply a polytheistic view with Elyon as the chief deity and with YHWH as one of the "sons of God." (3) The Greek could be explained as a translation of "sons of God" = "angels of God." However, the Greek may reflect how this passage was later exegeted since this text was used by the rabbis to explain how the nations of the world were placed under the control of seventy angels with YHWH retaining control over his people Israel.

D. Variant Readings and Scribal Practices

Textual critics in all fields recognize that when manuscripts were produced by hand and often copied on the basis of oral dictation the possibility of error was common. The attempt to discover and correct the types of mistakes produced in this manner is also a task of textual criticism. Sometimes, but not always, the versions aid in discovering where such mistakes have been made. The following examples illustrate the basic type of mistakes.

(1) *Wrong word division.* The Hebrew text of Amos 6:12, followed by the versions, asks the question: "Does one plow with oxen?" If the word "with oxen" *(bbqrym)* is divided into two words *(bbqr ym)* the text reads: "Does one plow a sea with oxen?" which certainly makes better sense and clearly fits the context.

(2) *Transposition of letters and words (metathesis).* When two letters in a word are exchanged this creates a new word. For example, the Hebrew of Ps 49:11 reads "their inward thought" *(qrbm)*. If one reads qbrm, this gives "their grave" (with some of the versions) and provides a better reading. Sometimes, a word seems to have gotten out of order. II Chron. 3:1 in Hebrew reads "which he had appointed in the place of David" *('shr hqn bmqm dwd)* whereas "in the place which David has appointed" *(bmqm 'shr hqn dwd)* seems to make better sense and is read by some of the versions.

(3) *Confusion of letters.* Some of the Hebrew letters look very similar in handwritten form. This is especially the case with *d* and *r*. Sometimes a wrong but similar letter was copied in a text. The countries Edom *('dm)* and Aram *('rm)* sometimes appear where one would expect the other. It has been frequently suggested, on the basis of some versions, that "cities *(ᶜrym)* are despised" in Is 33:8 should read "witnesses *(ᶜdym)* are despised" and this reading occurs in a manuscript from Qumran.

(4) *Confusion of words that sound alike.* In Hebrew, as in any language, there are words which sound alike although are different in meaning. The Hebrew words for "not" *(lô')* and "to him" *(lô')* were pronounced identically and seem to have been confused, for example, in I Sam 2:16 and Ps 100:3. In both cases, the Masoretes suggested a qere.

(5) *Omission (haplography) due to similar ending (homoeoteleuton) or similar beginning (homoeoarchton).* In copying texts, identical words or words with similar endings or beginnings can lead a copyist to omit material by jumping from one word to another. Gen 4:8 and I Sam 10:1, which have already been discussed, fall into this

category. In the following translation of a portion of II Samuel 14:30, the italicized words appear in the Greek and a fragment from Qumran but appear to have been lost from the Masoretic text by homoeoteleuton:

> So Absalom's servants set the field on fire. *The young men of Joab came to him with torn garments and reported that the servants of Absalom had set the field on fire.*

Sometimes what may have been omitted was only a phrase, an expression, a word, or a letter. For example, the Hebrew of Hos 4:19 reads "because of their sacrifices" (*mzbḥtm*) whereas some of the ancient versions read "because of their altars" (*mmzbḥtm*) which might suggest that a double m should have been written or read at the beginning of the word.

(6) *Additions made due to erroneous repetition (dittography).* A copyist could write twice what should have been written only once and thus produce a faulty text. The Masoretic text of II Sam 6:3-4 contains what appears to be a dittography (in italics):

> And they carried the ark of God upon a cart, a new one, and brought it out of the house of Abinadab which was on the hill. Uzzah and Ahio, sons of Abinadah, were driving the cart, *the new one, and brought it out of the house of Abinadab which was on the hill.*

(The text has been translated to preserve the Hebrew word order). The Greek and a fragment from Qumran do not contain the repeated material.

(7) *Various forms of textual expansion.* Additions could be made to the text in various ways: assimilation to parallel passages, addition of epithets, clarification of subjects and objects, conflation of readings, and so on. When a scribe copied a text, he was of course familiar

with material found elsewhere and sometimes may have inadvertently added material known from similar passages elsewhere. For example, the statement "to the priest" in Lev 6:6 may have been added due to the influence of Lev 5:18 since the phrase is missing in the Samaritan version. Common epithets of Yahweh in the Bible are "God of Israel" and "God of hosts." The versions vary as to the appearance of such epithets suggesting that those may have frequently been added. The name Nebuchadnezzar appears in the Hebrew text in eight places in the book of Jeremiah (27:6,8,20; 28:3,11,14; 29:1,3) but is missing in the Greek parallels to these texts. Elsewhere in Jeremiah the name is spelled Nebuchadrezzar. This fact plus the omission from the Greek would suggest that Nebuchadnezzar's name was added to the text. If a scribe was familiar with variant readings of a text, both readings or modified forms of those readings could be included in a text. Ez 1:20 reads: *"Wherever the spirit wanted to go,* they [the living creatures] went, *wherever the spirit wanted to go,* and the wheels rose along with them." The words in italics preserve slightly different forms in Hebrew and it may have been that the scribe was familiar with two readings and preserved them both. As was suggested earlier, the *qere* and *kethib* practice may also preserve variant readings. In some cases, a variant reading was written above the text in the Qumran manuscripts. If variant readings were noted, interlinearly or in the margins of texts, it would have been easy for the next copyist to have incorporated these into the text, thus producing a conflated text.

E. Rules and Principles in Textual Criticism

Old Testament textual criticism has always been pursued in the hope of determining and recovering the most original and authentic forms of the text. Is this possible and if so what are the rules for determining the best text? This question of course cannot be answered in any unqualified sense. There are no rules which can be applied universally. Seeing the problems is easier than supplying the solutions.

The Old Testment contains a number of duplicate texts (called deuterographs) where the same material appears in two or more different places: II Kings 18:13–20:19 = Is 36:1–38:22 = II Chron 32:1-20; II Kings 25:1-22 = Jer 39:1-10 = Jer 52:4-27; II Kings 25:27-30 = Jer 52:31-4; II Sam 22 = Ps 18; I Chron 16:8-36 = Ps 105:1-15 + Ps 96:1-13 + Ps 106:1, 47-48; Ps 14 = Ps 53; Ps 31:1-3a = Ps 71:1-3; Ps 60:7-12 = Ps 108:8-13. Even the duplicate passages do not agree in every textual detail. Are the differences in duplicate material the result of corruptions and mistakes in the written form of the text? Are the differences due to merely stylistic variations? Or do the differences reflect variations which were already in the material in its oral form before it became a written text? If the tendency of scribes was to harmonize and perhaps to conflate readings, are not the variants for that reason probably more original?

Texts of the Hebrew scriptures from Qumran are several hundred years older than the earliest extant Masoretic form of the text. Where these texts differ, is the Qumran material, being the oldest, to be taken as the more original text? Logically, this would appear to be the natural conclusion. There are a number of problems involved in such an assumption. (1) Textual critics have always known that the value of a manuscript cannot be based solely on the issue of date. (2) The Qumran evidence itself is ambiguous. Scrolls or fragments from the same caves differ radically from one another as in the case of Samuel, Isaiah, Jeremiah, and Psalms. There is no single textual tradition at Qumran. (3) The consonantal text of the Masoretes, if it goes back to a text standardized early in the second century CE, may be based on a tradition as ancient as the Qumran texts.

Books for which there are radically different texts

among the witnesses, as in the case of Job and Jeremiah, present special problems. Where textual traditions are so different, is it really possible to speak of the original, authentic text? To do so implies that at one time there existed the text of the book from which the various traditions or recensions developed. However, is it not possible that differences already existed in the tradition before it came to be written down? Or that from the beginning, when the materials were not yet considered as "scripture," there already existed a variety of traditions? (That religious communities were quite willing to live with diverging traditions is illustrated by the inclusion of Kings and Chronicles within the canon in spite of their divergent presentations of Israelite history). How many of these traditions perished in antiquity cannot be known. What we possess in the three major textual traditions that have survived—the Masoretic, the Greek, and the Samaritan—are three general traditions which achieved "the status of a *textus receptus* within the socio-religious communities which perpetuated them" (Talmon, *QHBT*, 41). These communities were, of course, rabbinical Judaism, the early church, and Samaritan Judaism. Interestingly enough, each of these communities established and authenticated its own distinctive canon of scripture. The attempt to argue that three Hebrew textual traditions developed in geographically distinct locales (the *Vorlage* of the Greek in Egypt, the *Vorlage* of the Samaritan in Palestine, and the *Vorlage* of the Masoretic in Babylonia) oversimplifies a much more complex situation and overtypifies the textual evidence. (For the theory of "local texts" see Albright, Cross, and Klein.)

In light of the numerous problems associated with the textual criticism of the Old Testament, is it possible to state any rules or principles for use in textual criticism in attempting to determine superior readings where there are multiple witnesses to the text? The following are perhaps some valid general principles.

(1) Textual criticism must begin, as did the discussion

in this chapter, with the Masoretic tradition. This tradition is, after all, the canonical form of the Hebrew scriptures. After the end of the first century, this textual tradition was the standardized text and was transmitted with care and under fairly controlled conditions.

(2) The most valuable texts for correcting the Masoretic text where problems exist are the Samaritan Pentateuch, the Qumran scrolls, and the Old Greek. Each of these has its own special problems and the attempt to discover "the earliest Greek text" is itself fraught with enormous problems. However, all three of these derive from the time prior to the standardization of the traditional Hebrew text form. At times, where these traditions contain material not found in the Masoretic text, they may not supply material which can be used to determine a reading or content "superior" to the Masoretic but rather a form of the tradition which paralleled what the rabbis selected as the authoritative text.

(3) The textual critic should assume that the original form of the traditional Hebrew text made sense. Where the text does not make sense, it is reasonable to assume that problems exist. It may be that none of the earliest witnesses makes sense (see the discussion of I Sam 14:41 above). When this is the case, textual criticism must involve a certain amount of conjecture or emendation.

(4) Variant readings among the texts must be evaluated and assessed individually, case by case. There are no blanket rules which are always applicable since the possibility for mistakes and corruption are manifold (see above, section D of this chapter).

Textual critics in all fields have worked with two general principles which certainly must be employed in biblical textual criticism:

(5) The more difficult reading should be assumed the superior reading. This principle is based on the assumption that if changes are made they generally aim at clarification, not confusion.

(6) The shorter reading should generally be assumed to

be the best reading. This principle is based on the assumption that the tendency was to expand and extend the text rather than to shorten the text. (This of course does not apply where haplography is suggested.) Ancient scribes, certainly before the standardization of the text, were more like editors than stenographers.

These principles are very general. This is due in no small part to the fact that textual criticism is an artistic science based on the employment of an informed common sense.

CHAPTER 3

The HISTORICAL-CRITICAL APPROACH TO THE OLD TESTAMENT

D. C. Allen, *The Legend of Noah: Renaissance Rational-*
ism in Art, Sciences and Letters (Urbana: University of
Illinois, 1943, ²1963); T. O. Beidelman, *W. Robertson*
Smith and the Sociological Study of Religion (Chicago:
University of Chicago, 1974); H. Bornkamm, *Luther and*
the Old Testament (Philadelphia: Fortress Press, 1969);
C. A. Briggs, *The Higher Criticism of the Hexateuch* (New
York: Charles Scribner's Sons, 1892, ²1897); J. E.
Carpenter, *The Bible in the Nineteenth Century* (London:
Longmans, Green and Co., 1903); J. E. Carpenter and G.
Harford, *The Composition of the Hexateuch* (London:
Longmans, Green, and Co., 1903); P. M. Casey, "Porphyry
and the Origin of the Book of Daniel," *JTS*
XXVII(1976)15-33; T. K. Cheyne, *Founders of Old*
Testament Criticism: Biographical, Descriptive, and
Critical Studies (London/New York: Methuen &
Co/Charles Scribner's Sons, 1893); B. S. Childs, "Psalms
Titles and Midrashic Exegesis," *JSS* XVI(1971)137-50; J.
Coppens, *The Old Testament and the Critics* (Paterson,
NJ: St. Anthony Guild, 1942); S. J. De Vries, "The
Hexteuchal Criticism of Abraham Kuenen," *JBL*
LXXXII(1963)31-57; idem, *Bible and Theology in The*
Netherlands: Dutch Old Testament Criticism under
Modernist and Conservative Auspices 1850 to World War
I (Wageningen: H. Veenman & Zonen, 1968). A. Duff,
History of Old Testament Criticism (London: Watts & Co.,
1910); F. W. Farrar, *History of Interpretation* (Lon-
don/New York: Macmillan/Dutton, 1886); H. W. Frei, *The*
Eclipse of Biblical Narrative: A Study in Eighteenth and
Nineteenth Century Hermeneutics (New Haven: Yale
University Press, 1974); V. Furnish, "The Historical
Criticism of the New Testament: A Survey of Origins,"
BJRUL LVI(1973-74)336-70; R. M. Grant, "Historical
Criticism in the Ancient Church," *JR* XXV(1945)183-96;
idem, *The Letter and the Spirit* (London/New York:
SPCK/Macmillan, 1957); idem, *A Short History of the*
Interpretation of the Bible (New York: Macmillan, 1963);
E. M. Gray, *Old Testament Criticism: Its Rise and Progress*

from the Second Century to the End of the Eighteenth (New York:Harper, 1923); H. Hailperin, *Rashi and the Christian Scholars* (Pittsburgh: University of Pittsburgh, 1963); E. G. Kraeling, *The Old Testament since the Reformation* (London/New York: Lutterworth/Schocken, 1955/1969); E. Krentz, *The Historical-Critical Method* (Philadelphia: Fortress Press, 1975); R. Loewe, "The Jewish Midrashim and Patristic and Scholastic Exegesis of the Bible," *SP* I(1957)492-514; *idem*, "The 'Plain' Meaning of Scripture in Early Jewish Exegesis," *Papers of the Institute of Jewish Studies London*, I, ed. J. G. Weiss (Jerusalem: Magnes Press, 1964)140-85; D. E. Nineham, ed., *The Church's Use of the Bible: Past and Present* (London: SPCK, 1963); J. S. Preus, *From Shadow to Promise: Old Testament Interpretation from Augustine to the Young Luther* (Cambridge: Harvard University Press, 1969); A. Richardson, *The Bible in the Age of Science* (London: SCM Press, 1961); B. Smalley, *The Study of the Bible in the Middle Ages* (2nd ed.; Notre Dame: University of Notre Dame, 1964).

Today when people study documents from past times, they attempt to discover a number of things about them. (1) Scholars seek to understand as much as can be known about the context out of which they came. This involves knowledge, where possible, about the author or authors; the historical period in which the writings originated; and the social, cultural, and economic circles to which their authors belonged or which made use of such documents. (2) Scholars try to understand what the texts meant for the ancient audiences to which they were addressed. (3) Attempts are made to determine the purposes served by the documents, such as why they were written in the first place and how they were utilized.

All of these concerns are factors which contribute to the historical-critical study of literature. Such an approach is applied to literature whether that literature be an Egyptian mythological text, an Akkadian code of law, or a

Roman inscription. The ultimate goal of such a pursuit is an understanding of the text in terms of its original composition, content, and audience.

In modern biblical study, the same interpretive analysis is applied to the biblical texts as would be applied to any other document from antiquity. This has not always been the case. In this chapter, we shall explore the limited use which was made of historical criticism in the early synagogue and church, how this approach was overshadowed in the early medieval period, how significant concern with the literal meaning of the scriptures gave birth to historical criticism, and how the method reached its place of dominance in the nineteenth century.

A. Literary Criticism in the Early Synagogue and Church

Ancient students and scholars were concerned with who wrote the biblical books, when, and for what purposes. Interests such as these are already reflected in some places within the Old Testament itself. For example, thirteen psalms contain short introductory statements specifying particular historical episodes in the life of David which were assumed to have provided the occasions for the compositions of the psalms. These psalms are, with the biblical passages which recount the episodes assumed noted in parenthesis: 3(II Sam 15:1-18:33); 7 (unknown); 18 (II Sam 22); 34 (I Sam 21:10-15); 51 (II Sam 11:1-12:14); 52 (I Sam 22:6-10); 54 (I Sam 23:14-24); 56 (I Sam 21:10-15; 27:1-4); 57 (I Sam 22:1; 24:1-7); 59 (I Sam 19:8-17); 60 (II Sam 8:3-8; 10:15-20); 63 (I Sam 24:1-7; II Sam 15:1-16:14); and 142 (I Sam 22:1; 24:1-7). These notations, which were not part of the original compositions, assume that David was the author of the psalms and demonstrate that editors of the material were concerned with such matters as the historical circumstances which gave rise to the writing of biblical texts. Their interest, however, was primarily exegetical. That is, the historical associations were employed as the means to expose the inner life of David for contemplation and imitation by the pious of a later age (see Childs).

Rabbinic scholars have provided us with incidental comments on the authorship of the Hebrew scriptures. This demonstrates that they had at least a minimum concern for historical criticism. However, rabbinic sources neither provide any discussion as to how the rabbis arrived at their conclusions about authorship nor provide any systematic discussion of the issues involved. The Babylonian Talmud contains the following statement about the authors of the scripture:

Who wrote the scriptures? Moses wrote his own book [the Torah or Pentateuch] and the portion of Balaam [Num 22–24 or some unknown work?] and Job. Joshua wrote the book which bears his name and [the last] eight verses of the Pentateuch. Samuel wrote the book which bears his name and the book of Judges and Ruth. David wrote the book of Psalms, including in it the work of the ten elders, namely, Adam, Melchizedek, Abraham, Moses, Heman, Yeduthun, Asaph, and the three sons of Korah. Jeremiah wrote the book which bears his name, the book of Kings, and Lamentations. Hezekiah and his colleagues wrote Isaiah, Proverbs, the Song of Songs and Ecclesiastes. The men of the Great Assembly wrote Ezekiel, the twelve minor prophets, Daniel, and the scroll of Esther. Ezra wrote the book that bears his name and the genealogies of the book of Chronicles up to his own time. . . . Who then finished it [the book of Chronicles]? Nehemiah the son of Hachaliah. (*Baba Bathra* 14b–15a)

Several comments should be noted with regard to this text. (1) The Hebrew word translated "wrote" could also mean what we would include in the verb "edit" and perhaps even "publish." (2) The book of Nehemiah is not mentioned but was probably understood as being noted in the final statement. (3) The Talmud contains different traditions about the authorship of the Psalms. Another list places David among the ten contributors to the Psalms:

Adam, Moses, Asaph, Heman, Abraham, Jeduthun, David, Solomon, the three sons of Korah, and Ezra (Baba Bathra 14b). (4) The Great Synagogue was believed to have had its origins during the days of Ezra and to have functioned as a forerunner to the later Sanhedrin. (5) The view that Ezra collected or produced the final form of all the Hebrew scriptures was also current in early Judaism (see above, pp. 32, 43). (6) The belief that Moses wrote the account of his own death was current in some circles in Judaism and was noted by Josephus (Antiquities IV 326) and Philo (On the Life of Moses II 291). (7) The interest in the authorship of the biblical books is primarily a theological, not a historical, concern.

The general outline of the above views on the authorship of the scriptures became widespread in both Judaism and Christianity. In both religious communities, the conclusions regarding human authorship of the scriptures were undergirded by the argument that behind the human writers stood divine authority. Revered authorship and divine inspiration combined to produce respect and awe before the sacred writings.

In the early history of Judaism and Christianity, there were some persons who attempted to study biblical materials from more developed critical-historical perspectives. Many scholars in pre-Christian times were literary critics who sought to determine the authenticity and date of documents and to establish the best form of texts. Many authors of the Hellenistic Age, which began with Alexander's conquest of the East, included sections on criticism in their writings. The works of Homer were frequently subjected to criticism, partly to establish the most authentic text but also to question the historicity of the works and their contents. Dio Chrysostom (about 40-115), in his oration Troica, sought to prove that the Trojan War never took place. Thus he denied the historical character of the Iliad and Odyssey.

Some Jews living in the Greco-Roman world were influenced by the documentary criticism practiced by their contemporaries. The Alexandrian author, Philo (about 20 BCE-50 CE), noted that there were Jews who doubted the historical reliability of their scriptures and even considered some of their contents to be myths. Other Jewish scholars, like Philo himself and his predecessor in Alexandria, Aristobulus (second century BCE), moved beyond the letter of the sacred writings and searched for allegorical and hidden philosophical meanings of the texts. In so doing, their treatment of the biblical materials was similar to the treatment of classical mythological texts by Greek allegorists.

Two persons who stood outside both Judaism and Christianity challenged the historicity and the widely assumed authorship of some of the books. The second-century pagan philosopher Celsus argued that much in the scriptures is unbelievable because it assumes the operation of the miraculous and is filled with absurdities. According to Origen (about 185-254), who wrote a work entitled *Contra Celsum*, Celsus argued that the Mosaic book of Genesis was based on sources borrowed from others. The flood story, for example, was a retelling of the "Deucalion narrative current among the Greeks." Celsus thus asserted that early Hebrew history and genealogies were the "same old story, received by most in the form of a myth."

Porphyry (about 232-303) was a Neo–Platonist philosopher and a virulent anti-Christian whose fifteen-book work against the Christians was condemned to the fire in 448. Porphyry pointed to many alleged inconsistencies in the New Testament gospels and attacked the Jewish and Christian interpretation and dating of the scriptures and especially the book of Daniel. In the preface to his commentary on Daniel, Jerome tells the following about Porphyry's analysis of the book:

Porphyry wrote his twelfth book against the prophet Daniel, asserting that the book inscribed with his name was written, not by him, but by some one who lived in Judaea in the days of

Antiochus Epiphanes [175-164 BCE], and that Daniel did not so much foretell future events as relate what had already taken place. That in fine all his narrative up to the time of Antiochus contained a true history; whatever opinions he advanced with respect to later events were false, since he did not know the future. (Text in Gray, 17-18, 209)

Thus Porphyry argued that the book of Daniel was a pseudepigraph (a book written under the name of another) produced during the Maccabean period. (On Porphyry and his possible dependence on Syriac-speaking Jews and Christians, see Casey.)

Some early Christians also engaged in historical criticism of the scriptures and disputed some of the opinions held about them. For example, Apelles, who was for a time a follower of the heretic Marcion (second century), argued on theological grounds against the inspiration of the Old Testament. The following quote illustrates his method of argumentation:

Did God know Adam would transgress his commandments or did he not? If he did not know, there is no declaration of his divine power; if however he knew and nevertheless gave orders which had to be neglected, it is not godlike to give a superfluous command. Yet he gave a superfluous command to that first-formed Adam, which he knew he would not keep at all. Yet God does nothing superfluous. Therefore the writing is not of God. (Text in Grant, 1945, 187-88)

Julius Africanus (about 170-245), who produced a major encyclopedia and world history, seems to have been the most thorough practitioner of biblical criticism in the ancient church. He applied criticism to determine the authenticity of certain passages in manuscripts of Homer's works and commented on the problems involved in the Matthean and Lukan genealogies of Jesus. In a letter written to his contemporary, Origen, Africanus demonstrates that he dealt critically with at least parts of the Old Testament. He sought to establish that the story of

Susanna originally formed no part of the book of Daniel but was in fact a late and fictitious work. He pointed to differences in style between Daniel and Susanna, to plays on words in the latter which only made sense if the work was originally composed in Greek, to historical improbabilities, and to the fact that Susanna was not a part of the scriptures in the Jewish canon. (On Africanus, see Grant, 1945, 190-93.)

B. Early Jewish and Christian Interpretation of the Old Testament

If some in Judaism and Christianity engaged in biblical criticism during the early centuries, why did this endeavor cease? There were perhaps a number of reasons. (1) Classical Greek higher education, which had fostered historical and source criticism, began to decline after the second century. Thus the influence of classical scholarship declined. There were fewer outside the faith to imitate and few converts who brought a classical heritage into the religious communities. (2) The religious communities considered such an approach to be dangerous and subversive of faith. People like Celsus, Porphyry and the later emperor Julian turned such learning against the faith. (3) The development of closed canons which were understood as divine revelation encircled the scriptures with an aura that discouraged any critical posture.

The most significant factor, however, was (4) the development of exegetical approaches to the scriptures which allowed for enormous speculation on the text with little or no regard for the historical or original meaning. Thus the historical background and history of the text as well as the author's intentions could be and often were ignored. These approaches were developed by the Pharisaic rabbis and the church fathers. Both of these groups inherited rich and varied exegetical traditions. Their predecessors had read the scriptures as eschatological predictions about the final times (at Qumran and most of the New Testament authors), as allegories or texts with hidden philosophical meanings (Philo, Book of Hebrews, and sometimes Paul), and/or as texts providing the laws and guide for the righteous and pure life before God (Sadducees and early Pharisaism).

Both the rabbis and the church fathers employed exegetical procedures which allowed the interpreter to find more than the literal meaning in a text. Among Christians, the "deeper" meaning of the text was sought and a distinction was made between the "letter" and the "spirit" (see II Cor 3:6). Just as the human person was composed of many elements—body, soul, and spirit—so also were the scriptural texts. The body of a text was its straightforward meaning, the soul its moral sense, and the spirit its mystical or allegorical meaning. This approach to the scriptures had several roots (see Grant, 1957). (1) One was the Greek allegorical treatment of epics and mythical materials which was widespread even in pre-Christian times. (2) The philosophical-allegorical interpretation of scripture used by Aristobulus and Philo had a great influence on Alexandrian Christianity. (3) Rabbinic exegesis, to be discussed below, was also a factor. (4) The discovery of multiple layers of meaning in the text was also employed to combat an overly simplistic view of scripture which read metaphoric, parabolic, and figurative language and expressions as if they were literally true.

This search for the "deeper" or "spiritual" meaning in the text was opposed to a limited extent by some church exegetes. Marcion, for example, insisted that the Old Testament was not a Christian book and that no amount of allegorical interpretation could turn it into one. In order to stress the difference between the God of the Old Testament and that of the New and between Judaism and Christianity, he argued for an absolutely literal reading of the texts. The so-called school of Antioch—whose most famous theologian was Theodore of Mopsuestia (about

350-428)—opposed excessive allegorical interpretation of the scriptures and argued that any deeper meaning must be based on the letter of the text. According to this approach, some Old Testament texts, such as Pss 2, 8, 45, and 110, were originally messianic and spoke of future events but other texts, like Ps 22, were historical and could only be applied typologically to Jesus. In the debates and discussions between the Alexandrians and Antiochenes, Jerome (331-420) occupied a middle position.

Within Christianity, the view that the true meaning of the Old Testament was the spiritual and deeper meaning lurking beneath the surface and pointing to Christ and his church triumphed. The following medieval verse demonstrates the church's approach to multiple layers of meaning in each text, an approach which was already fully developed by the fourth century:

> The letter shows us what God and our fathers did;
> The allegory shows us where our faith is hid;
> The moral meaning gives us rules of daily life;
> The anagogy shows us where we end our strife.
> (From Grant, 1963, 119)

In his discussion of Galatians 4, the monk John Cassian (about 360-435) demonstrates how the fourfold sense of scripture was applied. In commenting on Jerusalem, he wrote that literally or historically the name refers to a city of the Jews, allegorically it denotes the church of Christ, tropologically it indicates the human soul, and anagogically it signifies the heavenly City of God (see Preus, 21-22).

With every text capable of numerous meanings, the interpreter was never forced to take the text literally and critically; one could always seek refuge amid the higher pinnacles of spiritual exegesis. However, a critical stance over against the text was not really permissible. Augustine (354-430) expressed it this way:

If we are perplexed by an apparent contradiction in scripture, it is not permissible to say, the author of this book is mistaken;

93

instead, the manuscript is faulty, or the translation is wrong, or you have not understood. . . . Scripture has a sacredness peculiar to itself. In other books the reader may form his own opinion and perhaps, from not understanding the writer, may differ from him. . . . We are bound to receive as true whatever the canon shows to have been said by even one prophet or apostle or evangelist. (Contra Faustum Manichaeum II 5)

What the text "said" and "meant" when properly understood was, of course, expected to agree with the orthodox faith: "that which has been believed everywhere, always, by everyone."

Rabbinical exegesis, like Christian interpretation, was based on the belief that the Bible was God-given and totally consistent. At the same time, exegesis operated on the premise that no biblical passage could really contradict an accepted rabbinic article of belief. The biblical texts were searched, passages combined, and phrases and constructions associated so that traditional laws and new rules and regulations could claim biblical warrant. The responsibility of the biblical scholar was the proper understanding of the written text in light of the received and developing faith: "Search it [Torah] and search it, for everything is in it" (Mishnah, Aboth 5:22).

Various rules for the interpretation of scripture were devised. The best known were the seven rules associated with Hillel the Elder (last century BCE). These hermeneutical principles were utilized in making the scriptures apply to the contemporary situation. Some rabbis, such as Akiba (d. 134), argued that deeper meanings could be sought in practically every letter, particle, and grammatical construction of the biblical texts. Others, like Akiba's contemporary Rabbi Ishmael, contended that "the Torah speaks in human language" and sought to base interpretations on the sense of the text rather than words, letters, or syntax in the text. Their goals, however, were basically identical; namely, the desire to see the fullness of rabbinical thought and practice in the sacred text.

Thus early Jewish exegesis of the Old Testament encouraged an interpretation which sought for various senses in a single text, although this was more controlled and subdued when the text in question was legal in character. The memory-word (or mnemonic), *pardes*, was used to refer to such an approach. Each of the consonants in the word denoted a particular meaning to be found in the text: *peshat* (the plain meaning), *remez* (allusion or allegory), *derash* (the homiletical), and *sod* (the mystical or secret).

Significant differences existed between early Jewish and Christian approaches to the Old Testament although neither really sought to expound the literal historical meaning of the text in light of its original setting. However, for rabbinical scholars, the Old Testament laws and mode of life remained valid. They sought to adhere to the letter as well as the new understanding of the text. Thus the rabbis could speak of the "plain meaning" (the *peshat*) of the text over against its exposition (the *midrash*) (see Loewe). Thus the plain meaning of the text, which, however, did not correspond to what today is called the literal and historical meaning, was never really lost. Among Christians, the situation was different. The Old Testament was turned into a Christian book, a maneuver frequently accomplished by exegetical acrobatics that completely ignored the plain meaning of the text. Most of the Old Testament legal material was considered by Christians as no longer binding and thus there was no theological obligation to preserve the straightforward sense of this material.

C. Biblical Study from the Middle Ages to the Reformation

In medieval Judaism and Christianity, the general tendency in biblical interpretation continued to be the search for multiple meanings in each text. However, there were a number of developments which contributed to the subsequent rise of a historical-critical approach to the Old Testament. (1) First of all, among Jewish scholars, especially those in Spain, the study of biblical Hebrew grammar was placed on a scholarly footing. Such scholars as Menahem ibn Saruk (910-970), Judah ben David Hayyuj (about 1000), and Jonah ibn Janah (about 1000) were the forerunners in this development. (2) Commentaries which utilized grammatical insights and stressed the plain meaning were written by such scholars as Abraham ibn Ezra (1092-1167) and Solomon ben Isaac, better known as Rashi (1040-1105).

This grammatical and commentary work by Jewish scholars frequently bypassed the tradition which had accumulated around the biblical texts and stressed their natural meaning. At times, exegetes offered suggested emendations for improving the texts. Critical evaluations of Old Testament materials were also made. Moses ben Samuel Gikatilla (d. 1080) suggested that some of the psalms must have been written late in Israelite history and that the book of Isaiah is actually two works with the break coming between Is 39 and 40. Some writers were led to question the Mosaic authorship of the Pentateuch. Ibn Ezra had doubts about whether Moses was the author. Such biblical phrases as "Moses wrote," "the Canaanite was then in the land," and "beyond the Jordan" seemed to have raised doubts in his mind. Ibn Ezra does not comment on such problems in detail but notes here and there that "there is in this a mystery; let him who comprehends be silent."

In medieval Christianity, the Old Testament was understood in diverse ways but generally without regard to the original intention of the writers or the texts (see Preus). A number of factors should be noted about the medieval Christian treatment of the Old Testament. (1) As a rule, Christians accepted the continued and abiding value of the moral laws of the Hebrew scriptures but saw them in need of fuller understanding in light of the New Testament. (2) Christian meaning was assumed to be present in the words of Hebrew scripture, but this was a meaning given by God, the author of sacred scripture. (3) The Old Testament was a sign or figure of the New Testament and thus the New was the real meaning of the Old. (4) Where the Old was understood as promise about Christ and the church, it was assumed that the promises either were understood by ancient Israelites in a "carnal" or worldly fashion or else were already appropriated in a truly Christian, although chronologically pre-Christian, sense. (4) Interpretation which sought for several meanings in the texts, inherited from the early church, continued apace. Most commentators stressed four meanings, although for individual commentators the number could be lesser or greater.

Medieval Christianity was not devoid of commentators who sought to discover and expound the literal or historical sense of scripture. In its own way, scholastic theology contributed to this interest in the literal sense of scripture. Scholasticism utilized philosophical perspectives and rationalistic approaches in constructing its theological system. This meant that, unlike their predecessors, scholastic theologians did not require biblical exegesis to carry the full weight of their theology. Arguments and insights drawn from philosophy and natural theology became the foundation upon which theological systems were built. In addition, by assigning reason a dominant place in the theological enterprise, scholastic theologians made possible some objectivity by which an overly subjective reading and interpretation of scripture could be condemned. (On the use of the Bible by scholastic theologians and the role of literal interpretation in their exegesis, see Preus, 38-60 and Grant, 1963, 120-27.)

A number of scholars associated with the Abbey of St. Victor in Paris (founded in 1110) are noteworthy for their emphasis on the literal interpretation of scripture. Among the Victorines were Hugh (d. 1141), Richard (d. 1173), and Andrew (d. 1175), who attempted to provide their students with the necessary tools for Bible study (see Smalley, 83-195). They stressed the importance of geographical, historical, and scientific knowledge for understanding the scriptures and, above all, the need to know Hebrew and to pay attention to the literal sense of the texts. Hugh opposed an excessively allegorical reading of the text and those who disdained the simple meaning:

Do not despise what is lowly in God's word, for by lowliness you will be enlightened to divinity. The outward form of God's word seems to you, perhaps, like dirt, so you trample it underfoot, like dirt, and despise what the letter tells you was done physically and visibly. But hear! that dirt, which you trample, opened the eyes of the blind. Read Scripture then, and first learn carefully what it tells you was done in the flesh (text in Smalley, 93-94).

Hugh emphasized that the interpreter must heed "that which appears to have been certainly intended by the author" and "that explanation which is admissible in the context." Nonetheless, the significance of the historical and literal meaning of scripture for Hugh and the other Victorines was primarily its aid in the service of spiritual and theological exegesis (see Preus, 24-37). What they sought to do was to shift the emphasis. "The 'building' of exegesis had been growing top-heavy. Monks had concentrated on the 'upper story' and its 'painting'; scholars on the theological questions. The Victorines saved the whole structure by strengthening its basis" (Smalley, 196). In their re-emphasis of the literal meaning of scripture, the Victorines were dependent upon such patristic exegetes as Jerome but above all upon the exegesis and friendship of contemporary Jewish scholarship and scholars in twelfth century France (see Smalley, 149-72).

A later Christian theologian who, like the Victorines, was greatly influenced by Jewish scholarship, especially the commentaries of Rashi, was Nicholas of Lyra (see Preus, 61-71; Hailperin, 137-246). Nicholas (about 1270-

1349) a Franciscan born in Normandy, spent most of his years in Paris. His works, of which the most famous was a running commentary on the Old and New Testaments, were widely popular and later exerted an influence on Martin Luther. Of all medieval Christian scholars, Nicholas was the most proficient in Hebrew and the best acquainted with practically all forms of Jewish biblical studies. Nicholas gave lip service to the fourfold sense of scripture current in the exegesis of his day. In his exegesis, however, Nicholas emphasized two meanings: "The *outer* Scripture is the *sensus litteralis,* which is more exposed, because its signification comes from an immediate understanding of the words. The *inner* Scripture, however, is the *sensus mysticus,* or *spiritualis,* which is more hidden, because its signification comes from the *things signified* by the words" (quoted in Hailperin, 256-57). The *sensus litteralis* was the sense and the intention of the author. Nicholas recognized that the original author could speak in allegory or metaphor so that the literal sense was sometimes an expression of allegorical language. Nicholas stated the importance of the literal meaning in the following manner:

All of them [senses] presuppose the literal sense as the foundation. As a building declining from the foundation is likely to fall, so the mystic exposition, which deviates from the literal sense, must be reckoned unbecoming and unsuitable, or in a way less becoming, other things being equal, and less suitable. Those who wish to make proficiency in the study of Sacred Scriptures, must begin with the literal sense. . . . It must be observed likewise, that the literal sense has been much obscured by the method of exposition traditionally recommended and practiced by others who, though they may have said many things well, have yet touched on the literal but sparingly, and have so multiplied the mystical senses as nearly to intercept and choke it. (quoted in Hailperin, 257)

In order to recover the "literal sense as the foundation," Nicholas turned to the Hebrew text and Jewish exegetes,

99

especially Rashi. His commentary refers to Rashi on practically every page. So strong was his utilization of the work of Jewish exegetes that contemporaries could refer to him as the "Judaizing Lyra" and later generations debated whether he was not in fact a Jew.

The Hebrew Renaissance of the late eleventh to the early thirteenth century produced noteworthy advances in the study of the literal sense of the Hebrew scriptures. This movement affected some Christian exegetes, most notably the Victorines and Nicholas of Lyra. In 1312, the Council of Vienne decided to establish chairs of Hebrew and Arabic in the universities of Rome, Paris, Oxford, Salamanca, and Bologna. This was partially a positive reaction to the concern for a knowledge of Hebrew and Jewish exegesis. Involved in the decision, however, was also a desire to stem the "Judaizing" interpretation of the scriptures as well as the hope of propagating the Christian faith among nonbelievers (see Hailperin, 133-34, 253-54). Although the impact of Jewish studies upon Christians was lessened in the years following the Council of Vienne, due to increased anti-Judaic sentiment, it did not disappear entirely.

The Classical Renaissance, which began in Italy during the fourteenth century and spread northward, stimulated intellectual activity which would eventually have enormous consequences for biblical studies. With their recovery of classical culture, revived interest in the Greek language, and militant humanism, Renaissance scholars often took a critical approach toward the life and culture of their day and the traditions upon which these were based. Three elements in Renaissance thought and life had special significance for biblical studies.

(1) During the Renaissance, there developed a true sense of anachronism, that is, an understanding of the past as truly past. Medieval art and literature frequently lacked any truly historical perspective on the past which allowed one to understand the past as different in space and time from the contemporary. Some Renaissance

scholars rediscovered the past with its differences and on occasion embraced it with a passion and turned on the present with a vengeance. Petrarch (1304-1374), for example, wrote nostalgic letters to classical authors and heaped scorn upon the barbaric conditions of his own day. This renewed sense of the past as past was to contribute to the development of history as a discipline and was to make possible a recognition that the biblical documents were a part of that past and must be studied in light of their past historical context.

(2) Documentary criticism was a widely practiced art among Renaissance scholars. The most famous case of such criticism was the challenge to the authenticity of the so-called Donation of Constantine, which had been used by the papacy to claim temporal power. Lorenzo Valla (about 1406-1457) in 1439 amassed an overwhelming case against the genuineness of the document. However, his criticism was not unique, having been anticipated by Otto of Freising (about 1110-1158) and advocated independently by his contemporaries Nicholas of Cusa (about 1400-1464) and Reginald Pecock (about 1393-1461). Valla's case was epoch-making because he brought together a gamut of arguments drawn from philology, grammar, logic, geography, chronology, history, and law. This type of criticism was applied to numerous documents, both classical and Christian, in order to elucidate their origin and history. Although the Old Testament was not subjected to such analysis, nonetheless, documentary criticism was placed on a scientific footing and the technique lay at hand ready to be applied to the biblical texts.

(3) Renaissance humanists stressed the use of grammatical analysis as the means for understanding ancient texts. This meant that philology, grammar, and textual criticism were more important than tradition as interpretive tools. In Valla's annotations on the New Testament, first published by Erasmus in 1505, he argued that none of the words of Christ have been preserved since Christ spoke in

Hebrew and never wrote anything. Grammatical analysis meant that the biblical writings must be treated as literary sources like any other documents. Erasmus (1467-1536) drew the conclusion Valla only inferred: the trivial concerns of the grammarian are of more importance in understanding the biblical texts than the inquiries of theologians. This conclusion had far-reaching consequences since the difference between the grammatical analysis of a text and a theological interpretation of or gloss on the text is enormous. The former demands a literal and realistic reading of the sources which was not required by the latter.

The Protestant Reformation of the sixteenth century contributed significant developments which were to make historical criticism possible if not necessary, although the reformers themselves did not really engage in historical criticism. Three operating principles in the Reformation should be noted. (1) *Sola scriptura* was a keynote of the Reformation. This emphasis on the Bible as the rule and norm of faith returned the Bible to the center of the theological enterprise and thus broke with scholastic theology. In emphasizing the Bible, Luther and the other reformers stressed a literal interpretation of the scriptures. Luther declared: "The Holy Spirit is the plainest writer and speaker in heaven and earth, and therefore His words cannot have more than one, and that the very simplest, sense, which we call the literal, ordinary, natural, sense." He argued that heresies and errors in scripture had arisen out of disregard for the plain and simple meaning. In his earliest exegesis, Luther did not hold this view, but in his work on the Old Testament he was compelled toward the views of Nicholas of Lyra and his Judaizing exegesis (see Preus, 267-71). For Luther, the Old Testament became a book of promise; but his emphasis on the *sensus propheticus* meant that the Old Testament, in its literal but promissory meaning, had to be understood in light of the historical "Jewish" community to whom the promises had been made.

Luther, like other reformers, argued that "scripture itself by itself is the most unequivocal, the most accessible, the most comprehensible authority, itself its own interpreter, attesting, judging, illuminating all things." In other words, scripture must be interpreted by scripture. Both Luther and Calvin, however, recognized that at times scripture is contradictory. Luther's verdict was: "If a difficulty arises in regard to the Holy Scriptures and we cannot solve it, we must just let it alone." As we have seen, Luther returned to the Jewish canon as the content of the Christian Old Testament. He was critical of James, Jude, Hebrews, and Revelation in the New Testament and evaluated these on the basis of his "canon within the canon" ("what urges Christ"). Later Protestants, inheriting the reformers' emphasis on the Bible, would discover that when they encountered a difficulty in the text they were unable to "just let it alone."

(2) A second emphasis of the Protestant Reformation was its iconoclastic attitude toward tradition. All the reformers agreed that the church had gone wrong although they differed as to exactly when and how. As a result, they sought to restore the purity of the church and return to the origins. Such an attitude created a disregard or a hostility toward the traditions of the church which included the church's attitude toward scripture. Elements which the reformers believed had surreptitiously entered the church's faith and practice were fair game for criticism. The importance of this iconoclastic attitude of the reformers lies in the fact that it created a critical stance toward tradition, orthodoxy, and received opinions. During the Reformation period, this critical attitude was primarily applied to post-biblical traditions, but the way was prepared for extension of the criticism to the biblical literature itself.

(3) A third development in the Reformation was the growth of religious freedom. The reformers argued that a person could interpret and understand the scriptures aided by divine light or *fides divina*. On the one hand,

such an approach rejected authoritarianism in tradition, priesthood, and religious practice; on the other hand, it encouraged the appeal to private judgment. The right to exercise private judgment not only allowed an individual to form his own opinion but also made it possible to conclude compromises and accommodations with the developing thought and movements of the time. Theological and critical positions were thus capable of absorbing modernity often in the name of returning to and restoring antiquity. The reformers were certainly not pleased with some of the products which resulted from this religious freedom and even sought to suppress the radicals who camped in the shadows of their tents. The Socinians, for example, developed a moderate unitarian theology and argued that the veracity of the scriptures should be subject to rational judgment. Such modernity and accommodation antagonized the reformers.

The scientific revolution which peaked in the sixteenth and seventeenth centuries has probably been of more consequence to biblical studies, and to theology as a whole, than any other single phenomenon (see Furnish, 336-39). Customarily, the beginnings of this revolution are seen in the work of the Polish astronomer, Nicolas Copernicus (1473-1543), who advanced the theory that the earth was in motion rotating around the sun and that "the order and magnitude of the stars and all their orbs and the heaven itself are so connected that in no part can anything be transposed without confusion to the rest and to the whole universe" (from the preface to his De revolutionibus). Copernicus' work was later substantiated and elaborated by Galileo, Kepler, and Newton. The implications of the scientific method with its emphasis on the observation of natural phenomena, the employment of human reason, and the generalization of perceptual experience were first applied to the study of the physical universe in the fields of mechanics and astronomy. Gradually, the same methodology was applied to matters of historical research. Out of the development of the scientific approach to natural and historical data, four important conclusions developed. (1) Persons should have the right to exercise their reason even when such an undertaking challenges the inherited and sacred traditions from the past. (2) The universe operates in accordance with natural laws and principles. (3) Natural and human causes should be sought as the explanations for events and conditions in the natural and human worlds. (4) The past can be understood in terms of the present since what was possible once is possible still and what is incredible now has been incredible always.

The methodology and conclusions of the scientific approach quickly came into conflict with the church and its understanding of scripture. Both Galileo and Kepler realized that their scientific methodology and conclusions about the natural world posed serious consequences for theology and biblical interpretation (see Furnish, 340-41). Kepler (1571-1630) suggested that the biblical materials were not concerned with physics and astronomy, that is, with scientific matters, but with the theological dimensions of life. However, Kepler suggested that in some cases the new discoveries of science could be used in support of the Bible and he proposed, in 1606, that the Bethlehem star was actually the conjunction of Mars, Saturn, and Jupiter in the sign of Taurus in 6 BCE. Galileo (1564-1642) suggested that both nature and scripture are manifestations of God's word and that where experience and nature clash with scripture one must side with experience. Kepler sought to compartmentalize science and scripture, whereas Galileo's position actually provided the basis for placing science over against the scriptures. In its dogmatic reaction to and denunciation of Galileo, the church affirmed the dominance of theology and scripture over science and reason.

The scientific revolution was ultimately to produce a major reorientation in practically all aspects of life. When its implications were applied to philosophy by Francis Bacon (1561-1626) and Rene Descartes (1596-1650), it gave birth to doubt and skepticism as basic philosophical postures. When applied to historical data, the scientific approach sought for explanations "from below" rather than "from above," that is, in terms of human and natural causation rather than in supernatural categories. It should not be assumed, however, that science and religion were in conflict from the beginning. Many of the early scientists were men of piety and sought to reconcile their scientific knowledge with religious faith. For example, in the seventeenth century one of the most widely debated topics was Noah's flood. Exegetes, who were sometimes scientists as well, drew upon all the sciences of the time in order to substantiate the historicity of the flood and to understand it in rational terms (see Allen).

D. The Origins of the Historical-Critical Approach

In the seventeenth century, one finds expressions of the fundamental presuppositions which were to become the hallmarks of the historical-critical approach to the Old Testament. Among such presuppositions are the following: (1) The Bible is to be studied in the same critical manner as any other book. (2) The biblical material has a history of composition and transmission which can be elucidated by distinguishing the various circumstances through which the material passed. (3) Internal statements, characteristics of style, and repetitions make possible a denial of the assumption that a single author stands behind the Pentateuch. (4) Behind the various writings in the Old Testament must be discerned human authors who wrote with particular purposes and aims in mind. (On the seventeenth-century developments, see Briggs, 36-45; Carpenter-Hartford, 38-52; and Gray 75-115.)

The important figures in biblical criticism during the seventeenth century were the English philosopher

Thomas Hobbes (1588-1679), the Dutch Jewish philoso-
pher Benedict de Spinoza (1632-1677), the Dutch jurist
and theologian Hugo Grotius (1583-1645), the French
Catholic priest Richard Simon (1638-1712), the French
Protestant Isaac de la Peyrère (1592-1676), and the Swiss
Calvinist Jean le Clerc (1654-1736). Of these, Hobbes,
Grotius, and Spinoza were greatly influenced by the new
developments of their times produced by the scientific
thought and had moved away from the typical Jewish and
Christian views of religious authority and revelation.
Their biblical criticism was probably more a result than a
cause of this changed attitude.

Grotius' studies on the Bible were primarily concerned
with the New Testament. Three elements in his interpretation are worthy of note. (1) He argued that the biblical
writings were produced as the occasion required and in
accord with the time involved. They were the products of
and were influenced by limited historical settings. (2) He
compared the transmission of biblical texts with that of
classic writings. (3) Classical texts were employed in
elucidating the content of the biblical texts.

In his *Leviathan*, published in 1651, Hobbes proposed a
number of arguments against Moses as the author of the
Pentateuch and suggested that "in titles of books the
subject is marked as often as the writer." In his argument
that Moses did not write the Pentateuch, Hobbes had been
anticipated in the preceding century by Carlstadt (1520)
and Andreas Masius (1574). Hobbes, however, spelled
out many of the reasons for assuming post- or non-Mosaic
materials in the Pentateuch (many of these had already
been hinted at by Ibn Ezra). He argued that Gen 12:6 must
have been written when the Canaanite was not in the
land; Num 21:14 cites another work, and so on. Hobbes
concluded that Moses wrote what the scriptures themselves say he wrote (see Ex 17:14; 24:4; 34:28 and so on).
Hobbes attributed Deut 12-26 to Moses and considered
this to be the book discovered by the priest Hilkiah on the
basis of which Josiah carried out his reform in the seventh

century BCE (II Kings 22:8). In similar fashion, Hobbes sought to show that references such as "until this day" found throughout the historical books meant that these were written after the events they narrated (see the excerpts from Hobbes in Gray, 75-83). Hobbes suggested that a proper study of the Bible should be as follows: "The light that must guide us in this question, must be that which is held out to us from the books themselves; and this light, though it show us not the writer of every book, yet it is not unuseful to give us knowledge of the time wherein they were written" (Leviathan III 33). Such an approach assumes two things: (1) tradition must be bypassed and (2) the books must be studied and evaluated on the bases of their contents and internal evidence.

In 1655, Peyrère published a small treatise in Latin which appeared anonymously the following year in English translation with the title Men Before Adam (see Allen). His work reflects the impact which such a seemingly unrelated matter as world exploration could have upon biblical studies and theology. (The discovery of new lands with previously unknown animal life had already begun to cramp the quarters exegetes could assign the various species on the ark.) Basing his argument on Rom 5:12-14, Peyrère contended that the greater part of humanity had descended from neither Adam nor Noah. Such a hypothesis led him to an inquiry about the nature and date of the Pentateuch. Due to such factors as the reference to Moses' death, "unto this day," and so on, Peyrère concluded that Moses could not have written the Pentateuch. He wrote:

I need not trouble the reader much further, to prove a thing in itself sufficiently evident, that the first five books of the Bible were not written by Moses, as is thought. Nor need any one wonder after this, when he reads many things confus'd and out of order, obscure, deficient, many things omitted and displaced, when they shall consider with themselves that they are but a heap of copie confusedly taken.

Peyrère argued that Deut 2 (like Ps 108) reflected David's conquest of Edom and thus at least part of Deuteronomy "were written long after David's time." On this point, he anticipated a significant later development in historical critical study: the use of the historical books and Israelite history for understanding passages, sections, and documents in the Pentateuch.

In Spinoza, who changed his name from Baruch after being expelled from the Jewish community in Amsterdam (1656), multiple developments coalesced to produce the most outstanding biblical critic of the seventeenth century. He was thoroughly acquainted with late medieval Jewish learning (especially Maimonides and Ibn Ezra), with scientific thought, with the radical philosophy of Hobbes and Descartes, with the Renaissance distrust of tradition and distaste for stifling orthodoxy, and with a rationalistic view of the word of God and of religion as consisting of "love and obedience to God with the whole heart and mind, and in the practice of justice and charity to our neighbor." Spinoza declares in his *Tractatus theologico-politicus* (1670) that he set out to "examine the Scriptures anew, in a spirit of entire freedom and without prejudice, to affirm nothing as to their meaning and affirm nothing in the shape of doctrine, which I did not feel plainly set down in their pages." But he recognized that "they who hold the Bible, as it is, to be the handwriting of God, sent from heaven to men, will doubtless exclaim that I am guilty of the sin against the Holy Ghost, in contending that the Word of God is in parts imperfect, corrupt, erroneous, and inconsistent with itself. . . . " Spinoza, in addition to employing the suggestions of his predecessors for a non-Mosaic authorship of the Pentateuch, pointed to events which were "plainly impossible." His mathematical interests are apparent: "Jacob is found at a very advanced age, namely eighty-four, when he took Leah to wife; while, on the contrary, Dinah could scarcely have been seven when she was violated by Shechem; and Simeon and Levi, again scarcely twelve and eleven when they ravaged a city and put all the inhabitants thereof to the sword." His conclusion on the Pentateuch is that

Anyone who but observes that in these five books precept and narrative are jumbled together without order, and that one and the same story is often met with again and again, and occasionally with very important differences in the incidents— whosoever observes these things will certainly come to the conclusion that in the Pentateuch we have merely notes and collations to be examined at leisure; materials for history rather than the digested history itself.

Spinoza argued that the Bible was not really written to provide either philosophical and theological systems or the true course of historical events.

Scripture does not explain things by their secondary causes, but only narrates them in the order and the style which has most power to move men, and especially uneducated men, to devotion; and therefore it speaks inaccurately of God and of events, seeing that its object is not to convince the reason, but to attract and lay hold of the imagination.

He actually formulated a program for biblical criticism.

The history of the Scriptures . . . should teach us to understand the various vicissitudes that may have befallen the books of the prophets whose tradition has been handed down to us; the life, character and aim of the author of each book; the part which he played; at what period, on what occasion, for whom and in what language he composed his writings. Nor is that enough; we must know the fortune of each book in particular, the circumstances in which it was originally composed, into what hands it subsequently fell, the various lessons it has been held to convey, by whom it was included in the sacred canon, and, finally, how all these books came to be embodied in a single collection.

The most influential Old Testament critic of the seventeenth century was Richard Simon, whose *Critical*

History of the Old Testament (1678) had gone through four Latin, two English, and seven French editions by 1700, although attempts had been made to suppress the work before publication. Simon's work was addressed to the general educated audience and its translation into vernacular languages gave the work a more than normal circulation. His book dealt with three major concerns: (1) the Hebrew text from Moses to the present, (2) the translations of the Bible, and (3) the problem and method of translation which included a criticism of Old Testament interpretation from Origen to his own day. Simon seemed to have had three purposes in mind in writing his work. (1) The weaknesses and fallacies of other interpreters were analyzed. (2) He wished to show that the Protestant principle of *sola scriptura* was not as sound a principle as the Catholic system of reliance upon scripture, tradition, and church. This was due to the fact that the Bible is full of the "greatest difficulties." (3) He wished to introduce a critical approach to the scriptures which the difficulties in the text necessitated. He used "critical" and "criticism" throughout his work but argued that such terms are "proper to the art of which I am treating. These terms will come as no novelty to scholars, who have for some time been accustomed to their use in our language."

Simon argued that Moses was not the sole author of the Pentateuch. In analyzing the stories of creation and flood he pointed to repetitions and inconsistencies which were more than recapitulations. Gen 2 contains an account of the creation of man and woman that is remote from the account in Gen 1 and the flood stories repeat matters which would not have been necessary if only one author were involved. In addition one discovers differences in style—"Sometimes we find a very curt style and sometimes a very copious one, although the variety of the matter does not require it. . . ." Simon, therefore, suggests that various documents were used to produce the books of Moses.

With Simon, two factors in historical criticism of the Old Testament are raised to special prominence. (1) The Pentateuch is understood as a compilation of different documents. (2) Differences in style, repetitions within units, and similar phenomena attest to a diversity of authors and suggest the means for isolating documents. In other words, Simon not only recognized difficulties in the texts and indications of non-Mosaic authorship but also moved toward offering explanations of and solutions for these issues rather than commenting in general on biblical criticism.

In 1685, Jean le Clerc published an analysis and critique of Simon's work. He outlined, like Spinoza, the program of what was later to be called "higher criticism"; namely, the need and method for determining when a work was written, for what purposes, and so on. He argued against Simon's view that the Old Testament documents had been preserved by public recorders and official registers until they were later edited although with some disar- rangement and disorder. He likewise repudiated the suggestion that it was Ezra who finally edited the materials, a view found in Jewish tradition and alluded to by Spinoza. Le Clerc argued that the passages obviously written after Moses, the use of the term *nabi'* in Gen 20:7 (see I Sam 9:9), and other factors pointed to the monarchy as the period when the Pentateuch was produced. In addition, several factors, such as the use of the word Chaldea (Gen 11:28,31) and a knowledge of Mesopotamia (see Gen 2:11; 10:8-13; 11:1-9) suggested that the work was written by someone who had lived in Chaldea. On the basis of these arguments, le Clerc proposed that the Pentateuch was produced by the priest who returned from captivity to Samaria to teach the new inhabitants about Israelite religion (see II Kings 17:24-28). This priest combined the sources utilizing his own knowledge to meet a specific need. Le Clerc here demonstrates an important element in historical-critical study: the biblical documents were produced in specific historical situations to meet specific needs and to fulfill specific purposes.

The historical-critical approach to the Old Testament which developed in the seventeenth century was cautious, tentative, and precursory; but all the essential ingredients which were later to be developed fully were already present—a refusal to accept traditional interpretations or appeals to divine origin as authoritative, a stress upon the literal-grammatical sense of the text as the means for understanding its content, a reliance upon the internal evidence of the text as the basis for discussion of documentary integrity and authorship, and the search for historical and sociological situations as appropriate contexts for understanding the origin and use of the materials. Historical criticism, however, was practiced and espoused only by a few and its contact with the church—both Catholic and Protestant—and the synagogue was primarily only at the point of opposition. Advocates of critical study of the Bible did not rate any sustaining movement or any widely circulated literature. (Simon's work was something of an exception.)

The eighteenth century brought radical new developments in religion and witnessed a diversity of theological and philosophical systems competing with scholarly respectability in the intellectual marketplace. Tradition, social customs, and the operating regulations of the marketplace continued, however, to favor the more orthodox and less radical forms of Christian theism. The new impetus came primarily from English deism. This movement challenged the authority and orthodoxy of the established religious institutions, sought to eliminate the superstitious and mysterious from religious claims and practices, and reduced religion to those features which were understandable through reason, nature, and ethical reflection. The initial phase of the deistic controversy focused on the nature and possibility of historic revelation but moved to an examination of the specific Christian and biblical claims of the revelation of God in historical events and thus to an exploration of the factual quality of the events, especially miracles, reported in the Bible. English and American deists, such as Toland, Clark, Collins, Tindal, and Jefferson, advocated a system of natural and reasonable religion freed from most of the elements of supernaturalism. Attempts were made by these advocates of "religion within the bounds of reason" to come to terms with the biblical traditions by siphoning off the supernatural, the miraculous, and the unbelievable in order to leave, in a usable form, the distilled essence of a reasonable faith. In France, deism found an expression in Bayle, Voltaire, Rousseau, and Diderot which was much more virulent in its attack upon Christianity and the Bible. (Thomas Paine also belongs in this group.) French deists popularized what they understood as the inconsistencies, absurdities, and low morality in the Bible, especially the Old Testament. In Germany, the impact of deism was more directly related to the exegesis and interpretation of biblical texts than was the case in England and France and thus was of more immediate consequence for biblical studies. "Unlike the English discussion of the fact issue, which had by this time [latter half of the eighteenth century] become completely mired in the external evidence question [geological evidence for the flood and so on], the German scholars' procedure was therefore almost exclusively internal, i.e. literary-historical" (Frei, 56; see his discussion of the eighteenth century, 51-65). This was due to the fact that Germany had been less influenced by the developments in the Renaissance and the scientific revolution than either France, England, or Holland; and German theologians had more stringently adhered to the Protestant principle of scriptural authority. In addition, the major German academic institutions were created or came to prominence primarily in the eighteenth century and thus there was less influence of advanced secular education.

The influence of rationalistic humanism, mediated to Germany through English deism, did on occasion produce caustic attacks on the historicity and reliability of the Old Testament. For example, in the *Wolfenbüttel Fragments* by Hermann Samuel Reimarus (1694-1768), published after his death, there is an essay on the passage of the Israelites through the Red Sea. Reimarus pointed out the historical impossibilities in a literal acceptance of the text: 600,000 Hebrew men (Ex 12:37-38) plus their wives, children, the mixed multitudes, and animals leaving Egypt would give a figure of over 3,000,000 people, 300,000 oxen and cows, and 600,000 sheep and goats requiring over 5,000 wagons to carry their equipment and 300,000 tents for their housing. Marching ten abreast, such a number would have formed a column 180 miles long and have required nine days as a minimum to march through the parted sea.

The rationalistic spirit of the time was absorbed into Old Testament studies in Germany through the word of Johann David Michaelis (1717-1791), Johann Salomo Semler (1725-1791), and others in the last half of the eighteenth century.

At the Diet of Worms (1521), Luther had declared that he must be "convinced by the testimony of the scriptures or by clear reason." Clear reason now forced biblical criticism to become scientific and to examine the Old Testament apart from any special appeal to divine verbal or literary inspiration. Both Michaelis and Semler were directly influenced by English deism. By the time Johann Gottfried Eichhorn (1752-1827) published his three-volume introduction to the Old Testament (1780-1783), the humanistic argument that the literature of the Old Testament should be investigated like any other literature was on its way to becoming an integral part of the mainstream of German Protestant biblical study. (On Eichhorn, see Cheyne, 13-26; Gray, 148-56.)

E. Pentateuchal Criticism

In the critical study of the Hebrew scriptures, the Pentateuch occupied the center of attention throughout the eighteenth and nineteenth centuries. The primary focus of pentateuchal studies was the attempt to divide the material into its component sources, to determine the relationship of these sources to one another, and to assign them and their final combination to specific historical periods. Already in the seventeenth century, scholars had recognized the possible existence of sources or documents on the bases of varieties in language and style, contradictions and divergent points of view, duplications and repetitions, and signs of composite structure but had accomplished nothing overly constructive in the way of documentary criticism.

Between Simon and Eichhorn, an additional "pillar" had been added to support the hypothesis of documents in the Pentateuch: the use of different names for God. In 1711, Henning Bernhard Witter (1683-1715), a German pastor, published a commentary on the Pentateuch (which never reached beyond Gen 17:27) in which he isolated documents using differences in the divine name as one criterion. He showed that in Gen 1:1–2:4 Elohim is used as the divine name while in Gen 2:5–3:24 Jehovah (Yahweh) appears. These two sections not only used different names for the deity but, he concluded, are also parallel to one another. (A view already taken by Campegius Vitringa in 1683, and hinted at by Simon, but without resort to the argument from the divine names.) In 1753, Jean Astruc (1684-1766), a French physician expounded the same point. Astruc argued that Moses inherited two basic sources (one using Elohim, the other Yahweh) plus ten fragments which he combined into four parallel columns which were later combined to produce Genesis. (On Astruc, see Gray, 128-47.) Eichhorn utilized Astruc's discussion in his introduction and Semler incorporated the insights of Simon, and thus their roles in the history of pentateuchal criticism were never lost, a fate which did not befall Witter.

In the nineteenth century, some form of source criticism and post-Mosaic authorship were generally assumed in German scholarship. Controversy raged not so much over the use of the method but over the results. The basic issues discussed were (1) the assignment of material to the sources, (2) their order and relationship, and (3) the determination of their dating. Further developments had to take place before the so-called four-source theory of the Pentateuch came to be considered fully established.

In 1798, Karl David Ilgen (1763-1834) isolated seventeen documents in Genesis. He assigned these to three authors and thus three parallel sources: two utilizing the name Elohim and one employing the name Jehovah (Yahweh). In addition, he suggested that the Yahwistic source might be further divided into two different documents (on Ilgen, see Gray, 169-72). In 1805, Wilhelm Martin Leberecht de Wette (1780-1849) persuasively argued that the book of Deuteronomy differs radically from the rest of the Pentateuch and was the law book of Josiah's reformation carried out in 621 BCE, having been produced not long before that time (already anticipated in modern times by the Englishmen Hobbes, in 1651, and Parrish, in 1739). (On de Wette, see Cheyne, 31-53.) These developments laid the foundation for the four-source theory: two Elohistic writers, one Yahwistic, and the Deuteronomic. The association and dating of Deuteronomy to Josiah's reform provided an Archimedean point for the dating question and introduced the issue of the history of the legal material into the question. In an 1806 work, de Wette suggested that no trace of the Mosaic legislation, which later came to be designated "P," could be found in the historical books prior to Josiah's reform (Joshua–II Kings 21).

Attempts were made to explain the origin of the Pentateuch in terms other than the combination of parallel sources. One such approach was the "fragmentary hypothesis" advocated by the Englishman Alexander Geddes (1737-1802; see Gray, 173-83) and the German Johann Severin Vater (1771-1826). This view, which was shared by de Wette, assumed that the Pentateuch was

composed of numerous independent fragments of varying sizes which were combined to produce our present
work. Another view of the origin of the Pentateuch has
been designated the "supplementary hypothesis." This
theory assumes that a basic document, or one connected
strand, formed the nucleus of the Pentateuch to which
were added various materials in the course of time. This
theory is generally seen to have originated with Heinrich
Georg August Ewald (1803-1875; on him, see Cheyne,
66-118). Both the fragmentary and supplementary hypotheses had to be tested before scholars returned to the
documentary theory which assumed the existence of
parallel documents. The work of Hermann Hupfeld
(1796-1866) on the sources of Genesis, published in 1853,
shifted research back to the documentary theory.

The documentary approach to the Pentateuch had
isolated four sources in the Pentateuch, relying upon the
five pillars of documentary criticism: (1) the use of divine
names, (2) language and style, (3) contradictions and
divergencies within the text, (4) duplication and repetition of material, and (5) the evidence that different
accounts have been combined. The four sources isolated
ultimately came to be designated PJED. Of these, P and D
were the most easily isolated. P, which avoids the name
Yahweh until the time of Moses (see Ex 6:2-3, a central
passage in the documentary theory), was assumed to
consist of some narrative material (such as Gen 1, 17),
genealogical and chronological notices (like Gen 5), and
legal material (Ex 25-31; 35-40; most of Leviticus and
large portions of Numbers). D was located primarily in
Deuteronomy and was assumed to be the legislation used
by Josiah in his reform. J used the name Yahweh
throughout (see Gen 4:26) and was found primarily in
Genesis and Exodus. Parallel accounts to J (for example
Gen 20, which forms a parallel to Gen 12), which used the
name Elohim but did not possess the style and character
of P were attributed to E. Much of nineteenth–century
scholarship considered the order of the documents to be

the priestly document (P), the Yahwistic history (J; in German Yahweh appears as Jahweh), the Elohistic history (E), and the Deuteronomic code (D). The priestly source, since it provided the general chronological framework and the bulk of the legislation in Genesis-Numbers, was assumed to be the basic or foundation document into which the other documents were edited. The period of David or Solomon was generally considered the time of its origin.

Gradually, scholars began to argue that P was not the earliest but actually the latest of the four sources in the Pentateuch. This was suggested as early as 1833 by Eduard Reuss (1804-1891) in his lectures, in 1835 by Wilhelm Vatke (1806-1882) and Johann Friedrich Leopold George (1811-1873), in 1866 by Karl Heinrich Graf (1815-1869) and subsequently by numerous other scholars. There were a number of reasons for this redating which assigned P to the exilic or post-exilic period. (1) The laws in P were assumed to be later than those of D. For example, D argues for sacrifice at only one site while P presupposes only one place of sacrifice; in D, the Levites are priests but in P they are a lower order of the clergy. (2) The historical books (Joshua-II Kings) do not presuppose and do not reflect the history of a people that shows any acquaintance with the laws and narratives of P. (3) The prophets show no influence from the laws found in P. (4) If one assumed that Israelite life and history were regulated by the legislation of P, then the history that is presented in the Old Testament historical books is incomprehensible. However, if one places P late rather than early in that history, then Israelite history becomes understandable. The dating of the pentateuchal documents in the order JEDP became widely accepted at the close of the nineteenth century and represented the summation of the historical-critical and documentary study of the Old Testament. This approach was represented in England by bishop John William Colenso (1814-1883; see Cheyne, 196-204) and Samuel Rolles

Driver (1846-1914; see Cheyne, 248-372), in Scotland by William Robertson Smith (1846-1894; see Beidelman); in Holland by Abraham Kuenen (1828-1891; see De Vries); and in the United States by Charles Augustus Briggs (1841-1913). The most influential and best known exponent of the historical-critical approach to the Old Testament was Julius Wellhausen (1844-1918) whose *Prolegomena to the History of Israel*, first published in 1878, summarized and popularized, in an engaging and provocative fashion, the arguments for the historical-critical study of the Old Testament and for the order of JEDP for the documents of the Pentateuch (see *COTS*, 7-12; Coppens, 18-37).

The nineteenth century saw the triumph of the historical-critical approach to biblical studies. The victory was not won easily nor without battles and scars. Some called into question the whole procedure and believed themselves to be fighting more than a rear guard action while others challenged the results and conclusions of the approach. These developments we will note in the remaining chapters of this volume, but especially in chapter five.

chapter 4

OLD TESTAMENT
FORM CRITICISM

A. Alt, "The Origins of Israelite Law," in his *Essays on Old Testament History and Religion* (Oxford/Garden City: Basil Blackwell/Doubleday, 1966/1967)79-132; M. J. Buss, "The Study of Forms," *OTFC*, 1-56; W. M. Clark, "Law," *OTFC*, 99-139; J. L. Crenshaw, "Wisdom," *OTFC*, 225-64; *idem*, "Studies in Ancient Israelite Wisdom: Prolegomenon," *Studies in Ancient Israelite Wisdom*, ed. J. L. Crenshaw (New York: KTAV, 1976)1-45; G. Fohrer, "Remarks on Modern Interpretation of the Prophets," *JBL* LXXX(1961)309-19; E. Gerstenberger, "Psalms," *OTFC*, 179-223; H. Gunkel, *The Legends of Genesis: The Biblical Saga and History* (Chicago: Open Court, 1901; reissued with an introduction by W. F. Albright; New York: Schocken Books, 1964); idem, *What Remains of the Old Testament and Other Essays* (New York: Macmillan, 1928); idem, *The Psalms: A Form-Critical Introduction*, with an introduction by J. Muilenberg (Philadelphia: Fortress Press, 1967); *idem*, "The Israelite Prophecy from the Time of Amos," in *Twentieth Century Theology in the Making*, ed. J. Pelikan (New York: Harper & Row, 1969)48-75; A. R. Johnson, "The Psalms," *OTMS*, 162-209; R. Knierim, "Old Testament Form Criticism Reconsidered," *Int* XXVII(1973)435-68; D. A. Knight, "The Understanding of 'Sitz im Leben' in Form Criticism," *SBLSP I* (1974)105-25; K. Koch, *The Growth of the Biblical Tradition* (New York: Charles Scribner's Sons, 1969); L. Köhler, "Justice in the Gate," in his *Hebrew Man* (Nashville: Abingdon Press, 1956)127-50; W. E. March, "Prophecy," *OTFC*, 141-77; A. Olrik, "Epic Laws of Folk Narrative," *The Study of Folklore*, ed. A. Dundes (Englewood Cliffs: Prentice-Hall, 1965)129-41; G. M. Tucker, *Form Criticism of the Old Testament* (Philadelphia: Fortress Press, 1971); J. A. Wilcoxen, "Narrative," *OTFC*, 57-98.

The historical-critical approach to the Old Testament, as pursued in the second half of the nineteenth century, was largely occupied with source analysis and documentary study. These, however, were not conducted merely as an end in themselves. Documentary criticism, as in the work of Wellhausen, frequently served a prefatory function. It was the preliminary work which provided the raw material for understanding and writing the religious and political history of ancient Israel and early Judaism. It was also understood as an important aid to exegesis. One should note that Wellhausen's most important book on documentary criticism was called a *History of Israel* in its first edition and *Prolegomena to the History of Israel* in its second edition. This clearly illustrates the subsidiary nature of the discipline. Nonetheless, historical criticism in general and Wellhausen's followers in particular could at times become enmeshed in the methodology and focus on source analysis as an end in itself.

A. Hermann Gunkel and the Rise of Form Criticism

Near the end of the last century, a new impetus and approach to Old Testament studies developed which were spearheaded by the Old Testament scholar Hermann Gunkel (1862-1932). This new method is referred to in broad terms as "History of Religions." Form criticism was an important element in this new methodology. Dissatisfaction with the historical-critical or documentary approach was one of the significant factors in the rise of the history of religions approach. One of the members in this new movement, Hugo Gressmann (1877-1927) declared: "We are fed up with being treated with literary criticism only." This negative attitude toward documentary criticism with its obsession with external problems about dates, documents, and authors was in reality a positive desire for a greater appreciation of the biblical materials, for an esthetic and empathic understanding of the material.

The form-critical approach to the Bible, however, was a child of its time. Gunkel himself recognized this and pointed to four movements of his day, which he understood as advancements leading to altered perspectives and new approaches in Old Testament study. These four were described by Gunkel as neo-Romanticism, comparative religion, history of literature, and psychology. According to Gunkel, the neo-romantic or "impressionistic" movement saw colors and heard new sounds which manifested the inner life of man. Comparative religion provided a wealth of valuable material for comparison with the Old Testament. The history of literature offered the means to analyze literary forms in order to provide an empathic understanding of the literature from the past. Psychology allowed the investigator to seek for and appreciate an immediate perception of ancient man and his literature.

It is possible to see the rise of form criticism within the context of broad developments characteristic of the turn of the century (see Buss, *OTFC*, 31-38). (1) The period witnessed a philosophical shift away from the strong emphasis on novelty, individualism, and historicism which had generally been characteristic of the nineteenth century. A recognition of the importance of the community, the larger social nexus, classes, and institutional structures was widespread. This found reflection in politics, economics, and other areas. The writings of Karl Marx (1818-1883) and Nikolai Lenin (1870-1924) and the rise of various forms of socialistic thought reflect this trend as do the writings of Walter Rauschenbusch (1861-1918) and the rise of the "social gospel" in the United States.

(2) The social sciences—anthropology, sociology, and ethnology—as well as psychology were just beginning to exert a formative impact. The social sciences provided new theories concerning human behavior in general and the origin and function of religion in particular. As a rule, these tended to stress the social dimensions and functions of religion and to play down the significance of the individual.

(3) A further factor was the developing interest in and

field work among the so-called "primitive peoples." All types of data—including religious—were amassed, often in multivolume collections such as Sir James Frazer's *The Golden Bough*, concerning the practices, folk customs, tales, beliefs, and ceremonials of these people. It was generally assumed in such research that all religions contained common elements and features which made possible genuine comparative studies. As a rule, such field work and the collection of data led to a greater stress on religion as a function of the group and a greater appreciation of the role of ceremonials and rituals in religion and worship.

(4) The vast literature of other ancient near eastern cultures had become sufficiently known and extensive to make possible and even to encourage comparison with Old Testament literature. First Egyptian and then Akkadian texts became available, supplementing the previously utilized Islamic materials. (In spite of the discovery and decipherment of such texts chronologically nearer to ancient Israel in time, Wellhausen continued to insist that "the original gifts and ideas of the primitive Hebrews can most readily be understood by comparing Arabian antiquity.")

(5) A final factor important to an understanding of Gunkel's work was the development and application of genre studies and literary analyses to a broad spectrum of literature. Folklore had been studied extensively in terms of genre analysis. The beginnings had been made in a similar analysis of near eastern texts and Germanic literature was studied along typological lines. The insights of some earlier writers, such as the Englishman Robert Lowth (1710-1787) and the German romantic critics of rationalism, Johann Georg Hamann (1730-1788) and Johann Gottfried Herder (1744-1803), who had stressed the role of poetry and imagination in literature and folklife, were utilized by such biblical scholars as Karl Budde (1850-1935) and Eduard Reuss in a way that anticipated and paralleled Gunkel. (See for example,

Budde's essay, "Poetry (Hebrew)," *HDB* IV[1902] 2-11.)

There is no doubt that Gunkel was indebted to many of these interests and to other scholars in the development of his methodology. In his earliest writings, Gunkel had a habit of not employing footnotes very extensively in order to encourage a more popular reading of his works. This makes it difficult to trace his dependencies. Throughout his career, however, Gunkel preserved friendship with and employed the research of scholars whose interests encompassed several disciplines. In spite of Gunkel's predecessors and the fact that he shared in general and specific cultural and literary developments of his day, his importance in the history of biblical studies remains monumental. He was the first biblical scholar to stress the indispensability of "form-critical" concerns for an adequate interpretation of the Old Testament.

Much of Gunkel's approach also was no doubt influenced by his "artistic" and sensitive approach to literature. A recent Old Testament scholar has described Gunkel in the following manner:

While Gunkel recognized the validity of historical criticism as a legitimate, even necessary, discipline, he was convinced that it failed to answer many of the most natural and insistent questions raised not only by the modern reader, but by the biblical records themselves. . . . Imagination and insight into the manners and nuances of speech, appreciation and literary sensitivity, openness to the whole world of Near Eastern culture as it found expression in the great literary monuments, and withal a rare ability to identify oneself in spirit and empathy with the mind and mood of the biblical writers in all their manifold ways of speaking, made it possible for him . . . to press scholarly inquiry beyond the confines of source analysis and phenomenological scrutiny. He knew how to *listen* to a text, and always insisted that it be read aloud in order that the reader might the better discern its movement and direction, its rhythm and assonance, its key words and accents. Research for him was as much an art as a science. He was insistent upon permitting the biblical speakers to have their say in their own fashion. He was aware they were *human* beings, like ourselves, and was not

126

embarrassed in drawing upon contemporary history and everyday experience for the illumination of the ancient text. He recognized that in the pages of the Old and New Testament we have to do, not with literature in our modern understanding of *belles lettres,* but rather with extracts drawn from the daily life of persons and communities. (James Muilenberg in his preface to the English translation of Gunkel's *The Psalms,* iv)

The methodology which Gunkel pursued, and he did not use the term form criticism *(Formgeschichte),* was what he called literary history *(Literaturgeschichte)* and genre research *(Gattungsforschung).* The overall goal of such an endeavor was the desire to understand and appreciate the literature of ancient Israel in its totality, that is, in its functional relationship to the whole of the people's life and history. For Gunkel, this involved two tasks. (1) "The prime task of a history of literature in Israel must . . . be to determine the *literary types* represented in the Old Testament" (1928, 59). (2) "This study of the literary types, however, will only merit the name of Literary History when it attempts to get at the *history through which these types have passed"* (1928, 61).

What Gunkel meant by a literary type or genre *(Gattung)* was best expressed in writings published toward the close of his career. The following is a translation of a discussion he published in *ZAW* in 1924:

Every genre shows its individuality in defined characteristics:

(1) In a common store of thoughts and moods, which is carefully transmitted from generation to generation, despite the sundry changes in the customary spiritual quality that can be carried out at the hands of outstanding individual authors;

(2) In a traditional linguistic form, i.e., definite phrases, sentence structures, images, and so forth; that is the customary form which usually preserves the thoughts and can endure sometimes for many centuries; on this linguistic form we lay a special value because it is just this which is the easiest to recognize.

(3) A third characteristic of a genre is a definite *Sitz im Leben* of the people, in which it originally had its special place, out of

which just these thoughts and their forms of expression have arisen and in which they are therefore also to be understood, even if it is true that the genres in a more developed time, when writing came to dominance in the cultural life, had given up this oldest situation in favor of the written book.

Only where we have all three criteria preserved together, only where we can ascertain that definite thoughts in a definite form on a definite occasion were expressed have we the right to speak of a genre. (See also 1928, 115-16.)

Thus, for Gunkel every genre or literary type has a specific content and mood, a formal language of expression, and a setting in life.

Gunkel coined the phrase *Sitz im Leben* to designate the social context within which literary genres originated and were employed.

Every ancient literary type originally belonged to a quite definite side of the national life of Israel. Just as among ourselves the "sermon" belongs to the pulpit, while the "fairy-tale" has its home in the nursery, so in ancient Israel the Song of Victory was sung by maidens to greet the returning war-host; the Lament was chanted by hired female mourners by the bier of the dead; the Thora was announced by the priest in the sanctuary; the Judgment (*mishpat*) was given by the judge in his seat; the prophet uttered his Oracle in the outer court of the temple; the elders at the gate gave forth the Oracle of Wisdom. To understand the literary type we must in each case have the whole situation clearly before us and ask ourselves, Who is speaking? Who are the listeners? What is the *mise en scène* at the time? What effect is aimed at? In many cases a type is employed by a special class of speaker, and its use reveals of what class he is. Just as today a "sermon" implies a professional "preacher," so in ancient time the Thora and the hymn of worship were given through the priest, the oracular saying was uttered by the "wise men," and the lay was the utterance of a "singer." There may even have been a professional class of popular "story-tellers." (1928, 61-62)

According to Gunkel, the purpose of a literary history of

various types of genres from their earliest period until they reached their final canonical form (see 1928, 61-66). In the earliest usage, according to him, genres were short, oral, and originated in and were employed in general, communal life. Artistic and classical poetry, developed by professionals, gradually arose alongside the national and popular oral "literature." Imitations of both this oldest popular composition and classical creations developed at the hands of professional writers. Collections of popular and classical literature came into being as Israel moved into a more literary phase. Collectors gave structures and unity to literature derived from its oral stage. Creative personalities, such as the author of Job, put together large cycles of material as did the collectors of the historical traditions. In the final stages, different genres were combined and mixed.

Finally we come to the tragedy of Hebrew literature. The spirit loses power. The types are exhausted. Imitations begin to abound. Redactions take the place of original creations. Hebrew ceases to be the living language of the people. By this time the collections are grouped together into larger collections. The Canon has come into being. (1928, 66)

In the historical-critical approach, much emphasis was placed on documents and their authors. Gunkel shifted the attention away from the writers and collectors (although he argued that they must be understood as more than collectors) and concluded that the interpreter who begins with the author (and documents) begins to build the house with the roof. Before the end of the last century, Gunkel and Wellhausen debated this issue as well as the use of comparative material from other cultures to elucidate Old Testament material (see Knight, *RTI*, 74). This does not mean that Gunkel repudiated the historical-critical work of Wellhausen—he presupposed and built upon it.

The form-critical approach to the Old Testament can

best be illustrated by examining how this methodology is applied in the five main areas of Old Testament literature: narratives, psalms, prophecy, law, and wisdom. In the first three of them, Gunkel made by far the most outstanding individual contribution.

B. Form Criticism and the Narratives in Genesis

Gunkel's methodological essay on Genesis, translated into English as *The Legends of Genesis* (1901), formed the introduction to his commentary on the book(1901, ³1910; see J. A. Wilcoxen, *OTFC*, 57-69). Gunkel's starting point in his discussion was exegetical or hermeneutical: How should and can the narratives of Genesis be read and understood in light of the recognition that they are not "historical" documents? Gunkel concluded that they are legends and must be so read and appreciated.

Gunkel used several criteria to distinguish legend from history (see 1901, 1-12). (1) Mode of transmission: legends originally were transmitted in oral tradition, history in writing. (2) Subject matter: legends deal with things that interest common people and with private and family relations while history deals with public occurrences and matters of political importance. "History would be expected to tell how and for what reasons David succeeded in delivering Israel from the Philistines; legend prefers to tell how the boy David once slew a Philistine giant" (1901, 5). (3) Sources: legend depends upon tradition and imagination while history relies upon eyewitnesses and records. (4) Type of action narrated: legends frequently report things that are incredible— "violations of probability and even of possibility"—and involve the direct action of God or gods whereas history deals with the credible.

Consider especially the central position of the Second Book of Samuel, the history of the rebellion of Absalom, the most exquisite piece of early historical writing in Israel. The world that is there portrayed is the world that we know. In this world, iron does not float and serpents do not speak; no god or angel appears like a person among other persons, but everything happens as we are used to seeing things happen (1901, 10).

(5) Style and intent: history is prosaic and seeks to inform while legend is poetic and aims to please, to elevate, to inspire, to instruct, and to move.

He who wishes to do justice to such narratives [legends] must have some aesthetic faculty, to catch in the telling of a story what it is and what it purports to be. And in doing so he is not expressing a hostile or even skeptical judgment, but simply studying lovingly the nature of his material. Whoever possesses heart and feeling must perceive, for instance in the case of the sacrifice of Isaac [Gen 22], that the important matter is not to establish certain historical facts, but to impart to the hearer the heartrending grief of the father who is commanded to sacrifice his child with his own hand, and then his boundless gratitude and joy when God's mercy releases him from this grievous trial. And every one who perceives the peculiar poetic charm of these old legends must feel irritated by the barbarian—for there are pious barbarians—who thinks he is putting the true value upon those narratives only when he treats them as prose and history. (1901, 10-11)

The basic constituent unit in the Genesis narratives is, according to Gunkel, the particular legend: "popular legends in their very nature exist in the form of individual legends" (1901, 43; he quotes Reuss and Wellhausen who had already advanced a similar view). In the first edition of his commentary, Gunkel discussed the form of the individual legend but not in a very systematic fashion (see 1901, 37-87). By the time of the third edition (1910), Axel Olrik had published his influential essay on epic laws of folk narrative, first presented as a lecture in Berlin (1908), where Gunkel was a professor at the time. In many ways, Gunkel's analysis of biblical legends had already relied upon similar assumptions to those of Olrik and he expressed his agreement with Olrik, making frequent reference to his essay in the 1910 edition. The most important of Olrik's laws about the composition of oral literature (myths, songs, heroic sagas, and local legends) and the characteristics Gunkel anticipated or stressed may be outlined as follows:

(1) *Law of opening and closing.* The legend does not begin or end abruptly. It moves from calm to excitement and returns to calm. [Gunkel: "The narrative always opens in such a way that one recognizes that something new is about to begin; and it closes at the point where the complication that has arisen is happily resolved: no one can ask, What followed?" (1901, 44; but see p. 69 where he speaks of legends ending with a sudden jolt.)]

(2) *Law of repetition.* In traditional oral narrative, repetition provides emphasis, builds tension, and fills out the narrative. [Gunkel: ". . . to postpone the catastrophe and intensify the interest . . . to repeat the same scene twice . . ." (1901, 83).]

(3) *Law of three.* Storytellers generally work with three as the maximum number of characters and delight in a threefold repetition of events.

(4) *Law of two to a scene.* Legends are always polarized and this is reflected in the characterizations and descriptions. Generally there are no more than two characters, often in contrast, in a single scene. [Gunkel: "The narrator of the legend, unlike the modern novelist, could not expect his hearers to be interested in many persons at once, but on the contrary, he always introduces to us a very small number. Of course the minimum is two, because it takes at least two to make a complication of interests. . . . it is rare that all the persons of the story appear at once, but only a few, usually only two . . ." (1901, 49-50).]

(5) *Law of the twin and contrasts.* Narrators sometimes use twins or two persons, frequently depicting the characters in sharp contrast.

(6) *Law of schematization*. Characters appear in a certain order and the legend follows certain formulas and structures: attributes are expressed in action, only essentials are narrated, and the narrative is single-stranded, refusing to go back in order to fill in missing details. [Gunkel spoke of "the brevity of legends," "their extraordinary sharpness," "condensed and effective," "systematic arrangement of parts," "succession of scenes," "everything is subordinated to the action."]

(7) *Law of one or more major scenes*. In the main scene(s), the actors confront one another in sculptured situations.

(8) *Law of logic*. Themes presented must exert an influence upon the plot. [Gunkel spoke of the balance of parts, the absence of superfluous detail, the succession of scenes, and that "the remarks which the narrator does introduce are an essential part of the narrative."]

(9) *Law of unity of plot*. Loose organization and uncertain action are anathema to the legend and are signs of literary works. [Gunkel: The legend relies upon clearness in which the elements are "easily grasped and the relation of which to one another is perfectly plain. And these outlines are never painfully forced, but seem to have come quite as a matter of course from the nature of the subject" (1901, 48).]

(10) *Law of concentration on a leading character*. In a legend, generally one character occupies the central interest of the story. [Gunkel: "The hearer does not have to ask many questions to learn which of the personages should receive his especial attention; the narrator makes this very plain to him by speaking most of the chief personage. . . .In many cases it is the destinies of a single leading personage that we pursue . . ." (1901, 53-53).]

Gunkel distinguished a variety of legends in Genesis. There are two main groups: mythical legends about the origin of the world and its beginnings (Gen 1-11) and legends about the patriarchs of Israel (Gen 12-50). Mythical legends are the oldest since "legend as a literary variety has its origins in myths" (1901, 14). There are a number of distinctions between the two classes.

1) They differ in subject matter: mythical sagas [legends] deal with the origins of the world and of men; patriarchal, with the ancestors and the origin of Israel. 2) They differ in their spatio-temporal setting: mythical sagas are remote in time and space; patriarchal sagas treat events of Canaan and its neighbors. 3) Particularly do they differ in their main actors: the first have God or the gods as actors; the latter, men, though occasional divine appearances may be included. Under this same point might fall another important criterion: 4) the mythical sagas are polytheistic in their religious orientation; the patriarchal sagas are monotheistic. Finally, 5) some differences in origin can be distinguished: mythical sagas originate as answers to universal questions, that is, questions about natural phenomena throughout the world and about man qua man; patriarchal sagas originate in questions about tribal history and natural phenomena local to Canaan and its environs. (Wilcoxen, 61)

Gunkel subdivided the patriarchal legends into historical, ethnograhic, and etiological legends. Historical legends reflect some historical occurrence, although the legend has frequently veiled the historical memory so that it is impossible to determine the time, place, or actors in the event. Examples of historical legend are Abraham's treaty with Abimelech at Beersheba (Gen 21:22-34), which reflects some actual treaty between Israelites and Philistines; the rape of Dinah (Gen 34), which reflects the struggle of Israelite tribes against the Canaanite city of Shechem; and the various stories of migration (Abraham, Rebecca, and Jacob from the north; Abraham and Jacob's descent into Egypt). Examples of ethnographic legend are the Jacob and Esau stories where the common features are tribal and race relationships and presuppose no actual historical events.

Gunkel distinguished various types of etiological legends but all tell a fictitious story in order to answer the questions, "Why?" and "How?" (1) Ethnological etiologies seek to explain certain circumstances in the life of a people: Why Canaan is the servant of his brothers (Gen 9:20-27), why the children of Lot dwell in the East (Gen 13:2-13), and so on. A constant ethnological interest concerns how Israel came to have Canaan:

The legends tell in many variations how it came about that the patriarchs received this particular land: God gave it to Abraham because of his obedience [Gen 12:1-3]; when on the occasion of the separation at Bethel, Lot chose the East, the West fell to Abraham [Gen 13:2-13]; Jacob obtained the blessing of the better country from Isaac by a deception [Gen 27:1-40]; God promised it to Jacob at Bethel [Gen 28:11-17], and so on. (1901, 26)

(2) Etymological etiologies explain the name of something: legends tell why Jacob is "heelholder" (Gen 25:26); Zoar means "trifle" (Gen 19:20-22); Beersheba is "the well of seven" (Gen 21:28-29); Isaac refers to laughter (Gen 18:12); and so on.

(3) Ceremonial or cultic legends tell of the origin of cult places and practices: Why does one sacrifice a ram instead of a child (Gen 22)? Why is a limping dance performed at Penuel (Gen 32:31-32)? Why is the stone at Bethel anointed (Gen 28:11)?

(4) Geological etiologies explain the uniqueness of a locality: why is the Dead Sea region so desolate (Gen 19)? Why is there a womanlike statue of salt near its shore (Gen 19:26)?

Gunkel realized that some of the Genesis narratives could not be placed into any of his types and that frequently the same narrative may contain several features of various types of legends or various types of legend may be combined. The narrative of the flight of Hagar (Gen 16) contains ethnographic features (the life of Ishmael), ethnological interests in describing the conditions which produced the life of the Ishmaelites, cultic concerns (the explanation of Lahai-roi), and etymological elements in the explanation of names. He pointed out that etymological elements never appear alone in the Genesis narratives but always in conjunction with other features; that is, they are more motifs than an independent type.

Gunkel had a number of things to say about the origin and *Sitz im Leben* of the individual legends of Genesis. (1) The exact origin of the narratives can no longer really be discovered. Most of the material in Gen 1–11 was seen as ultimately Babylonian in origin and the patriarchal legends as primarily Canaanite although the Joseph story may reflect some Egyptian influence. Some of the legends (Dinah, Gen 34; Tamar, Gen 38; Reuben, Gen 35:22; and those set in the southern Negeb) may have been Israelite in origin (1901, 92-93). Thus Israel adopted and adapted legends from diverse backgrounds. (2) The narratives were obviously the original creations of individuals, but this was so far in the past that one should speak of the legends as folk literature. (3) As to their *Sitz im Leben* in folk culture, Gunkel spoke in rather general terms. "The common situation which we have to suppose is this: In the leisure of a winter evening the family sits about the hearth; the grown people, but more especially the children, listen intently to the beautiful old stories of the dawn of the world, which they have heard so often yet never tire of hearing repeated" (1901, 41). Gunkel also spoke of professional storytellers, familiar with the old songs and legends, who wandered about the country especially during the time of popular festivals. (He assumed that the prose narratives which we now possess may have once existed in rhythmic form for singing; 1901, 41). Many of the cultic legends were probably told at the sanctuary or at the time of the festival involved. All the greater sanctuaries may have possessed their story of how the place became holy just as each festival had its cultic legend (for example, the exodus legend was told at Passover). Gunkel, however, assumed that the sanctuary and festival legends were later explanations of already existing phenomena (1901, 32-33).

If the legends were originally short, oral, self-contained, and independent units, how did they move from that stage to the form in which we now have them in the scriptures? Already in the oral stage, Gunkel argued, legends attracted one another so that legend-cycles were formed. Traveling storytellers and pilgrimages to sanctuaries provided occasions for such combinations. Legends concerned with the same character, similar themes, and/or related historical occurrences came together to form cycles already at the oral stage. The same "person" could take on several legends and characterizations: at Penuel (Gen 32:22-32), Jacob is the hero who challenges God himself; in the Jacob-Esau stories he is shrewd but cowardly; and the Jacob to whom God appears at Bethel is even different again. These cycles of legends, such as Abraham-Lot and Jacob-Esau, could be further expanded by the incorporation of additional legends such as Abraham's journey to Egypt (Gen 12:4-20) and the Jacob-Laban legends (Gen 29:15-32:1). The following quote illustrates Gunkel's concept of how the cycles developed:

Jacob is originally the type of the shepherd who ousts the hunter. With reference to the name Jacob, it is simply a proper name of that period, such as the heroes of German folk-tales also bear. We find it as such in Babylonian literature. The name Jacob (Jaqubum) is abbreviated from Jacob-el (Jahqub-il, Jaqub-il), and it occurs in the time of Hammurabi. That it was also known in the West we learn from the list of Thutmosis III (*circa* 1500 B.C.), where it appears as the name of a Canaanite town. Names of similar formation in Canaan are also to be found in the Tel-el-Amarna period. Thus it is not surprising to find this same name in an ancient Hebrew folk-tale. The objection—raised more than once in recent years—that Jacob was not a Canaanite name, has little force, for, after all, we know practically nothing of the names from that primitive time. And why should the folk-tale be confined to the commonest names? Regarding the name Esau we can say nothing at all. Whether it is in any way connected with the Phoenician Usoos, the hunter and the enemy of the brother Samemrumos, must be left an open question.

The subsequent history of the Jacob figure was probably as follows:

First of all, to Jacob, who outwitted Esau, was referred a second story, which dealt likewise with a young, clever shepherd. In this way the *Laban story* was added.

Simultaneously, a continuation was invented for the Esau story [Gen 32:3–33:17]. . . .

The biggest step, however, was taken when Jacob was declared to be the ancestor of Israel. At that period a new meaning was given to the older tales—Esau was identified with Edom and Laban with Aram. At the same time the name Jacob was inserted into a whole series of other tales which dealt with the tribes and with the holy places of Israel. The complete figure thus arose by the addition of the Israel tradition to the Jacob tradition. (1928, 184-86. His entire essay in this volume ["Jacob," 150-86] provides an excellent view of Gunkel's work on the legends.

At the same time, a single legend could be expanded through the addition of speeches, extended descriptions, and so forth to produce what Gunkel called a "novella." This reflects a later stage in legend form and is represented by the Joseph story (Gen 37; 39-50) and to a lesser extent by such texts as Gen 20; 24. The creation of legend cycles and novellas was followed by the collection of this material into the sources of the Pentateuch (J, E, P). Here Gunkel stresses that the Yahwist and Elohist are not authors in our (or Wellhausen's) sense of the term but were collectors and are to be understood as schools of narrators. The period of the formation of the legends came to an end in premonarchic times. The early monarchy saw the legends "remodeled" into more national legends. By about 900 BCE, the legends had reached the basic form which we have today although in their later J and E form and subsequent redactions, some alterations and additions continued to be made.

Gunkel recognized that the secondary character of the overall structure of the Genesis traditions and their earlier legendary form make it impossible to use the traditions in Genesis to reconstruct a patriarchal history. According to Gunkel, most of the legends do not assume any historical events whatever which might have engendered the events whatever which might have engendered the legends. The preliterary stage of the traditions cannot be expected to preserve adequately historical memories even where events are involved since "oral tradition cannot remain uncorrupted for any length of time and is therefore inadequate to be the vehicle of history" (1901, 4).

C. Form-Critical Study of the Psalms

Gunkel's form-critical study of the psalms (see Johnson, 162-81) made two important contributions which have dominated research since his time: (1) his analysis and classification of the psalms into their literary types and (2) his association of many of the psalms with worship services in the cult. He was not the first to analyze the psalms into their types or to point to the cult as their place of usage. However, he was the first to employ these perspectives fully as interpretive principles for understanding the psalms. Gunkel recognized that "in the earliest history of man all religion existed only in the form of the worship service, while a cultless piety developed only later" (1967, 5). The earliest psalms were therefore composed for the cult. Although he never assumed that all the present biblical psalms were written for and used in the cult, he did gradually assume this for many of the psalms. In some of his earliest writings on the subject, he assumed that only a small fraction of our Psalter was originally composed for the cult (see 1967, 5). Utilizing his criteria for determining a genre, Gunkel divided the psalms into five main types.

The largest single class of psalms according to Gunkel was the psalms of lament (1967, 19-22; 33-36). The components of this type psalm are:

(1) *The invocation or address to the diety* often with a personalizing appellation such as "Yahweh, my God" or "my God" and frequently with an initial statement of plea.

139

(2) The *complaint* in which the worshiper describes the conditions of his distress.

(3) The *petition or request for help* which forms the heart of the lament, generally stated in an imperative form. Sometimes this section appears in the form of a wish with Yahweh spoken of in the third person. The petition or request prayed for the rescue and redemption of the worshiper and for the destruction of his enemies.

(4) The *motivations for divine intervention* which contain references to such things as the grace and the righteousness of God.

(5) The *affirmation of confidence* which contains the worshiper's statements of his confidence in the divine ability to help. These might be addressed with references to Yahweh in either second or third person.

(6) *Assertion of innocence or confession of sin.*

(7) *Conclusion* often expressing a statement of assurance and/or a vow plus hymnic elements.

Gunkel assigned the following psalms to this type: 3; 5; 6; 7; 13; 17; 22; 25; 26; 27:7-14; 28; 31; 35; 38; 39; 42; 43; 51; 54; 55; 56; 57; 61; 63; 64; 69; 70; 71; 86; 88; 102; 109; 120; 130; 140; 141; 142; 143. Gunkel associated what he called "psalms of confidence" (4; 11; 16; 23; 27:1-6; 62; 131) with this class and saw them as independent expressions of the affirmation of confidence (number 5 above). The individual psalms of lamentation have a "very pronounced style; almost invariably the same thoughts and images recur. The peculiar and recurring situation in this psalm type is that of the supplicant who, in the midst of some illness which is a matter of life and death, must at the same time complain about his enemies who are persecuting and slandering him" (1967, 19-20).

A second class of psalms are the individual thanksgiving psalms (18; 30; 32; 34; 40:2-12; 41; 66; 92; 116; 118; 138). These psalms, according to Gunkel, were used in rituals of thanksgiving sacrifice as references in them to sacrifice and fulfillment of vows suggest. The following elements appear in these psalms:

(1) *Introductory statement of thanksgiving or praise.*
(2) *Description of the distress and redemption* from which the person had been saved. This might contain references to God in the second or third person.
(3) *Confession of Yahweh as redeemer.*
(4) *Proclamation of thanksgiving sacrifice.*
(5) *Conclusion,* often containing hymnic or petitionary elements.

In describing the usage of these psalms, Gunkel wrote:

The scene which we must try to visualize is something like this. The person who is to offer the sacrifice prostrates himself before the temple (Ps 138:2). A number of relatives and acquaintances who expect to participate in the sacred meal stand around him (Ps 22:26). Then, with a sacred goblet in his hand (Ps 116:13) and prior to the actual sacrifice, he sings his song with a loud voice. He may turn first to the bystanders and say something to this effect: "Listen, this is the way it was with me; so now thank Yahweh with me." (1967, 17-18)

A third main psalm type isolated by Gunkel is the hymn (1967, 10-13, 30-31). This type contains the following elements:

(1) *Introductory call to praise* (which was originally addressed to the choir, nation, or other praising group) *or an affirmation of praise.*
(2) The *main body* of the hymn praising Yahweh's attributes and deeds. These might be given expression in the form of participial phrases, separate sentences, rhetorical questions, or other grammatical forms.
(3) *Conclusion* which might parallel the introductory formula or express a wish, petition or blessing.

Gunkel argued that the hymn was originally intended for use in worship at the sanctuaries, especially at the great and important annual festivals and national celebrations. Pss 8; 19; 29; 33; 46; 48; 65; 67; 68; 76; 84; 87; 96; 98; 100; 103; 104; 105; 111; 113; 114; 117; 122; 135; 136; 145; 146; 147; 148; 149; 150 were placed in this class. Pss 47; 93; 96:10-13; 97; 99 were classified by Gunkel as "enthronement songs" or special hymns looking forward to the ultimate enthronement of God as king.

A fourth type of psalm is the category of communal laments (1967, 13-15, 32-33). In describing the elements of this type, Gunkel wrote:

The content of these laments may be divided into three parts. First, there is the lament proper, the purpose of which is to move Yahweh to compassion. . . . Then comes the prayer to Yahweh to remove the calamity, whatever it may be. At this point, all kinds of arguments are put before Yahweh with the intent of moving him to think graciously upon his people and intervene in their behalf. Here belong especially the reminders of their close relationship with Yahweh, which he should not forget, or the memory of the past, in which he has so often helped them. Finally, there is the certainty of hearing. (1967, 32)

These communal laments (44; 74; 79; 80; 83; and, to a lesser degree, 58; 106; 125) were employed on days of community fasts proclaimed and observed when the whole community was threatened with some major calamity such as drought, famine, war, pestilence, and foreign invasion. The community assembled at the sanctuary, and along with signs of fasting, wearing sackcloth and ashes, weeping and wailing, and sacrifice, poured out its soul to Yahweh in pleas for deliverance. In the communal laments "the woeful plight of the people is depicted; it is bewailed and lamented with copious tears. These are the vengeful cries of a tormented people, affronted in that which they consider most holy" (1967, 32).

A fifth class of psalms, according to Gunkel, are the royal psalms (2; 18; 20; 21; 45; 72; 101; 110; 132; 144:1-11). He recognized that this classification was not strictly a form-critical assessment since the only unifying elements in these psalms was the fact that all of them were concerned in one way or another with the king.

Psalm 20 was performed by the royal choir when the king went forth to battle. The royal lament, Psalm 144:1-11, is to be assigned to the same setting. Psalm 18 is the thanksgiving prayer of a king upon his return from a campaign. Psalm 45 is a spirited and very ancient song sung to glorify the wedding of the sovereign. A song performed in the royal sanctuary on the occasion of the anniversary of the establishment of that sanctuary and of the founding of the kingdom is Psalm 132. Most frequent are those poems which were sung at the king's enthronement or at the annual royal festival (Pss 2, 21, 72, and 110); on the day of his enthronement the king himself made a solemn vow [Ps. 101]. (1967, 24)

In addition to these five major psalms genres, Gunkel noted the following minor types: pilgrimage (84; 122), victory songs (partially preserved in 46; 48; 66; 76; 118), communal thanksgiving (66:8-12; 67; 124; 129), legendary (78; 105; 106), wisdom (1; 37; 49; 73; 112; 127; 128; 133), liturgies and dialogues (15; 24; 134; 121), and mixed psalms (40; 89; 90; 107; 108; and so on).

D. Form-Critical Study of the Prophets

Gunkel's interest in the prophets and prophetical literature spanned the whole of his career. Unfortunately, he never devoted a systematic and extensive study to the form criticism of prophecy, comparable to his major introduction to the psalms, which would have allowed him occasion to express his views fully. At the same time, he never produced a commentary on any prophetical book which would have revealed his methodology at work as in his Psalms and Genesis commentaries. Most of his essays on the prophets are very brief and introductory in character and he discusses form-critical questions only as one element in an overall view of prophecy.

In discussing the prophetical materials form-critically, Gunkel stressed that the prophets were originally speakers and not authors. They began their messages with a call "to hear," not "to read." For Gunkel, the original prophetic address was a future-oriented word. In the earliest form of prophecy, such words were probably spoken as a response to an inquiry. When persons reached their wits end, they turned to God with questions about everyday life: dreams (Gen 41), sickness (II Kings 1), siege (II Kings 7:1), journeys (Judg 18:5), battle (I Sam 14:18, 34). Appeal in such cases was directed to "men of God" of whom the prophets were one type. Questions about the future were addressed to the prophet who in the form of prophecies and predictions foretold the future. "There never arose a prophet in Israel whose first saying was not the foretelling of an event of the immediate future" (1969, 69).

Since the early prophets were ecstatic persons (see below, pp. 254-60), their behavior—they screamed, cried out, slavered—and speech were passionate and ecstatic. Such a view led Gunkel to conclude:

> The *short enigmatic words and combinations of words* such as Jezreel, Lo-ammi, Lo-ruhamah (Hosea [1:2-9]), Emmanuel, Shear jashub (Isaiah [7:14, 3]), Maher-shalal-hash-baz—'the spoils speed, the prey hastes' (Isa. 8:1), Rahabhammoshbath ('Rahab who sits still', the bound dragon of chaos; Isa. 30:7) are examples of the very earliest prophetic style. (1969, 64-65)

In addition to its futuristic and ecstatic character, according to Gunkel, the earliest prophetic style was characterized by brevity. For him, the oldest units of prophetic style are likewise the shortest. The appearance of prophetic oracles or sayings that extend to two, three, or more lines already suggests a major development in prophecy. Since each prophetic utterance possessed a customary and conditional extent, the discovery of the true limits of the individual, originally independent, oracles is of particular importance. These, of course, may not coincide with the present chapter and verse division of the scriptures.

Since it is characteristic of every literary category, that the units within the category are of a specific form and extent, and since if these units are not identified, it is impossible to understand the style in question, the study of the style of the prophets must begin with the units in which their utterances were made. This study is all the more valuable, in that in general they are not indicated in the tradition of the text we possess, and many scholars, who have not yet realized the necessity of this task, and following modern ideas of style, still think in terms of units which are much too large and display great uncertainty in the distinguishing and identification of the passage. (1969, 64)

Also, the original prophetic oracle was poetic and metrical in character.

Of its nature, enthusiastic inspiration speaks in poetic form, and rational reflection in the form of prose. Consequently, in form the prophetic speech was originally a poem. People like the prophets, who received their ideas in times of exalted inspiration, and uttered them under the impulse of an over-flowing emotion, could only speak in poetic rhythms. (1969, 66)

A further characteristic of the earliest prophetical oracles noted by Gunkel was their mysterious quality: "revelations were received in mysterious times of ecstasy; they appeared obscure and shadowy before the soul of the prophet. This is faithfully reflected in the style of the visions of the future, and explains the strange demonic and enigmatic tones of these passages" (1969, 69). In addition, "the prophets often consciously concealed even what was clear to them" (1969, 70). "The prophets received their revelations in mysterious hours of ecstasy and would have considered it unbecoming in them to desecrate God's secrets by exposing them to the full light of day" (1928, 131). In discussing the mysterious quality of early Hebrew prophecy, Gunkel refers to the enigmatic words spoken by the oracle of the Delphic Apollo which suggests that his interpretation was influenced by the understanding of "prophets" in Greek culture. Thus the prophets avoided specific names, used approximate or generalized numbers, indirect expressions, concrete but imprecise imagery, allegorical and mythological references, and special names (see 1969, 69-71).

Another characteristic noted by Gunkel was a certain syntactical style. A basic tenet of his form-critical approach was the argument that fixed genres favor certain syntactical constructions. Characteristic of prophetic address is the use of the future tense or prophetic perfect in which the predicted is treated as already having happened, of address in the second person reflecting the prophet's function as messenger coming face to face with those to whom Yahweh had sent him, of the imperative which is genuinely prophetic and through whose usage the prophet felt justified in giving commands to the whole world in the name of Yahweh, and of questions which reflect the use of inquiries as the prophet's means of understanding his initial revelation (1969, 72-73). Generally the prophetic oracle was spoken as if it was the word of Yahweh himself. "Here the prophet regards himself as the 'messenger' of Yahweh—a favorite and characteristic image from an early period—and just as a messenger reports the words of his master exactly as he has heard them from him [Gunkel refers to II Sam 3:12-16; 19:12], so the prophet also has the right to speak in the first person in the name of Yahweh himself" (1969, 67).

In addition to these general characteristics, Gunkel spoke of prophetic address as characterized by a jumpy style, extraordinarily concrete descriptions and imagery, and great passion. Thus for Gunkel, the oldest prophetic style of address was short, future-oriented, ecstatically colored, poetic, metrical, mysterious, sometimes jumpy, passionate, and dominated by certain syntactical constructions.

146

This oldest prophetic style, according to Gunkel, could take the form of either a promise (*Verheissung*) or a threat (*Drohung*), depending on whether the word about the future was of good or evil omen. Corresponding to these were of course the two types of Israelite prophecy—salvation and judgment prophecy—which at almost every period existed side by side. In explicating the coming threat and doom, the prophets utilized the reproach (*Scheltwort*). Prophets "were not satisfied merely with foretelling the future, although this always remained their principal purpose; but they also began to give the *ethical reason* why what they had prophesied had to come to pass" (1969, 74). Gunkel understood the use of the reproach as an inter-prophetical development, although he considered it to be more characteristic of classical than earlier prophecy.

The earlier prophets prophesied individual events in the immediate future; the later literary prophets certainly did not cease to speak in the first instance of the future, but they were able to do more than this: they were capable of giving the reasons why Yahweh was sending the event they prophesied; they knew his thoughts and they felt his moods. (1969, 53)

The reproach or the reason offered for the coming judgment belongs with the threat; the former contains the exposition of the sin and the latter contains the announcement of the coming judgment. Sometimes the reproach precedes the threat, which is introduced by "therefore":

Reproach: "They do not know how to do right," says Yahweh,
"those who store up violence and robbing in their strongholds."
Therefore
Threat: thus says Yahweh God:
"an adversary shall surround the land, and bring down your defenses from you,

147

and your strongholds shall be plundered."
(Amos 3:10-11)

The threat could also precede the reproach which was then introduced by "because":

Thus says Yahweh:

Threat: "For three transgressions of Damascus,
            and for four, I will not revoke the
            punishment;
            because
Reproach: they have threshed Gilead with threshing
            sledges of iron."
            (Amos 1:3)

Gunkel noted that the prophets followed no consistent pattern in this regard; they could move from reproach to threat and back to reproach again and vice versa. When the reproach appears first, it is often introduced by such words as "woe" or "hear." Entire books, such as Amos (excluding 9:11-15), consist of essentially these two elements—the threat and the reproach. At times, the prophets simply denounced the people, that is, the reproaches appear independent of any other element (see Is 1:2-3, 4-9; Jer 2:10-13). Gunkel considered this use of the reproach to expose sin as a new, uniquely prophetic genre.

In addition to promises, threats, and reproaches and various combinations of these, the prophets also uttered exhortations *(Mahnen* or *Mahnrede)* and preached repentance since there steals into every man's heart a little "perhaps" and because every legitimate prophet had as his final goal the conversion of the people from their evil ways.

It was an ancient prophetic practice to answer questions and give advice (Jer. 42:1ff.; Zech. 7:1ff.; Micah 6:6ff.); making use of this right, the prophets uttered *exhortations,* and so found an opportunity of developing their great religious and ethical ideas in a positive sense. . . . (1969, 74-75)

In proclaiming their message, the prophets borrowed and adapted a wide range of nonprophetical genres. On the basis of content, Gunkel spoke of the incalculable variety of prophetic words: "promises and threats, descriptions of sin, exhortations, priestly injunctions, historical descriptions, disputes, songs of every kind, both religious songs and imitations of secular songs, songs of lamentation and rejoicing, short lyrical passages, and whole liturgies, parables, allegories etc" (1969, 68). The reason the prophets adopted such a wide range of alien genres was "their burning desire to gain power over the minds of their people. The fact that they mastered such an extraordinary number of literary categories is a sign of the zeal with which they struggled with the hearts of their people" (1969, 68-69). This broadening of the prophetic employment of genres beyond the promise, threat, reproach, and exhortation was involved in the fact that the prophets, on the one hand, developed into poets, and, on the other hand, became preachers, teachers, and thinkers (see 1969, 73-75). As poets and preachers, the prophets filled out the other forms of prophetic address with a "marvelous profusion" of genres borrowed from practically every area of Israelite life.

E. Form Criticism and Old Testament Laws

Gunkel's work on the narratives of Genesis, his analysis of psalms types and their *Sitz im Leben*, and his form-critical discussion of prophetic genres have remained the starting point of Old Testament form-critical studies. Albrecht Alt (1883-1956) applied Gunkel's concerns to the Old Testament legal materials in order to go behind the literary compilations of laws and to discover the characteristic forms and functions.

The methods of literary criticism alone do not suffice to lead us directly to the oldest forms, for they can only show us older literary versions of the laws, and the oldest written forms which

149

we can isolate with any degree of probability seem bound in any case to be secondary productions, quite distinct from the first promulgation of the laws. The making of the law is basically not a literary process at all, but part of the life of a commnity. (86 [110 in American ed])

In his basic study of Old Testament law, first published in Germany in 1934, Alt divided Israelite laws into two basic types: casuistic and apodictic. Casuistic laws, sometimes referred to as case or conditional laws, contain an introductory conditional clause which generally begins with "if" or "when" and provide an instance or case. This is then followed by a clause stating the consequence or penalty generally introduced by "then" or "he" or "the one" (see the examples in Ex 22:1-17). Alt argued that Israel shared this type of law with general near eastern culture and probably inherited such laws from the Canaanites. He offered three arguments to support the Canaanite background for such law. (1) "Its formal characteristics . . . are the same as those of the legal codes in other nations of the Ancient East. . . ." (2) "The content of the Israelite casuistic law has as its background throughout the culture first adopted by the people of Israel when they settled in Palestine." (3) "It does not take national or religious considerations into account, and has a secular outlook which is easier to reconcile with polytheistic than with monotheistic thought." (98 [125-26]) Alt argued that this type of law with its specified cases was utilized "in the exercise of normal jurisdiction," "in the work of the ordinary courts." (91[116]) Casuistic laws originated and were employed in the courts themselves in the execution of justice. Such justice was administered on the local level, in the "city gate" (see Köhler), by ordinary citizens as representatives of the community.

Apodictic laws, according to Alt, could begin with a reference in the second person ("You shall or shall not . . ."; see Ex 23:14-19), with a Hebrew participle ("whoever . . . "; see Ex 22:19-20), or with a curse ("cursed be he who . . . "; see Deut 27:15-26). Alt took this type of law to be characteristically Israelite, to be concerned with the sacral realm or religious matters, and to be free of any Canaanite influence. Alt assumed that such laws were proclaimed by religious officials on public occasions.

The apodeictic law provides the central text for a sacral action involving the whole nation, and those who proclaim it are the mouthpiece of Yahweh, the levitical priests, whose task in the assembly of the whole nation was by no means only to conduct the worship of Yahweh, but who also carried out the function, at least equally important, of making his demands known to Israel. (125[161])

The origin of the proclamation of the apodeictic law, placing an obligation on the whole nation, at the Feast of Tabernacles, is a regular *renewal of the covenant* between Yahweh and Israel . . . .(129[166-67])

Since the worship of Yahweh, with which the apodeictic law is inseparably linked, clearly originates from the desert, we can presume the same source for the basis of the apodeictic law, if not for the extant examples in their present form. (131[169])

F. Form-Critical Study of Wisdom Literature

A fifth major type of Old Testament literature—in addition to narrative, psalm, prophecy, and law—is what has been broadly labeled wisdom literature. Proverbs, Job, and Ecclesiastes in the Hebrew canon are placed in this category. Form critical work on wisdom literature— as with other types of Old Testament literature—has sought to determine the primary forms characteristic of wisdom and to ascertain where such forms had their origin and usage (see Crenshaw).

The simplest unit in wisdom literature is, of course, the single proverb. This can be a one-line saying complete in itself: "Let not him that girds on his armor boast himself as he that takes it off" (I Kings 20:11). The wisdom literature, however, does not consist simply of single sayings or proverbs such as one finds as the primary content of Prov 10:1-22:16. Units are also found which are much larger, more complex, and less proverbial in style. Crenshaw has divided the wisdom material into eight basic categories or genres: (1) proverbs (see the book of Proverbs); (2) riddle (Judg 14:10-18, but probably elsewhere: see Prov 5:1-6, 15-23; 6:23-24; 16:15; 20:27; 23:27, 29-35; 27:20); (3) fable (Judg 9:8-15; Num 22:21-35; Gen 37:5-11), and allegory (Prov 5:15-23; Eccl 12:1-6); (4) hymn (Prov 1:20-33; 8); (5) dialogue (Job); (6) confession or autobiographical narrative (Prov 4:3-9; 24:30-34; Eccl 1:12-2:26; 8:9-9:1); (7) lists or *onomastica* (Job 38); and (8) didactic poetry (Pss 37; 49; 73; 139) and narrative (Prov 7:6-23).

That wisdom, in its proverbial form, had its origin and usage in the family and clan is a widely held assumption. In addition to this, it is assumed that the royal court and schools in ancient Israel were concerned with and fostered the educational and philosophical interests reflected in wisdom literature. On this issue, Crenshaw has written:

It can be stated that wisdom literature is of four kinds: (1) juridical, (2) nature, (3) practical, and (4) theological . . . . Similarly, there exist (1) family/clan wisdom, the goal of which is the mastering of life, the stance hortatory and the style proverbial; (2) court wisdom, with the goal of education for a select group, the stance secular, and method didactic; and (3) scribal wisdom, with the aim of providing education for everyone, a stance that is dogmatico-religious, and a dialogico-admonitory method. (*OTFC*, 227)

G. Issues in Contemporary Form-Critical Study

Old Testament form criticism has made significant and lasting contributions to biblical studies and established itself as an important and indispensable tool. In recent years, some problems in form-critical research have been noted and should be commented on briefly (see Fohrer, Knierim, and Knight).

(1) Gunkel assumed a very simplistic developmental process in his genre analysis. He argued that the purest and shortest form of a particular type was the oldest. He concluded that the original prophetic word was a short enigmatic saying. From single sayings, there developed oracles composed of complete sentences, several lines, and finally long sermons. Similarly, the prophets developed from ecstatics, to orators, to poets, preachers, teachers, and thinkers. The prophetic traditions developed from oracle sayings, to small collections, to pamphlets, to books. The earliest narratives were assumed to be brief and episodic partly because of the inability of the Israelite storyteller to produce extended narratives and partly due to the short attention span of his hearer! Such assumptions by Gunkel overly systematize and simplify the development of genres while no doubt preserving some elements of truth. Gunkel's view that the final stage or stages of the process was a degeneration has frequently produced a certain disdain for the final written form of a text.

(2) Gunkel's emphasis and stress on the individual unit frequently led to extreme dissection of the biblical text. Scholars, for example, have discovered as many as forty or fifty individual units in the short book of Amos. Surely one cannot assume that each of these units possessed its own structure, content, mood, and *Sitz im Leben*. Just as documentary critics sometimes divide the text into a senseless multitude of sources and redactions, so form critics sometimes divide the material into a meaningless mass of individual units.

(3) The problem of determining the actual life setting, or *Sitz im Leben*, for the various genres has proved to be enormous. Frequently Gunkel limited himself to very general comments on this matter. He spoke of stories being told around the evening campfire or on festival occasions and of the prophets delivering their oracles in

the market place or in the temple court. These, however, do not produce very conclusive or very helpful results with regard to the material's original usage. Some scholars have gone in the opposite direction and attempted to reconstruct the original life setting in great detail but often with little supportive evidence.

(4) As a rule, form-critical studies, and this was the case with Gunkel, have focused on the oral stage lying behind the written text. However, the Old Testament is a collection of books, and books are the product of literary activities. In many cases, an oral or preliterary stage may be discovered behind the written text, but this may not necessarily be the case. At any rate, the literary stage is the only one we possess. Form-critical concern with the oral phase must not be seen as the final effort in biblical interpretation.

CHAPTER 5

THE PENTATEUCH

W. Brueggemann, "Yahwist," *IDBS*, 975-75; *idem* and H. W. Wolff, *The Vitality of Old Testament Traditions* (Atlanta: John Knox Press, 1975); U. Cassuto, *The Documentary Hypothesis and the Composition of the Pentateuch* (Jerusalem: Magnes Press, 1961); F. M. Cross, *Canaanite Myth and Hebrew Epic: Essays in the History of the Religion of Israel* (Cambridge: Harvard University Press, 1973); J. I. Durham, "Credo, Ancient Israelite," *IDBS*, 197-99; I. Engnell, *A Rigid Scrutiny* (Nashville: Vanderbilt University Press, 1969) = *Critical Essays on the Old Testament* (London: SPCK, 1970); R. Frankena, "The Vassal-Treaties of Esarhaddon and the Dating of Deuteronomy," OTS XIV(1965)122-54; T. E. Fretheim, "Elohist," *IDBS*, 259-63; A. W. Jenks, *The Elohist and North Israelite Traditions* (Missoula: Scholars Press, 1977); Y. Kaufmann, *The Religion of Israel: From the Beginnings to the Babylonian Exile* (Chicago/London: University of Chicago Press/George Allen & Unwin, 1960); K. A. Kitchen, *Ancient Orient and Old Testament* (London/Chicago: Tyndale House/InterVarsity Press, 1966); B. A. Levine, "Priestly Writers," *IDBS*, 683-87; H. Lindsell, *The Battle for the Bible* (Grand Rapids: Zondervan, 1976); D. J. McCarthy, *Old Testament Covenant: A Survey of Current Opinions* (Oxford/Atlanta: Basil Blackwell/John Knox Press, 1972); G. Maier, *The End of the Historical-Critical Method* (St. Louis: Concordia Press, 1977); G. F. Moore, "Tatian's Diatessaron and the Analysis of the Pentateuch," *JBL* IX(1890)201-15; E. W. Nicholson, *Deuteronomy and Tradition* (Oxford/Philadelphia: Basil Blackwell/Fortress Press, 1967); M. Noth, *A History of Pentateuchal Traditions* (Englewood Cliffs: Prentice-Hall, 1972); R. M. Polzin, *Biblical Structualism: Method and Subjectivity in the Study of Ancient Texts* (Philadelphia/Missoula: Fortress/Scholars Press, 1977); G. von Rad, *The Problem of the Hexateuch* (Edinburgh/New York: Oliver & Boyd/McGraw-Hill, 1966); R. Rendtorff, "The 'Yahwist' as Theologian? The Dilemma of Pentateuchal Criticism,"

JSOT III(1977)2-9; D. Robertson, "Literature, Bible as," *IDBS*, 547-51; S. Sandmel, "The Haggada within Scripture," *JBL* LXXX(1961)105-22; H. H. Schmid, "In Search of New Approaches in Pentateuchal Research," *JSOT* III(1977)33-42; R. J. Thompson, *Moses and the Law in a Century of Criticism since Graf* (Leiden: E. J. Brill, 1970); J. H. Tigay, "An Empirical Basis for the Documentary Hypothesis," *JBL* XCIV(1975)329-42; J. Van Seters, "Confessional Reformation in the Exilic Period," VT XXII(1972)448-59; *idem, Abraham in History and Tradition* (New Haven/London: Yale University Press, 1975); G. Vink, "The Date and Origin of the Priestly Code in the Old Testament," OTS XV(1969)1-144; N. E. Wagner, "Pentateuchal Criticism: No Clear Future," *CJT* XIII(1967)225-32; *idem,* "Abraham and David?" in *Studies on the Ancient Palestinian World,* ed. J. W. Wevers and D. B. Redford (Toronto: University of Toronto Press, 1972)117-40; M. Weinfeld, "Deuteronomy—The Present State of the Inquiry," *JBL* LXXXVI(1967)249-62; J. Wellhausen, *Prolegomena to the History of Israel* (Edinburgh: A. & C. Black, 1885); F. V. Winnett, "Re-examining the Foundations," *JBL* LXXXIV(1965)1-19; E. J. Young, *An Introduction to the Old Testament* (Grand Rapids: Wm. B. Eerdmans, 1949, [3]1964).

The Old Testament Pentateuch, or Torah, combines narrative and legal materials with occasional poetic sections. The narrative material tells the story of human history from Adam to Abraham, then recounts the fate of Abraham and his descendants (primarily the ancestors of Israel) until the period just before the conquest of the territory west of the Jordan River. The legal material primarily appears as two large blocks: the revelations given while the people are encamped at Mt. Sinai (Ex 19–40; Leviticus; Num 1:1–10:10) and Moses' proclamation of the laws in Moab just before the conquest (Num 22-36 and Deuteronomy). At other places, laws, commands, and legal ordinances appear (see Gen 1:28-29;

9:1-7; 17:9-15 and throughout the journeys recorded in Num 10:10–21:35).

That Moses was the author of the Pentateuch was a firm belief shared by Judaism and Christianity—synagogue and church—throughout much of their history. Before more modern times, problems in the text which cast doubt on the validity of this traditional assumption were only rarely noted even though the Pentateuch itself nowhere claims Moses as its author. In the sixteenth and seventeenth centuries, persons became increasingly aware of internal references in the Pentateuch which contain contradictions, anachronisms, stylistic variety, and indications of editorial activity.

Mosaic and single authorship of the Pentateuch came to be challenged on a number of grounds. (1) As anachronisms, scholars pointed to the account of Moses' death (Deut 34; both Philo [On the Life of Moses II 291] and Josephus [Antiquities IV 326] defended Moses as the prophetic author), to the anachronistic reference to the city of Dan (Gen 14:14; see Judg 18:29), to Gen 36:31, which assumes knowledge of the Hebrew monarchy, to references to Canaanites still in the land (Gen 12:6; 13:7), to the Philistines (Gen 21:34; 26:14-18; Ex 13:17), and so on—all of which suggest a post-Mosaic date. (2) Multiple accounts of the same events were noted: Beersheba is so named on two occasions (Gen 21:31; 26:33); reference to the naming of Bethel appears in two passages (Gen 28:19; 35:15); Jacob's name is twice changed to Israel (Gen 32:28; 35:10); on three occasions a patriarch passes off his wife as his sister (Gen 12:10-20; 20; 26); and, in a span of nine verses, Moses is called to go up and goes up Mt. Sinai three times (Ex 24:9-18) without ever coming down; and so forth. (3) Disagreements between narratives were frequently pointed out: the character and order of creation differ between Gen 1:1–2:4a and 2:4b-25, the flood story contains contrary statements about the number of animals taken into the ark (compare Gen 6:19-20 with 7:2, 8-9), and so on. (4) Differences in the laws have been noted: Ex 20:24 allows for altars to be built at every place God appoints, but Deut 12:14 forbids altars except at a single and centralized sanctuary. Ex 21:2-11 stipulates that female slaves are not to be released after six years, while Deut 15:12 stipulates they are to be. Ex 28:1 limits the offering of sacrifices to the descendants of Aaron, but Deut 18:7 permits this service to any Levite. Ex 12:8-9 requires that the Passover lamb be roasted whole, while Deut 16:7 specifies that it be boiled, etc. (5) Some texts specify that God was known and worshiped by the name Yahweh from earliest times (see Gen 4:26), while elsewhere it is claimed that this name was only revealed at the time of Moses (see Ex 6:2-3). (6) Various differences in style and in the concept of God (compare Gen 1:1–2:4a with 2:4b-25) have been noted as suggesting diversity of authorship.

A. Wellhausen and Classical Source Criticism

The four-source theory (JEDP) of the origin of the Pentateuch was worked out in the nineteenth century in an attempt, first of all, to deal with the problems inherent in the biblical text, secondly, to make sense of the history of Israel presented in the historical books, and, thirdly, to make understandable the Old Testament, which was "practically a sealed book even to thoughtful people" who did not possess "the historical key to the interpretation of that wonderful literature" (W. R. Smith, in Wellhausen, vii). The classical exposition of the source analysis of the Pentateuch, which goes back to Reuss, Graf, and Kuenen, was worked out by Julius Wellhausen. Regarding JE as a single tradition, Wellhausen described the primary issues and his approach in the following manner:

The point is not to prove that the Mosaic law was not in force in the period before the exile. There are in the Pentateuch three strata of law and three strata of tradition, and the problem is to place them in their true historical order . . . in the comparison of them with the ascertained facts of Israelite history. . . . After laboriously collecting the data offered by the historical and prophetical books, we constructed a sketch of the Israelite history of worship; we then compared the Pentateuch with this sketch, and recognised that one element of the Pentateuch bore a definite relation to this phase of the history of worship, and another element of the Pentateuch to that phase of it. This is not putting logic in the place of historical investigation. . . . I always go back to the centralisation of the cultus, and deduce from it the particular divergencies. . . . I attach much. . . . weight. . . to the change of ruling ideas which runs parallel with the change in the institutions and usages of worship; . . . . Almost more important to me than the phenomena themselves, are the presuppositions which lie behind them. (366-68)

Criticism has not done its work when it has completed the mechanical distribution [of the materials to their sources]; it must aim further at bringing the different writings when thus arranged into relation with each other, must seek to render them intelligible as phases of a living process, and thus to make it possible to trace a graduated development of the tradition. (295)

Focusing on the history of Israelite religion, Wellhausen sought to show how the three strata of the law and the three strata of tradition depict five central issues involved in worship and cultic life. In all five areas, the strata show a progression and development which allow the historian and source critic to place the sources in relative chronological relationship to one another. For Wellhausen, JE reflects the same religious situation as the book of the covenant (Ex 21–23) and the "law of the two tables" (Ex 34); D is, of course, found in Deuteronomy; and P incorporates the cultic and priestly legislation in Ex 25–31; 35–40; Leviticus; and Num 1:1–10:10. The accompanying chart illustrates how he saw the relationships of the strata on five cultic issues.

Wellhausen argued that the reform of Josiah in the late seventh century was the first occasion in Israelite history when only one sanctuary was considered legitimate and all others were to be destroyed (so also de Wette and others; see II Kings 22-23). Thus D (the book or earlier

	Sanctuary	Sacrifice	Feasts	Clergy	Clergy Income
JE	Multiplicity of altars and sanctuaries.	Assumed but spontaneous and nature-oriented.	Agricultural festivals; joyous celebrations.	No distinction between clergy and laity.	Priestly share of offerings not regulated.
D	One place of worship commanded.	Generally like JE. (Ezekiel shows attempts to regulate.)	Generally like JE (Passover and Unleavened Bread combined).	All Levites are priests of the altar.	Some regulation of the priestly dues from people.
P	One place of worship presupposed.	Regulated; propitiation stressed; concern with how, and by whom.	Regulated by the calendar not harvests; Day of Atonement added.	Levites are a lower order; only Aaronites are priests.	Extreme regulation of sacrifices, tithes, and other priestly benefits.

version of Deuteronomy) belonged to and was written during this period. Since P (the priestly material in the Pentateuch) is later than both D and Ezekiel 40–48, this stratum comes from after the exile. P and the final form of the Pentateuch were associated with the reforms of Ezra and Nehemiah in the mid-fifth century. J and E were assumed to be earlier than D and to reflect the status of religious and cultic life prior to the great prophetic movement in the second half of the eighth century. It was the great classical prophets who, in taking offense at cultic life, laid the foundations for the Deuteronomic reformation and its stress on the centralization of worship and restriction of sacrifice to one place.

The language held by these men [Amos and Hosea] was one hitherto unheard of when they declared that Gilgal, and Bethel, and Beersheba, Jehovah's favourite seats, were an abomination to Him; that the gifts and offerings with which He was honoured there kindled His wrath instead of appeasing it; that Israel was destined to be buried under the ruins of his temples. . . . Their zeal is directed, not against the places, but against the cultus there carried on, and, in fact, not merely against its false character as containing all manner of abuses, but almost more against itself, against the false value attached to it. (23)

The Deuteronomic legislation is designed for the reformation, by no means of the cultus alone, but at least quite as much of the civil relations of life. The social interest is placed above the cultus, inasmuch as everywhere humane ends are assigned for the rites and offerings. In this it is plainly seen that Deuteronomy is the progeny of the prophetic spirit. Still more plainly does this appear in the *motifs* of the legislation; according to these, Jehovah is the only God, whose service demands the whole heart and every energy; He has entered into a covenant with Israel, but upon fundamental conditions that, as contained in the Decalogue, are purely moral and of absolute universality. Nowhere does the fundamental religious thought of prophecy find clearer expression than in Deuteronomy,—the thought that Jehovah asks nothing for Himself, but asks it as a religious duty that man should render to man what is right, that His will lies not in any unknown height, but in the moral sphere which is known and understood by all. . . . The final outcome of

Source Analysis of Genesis

	P	J	E
PRIMEVAL HISTORY			
(Gen1–11) Creation to Noah	1:1–2:4a	2:4b-4:26	
	5:1-28	5:29	
	5:30-32	6:1-8	
Flood	6:9-22	7:1-5	
	7:6	7:7-10	
	7:11	7:12	
	7:13-16a, 17a		
		7:16b, 17b	
	7:18-21	7:22-23	
	7:24		
	8:1, 2a	8:2b, 3a	
	8:3b-5	8:6	
	8:7	8:8-12	
	8:13a	8:13b	
	8:14-19		
Epilogue		8:20-22	
	9:1-17		
Noah's curse, blessing		9:18-27	
	9:28-29		
Table of nations	10:1-7	10:8-19	
	10:20	10:21	
	10:22-23, 24	10:25-30	
	10:31-32		
Tower of Babel		11:1-9	
Genealogy, Shem-Abraham	11:10-27	11:28-30	
	11:31-32		
PATRIARCHAL HISTORY			
(Gen 12–50) *Abraham Cycle*			
(Gen 12:1–25:18) Call of			
Abraham		12:1-4a	
	12:4b-5	12:6-9	
In Egypt		12:10-13:1	
Separation from Lot		13:2-5	
	13:6	13:7-11a	
	13:11b-12	13:13-18	
Abraham's victory			
(Gen 14, special tradition)			
Covenant with Abraham		15:1-2	
			15:3a
		15:3b-4	15:5
		15:6-12	15:13-16
		15:17-21	
Ishmael's birth	16:1a	16:1b-2	
	16:3	16:4-14	
	16:15-16		

	P	J	E
Covenant of circumcision	17:1-14		
Promise of son	17:15-27		
Destruction of Sodom		18:1–19:28	
	19:29		
Lot's daughters		19:30-38	
Abraham in Gerar		20:1a	20:1b-18
Isaac and Ishmael	21:1b-5		21:6
		21:7	21:8-21
Abimelech			21:22-34
Testing of Abraham			22:1-19
Abraham's later years		22:20-24	
	23:1-20		
Isaac's bride		24:1-67	
Keturah		25:1-6	
Abraham's death	25:7-11a	25:11b	
Ishmael's descendants	25:12-18		
Jacob Cycle (Gen 25:19–36:43)			
Birth of Esau and	25:19-20	25:21-26a	
Jacob	25:26b	25:27-34	
Isaac stories		26:1-33	
	26:34-35		
Stolen blessing		27:1-45	
Jacob's exile	27:46–28:9		
Jacob's dream		28:10	28:11-12
		28:13-16	28:17-18
		28:19	28:20-22
Arrival in Aram		29:1-14	
Leah and Rachel		29:15-30	
Jacob's children		29:31-35	30:1-3
		30:4-5	30:6
		30:7-16	30:17-19
		30:20-21	30:22-23
		30:24	
Jacob's wealth		30:25-43	
Jacob's flight, covenant		31:1	31:2
with Laban		31:3	31:4-16
		31:17	
	31:18	31:19a	31:19b
		31:20-23	31:24-25a
		21:25b	31:26
		31:27	31:28-29
		31:30a	31:30b
		31:31	31:32-35
		31:36a	31:36b-37
		31:38-40	31:41-45
		31:46-49	31:50
		31:51-53a	31:53b-55
Angel of Mahanaim			32:1-2
Preparation for Esau		32:3-13a	32:13b-21
Jacob at Penuel		32:22-32	
Meeting with Esau		33:1-3	33:4-5
		33:6-7	33:8-11
		33:12-17	

	P	J	E
Arrival at Shechem	33:18a	33:18b	33:19-20
Rape of Dinah		34:1-31	
Jacob's return to			35:1-5
Bethel	35:6		35:7-8
	35:9-13		35:14
	35:15		
Birth of Benjamin			35:16-20
Jacob's sons		35:21-22a	
	35:22b-26		
Isaac's death	35:27-29		
Edomite lists 36:1-14			
(15-43 later addition to P)			
History of Jacob's Sons			
(Gen 37–50)			
Joseph's dream and	37:1-2	37:3a	37:3b
results		37:4-21	37:22-24
		37:25-28	37:29-36
Judah and Tamar		38:1-30	
Temptation of Joseph		39:1-23	
Joseph in prison		40:1	40:2-23
Pharaoh's dreams, Joseph's			41:1-33
rise		41:34a	41:34b, 35a
		41:35b	41:36-40
		41:41-45	
	41:46a	41:46b	41:47-48
		41:49	41:50-54
		41:55-57	
Brothers' first trip			42:1a
to Egypt		42:1b	42:2-3
		42:4-5	42:6-7
		42:8-11a	42:11b
		42:12	42:13-26
		42:27-28a	42:28b-37
		42:38	
Second trip		43:1-34	
Testing of the brothers		44:1-34	
The recognition		45:1	45:2-3
		45:4-5a	45:5b-15
		45:16-28	
Jacob in Egypt			46:1-5a
		46:5b	
	46:6-27	46:28–	
		47:5a	47:5b-6a
		47:6b	47:7-12
		47:13-26	
	47:27-28	47:29-31	48:1-2
	48:3-6		48:7-22
Blessings of Jacob 49:1a (1b-28;			
special tradition)			
Jacob's death, burial	49:29-33		
		50:1-10a	50:10b-11
	50:12-13	50:14	
Joseph's last days			50:15-26

the Deuteronomic reformation was principally that the cultus of Jehovah was limited to Jerusalem and abolished everywhere else,—such was the popular and practical form of prophetic monotheism. (487-88)

Wellhausen and the nineteenth-century source critics made their strongest case in regard to the deuteronomistic and priestly strata in the Pentateuch. The Deuteronomic material (D) was firmly anchored to the reform of Judean religion carried out by Josiah and the priestly material was related to the reconstitution of Judaism after the return from Babylonian exile. It was assumed that the parallel sources J and E were combined sometime before the reform of Josiah and then subsequently combined with D by another redactor. P—"the scarlet thread on which the pearls of JE were hung" (Wellhausen, 332)—finally provided the framework for the entire Pentateuch, which was publicly accepted as authoritative in conjunction with the post-exilic reformation of Ezra.

Source critics tended to assume that the documents J, E, D, and P were the creative products of particular authors. This does not mean that the authors were considered the creators of the content found within the sources. Wellhausen stressed that older traditions—myths, songs, stories—were utilized by the authors of the documents. Nonetheless, the importance of the authors is strongly stressed, as the following quote illustrates:

When the subject treated is not history but legends about pre-historic times, the arrangement of the material does not come with the materials themselves, but must arise out of the plan of a narrator. . . . From the mouth of the people there comes nothing [but the detached narratives, which may or may not happen] to have some bearing on each other: to weave them together in a connected whole is the work of the poetical or literary artist. (Wellhausen, 296)

The presentations of the earliest of Israelite history, according to the critics, were colored by the times in which the sources were written and therefore cannot be utilized as straightforward historical documents.

> We attain to no historical knowledge of the patriarchs, but only of the time when the stories about them arose in the Israelite people; this later age is here unconsciously projected, in its inner and outward features, into hoar antiquity, and is reflected there like a glorified image. (Wellhausen, 318-19)

Although Wellhausen concluded that "the longer a story was spread by oral tradition among the people, the more was its root concealed by the shoots springing from it," he nevertheless argued that "the popular fancy plays as it wills; yet it does not make such leaps as to make it impossible to trace its course" (326). Thus, he was able to reconstruct a significant role for Moses in Israelite history in spite of the long process through which the traditions had passed.

> Within the Pentateuch itself . . . the *historical* tradition about Moses (which admits of being distinguished, and must carefully be separated, from the *legislative*, although the latter often clothes itself in narrative form) is in its main features manifestly trustworthy, and can only be explained as resting on actual facts.
>
> From the historical tradition, then, it is certain that Moses was the founder of the Torah. . . . He was the founder of the nation out of which the Torah and prophecy came as later growths. He laid the basis of Israel's subsequent peculiar individuality, not by any one formal act, but in virtue of his having throughout the whole of his long life been the people's leader, judge, and centre of union. (438-39)

B. Reactions to Documentary Analysis

Following Wellhausen's engaging and captivating presentation of the documentary analysis of the Penta-teuch, source criticism cast its shadow through the length and breadth of Old Testament studies (for a history and discussion of the issues, see R. J. Thompson). Four basic reactions developed as responses to the Graf-Wellhausen theories: (1) strong opposition to and denial of the methodology, (2) full acceptance of the methodological approach accompanied by even further demarcation and analysis of pentateuchal sources, (3) general acceptance of the approach but uneasiness about the analysis of the sources and/or their dating, and (4) dissatisfaction with the critical focus on source analysis, on linguistic and philological concerns, and on matters such as dating, compilation, and editorial activity to the exclusion of the theological interests of the sources.

(1) Negative reactions to documentary criticism were exceptionally strong, especially in British and American circles and among Roman Catholics in general. Many voices were raised against "German infidelity" and this "dark side of the Enlightenment" which treated the Bible as if it were an ordinary book and flouted traditional views. The critical treatment of the Bible was seen as a frontal attack on many of the church's confessional statements about the scriptures. (Wellhausen recognized the clash between scientific study and confessional statements about the Bible and thus resigned as a theological professor of Old Testament at Griefswald in 1882.) Many ecclesiastical statements, like the Westminster Confession of 1647, had declared that the sacred scriptures were "given by inspiration of God to be the rule of faith" and that the "authority of Holy Scripture for which it ought to be believed and obeyed dependeth not upon the testimony of any man or Church but wholly upon God (who is truth itself) the author thereof; and therefore it is to be received because it is the word of God." Few confessional statements had gone as far as the Helvetic Concensus of 1675, in which many of the Swiss churches declared that God had watched over the writing of the word with such great care that even the vowel points and accents in the Hebrew text were inspired.

Many conservative scholars have opposed source

criticism on the grounds that such a challenge to the unity and Mosaic authorship of the Pentateuch denies the supernatural origin of the Bible (its inspiration) as well as its supernatural contents (its inerrancy or infallibility); that is, they have appealed to the "traditional" view of the scriptures, a view which received its classical formulation in the seventeenth century, and have argued that any departure from that position can only undermine faith. The stress on the uniqueness of the Bible can lead to the assumption that the use of the historical-critical approach in biblical studies is illegitimate.

For God's revelation we cannot just apply "the" historical method generally used in historiography. Rather, if one wants to allow even for the possibility of divine revelation, one must decide at the start to put aside the principle of analogy, which permits no exceptions, and obediently give way to the sovereignty of God. (Maier, 58)

Coupled with the denial of the use of the historical-critical method, there is frequently the argument that what the Bible says is true and for the faithful must be believed in its entirety.

(The Bible) communicates religious truth, not religious error. But there is more. Whatever it communicates is to be trusted and can be relied upon as being true. The Bible is not a textbook on chemistry, astronomy, philosophy, or medicine. But where it speaks on matters having to do with these or any other subjects, the Bible does not lie to us. It does not contain error of any kind. (Lindsell, 18)

In his 1893 encyclical, *Providentissimus Deus*, Pope Leo XIII strongly opposed the critical approach to biblical studies, repudiated "the Rationalists, true children and inheritors of the older heretics," and condemned " 'higher criticism,' which pretends to judge of the origin, integrity, and authority of each book from internal indications alone." Leo declared that it was "absolutely wrong and forbidden either to narrow inspiration to certain parts only of Holy Scripture or to admit that the sacred writer has erred" since "God, the Creator and Ruler of all things, is also the Author of the Scriptures—and that, therefore, nothing can be proved either by physical science or archaeology which can really contradict the Scriptures." He called for the training of biblical specialists, educated in Oriental languages, natural sciences, and history who could defend the scriptures according to the faith and tradition of the church.

The charge that Wellhausen and the source critics applied philosophical and evolutionary presuppositions to the history of Israelite religion has been used to discount the validity of source analysis. Wellhausen assumed that Israelite religion had developed through three phases: (a) the stage of primitive religion character- ized by primitive sentiments, a spontaneous and simple faith, and a nature orientation; (b) the stage of ethical concerns and consciousness intiated by the prophets; and (c) the stage of ceremonial and ritual religion influenced by the priestly legislation and separated from an orientation to nature. This schematization has been seen as an imposition of alien categories upon the Bible.

Objections to the genuineness of any portion of the Pentateuch which are based upon a theory of the evolutionary development of Israel's religious institutions must be rejected. It is becoming abundantly clear that the reconstruction of Israel's history which is associated with the name of Wellhausen is based upon Hegelian philosophy. . . . To give to such a philosophy of history a priority over the express claims of sacred Scripture is not to be scientific. Hence, since the development hypothesis, as it has generally been presented, rejects the special, supernatural intervention of God in the history of Israel, it must be rejected as unscientific and as incapable of correctly explaining the facts. (Young, 151)

The widely divergent expositions of the documentary hypothesis and the contrasting analysis of the sources (see section 2 below) have been seen as arguments against the authenticity of the method. If the Pentateuch developed as the hypothesis assumes, then scholars should be able to agree on the manner in which the materials developed. Some interpreters suggest that it is easier to accept and handle the difficulties involved in the assumption of Mosaic authority than it is to accept the difficulties involved in the documentary hypothesis.

There are, of course, difficulties in the position that Moses himself wrote the Pentateuch. But these seem to be almost trifling when compared with the tremendous difficulties that emerge upon any alternate theory of composition. There are, however, certain factors which have not received sufficient consideration.

(i) For one thing, it is perfectly possible that in the compilation of the Pentateuch Moses may have made excerpts from previously existing written documents. If he did so, this fact may account for some of the alleged difficulties that appear. For example, it might *in certain cases* explain the use of the divine names in Genesis.

(ii) On the other hand we must remember that the Bible, when considered in its human aspect, is an Oriental book. Now, parallels from antiquity show that the Oriental mind did not always present his material in the so-called logical order of the Occidental. The fact that the Pentateuch is, considered from the human side, a product of the Orient, may to some extent account for its form. One thing at least is clear. The elaborate 'scissors-and-paste' method which the documentary analysis postulates is without parallel anywhere in the ancient Oriental world.

(iii) Furthermore, we may ask, who in Israel's history was better prepared than Moses to write the Pentateuch? He had the time and also the training and learning to do so. Also, as human founder of the theocracy, he had the information that was requisite. The Pentateuch exhibits an inner plan and structure that betray a great mind. Who, better than Moses, could have produced such a work?

More than two hundred years of exhaustive study have been unable to produce a satisfactory substitute for the time-honoured biblical view that Moses himself was the human author of the Law. Hence, we cannot do better than to regard the Pentateuch as the product of the great lawgiver of Israel. (Young, 153)

All of the five pillars upon which the structure of documentary hypothesis rests (see above, pp. 116, 118) have been challenged at one time or another. U. Cassuto, for example, sought to show that "all these pillars were without substance" and that the "imposing and beautiful edifice" which scholars had erected thereon and lavishly decorated "has, in reality, nothing to support it and is founded on air" (Cassuto, 100). For example, he argued that perfectly plausible reasons existed for the variations in the names used for God and that none of these presupposed diverse documents.

In each case the Torah chose one of the two Names according to the context and intention, precisely as follows:

It selected the name YHWH when the text reflects the Israelite conception of God, which is embodied in the portrayal of YHWH and finds expression in the attributes traditionally ascribed to Him by Israel, particularly in His ethical character; it preferred the name 'Elōhīm when the passage implies the abstract idea of the Deity prevalent in the international circles of 'wise men'—God received as the Creator of the physical universe, as the Ruler of nature, as the Source of life.

The Tetragrammaton is used, when expression is given to the direct, intuitive notion of God, which characterizes the simple faith of the multitude or the ardour of the prophetic spirit; the name 'Elōhīm, when the concept of thinkers who meditate on the lofty problems connected with the existence of the world and humanity is to be conveyed.

The name YHWH occurs when the context depicts the Divine attributes in relatively lucid and, as it were, palpable terms, a clear picture being conveyed; 'Elōhīm, when the portrayal is more general, superficial and hazy, leaving an impression of obscurity.

The Tetragrammaton is found when the Torah seeks to arouse in the soul of the reader or the listener the feeling of the sublimity of the Divine Presence in all its majesty and glory; the name 'Elōhīm, when it wishes to mention God in an ordinary manner, or when the expression or thought may not, out of reverence, be associated directly with the Holiest Name.

The name YHWH is employed when God is present to us in His personal character and in direct relationship to people or nature; and 'Elōhīm when the Deity is alluded to as a Transcendental Being who exists completely outside and above the physical universe.

The Tetragrammaton appears when the reference is to the God of Israel relative to His people or to their ancestors; 'Elōhīm, when He is spoken of in relation to one who is not a member of the Chosen People.

YHWH is mentioned when the theme concerns Israel's tradition; and 'Elōhīm, when the subject-matter appertains to the universal tradition.

Sometimes, of course, it happens that two opposite rules apply together and come in conflict with each other; then, as logic demands, the rule that is more material to the primary purport of the relevant passage prevails. (Cassuto, 31-32)

An additional argument used against the documentary analysis of the Pentateuch condemns the approach as a reflection of modern attitudes which are totally inapplicable when applied to ancient times. It assumes a book-understanding of literature which, it is claimed, did not exist in antiquity.

It is not necessary for a person to have a very profound understanding of the similarities between the various cultures of the ancient Near East to be able to see that the whole literary-critical system is based upon a complete misunderstanding of the actual situation. It reflects a modern, anachronistic *book view,* and attempts to interpret ancient biblical literature in modern categories, an *interpretatio europaeica moderna.* (Engnell, 53)

Finally, opponents of source criticism have argued that the redaction, conflation, and editorial treatment of documents, such as is assumed by source critics, is without parallel in the culture of the ancient Near East.

The documentary theory in its many variations has throughout been elaborated *in a vacuum*, without any proper reference to other Ancient Oriental literatures to find out whether they had been created in this singular manner. . . . Hebrew literature shows very close external stylistic similarities to the other Ancient Oriental literatures among which (and as part of which) it grew up. Now, nowhere in the Ancient Orient is there anything which is definitely known to parallel the elaborate history of fragmentary composition and conflation of Hebrew literature (or marked by just such criteria) as the documentary hypotheses would postulate. And conversely, any attempt to apply the criteria of the documentary theorists to Ancient Oriental compositions that have known histories but exhibit the same literary phenomena results in manifest absurdities. (Kitchen, 114-15)

(2) The documentary approach to the Pentateuch has been accepted by a majority of Old Testament scholars. Research in this area has witnessed attempts to extend the limits of the documents into the historical books (Joshua to II Kings), to divide JEDP further, and to defend the source theory against its detractors.

Many attempts have been made to trace some of the pentateuchal documents into Joshua and Judges and even to see them as extending as far as the narrative history of the monarchy (see further, below pp. 202-6). Far more effort has been expended on attempting to subdivide further the four basic strands of pentateuchal material. In reading any major Old Testament introduction, one encounters references to such sigla as J^1, J^2, E^1, E^2, P^1, and P^2 or their counterparts which testify to this effort. The attempts to define further the proposed documents are based on the assumption of parallel narratives and are not just ways of dealing with what are assumed to be additions or elaborations. Von Rad, for example, after extensive study of P, concluded that what is generally assigned to this source should be broken down into two parallel strands which extend throughout the Hexateuch (Genesis–Joshua).

A more widespread effort to discover a fourth narrative

strand in the Pentateuch, in addition to J, E, and P, has focused on the material contained in J. In the material assigned to this source there are a number of elements which interrupt a unified perspective. For example, the Adam-Eve story (Gen 2:4b–3:24) assumes an unpopulated world whereas the Cain-Abel story, which now follows (Gen 4), assumes a populated world where people would want to slay Cain and where he could choose a wife. Further, the genealogy of Cain (in Gen 4) and that of Seth (in Gen 5) are mutually exclusive. Similar divergencies are noted elsewhere. The most widely acknowledged attempts to isolate a fourth narrative strand in the Pentateuch are the following:

L = a "lay" source isolated by Otto Eissfeldt; assumed to begin with Gen 2:4b and to extend throughout Genesis and Exodus but including some passages in Numbers; very primitive; sympathetic to nomadic life–style; oldest narrative source of the Pentateuch (dated about 950-850 BCE according to Eissfeldt).

N = a "nomadic" source stratum isolated by Georg Fohrer; similar in content to Eissfeldt's L, understood by Fohrer as later than and a reaction to J; probably originated in southern Judah; reflects a shepherding, nomadic approach to life and opposition to urban and settled life and civilization; dated about 800 BCE.

S = a "Seir" (Edomite) or "Southern" source isolated by Robert H. Pfeiffer; found only in Genesis; contained the non-P material in Gen 1-11 on the origin and development of mankind and the account of the origins of the peoples living in southern Palestine and Trans-Jordan (parts of Gen 14–35; 38; 36); concluding with an account of the history of Edom; the material in Gen 1–11 was Edomite in origin; the remaining material was Jewish midrash; the source was integrated with the Pentateuch very late, just before the final edition of the "Law of Moses" was issued (about 400 BCE).

K = A "Kenite" source isolated by Julian Morgenstern; a fragmentary account of the oldest version of the exodus narrative; oldest document of the Hexateuch; contains the small "book of the covenant" in Ex 34; was the basis of Asa's reform (see I Kings 15:9-15) in 899 BCE.

(For a description of these hypothetical sources, see the standard Old Testament introductions by Eissfeldt, Fohrer, Pfeiffer, and Morgenstern, "The Oldest Document of the Hexateuch," *HUCA* IV (1927)1-138.)

Source critics of the Pentateuch have sought in a number of ways to defend the documentary approach and to illustrate that documents were transmitted, conflated, and edited in antiquity as assumed by the hypothesis. Obviously, the strongest arguments advanced by the theory's supporters are that it takes into consideration and offers an explanation for internal problems within the Pentateuch itself and that the theory allows the interpreters to correlate the documents and law codes, at least provisionally, with the course of Israelite and Jewish history as this can be reconstructed from the historical books of the Old Testament. In addition, various other arguments have been advanced.

(a) Within the Old Testament itself, duplicate and parallel texts have been preserved, for example, II Sam 22 = Ps 18; Ps 14 = Ps 53; II Kings 18:13-20:19 = Is 36:1-39:8; and I-II Chronicles parallels Genesis to II Kings. In all of these, significant variations exist which suggest that traditions could be handed down in different forms. The books of Chronicles, which parallel the books of Kings, most clearly demonstrate how theological and political interests could influence the treatment of earlier traditions. At times, the Chronicler reproduces the books of Kings verbatim; at other points, the material has been rewritten and supplemented (from another source?).

(b) References to works from which extracts have been excerpted and incorporated into the biblical texts occur in places in the Old Testament: Num 21:14 refers to the book of the Wars of Yahweh, and Josh 10:12-13 and II Sam 1:17-27 speak of material taken from the Book of Jashar. These references suggest that earlier works were utilized in later compositions as postulated by the documentary hypothesis.

(c) The differences between the Greek and Hebrew versions of several Old Testament books such as Jeremiah and Job (see above, pp. 67-69) demonstrate that similar bodies of traditions could be transmitted (like J and E?) in different versions in the same community. That the book of I Esdras in the LXX canon parallels the end of Chronicles, the book of Ezra, and a small section of Nehemiah suggests that different works could be produced by combining material from other works.

(d) The pseudepigraphical book of Jubilees (a radical revision and rewrite of Genesis 1–Exodus 12) and the Genesis Apocryphon from Qumran demonstrate that traditions and documents were frequently rewritten, expanded, edited, and supplemented in Judaism.

(e) Writing in 1890, G. F. Moore argued that Tatian's Diatessaron provides an analogy to the combination of sources to produce the Pentateuch. About 170 CE, Tatian produced a harmony of the four gospels by weaving together the gospel material to produce what amounted to a highly eclectic work. Moore suggested that this forms a parallel to the combination of JEDP to produce the Torah and that such redactional techniques as those used by Tatian and compositional signs similar to those in the Diatessaron can be seen in the Pentateuch.

(f) Recently, Tigay has attempted to demonstrate that the method of composition assumed by the documentary hypothesis is clearly evident in some of the fragments of the book of Exodus from Qumran and in the parallel texts of the Samaritan Pentateuch. As is well-known, some of the episodes narrated in Exodus are described in different fashion in Deuteronomy. In some Qumran fragments and in places in the Samaritan Pentateuch some of the material from Deuteronomy has been incorporated into the Exodus texts. For example, Ex 18:21-27 has been supplemented with material drawn from Deut 1:9-18, and Ex 20:18-26 conflated with material from Deut 5:24-31. In these cases, the scribes producing the conflated text had two separate and different sources upon which to draw. They integrated the material, incorporating complimentary variant forms, preserving a maximum amount of the material, dropping material only when it was duplicated or insignificant, revising minimally the texts, and altering material only to make sense of the newly conflated and interpolated text. This is an analogous process to that assumed by source critics when they speak of conflation, supplementation, interpolation, and redaction of parallel sources. Those who conflated and edited the Qumran texts were not as free, it is assumed, as their predecessors; for the former's work with more revered texts made it impossible to drop material to avoid outright redundancy.

(3) While accepting the general documentary approach to pentateuchal studies, some interpreters have sought to modify the classical four-document scheme and the dating of Wellhausen. Three developments in this area have been especially significant.

(a) The narrative document E, since its isolation and separation from P, has been considered very fragmentary and incapable of providing a continuous narrative. While some scholars have continued to consider E as a northern document parallel to J but less fully preserved (see Fretheim and Jenks), others have seen E as only a later supplementation of J or modifications of J materials. The issues remain open and debatable.

(b) Radical changes have been proposed in attempting to understand the nature and date of J. For Wellhausen and early source critics, J represented an early (eighth century) and primitive form of religious faith and Israelite history. Gradually, J came to be understood as a very sophisticated theological work and was widely dated to the Solomonic age (tenth century) although no strong case was ever made for such a dating (see section 4 below).

(c) Heated debate has revolved around the dating, origin, and nature of D and the Deuteronomic traditions (see Weinfeld and Nicholson). Attempts have been made to date the work much earlier than the reform of Josiah; some scholars have suggested an origin as early as the days of Samuel. A few have dated D to the post-exilic community and pointed to its ideological and impractical character. While most scholars today would see at least an early form of D as the law code utilized in Josiah's reform, a wide variety of proposals are suggested for its provenance; circles closely related to the prophets, groups from Israel who came south after the fall of Samaria, Levitical priests and/or the "people of the land" living in the Judean countryside, the Jerusalem priests, and royal officials and statesmen associated with the Jerusalem court working without/with Josiah's knowledge. Of special importance is the question of the relationship of D to the books of Joshua through II Kings (see below, pp. 206-18).

(4) A major reaction to Wellhausen's source analysis came from those who were discontent with primarily documentary studies to the exclusion of concern for theological matters. In contemporary studies, interest in the theology of the sources has come to be a dominant concern.

Recent Old Testament research shows a notable change in the assessment of the 'sources' of the Pentateuch. Earlier generations of scholars were concerned to examine, as carefully as possible, the *literary* demarcation between the individual, written sources, to study their use of language, to determine the date of their origin and finally to describe the process of editing and compilation. In more recent times, it is remarkable how all these problems have fallen into the background. Instead, there predominates a strongly marked interest in the *theology* of the written sources of their authors. Indeed, the characteristic element of the written sources is frequently seen in the fact that they are theological works. (Rendtorff, 2)

In order to understand and to appreciate fully this concern with the theology of the pentateuchal sources, it is necessary to examine the work of a number of scholars who have operated along lines laid down by Hermann Gunkel.

C. The Contributions of the History of Tradition Approach

Gunkel and other like-minded scholars, working with genre analysis and a history of religions approach, set out to offer an aesthetic and sensitive exposition of Old Testament literature which would provide a supplement and alternative to purely documentary analysis. Gunkel's work established not only the form-critical approach to biblical study but also engendered a methodology subsequently designated history of tradition (or tradition criticism). This approach seeks to recover the process and fortune through which traditions passed and developed from their earliest ascertainable form to their final textual expression.

In his analysis of the narratives of Genesis, Gunkel had come to the following conclusions:

(1) The earliest form of the narrative traditions were short, self-contained, independent units—sagas (legends), myths, folk-tales.

(2) These units can be isolated and studied in terms of the rules of general folklore research.

(3) The individual units had their origin and usage in the folk culture of ancient Israel.

(4) In the process of transmission, traditions could be developed, expanded, altered, and reinterpreted.

(5) Already at the oral stage, originally independent traditions were brought into association to produce cycles of oral literature.

(6) "J" and "E" should not be considered as individual

authors but as schools of narrators who collected materials that had evolved in the course of history. The type of analysis utilized by Gunkel in his study of Genesis was subsequently applied to the other narratives of the Pentateuch by such scholars as Eduard Meyer (1855-1930) and Hugo Gressman (1877-1927).

Two scholars, Gerhard von Rad (1901-1971) and Martin Noth (1902-1968), have most fully developed Gunkel's approach while, like Gunkel, accepting the general methodology and results of source criticism. In 1938, von Rad published a monograph on the problem of the Hexateuch, an essay whose impact on twentieth-century Old Testament study has been almost unparalleled. The stages in the long development which produced the Hexateuch (Genesis through Joshua) is the work's center of focus. The problem and approach, as he envisioned them, must be viewed against the results arrived at by Wellhausen, Gunkel, and their successors: (1) the literary documents or strata of the Pentateuch (Hexateuch) had been analyzed into ever increasing fragmentary sources while (2) form criticism had attempted to isolate the smallest units of tradition and to trace their history, yet (3) neither of these approaches had done much to explain the organic structure and overall unity of the Pentateuch. Von Rad set out to deal with the question of how the Hexateuch in its present form—the final literary form—came into being.

Von Rad viewed the Hexateuch as a historical creed that gave expression to Israel's faith and whose basic contents and outline are rather simple.

God, who created the world, called the first ancestors of Israel and promised them the land of Canaan. Having grown in numbers in Egypt, the people of Israel were led into freedom by Moses, amidst miraculous demonstrations of God's power and favour, and after prolonged wanderings in the desert were granted the promised land. (2)

Von Rad advocated the thesis that the final form of the Hexateuch was the outgrowth and intricate elaboration of an early brief credo. He isolated forms of this credo or confessional creed in Deut 26:5b-9; 6:20-24; and Josh 24:2b-13. Characteristic of these credos was their employment of three of the major traditional complexes of the Hexateuch, although it was the last which dominated: (1) the patriarchs to whom the land was promised, (2) the exodus from Egypt accompanied by God's divine manifestations, and (3) the settlement in the promised land. Completely lacking from these credos are any references either to the traditions reflected in Gen 1–11 or to the Sinai materials. Von Rad concluded that the absence of any mention of the events at Sinai in these credos suggests that "the canonical redemption story of the exodus and settlement in Canaan on the one hand, and the tradition of Israel's experiences at Sinai on the other, really stand over against each other as two originally independent traditions . . ." (13).

Von Rad located both of the tradition complexes—the exodus-settlement and the Sinai-covenant—in the worship of the Israelite cult but in different cultic contexts. The credo focusing on the settlement theme was understood by von Rad as the cult-legend for the Feast of Weeks celebrated at the ancient shrine at Gilgal, a holy place associated with the conquest and settlement in Joshua (see especially Josh 3–5). The essential characteristic of the cult-legend is that it takes, according to von Rad,

. . . Definite, objective basic facts of the common faith and actualises them to furnish the content and the central feature of a cultic festival. . . The cult-legend provided the historical justification which enabled Israel to adopt as its own the ancient Canaanite festival, and from the standpoint of the old Yahwistic faith, it offered quite the handiest method of appropriating an agricultural festival. By the use of the creed, the congregation acknowledges the redemption sovereignty of Yahweh, now seen as the giver of the cultivable land. (43)

In other words, the settlement credo was used by the Israelites in their ritual celebration of taking possession of the promised land—originally observed at Gilgal—and in the process there occurred the "Israelitizing" of the old Canaanite harvest festival, the Feast of Weeks observed in the late spring.

The Sinai tradition was understood by von Rad as the cult-legend of the fall Feast of Booths as originally celebrated at Shechem. He argued:

It is evident that such material [the Sinai complex] does not exist in some nebulous sphere of piety, not is it the creation of a more or less personal religiosity; it belongs to the official worship, and is in fact fundamental to the worshipping community. Its function therefore is to be sought in the public religious activity of the community, that is to say, in the cultus. (21)

Basing his conclusion upon an earlier work of Mowinckel who had argued that the Sinai material, in light of Pss 50 and 81, was part of the fall festival, von Rad outlined the cultic celebration reflected in the Sinai story as follows:

One can picture the sequence: there is a preparatory hallowing, i.e. a ritual cleansing of the assembly; the assembly draws near to God at the blast of the trumpets; God declares himself and communicates his demands; sacrifice is offered and the covenant is sealed. (21)

A structure similar to the Sinai tradition was observed by von Rad in the reconstructed Shechem covenant festival and the book of Deuteronomy.

Exodus	Shechem Ceremony	Deuteronomy
1. Exhortation (Ex 19:4-6) and historical recital of the events at Sinai (Ex 19ff).	1. Joshua's allocution (Josh 24:14 ff) and the assent of the congregation (Josh 24:16ff, 24).	1. Historical presentation of the events at Sinai, and paranetic material (Deut 1–11).
2. Reading of the Law (Decalogue and Book of the Covenant).	2. Proclamation of the law (Josh 24:25; Deut 27:15ff).	2. Reading of the Law (Deut 12:1–26:15).
3. Promise of blessing (Ex 33:20ff).	3. Sealing of the covenant (Josh 24:27).	3. Sealing of the covenant (Deut 26:16-19).
4. Sealing of the covenant (Ex 24).	4. Blessings and covenant (Deut 27:12-13; Josh 8:34).	4. Blessings and Curses (Deut 27ff).

This similarity between the structure of Deuteronomy and the Sinai-Shechem covenant ritual convinced von Rad that Deuteronomy was a "rather baroque agglomeration of cultic materials, which nevertheless reflects throughout one and the same cultic occasion."

(Deuteronomy) is the outcome of a very long process of literary crystalisation, which returns in the end to a monumental unity of structure. . . . In its massive final form the book bursts all cultic bounds, and yet retains the pattern of hortatory allocution, reading of the Law, sealing of the covenant, blessing, and curse. (33)

If the settlement tradition and the Sinai complex were originally completely distinct and independent of each other, how did the hexateuchal structure in which they are combined come into being? For von Rad, the answer lies in the work of the Yahwist, who creatively "gathered up the materials which were becoming detached from the cultus, and compacted them firmly together within a literary framework" (50). Thus, von Rad consciously differed from Gunkel, who had seen the Yahwist as primarily a collector and a servant of the traditions and not a creative author-theologian.

Von Rad argued that the Yahwist's great theological work was constructed upon the basic support of the settlement tradition. Into the general structure of this credal confession, the Yahwist incorporated many subsidiary traditions. His great narrative construction, however, was produced by three major innovative steps: (1) The Yahwist incorporated the Sinai complex and thus fused this with the settlement tradition.

The former bears witness to Yahweh's generosity, but over against this, at the very heart of the Sinai tradition, is the demand of Yahweh's righteousness. Thus by its absorption of the Sinai tradition the simple soteriological conception of the Settlement tradition gained new support of a powerful and salutary kind. Everything which the Yahwist tells us, as he unfolds the plan of his tradition is now coloured by the divine self-revelation of Mt. Sinai. . . . The blending of the two traditions gives definition to the two fundamental propositions of the whole message of the Bible: Law and Gospel. (54)

(2) The patriarchal tradition (see Deut 26:5) was greatly expanded and developed by the Yahwist. Building upon the old concepts of the god of the fathers and the promise of the land, the patriarchal deposit was elaborated by the inclusions of various sagas and saga cycles. The traditional material was ordered and supplemented to stress Yahweh's guidance of his chosen, the patriarchs as recipients of promises which found their fulfillment in the settlement, and the patriarchal covenants as the promise to which the Sinai covenant was the fulfillment. (3) The primeval history (the J material in Gen 2–11) was added as a prologue and introduction to weld together the early history of the world and the history of redemption. The various traditions in the primeval history, according to von Rad, were coordinated and structured by the Yahwist to show the growth of sin and decay in the world and God's forbearing grace and redeeming activity which forgive and sustain at the same time that God punishes. The call of Abraham in Gen 12:1-3, which was a free formulation by the Yahwist, provides the answer to the problem posed in Gen 2–11, the issue of God's relationship to the nations of the world. The Yahwist submits that the answer to the problem is to be seen in "the meaning and purpose of the redemptive relationship which Yahweh has vouchsafed to Israel," represented in Abraham. Thus the Yahwist provides the "aetiology of all Israelite aetiology."

He proclaims, in a manner which is neither rationally justifiable nor yet capable of detailed explanation, that the ultimate purpose of the redemption which God will bring about in Israel is that of bridging the gulf between God and the entire human race. (66)

Finally, von Rad confronted what he called the "theological problem of the Yawhist." The issues, as he saw them, are: (1) How do the traditions which had their setting in the cult function in their new setting in the Yahwistic history? (2) In what historical and cultural context does the Yahwist belong? (3) How does the Yahwist understand the relationship between Israel and Yahweh's activity in terms of the promise-fulfillment motif?

(1) Von Rad argued that the ancient cultic material which was utilized by the J writer has lost all its original cultic interest. The traditions have undergone a secularization; the materials have been completely detached from the cult and "have been 'historicised': their inner content has actually been removed bodily from its narrow sacral context into the freer atmosphere of common history" (68). As long as the traditions were bound to the cult, the sphere of God's activity was seen in the sacral, cultic institutions. In the Yahwist's work, the stress is on God's direction and ordering of history—common history—toward the goal of redemption.

In a word, *the main emphasis in God's dealings with his people is now to be sought outside the sacral institutions.* God's activity is now perhaps less perceptible to the outward sight, but it is actually perceived more fully and more constantly because his guidance is seen to extend equally to every historical occurrence, sacred or profane, up to the time of the Settlement. (71)

(2) The "secularization" and the theological thrust of the Yahwistic history were related by von Rad to the time of Solomon, when an age of Israelite Enlightenment provided the people with a new and revolutionary understanding of themselves and their status in the world (see below, pp. 190-92).

(3) For the Yahwist, the issue of the settlement was conceived in terms of the entire twelve tribes of Israel (the old Gilgal creed was limited in usage to a much smaller

group) and was understood as reaching its fulfillment in the conquests and consolidation of "greater Israel" by David. God's care for Israel and the fulfillment of the promise had reached their apogee in the time and activity of David. Under David, the age-old aspirations and tribal claims had achieved a territorial realization that exceeded even the old expectations.

What more obvious course was there than to claim for David's successes the authority of those ancient ordinances? The events of David's reign could forthwith acquire a profound religious significance. Age-old decrees of Yahweh were recalled and David was seen to be the agent of God's will. (72)

A second major history of tradition investigation of the Pentateuch is found in the work of Martin Noth, originally published in 1948. According to him, a traditio-historical analysis demonstrates that the earliest pre-literary material in the Pentateuch was given expression in "certain statements of faith, grounded in the cult and formulated in a confessional manner, which constituted the roots from which in time, like a mighty tree, the Pentateuch grew" (following von Rad).

These confessional statements had as their contents certain *basic themes* derived from Israel's own history which God had directed in a special way. These themes were not added to one another all at once in order to form the basis for the further expansion of the Pentateuchal tradition, but rather were joined step by step in a definite sequence which can still be determined in general. We can therefore put these themes in a definite order according to their traditio-historical priority . . ., thereby gaining at the same time a general view of the development of the Pentateuchal tradition. (46)

These basic major themes, listed by Noth in the order of their priority, are:
  (1) *Guidance out of Egypt* (47–51). This theme was the primary confession of Israel as illustrated in its repeated and often independent appearance in

statements of faith scattered throughout theTestament and in its fixed formulaic and hymnic style. As such, it constitutes "the kernel of the whole subsequent Pentateuchal tradition." From its beginning, this confessional statement that "Yahweh brought/led Israel out of Egypt," was a "common confession of all Israel." The historical occurrence which may lie behind this confession can no longer be analyzed but it could not have been an experience undergone by the united Israelite tribes since these were essentially constituted in the course of the occupation of Palestine. "Thus one will have to assume that later on the clans who experienced the events in Egypt and at the Sea from time to time became part of the associations of Israelite tribes which banded together and occupied the land. Moreover, they probably became involved in a number of tribes and tribal groups rather than in just one tribe. As a result what they experienced was disseminated in wider circles of Israel and enthralling those who had not originally participated with its unique character and power, came to be a basic tenet of faith belonging to all Israelite tribes."

(2) *Guidance into the Arable Land* (51–54). The settlement or occupation was an addition to and an expansion of the Exodus theme. Originally, no doubt, each tribe possessed separate memories and conceptions of how it occupied its territory in Palestine. The form of the occupation narrative in its all-Israelite expression was due to the influence of the tribal groups settled in the central Palestinian hill country where occurred the early gatherings of the tribal groups at a central sanctuary.

(3) *Promise to the Patriarchs* (54–58). This theme had a very complicated and unique development. Various early traditions about the promise of land made by the God of the fathers, originally given outside

the promised land, were part of local clan cults. The figure of Jacob, associated with central Palestinian tribes, was the first introduced into the pentateuchal tradition. The southern tribes contributed the figures and traditions of Abraham and Isaac, and the Joseph story was an accretion from the central Palestinian stage in pentateuchal formation.

(4) *Guidance in the Wilderness* (58–59). This theme, although represented by numerous individual narratives, was neither very important nor independent and seems never to have had any cultic rootage. According to Noth, this theme had its origin among the southern tribes who lived in geographical proximity to the wilderness.

(5) *Revelation at Sinai* (59–62). This theme was the last in the series to be added to the other themes. This is evident in the theme's absence from the earliest confessional statements (so also von Rad and others) and the fact that the theme intrudes into the wilderness theme in the Pentateuch (at Ex 18, the Hebrews are at Kadesh, then follows the Sinai material, after which the Kadesh location is resumed; so already Wellhausen, 342-45). The Sinai material was based on the legend used in the covenant-making or renewal ritual. Although the theme seems to have been a contribution of the southern tribes, according to Noth, it seems also to have originally and inherently been oriented to an all-Israelite perspective.

In addition to Noth's attempt to isolate the origin and basic themes in the Pentateuch, he sought to demonstrate how these themes were combined and expanded to produce the present Pentateuch. The following of his theses are noteworthy. (1) The combination of these diverse themes from different backgrounds took place during the time between the settlement and the beginning of the formation of the state, that is, during the period of the Judges when Israel existed as a twelve-tribe league (see below, p. 229). (2) Lying behind both J and E was this common tradition from the premonarchic period in which the themes had been combined and expanded. Noth designated this common traditional basis "G" (for *Grundlage*) and concluded that where J and E contain common material, this goes back to G. Thus the really creative epoch in the formation of the pentateuchal tradition was the time of prestate tribal life (38–45). (3) To penetrate behind the independent themes and traditions in order to speak about the historical events they reflect or to discuss the history of "Israel" before the occupation of the land is impossible and, at any rate, "a common history experienced by the twelve tribes before the occupation of the land . . . never existed" (252-59). (4) Even a figure like Moses, who now plays a major role in the exodus-to-settlement traditions, was introduced into the themes secondarily. The surest historical tradition about Moses is his grave and burial in Trans-Jordan. Moses seems to have been a figure revered in the circle of the central Palestinian tribes and to have been associated first of all with the "guidance into the arable land" theme (156-75). (5) The final form of the Pentateuch has the P narrative as its literary basis and this P narrative was enriched by material drawn from a form of J which had already been expanded through the incorporation of E elements (8-19, 248-51). (6) Although the authors of the three major pentateuchal strands (J, E, and P) already found at hand not only the narrative materials but also their arrangement and combination, they should still be considered authors and each of the pentateuchal sources should be seen as the work of a single writer (228-29).

D. The Theology of Pentateuchal Traditions and Sources

The work of von Rad raised the issue of the theology of the pentateuchal sources to special prominence. According to him, and to Noth, who spoke of authors of the sources, a dominant concern of the traditions was theological. This was true even at the stage when they were still tied to the cult but became even more the case when the individual traditions were drawn into the arena of the theological and confessional credos. Such a view represents a significant departure from Gunkel, who saw exegesis as primarily an artistic endeavor and spoke of the teaching and entertainment quality of the traditions, and from Wellhausen, who saw exegesis in more of a "scientific" and historical perspective. (It should be recalled that von Rad's stress on the theological concerns of Old Testament materials and this theology's relevance was first pursued in the 1930s in Nazi Germany, where both Judaism and Old Testament faith were strongly under attack.)

Interest in pursuing von Rad's concern for the theology of the pentateuchal sources has been characteristic of many recent scholars. Representative of this approach are Hans Walter Wolff, a German, and Walter Brueggemann, an American, who both speak of the message or proclamation (kerygma) of the sources. Discussing the Yahwist, Wolff claims: "To speak of a 'kerygma' for the entire work is justified, in that: the work brings (1) a message from God, which (2) has the character of a claim, that (3) is aimed at a specific hour in history" (Bruggemann-Wolff, 137, note 62). Understanding the theological thrust of the Yahwist against the background of the Davidic-Solomonic state, Brueggemann has summarized the theology of this source as follows:

The promise-fulfillment dynamic serves J's purposes of fidelity to tradition, and at the same time provides relevance to the cultural, theological crisis of the tenth century. The Yahwist was able to look back to show that promise is the driving power of the narratives, that the narratives state not only what is but what is to be. J subtly affirmed that the long-standing promises were now being actualized in the Israel of David and Solomon.

(a) The ancient promise of a son and heir (Gen. 18:10) is now gloriously fulfilled in the royal son, Solomon (cf. II Sam. 12:24). (b) The ancient promise of the land (Gen. 12:1; 13:14-15) is now fulfilled in the empire, which controlled the land bridge of the Fertile Crescent (I Kings 4:24). (c) The great name (reputation) long ago promised to these nobodies (Gen. 12:2) is now fulfilled in Solomon (I Kings 1:47; 10:1-10), who became the envy of both his followers and his adversaries. (d) The ancient promise of blessing to other nations by means of Israel (Gen. 12:3) is affirmed. Israel now possesses resources, means, and opportunity to bring a blessing to her neighbors (cf. I Kings 4:20-21), but she also has the capacity to bring a curse (Gen. 12:10-20). . . .

J has imposed a distinctive theological reading on the history of Israel, interpreting it in terms of blessing and promise. Through this interpretation, J has provided important responses to the Solomonic situation, when Israel experienced a crisis of theological categories.

a) Solomon was tempted to be like others and to secure his own existence (cf. Gen. 11:1-9; and even 12:10-20). J makes subtle protest against any self-understanding in which Israel denied its role as a bearer of blessing. J rejects the syncretism which is content to settle for the ways of the world (the other cultures), which places no credence in the power of promise to direct life, and which makes no investment in blessing in a world seduced by curse.

b) Monarchy constituted a problem in Israel because it was an alien institution without traditional legitimization. J presents it as a way to implement Israel's peculiar identity. In depicting Abraham as a prototype of Israelite kings, J presents the royal establishment as a bearer of blessing in a world organized against blessing. Even in Israel, however, kings do not act this way and are bearers of curse, but J holds out another possibility.

c) The royal-urban myths in Solomon's time invited a royal regime to claim theological absolutism for itself (cf. Gen. 3; 4; 6-9; 11:1-9). J resisted such a temptation; when J speaks of Israel, as he finally does in Gen 12ff., he does not utilize ancient Near Eastern myth but instead has recourse to Israel's old traditions. As blessing answers curse, so Israel's communal memory responds to the world's myth. Clearly J defines Israel by old tribal memories which he shows to be relevant even in the new situation.

d) J affirms that the well-being of Israel and the performance of her historic mission are understood, not in terms of royal policy, enlightened though it may be, but in terms of the abiding promises of Yahweh which kings can neither invent nor void. Thus J issues a mighty protest against undue managing of history by the royal regime. (*IDBS*, 973-74)

The theology of the Elohistic source has not enjoyed the extensive treatment given that of J. The rather fragmentary nature of this source and the difficulty of hypothesizing a firm setting have made scholars more reticent to engage in theological speculation. A northern origin has generally been assumed (Jenks; but see Noth, 229-30) and a date in the ninth century is frequently espoused (see Fretheim, 260-61 and Wolff-Brueggemann, 67-82). During the ninth century, ancient Israel was threatened with syncretistic tendencies and the books of Kings present the times in terms of a life and death struggle between Yahwism and Baalism (see I Kings 17–II Kings 8). Wolff sees the characteristic component in E to be a call to "fear God." He postulates three primary theses about the work and its theology.

The most prominent theme of the Elohist is the fear of God. By means of traditional materials from salvation history the Elohist wanted to lead the Israel of his day through the events in which they were tempted and bring them to new obedience and to new disobedience.

The Elohist linked the separate traditional accounts together by dialogues which reveal a highly developed skill in composition. References to scenes that are not preserved imply later editing by someone else. The links show that over a long period of time God led his people through a series of tests of their obedience.

The interpretation which the Elohist gave the traditional materials of Israel can be best explained as an outcry against the syncretism following the time of Elijah. During that period Israel faced some of its greatest cultic, political, and social temptations. (Brueggemann-Wolff, 75, 80, 81)

The theology of the priestly work (on D, see pp. 206-7) has been interpreted against the background of exilic or post-exilic times after the demise of the Judean state and political autonomy. Although Kaufmann has advocated an early, pre-D date for P, he has been followed by very few (for the issues, see Levine). The central thrust of the priestly work lies in its depiction of "Israel" as a sacred, cultic community organized around the Jerusalem temple, which is represented in P by the wilderness tabernacle. The life of the community and the presence of God are to be found in existence oriented toward purity of life and ritual practice which give experience to the affirmation, "I, Yahweh, will be your God and you shall be my people." If the priestly work was produced in the exile, then it was "a program written in preparation for and in hope of the restoration of Israel" (Cross, 325) stressing "that the promise of the land of blessing still endures and will be realized soon" (Bruggemann-Wolff, 113). This would mean that the work was a programmatic project for a restored community similar to that of Ez 40–48. On the other hand, if P emanated from the life of the restored Jewish community following the exile, it was a work "no longer concerned with the crisis of the exile and its temptation to abandon the faith" but one preoccupied "with the creation of a new sense of order and stability in the universe, in the world of nations and history, and in the cultic community of the new 'Israel' " (Van Seters, 1975, 292). Nonetheless, it would still have been a programmatic production whose full implementation was still to be realized (so Vink).

E. Contemporary Issues in Pentateuchal Studies

During the past few years, many of the major conclusions of both documentary criticism and the history of traditions approach, as well as their methodological assumptions, have been seriously challenged.

Pentateuchal studies may now be described as in a state of anxious disarray or as on the move, but in a new and fruitful direction, depending upon one's perspective. In the present stage of discussion, it is possible only to speak of some past assumptions which have been challenged as no longer feasible and to point out some of the new emphases in research. The exact contours of future research are still uncertain.

(1) Von Rad's assumption that ancient confessional credos provided the structual outline of the Pentateuch has been seriously questioned (see Durham). Practically all of the texts which he used to reconstruct such credos are very late in their present form and there is no real way to prove that such credos provided an architectural framework whose completed structure was the final form of the Pentateuch. Credo-like material is apt to assume rather than predate the final pentateuchal form.

(2) Noth's argument that, prior to the formation of the state, "Israel" existed as a twelve-tribe league within which independent themes were united to form G (or what Cross calls the epic tradition of the tribal league) can no longer be upheld (see A. D. H. Mayes in *IJH*, 297-308). The biblical texts simply do not support such a reconstruction of early Israelite history. The same may be said of Cross's conclusion that "Israel's religion emerged from a mythopoeic past under the impact of certain historical experiences which stimulated the creation of an epic cycle and its associated rites of the early time" (Cross, viii) since the "historical experiences" of patriarchs, exodus, wilderness wanderings, and conquest are all now called into question.

(3) Covenant theology and covenant-renewal festival (see below, pp. 268, 303) as components in early Israelite life and faith, even in the early monarchical period, have also been questioned (see McCarthy). It has been argued that the concept of a national covenant between Israel and Yahweh, as assumed in the exodus-Sinai materials, came into prominence only late in the monarchical period,

during the Deuteronomic era, and was modeled on the relationship between Israelite kings and their Assyrian overlords (see Frankena).

(4) The association of a Yahwistic history with a tenth-century Israelite enlightenment in the reigns of David and Solomon has been strongly disputed in recent literature (see, for example, Winnett, Wagner, 1972). The exposition of the Yahwistic theology, as reflected in the works of von Rad, Brueggemann, and Wolff, would be seriously rebutted by any redating of the Yahwist. Such scholars as Van Seters have recently argued that the Yahwistic theology reflected in the patriarchal stories should be dated to the exile, at a time when the promise and possession of the land were significant issues and therefore to be dated after D.

The confession of Yahweh as the God of the patriarchs and the association of the promises to the fathers with the patriarchs is a specific development of Israel's sacred traditions during the exilic period and directly related to the needs of that period. The identity crisis which the exile created both for Israel and for Yahweh, her God, demanded a new traditional basis which was formulated in terms of the patriarchs. The "god of the fathers" religion and the promises of land and numerous progeny which are integrally related to it, are not the remnant of an early pre-settlement religion of landless nomads, but the basic components of an exilic religion of homeless exiles. Furthermore, the JE corpus in the Pentateuch which reflects this development of Israel's sacred tradition in the direction of giving a national identity to the patriarchs must be post-deuteronomic and exilic. (Van Seters, 1972, 459)

(5) Many scholars no longer want to speak of parallel documents or sources but of traditions which were augmented, supplemented, and annotated in the course of time. Sandmel, for example, speaks of traditions which

were embellished or modified in a manner similar to later Jewish haggada—"the fanciful retelling of tales"—perhaps in both oral and written form. Rendtorff and Schmid, in a manner somewhat like that of Engnell, argue that source criticism and tradition criticism are incompatible as they have been traditionally understood. Rendtorff concludes that the pentateuchal scheme in which creation, patriarchs, exodus-Sinai, wilderness, and conquest traditions were joined together cannot be placed in pre-Deuteronomic times. What he proposes is that the diverse traditions developed independently into larger units until major blocks of material existed. These were then literarily joined very late in the life of the community. Van Seters speaks of the supplementation of a set of traditions (in the Abraham stories) to produce sources but under conditions in which "each succeeding source is directly dependent upon, and supplements, the earlier tradition" (1975, 311).

(6) Finally, there is renewed interest in the understanding and exposition of the text in its received, final form. Broadly, this approach may be designated a "new literary criticism" and has many points of contact with the older "Bible as literature" approach (see Robertson). Many expressions of this new interest have been influenced by modern structualism (see Polzin, 1-53). New literary criticism "is part of a turning away from a preoccupation with history and a turning toward a concern with language" and thus it stresses "such fields as linguistics and semiology (the study of the use and meaning of signs) for basic presuppositions and methodological tools" (Robertson, 547).

CHAPTER 6

THE
HISTORICAL BOOKS

P. R. Ackroyd, "History and Theology in the Writings of the Chronicler," *CTM* XXXVIII(1967)501-15; *idem*, "The Deuteronomic History," in his *Exile and Restoration* (London/Philadelphia: SCM Press/Westminster Press, 1968)62-83; *idem*, "The Theology of the Chronicler," *LTQ* VIII(1973)101-16; *idem*, "The Chronicler as Exegete," *JSOT* II(1977)2-32; Y. Aharoni, *The Land of the Bible: A Historical Geography* (London/Philadelphia: Burns & Oates/Westminster Press, 1966); A. G. Auld, "Judges I and History: A Reconsideration," VT XXV(1975) 261-85; R. L. Braun, "The Message of Chronicles: Rally Round the Temple," *CTM* XLII(1971)502-14; *idem*, "Solomonic Apologetic in Chronicles," *JBL* XCII(1973) 503-16; W. Brueggemann, "The Kerygma of the Deuteronomistic Historian," Int XXII(1968)387-402; R. A. Carlson, *David, the Chosen King: A Traditio-Historical Approach to the Second Book of Samuel* (Stockholm: Almqvist & Wiksell, 1964); F. M. Cross, "The Themes of the Books of Kings and the Structure of the Deuteronomistic History," in his *Canaanite Myth and Hebrew Epic* (Cambridge: Harvard University Press, 1973)274-89; *idem*, "A Reconstruction of the Judean Restoration," *JBL* XCIV(1975)4-18 = Int XXIX[1975] 187-203); D. N. Freedman, "Deuteronomic History," *IDBS*, 226-28; *idem*, "The Chronicle's Purpose," *CBQ* XXIII(1961)436-42; J. Gray, *I & II Kings: A Commentary* (London/Philadelphia: SCM Press/Westminster Press, 1964, ²1970); S. Japhet, "The Supposed Common Authorship of Chronicles and Ezra-Nehemiah Investigated Anew," VT XVIII(1968) 330-71; *idem*, "Chronicles, Book of," *EJ* V 517-34; R. W. Klein, "Ezra and Nehemiah in Recent Studies," *MD*, 361-76; N. Lohfink, "Deuteronomy," *IDBS*, 229-32; J. L. McKenzie, *The World of the Judges* (Englewood-Cliffs/London: Prentice-Hall/G. Chapman, 1966); A. Malamat, "The Danite Migration and the Pan-Israelite Exodus-Conquest: A Biblical Narrative Pattern," *Biblica* LI(1970)1-16; A. D. H. Mayes, *Israel in the Period of the Judges* (London: SCM Press, 1974); T. N.

D. Mettinger, *King and Messiah: The Civil and Sacral Legitimation of the Israelite Kings* (Lund: CWK Gleerup, 1976); J. D. Newsome, Jr., "Toward a New Understanding of the Chronicler and His Purposes," *JBL* XCIV(1975)201-17; E. W. Nicholson, "Deuteronomy and the Deuteronomist," in his *Deuteronomy and Tradition* (Oxford/Philadelphia: Basil Blackwell/Fortress Press, 1968)107-18; R. North, "Theology of the Chronicler," *JBL* LXXXII(1963)369-81; J. F. Priest, "Etiology," *IDBS*, 293-95; G. von Rad, "The Deuteronomistic Theology of History in the Books of Kings," in his *Studies in Deuteronomy* (London: SCM Press, 1953)74-91; *idem*, "The Beginnings of Historical Writing in Ancient Israel," in his *The Problem of the Hexateuch* (Edinburgh/New York: Oliver and Boyd/McGraw-Hill, 1966)166-204; M. G. Rogers, "Judges, Book of," *IDBS*, 509-14; M. Smith, *Palestinian Parties and Politics that Shaped the Old Testament* (New York: Columbia University Press, 1971); S. Talmon, "Ezra and Nehemiah," *IDBS*, 317-28; M. Weinfeld, *Deuteronomy and the Deuteronomic School* (London: Oxford University Press, 1972); M. Weippert, "Canaan, Conquest and Settlement of," *IDBS*, 125-30; R. N. Whybray, *The Succession Narrative: A Study of II Sam. 9-20 and I Kings 1 and 2* (London: SCM Press, 1968); H. G. M. Williamson, *Israel in the Books of Chronicles* (Cambridge: Cambridge University Press, 1977); H. W. Wolff, "The Kerygma of the Deuteronomistic Historical Work," in W. Brueggemann and H. W. Wolff, *The Vitality of Old Testament Traditions* (Atlanta: John Knox Press, 1975)83-100.

The Pentateuch, in its final form, was edited as a historical document. That is, the books of the Torah are structured so as to tell the story, first, of mankind and, second, of the "chosen" line down to the time just prior to the entry into Canaan. This history is bound together through chronological and genealogical statements.

In addition to the Pentateuch, there are other historical

works in the Old Testament. Joshua–II Kings, the Former Prophets, picks up the story with the people in Trans-Jordan and continues the account down to the thirty-seventh year of the exile of king Jehoiachin (about 561 BCE). In addition to the Former Prophets, two other historical works are found in the Old Testament. I–II Chronicles begins with Adam and then presents the story of the chosen people down to the first year of the Persian king Cyrus (538 BCE). Ezra–Nehemiah begins its history with Cyrus and narrates the fate of the Jewish community through the reforming activity of Ezra and Nehemiah.

A. Pentateuchal Sources in the Former Prophets?

A number of considerations suggest that the Former Prophets should be seen as the continuation of the Pentateuch and therefore should be understood as simply the extension of the pentateuchal story. As such, the Pentateuch and Former Prophets would form a continuous historical work. If this be true, then one would expect the sources or documents of the Pentateuch, if these ever existed, to be continued in the Former Prophets.

A number of arguments have been used to support the contention that the Former Prophets should be viewed as merely a continuation of the pentateuchal materials and not as an independent work and that the earlier sources of the Pentateuch can still be seen in these books. First of all, the book of Joshua resumes the story at the point where Deuteronomy ends. Deut 34 tells of the death of Moses and his burial in an unknown grave in Moab. The book of Joshua begins with the account of Joshua's assumption of leadership after the death of Moses. Joshua's leadership of the people is already anticipated in Num 27:12-23 and Deut 34:9 and this would suggest a very close, perhaps literary, relationship of the Pentateuch with Joshua.

Secondly, much of the Pentateuch assumes what in the story only becomes reality in Joshua—the possession of the land. However one views the nature and origins of the traditions in the Pentateuch, it must be admitted that they anticipate, even presuppose, the Israelite occupation of Canaan. Without the continuation of the narrative in Joshua, the Israelites are left outside Canaan and the promise of the land is left without any realized fulfillment.

Thirdly, parallel and often contradictory traditions in the Former Prophets have been viewed as evidence of parallel sources or documents. These have frequently been understood as the continuation of sources isolated in the Pentateuch. One of the clearest cases of differing presentations is found in the conquest traditions. In the first twelve chapters of Joshua, the conquest is pictured as a swift and destructive undertaking from across the Jordan River. All the tribes participate under the leadership of Joshua. A grand strategy of attacks—in the center, south, and north of Canaan—produces a complete possession of the land. Except for groups that aided the invaders (Josh 6:22-25) or else made treaties of peace with the newcomers (Josh 9), all the entire population was annihilated. The following passage summarizes this perspective:

So Joshua took all the land, the hill country and all the Negeb and all the land of Goshen and the lowland and the Arabah and the hill country. . . . There was not a city that made peace with the people of Israel, except the Hivites, the inhabitants of Gibeon; they took all in battle. For it was Yahweh's doing to harden their hearts that they should come against Israel in battle, in order that they should be utterly destroyed, and should receive no mercy but be exterminated, as Yahweh commanded Moses. (Joshua 11:16-20)

This view which assumes that "Joshua left none remaining, but utterly destroyed all that breathed" (Josh 10:40) contrasts sharply with the picture of the occupation of the land presented in the opening section of the book of Judges. In this account, which is placed after the death of Joshua, the settlement takes place with no single leader, tribes operate individually or in limited cooperation, groups participate that were only loosely connected with Israel, much of the invasion takes place from the south, only the hill country is taken, the Canaanites are not slaughtered, and much land and many cities are not conquered (see Judg 1:1-36). Only "when Israel grew strong" did the invaders "put the Canaanites to forced labor, but did not utterly drive them out" (Judg 1:28).

A further example used to argue for parallel sources in the Former Prophets is the literature on the origin of the monarchy. In I Sam 8-12, there appears to be at least two major accounts of the rise of Saul to kingship (see Wellhausen, *Prolegomena*, 247-56). In one account, found in I Sam 8; 10:17-27; 12, there is a decidedly antimonarchical attitude. The adoption of a monarchical form of government is depicted as the result of human clammering for "a king like all the nations." Both Yahweh and the prophet Samuel are strongly opposed to the establishment of a monarchy and see it as a challenge to Yahweh's role as king. Samuel makes two speeches to the people opposing their cries for an earthly monarch. Finally, Samuel and Yahweh concede to the pleas of the people but only after Samuel homiletically harangues the Israelite hosts who confess: "we have added to all our sins this evil, to ask for ourselves a king" (I Sam 12:19).

A second version of the origin of kingship, found in I Sam 9:1–10:16; 11, takes a much more favorable attitude toward the monarchy. In this narrative, kingship is instigated by Yahweh and Samuel, who seek out Saul. Samuel anoints Saul in secret as the future ruler and then, after Saul rescues the city of Jabesh-Gilead from the Ammonites, participates in the coronation of Saul at Gilgal.

The narratives about the conquest of Canaan and the rise of kingship are only two examples among others which have led scholars to assume parallel accounts for the whole or major parts of the Former Prophets. Many scholars have attempted to isolate these so-called parallel accounts but, in the Former Prophets, there has been far less unanimity of opinion than is the case in pentateuchal studies.

One approach to this issue assumes that the five books of the Pentateuch and the books of Joshua, Judges, I and II Samuel, and I and II Kings once simply formed a single connected work which was only subsequently divided into nine separate books. According to this view, the sources of the Pentateuch, or at least some of them, continue throughout the Former Prophets. One scholar, for example, argued that J concluded in I Kings 12:19 and that E continued through II Kings 25:30. Another has seen J extending to the material on Hezekiah (II Kings 20) and E including the traditions through the time of Josiah (II Kings 23). Both of these analyses would place J and E very late in history.

There has been more general acceptance of the view that the pentateuchal sources once contained accounts of the conquest and therefore extended into Joshua and the beginning of Judges. This would mean that the sources carried the story of Israel's beginnings into the period of the settlement and thus narrated the fulfillment of the promise that the descendants of the patriarchs would possess the land of Canaan. Thus one should speak of a Hexateuch and hexateuchal sources rather than of a Pentateuch and pentateuchal sources.

Judg 1 plus other passages on the settlement (Num 21:1-3; 32:39,41-42; Josh 11:13; 13:13; 17:14-18) have frequently been considered to represent J or the Yahwistic historian's version of the settlement. This version described an invasion that was not unified and a conquest that was not completely successful. The material in Josh 2–11, which narrates the battles for the promised land, has been treated as E's version of the conquest. Perhaps Josh 24 could be seen as the conclusion of the E hexateuchal source. The detailed tribal allotments in Josh 13–21 have been assigned to the P source and viewed as that document's description of the realization of the promise of the land.

The attempt to trace the pentateuchal sources into the books of the Former Prophets has not been abandoned entirely. However, more and more arguments have been advanced which make such a tracing more difficult. For example, Judg 1 can hardly be considered a real unified portrayal of the conquest. Contradictions exist in the text (compare Judg 1:8 with 1:21); much of the material is of a purely legendary nature (Judg 1:5-7); and it is as much a "negative conquest" as a conquest tradition (see Judg 1:27-33). Such factors make it difficult to see the tradition as a source's description of the fulfillment of the promise of the land (for further problems in the chapter, see Auld). Even more problems confront any attempt to isolate the continuation of pentateuchal sources beyond Judg 1.

B. The Deuteronomistic History

The influence of the theological perspectives found in Deuteronomy upon Judges–II Kings has long been recognized. Wellhausen, for example, writing about the tradition in these books, declared that "the whole area of tradition has finally been uniformly covered with an alluvial deposit by which the configuration of the surface has been determined" (*Prolegomena*, 228). This "alluvial deposit" was understood as reflective of the thorough revision of the earlier traditions by the deuteronomistic of the exilic period. (The term *deuteronomistic* is used to suggest the general similarity of this exilic stream of thought with the earlier Deuteronomic thought embodied in D.)

In order to appreciate this deuteronomistic redaction, the main features of Deuteronomy (or D) must be noted. Central to Deuteronomic thought is the concept of a covenant between Yahweh and Israel. The impact of covenant thought was widespread and pervasive throughout the Near East during the days of the Assyrian empire and there is good reason to assume "that the authors of Deuteronomy were influenced in their covenant theology by Assyrian patterns of thought and institutions" (Lohfink, 231; see Weinfeld, 59-157). D, to be identified with an early form of the book of Deuteronomy, applied this covenant form to the relationship between Israel and her God and stressed that there is one God (Yahweh) who has chosen one people (Israel) with whom He has joined in covenant and given the land of promise (Canaan) requiring that Israel obey the one law (the Deuteronomic code) which includes worship in one cult and at one central sanctuary (understood to be Jerusalem). Promise of a good life in the land is presented as reward to the elect who obey the one law, and curses and punishments are announced for those who disobey the covenant stipulations. Obvious deuteronomistic passages in the Former Prophets take these Deuteronomic perspectives for granted.

In a volume published in 1943, Martin Noth argued that all the Former Prophets, Joshua through II Kings, form a unified historical work which he called the "Deuteronomistic History." According to him, a highly creative author in the exile took an early form of the book of Deuteronomy, prefixed a deuteronomistic introduction (now found in Deut 1:1-4:43) and then utilizing and editing earlier traditions produced Deuteronomy–II Kings as a unified compositional work. This work, according to Noth, sought to demonstrate that Israelite and Judean history, which climaxed in the fall of Samaria and Jerusalem and the resultant exiles, was the story of human idolatry and apostasy followed by divine retribution. The work demonstrated that the doom of the two nations was the inevitable fulfillment of God's promised curses for failure to live according to the stipulations of the Deuteronomic legislation. The work of Noth has formed the point of departure for most subsequent study of the Former Prophets as it will be for the following discussion.

According to Noth, the deuteronomistic historian divided the history of Israel into five major periods: (1) the history of the Mosaic period, (2) the period of the conquest, (3) the age of the Judges, (4) Saul, David, and Solomon, and (5) the era of Israelite and Judean kings.

Throughout the Deuteronomistic History, special emphases as well as the reflection of Deuteronomic theology can be seen. These are apparent in the selection and use of traditional material, but above all in speeches, prayers, and reflective comments found at significant points in the work. In the narrative account of the five major historical epochs, deuteronomistic perspectives are strategically incorporated to provide a theological prism through which the course of Israelite history and life are to be viewed. This deuteronomistic material constitutes a theological framework for the narratives. The following important passages demonstrate and illustrate the deuteronomistic editorial activity which now structures the work.

(1) *The Speech of Moses in the Land of Moab (Deut 1–4).* This speech is envisioned as having been presented to the assembled Israelites just prior to the crossing of the Jordan River. Deut 1–3 provides a historical resume of "recent" events which retells the story of Israel's march from Mt. Horeb (Sinai?) to the hills of Moab, but in a form different from the account found in the book of Numbers. The account in Deut 1–3 narrates the people's continuous disobedience and the demise of the generation that left Egypt (see Josh 5:4; but compare Deut 8:1-10). In a very sermonic fashion, Deut 4:1-40 proclaims Yahweh's love expressed to Israel in his divine election of one nation. Yahweh's love was manifested in his deliverance of the people from Egypt and in his gift of the land to them (Deut 4:32-39). The sermon appeals to the people to obey the statutes and ordinances of the law: "You shall not add to

the word which I command you, nor take from it; that you keep the commandments of Yahweh your God which I command you" (Deut 4:2). The purpose of Yahweh's redemption and the gift of the law is to create a people disciplined to his service and who knows that "Yahweh is God; there is no other besides him." The sermon concludes with an appeal and a promise. "Therefore you shall keep his statutes and his commandments, which I command you this day, that it may go well with you, and with your children after you, and that you may prolong your days in the land which Yahweh your God gives you for ever" (Deut 4:40).

(2) *Joshua's Speech at the time of the Settlement (Josh 23).* The book of Joshua presents the story of the Israelite conquest of Canaan—the fulfillment of Yahweh's promise to give his people a land.

Thus Yahweh gave to Israel all the land which he swore to give to their fathers; and having taken possession of it, they settled there. And Yahweh gave them rest on every side just as he had sworn to their fathers; not one of all their enemies had withstood them, for Yahweh had given all their enemies into their hands. Not one of all the good promises which Yahweh had made to the house of Israel had failed; all came to pass. (Josh 21:43-45)

Joshua's farewell speech emphasizes God's fidelity to his promises (Josh 23:14), challenges the people to observe "all that is written in the book of the law of Moses (Deuteronomy), turning aside from it neither to the right hand nor to the left" (Josh 23:6), and appeals to the people to love God, that is, to show their gratitude for salvation by observing the commandments (Josh 23:11). The speech warns Israel about mixing and intermarrying with the remnants of the nations (Josh 23:7,12) and worshiping other gods (Josh 23:7,16). Just as God has been faithful to give the land to the people as a possession, so God will bring down upon them the evil things, the curses (see Deut 28:15-68), and remove them from the land if they are disobedient.

But just as all the good things which Yahweh your God promised concerning you have been fulfilled for you, so Yahweh will bring upon you all the evil things, until he has destroyed you from off this good land which Yahweh your God has given you, if you transgress the covenant of Yahweh your God, which he commanded you, and go and serve other gods and bow down to them. Then the anger of Yahweh will be kindled against you, and you shall perish quickly from off the good land which he has given you. (Josh 23:15-16)

(3) *Theological Reflection on the Period of the Judges* *(Judg 2:11-23)*. Prior to the narratives providing a history of the time from the settlement to the beginning of the monarchy (Judg 3–I Sam 12), the editor provides a theological preview of the course which this history will follow. According to the writer, Israel will constantly pass through cycles of obedience and good times, disobedience and oppression. The following is the pattern within which the materials are edited and through which the history is viewed:

(a) As long as the divinely ordained ruler (judge) is alive, the people are faithful in their worship of Yahweh and enjoy peace and prosperity.

(b) With the death of the ruler, "the people do what was evil in the eyes of Yahweh," forsaking him and the covenant and serving the gods of the surrounding peoples or those of the "remnant of the nations" which remained in the land.

(c) The anger of Yahweh is kindled against the people and he gives them over to their enemies who oppress them.

(d) When the people cry out in repentance to Yahweh, he raises up a leader to save them from those who afflicted and oppressed them.

(e) As long as the deliverer was alive, the people were saved from their enemies, but upon the death of the judge the cycle was repeated.

(4) *Samuel's Speech at the Establishment of the*

210

Monarchy (I Sam 12). For the deuteronomistic historian, the end of the period of the judges and the beginning of the monarchy was a particularly significant stage in Israel's history. Accordingly, the primary human actor in that transition, the prophet Samuel, addresses the people in good deuteronomistic theology. Samuel's speech rehearses the great redemptive past in which God acted to redeem his people, granting them the gift of the land (I Sam 12:6-11). The speech stresses the people's demand for a king, which Yahweh is willing to grant but only as a concession (I Sam 12:12-17,19). The deuteronomistic historian has Samuel warn the people of the need for renewed diligence in light of the new political condition in Israel—a condition fraught with the dangers of disobedience and apostasy.

> If both you and the king who reigns over you will follow Yahweh your God, it will be well; but if you will not hearken to the voice of Yahweh, . . . then the hand of Yahweh will be against you and your king. . . . Fear not; you have done all this evil, yet do not turn aside from following Yahweh, but serve Yahweh with all your heart; and do not turn aside after vain things which cannot profit or save, for they are vain. For Yahweh will not cast away his people, for his great name's sake, because it has pleased Yahweh to make you a people for himself. (I Sam 12:14-15, 20-22)

(5) *Nathan's Oracle and the Prayer of David (II Sam 7)*. With the rise of David to power, the usurpation of the throne from the family of Saul, and the establishment of Jerusalem as a political and religious capital, Israelite history entered a new phase. The Deuteronomist addressed this new situation in the present form of the traditions found in II Sam 7. With the reign of David and the development of the concept of his family as the elect and eternal dynasty, a new political and religious dimension was introduced into Israelite life. Along with the concept of the chosen Davidic dynasty went the idea

of Jerusalem as the sacred city and Yahweh's dwelling place. In the oracle of Nathan, David is promised that his house (= dynasty) will be established after him (unlike Saul's). In David's prayer, he thanks Yahweh for the promise of his dynasty's eternity:

O Yahweh God, thou art God, and thy words are true, and thou hast promised this good thing to thy servant; now therefore may it please thee to bless the house of thy servant, that it may continue for ever before thee; for thou, O Yahweh God, hast spoken, and with thy blessing shall the house of thy servant be blessed for ever. (II Sam 7:28-29)

The successor(s) to David, however, have their future circumspectly hedged by the Deuteronomist—their future fortune is tied to their fidelity and obedience:

I [Yahweh] will be his father, and he shall be my son. When he commits iniquity, I will chasten him with the rod of men, with the stripes of the sons of men; but I will not take my steadfast love from him, as I took it from Saul, whom I put away from before you. And your house and your kingdom shall be made sure for ever before me; your throne shall be established for ever. (II Sam 7:14-16; see the more obvious references to the law and obedience in David's farewell words to Solomon in I Kings 2:1-4.)

(6) *King Solomon's Prayer at the Dedication of the Temple (I Kings 8:22-53)*. The construction of the temple under Solomon first comes into view in the deuteronomistic scheme in Nathan's oracle to David which has Yahweh say: "When your days are fulfilled and you lie down with your fathers, I will raise up your offspring after you, who shall come forth from your body, and I will establish his kingdom. He shall build a house for my name . . ." (II Sam 7:12-13). The temple and its fate, along with Davidic kingship, are dominant concerns of the Deuteronomist throughout the books of Kings. The prayer of Solomon reiterates the Davidic theology in its conditional form (I Kings 8:23-26). The older concept of the temple as

the dwelling place of Yahweh (I Kings 8:12-13) is modified to conform to Deuteronomic theology in which the divine name rather than God himself dwells in the temple (I Kings 8:27-30; compare Deut 12:5, 21). The general tone of Solomon's prayer stresses the issue of disobedience and the possibility of divine forbearance in light of disobedience. The blessing of Solomon which stands outside the prayer proper gives expression to the past fidelity of Yahweh but stresses the uncertainty of Israel's potential for obedience.

Blessed be Yahweh who has given rest to his people Israel, according to all that he promised; not one word has failed of all his good promise, which he uttered by Moses his servant. Yahweh our God be with us, as he was with our fathers; may he not leave us or forsake us; that he may incline our hearts to him, to walk in all his ways, and to keep his commandments, his statutes, and his ordinances, which he commanded our fathers. Let those words of mine, wherewith I have made supplication before Yahweh, be near to Yahweh our God day and night, and may he maintain the cause of his servant, and the cause of his people Israel, as each day requires; that all the peoples of the earth may know that Yahweh is God; there is no other. Let your heart therefore be wholly true to Yahweh our God, walking in his statutes and keeping his commandments, as at this day. (I Kings 8:56-61)

(7) *Theological Reflection on the Fall of Samaria (II Kings 17:7-23).* The fall of Samaria to the Assyrians in 722 BCE meant the end of the northern state of Israel and exile for many of her citizens. In his theological peroration on Samaria's fall the Deuteronomist points to several reasons for its calamity: (a) the Israelites were guilty of apostasy before Yahweh (II Kings 17:7-12); (b) they refused to listen to Yahweh's prophets whom he sent to call them to repentance and obedience (II Kings 17:13-14); (c) they despised Yahweh's commandments and the covenant and engaged in illegal worship (II Kings 17:15-17); and (d) they walked in the sins of King Jeroboam who led Israel

away from Jerusalem and from the house of David (II Kings 17:21-23).

> Yahweh was very angry with Israel, and removed them out of his sight; none was left but the tribe of Judah only. . . . Yahweh removed Israel out of his sight, as he had spoken by all his servants the prophets. So Israel was exiled from their own land to Assyria unto this day. (II Kings 17:18, 23)

Throughout the Deuteronomistic History, and especially in the passages noted above, the ultimate disobedience of the people and God's judgment are presupposed. That is, the work assumes the fall of Samaria and Jerusalem and both the Israelite and Judean exiles. Moses is already made to speak about the exile when the chosen will be scattered among the peoples and left few in number among the nations where Yahweh will drive them (Deut 4:27). Joshua refers to the possibility of perishing from off the good land which Yahweh has given them (Josh 23:13, 16). Samuel warns Israel: "If you still do wickedly, you shall be swept away, both you and your king" (I Sam 12:25). Solomon's prayer is permeated with the certainty of exile (I Kings 8:34, 46). Even the ruin of the temple is predicted in Yahweh's word to Solomon shortly after the dedication of the temple (I Kings 9:6-9). The entire Deuteronomistic History is permeated by this warning against disobedience, the people's lack of obedience, and God's judgment. In the books of Kings, the prophetic word and its fulfillment are a significant characteristic of the work (see von Rad, 78-82). "The Deuteronomist saw and wished his readers to see a direct relationship between the word of Yahweh as spoken by the prophets and the events of Israel's history" (Nicholson, 117). Deuteronomy, of course, had considered Moses to be the prophet preeminent (see Deut 18:15-22).

In its present form, the Deuteronomistic History clearly sets out to offer an apologetic theodicy. Israel's and Judah's history had ended in calamity. Why this was the case when Yahweh had chosen them and loved his chosen above all the peoples on earth is the central theological issue of the work. The work was thus written among the national ruins of God's chosen people; when statehood, monarchy, and temple had been destroyed; when those to whom the land had been promised were scattered among the nations; and when the land itself—God's gift—was overrun by foreigners.

Noth understood the Deuteronomistic History as a story of unrelieved doom and destruction—"as a mono-chromatic picture of unmitigated judgment" (Cross, 277). The author intended to demonstrate why such calamity had befallen God's people by showing that Israel and Judah had constantly been confronted with the law at every stage of history but had constantly not lived in accordance with the Deuteronomic demands. The calami-ty was not a tragedy; it was judgment. The deuterono-mistic author placed the question "why?" upon the lips of the nations and then answered his question:

"Why has Yahweh done thus to this land? What means the heat of this great anger?" Then men would say, "It is because they forsook the covenant of Yahweh, the God of their fathers, which he made with them when he brought them out of the land of Egypt, and went and served other gods and worshiped them, gods whom they had not known and whom he had not allotted to them; therefore the anger of Yahweh was kindled against this land, bringing upon it all the curses written in this book; and Yahweh uprooted them from this land in anger and fury and great wrath, and cast them into another land, as at this day." (Deut 29:24-28; see I Kings 9:6-9)

More recent study has sought to modify Noth's picture of the purpose of the Deuteronomist. Stress has been laid, by von Rad and Wolff, on the calls for rededication to the law and the hopeful expectations found in the work. For the historian, the judgment of Yahweh was not the last word. Several passages make clear that the writer held out hope for the scattered people and called for reaffirmation of faith and recommitment to the law; divine forgiveness and mercy stood over against the judgment (see Deut 4:29-31; I Kings 8:46-53). The clearest evidence of this expectation about the future is to be found in Deut 30:1-10. This passage outlines the religious needs for the time "when all these things come upon you, the blessing and the curse, which I have set before you, and you call them to mind among all the nations where Yahweh your God has driven you." For the Deuteronomist, the same Moses that proclaims the blessing and the curse can announce the future beyond the judgment. Several points in this passage are noteworthy. (1) The people are called to return to Yahweh and hear his voice. (2) They are promised that God will reverse their fate and gather the scattered from the farthest reaches and return them to the land their fathers possessed. (3) Back in the land a future more prosperous and numerous would await them. (4) God would even change their "disposition" and inner nature—circumcising their hearts so they could love Yahweh with heart and soul. (5) The curses would be taken from Israel and placed upon the foes and enemies who had persecuted the chosen.

Scholars have long debated whether there was only one edition of the Deuteronomistic History (most assume that the traditions were given some reinterpretation through additions and new emphases, even after the exilic period). Several arguments have been advanced in support of two editions of the work—one pre-exilic and a second exilic or postexilic. (1) The availability of documents which the Deuteronomist may have used in composing the history (see the next section) would seem more likely before than after the fall of Jerusalem. (2) There is no sermonic peroration or theological reflection on the fall of Jerusalem, parallel to that on the fall of Samaria, which one might expect in light of the author's view of history as divine judgment. (3) In several passages, the expression "until this day" seems to assume the existence of the Judean state and thus a time prior to the exile. (4) The death of Josiah, narrated in II Kings

23:28-30, does not agree with the prediction of his end noted in the words of the prophetess Huldah in II Kings 22:18-20.

Recently, Cross has argued that the first edition of the Deuteronomistic History was "written in the era of Josiah as a programmatic document of his reform and of his revival of the Davidic state. In this edition the themes of judgment and hope interact to provide a powerful motivation both for the return to the austere and jealous god of old Israel, and for the reunion of the alienated half-kingdoms of Israel and Judah under the aegis of Josiah" (287). Cross distinguishes two major themes in the books of Kings which he relates to the time of Josiah. One the one hand, there is the theme of the sin of Jeroboam, the first king of a separate Israel, whose religious practices led to the eventual judgment of God, the demise of Israel, and the destruction of Samaria (see I Kings 11:26-38; 12:26-33; II Kings 17:7-23; compare I Kings 13:33-34 with II Kings 17:21-23). On the other hand, there is the theme of the faithfulness of David, the eternity of his dynasty, and the sacredness of Jerusalem (see II Sam 7:16; I Kings 11:12-13, 32-36; 15:4; II Kings 8:19; 19:34; 20:6). In I Kings 13:1-5, Josiah is even predicted as the son of David who would destroy the altar of Jeroboam at Bethel. This second theme, according to Cross, reaches its climax in the account of Josiah's reform and his program for reuniting Israel and Judah under a single Davidic ruler (II Kings 22:1-23:25).

In Josiah who cleansed the sanctuary founded by David and brought a final end to the shrine founded by Jeroboam, in Josiah who sought Yahweh with all his heart, the promises to David were to be fulfilled. Punishment and salvation had indeed alternated in the history of Judah . . . as in the era of the Judges. Yahweh has afflicted Judah, but will not forever. (Cross, 284)

According to Cross's reconstruction, the later exilic editor laid the blame for Jerusalem's fall on Manasseh, considered the wickedest king in Judah (II Kings 21:2-15;

24:3-4), and added other passages which speak of the fall of Jerusalem, exile, and the carrying away of the Davidic king.

There seems to be valid reason for assuming a pre-exilic edition of the Deuteronomistic History. Cross, unlike other scholars who have argued for an edition in the age of Josiah, has offered the best arguments and theological rationale for its specific setting and function. Gray's argument that the pre-exilic edition belongs to the time between the outbreak of Jehoiakim's revolt against Nebuchadrezzar in 598 and his death in 597 (see II Kings 24:1) explains the lack of a detailed discussion of Jehoiakim's revolt and the dating of the fall of Jerusalem to the eighth year of Nebuchadrezzar (II Kings 24:12), which is the first dating in the books of Kings by a foreign chronology and should not be excluded from consideration (see Gray, 7, 753).

The final and definitive form of the Deuteronomistic History, however, was the product of an exilic perspective. Like most literary works in the ancient world, the history closes on a hopeful, optimistic note—the release of Jehoiachin from prison. Von Rad has argued that one should see in this release an expression of messianic hopes for the return and re-establishment of Davidic dynasty in Jerusalem—a glimmer of confidence in the belief that David's throne would be established forever.

C. Pre-Deuteronomistic Materials in the Former Prophets

Clearly, the historian did not create all the traditions found in the Former Prophets. In various places, references are made to existing sources upon which the historian claims to have depended or to which he refers his readers. For example, Josh 10:13 and II Sam 1:18 refer to the Book of the Upright, while I Kings 11:41 speaks of the Book of Acts of Solomon. Throughout the books of

Kings, reference is made to the Book of the Chronicles of the Kings of Judah or Israel. Is it possible to determine and isolate some of the traditions employed by the Deuteronomistic History? In section B above, several of the distinctive deuteronomistic passages were noted. When the obvious deuteronomistic material has been isolated in the Former Prophets, what remains? What can be said about these non-deuteronomistic traditions?

(I) *The Book of Joshua.* The book of Joshua consists of two major blocks of material: traditions about the conquest of the land (chapters 2–12) and lists on the allotment of territory to the tribes (chapters 13–21). In addition to these sections and the clearly Deuteronomistic materials (chapters 1 and 23), there also appears material about the establishment and practice of the Yahwistic cult (8:30-35; 22; 24).

In the conquest traditions in Josh 2–12, most of the individual stories pertain to territory occupied by the tribe of Benjamin. Only in Josh 10:16–12:24 does territory outside of Benjamin come into the picture. This would suggest that the conquest traditions in Josh 2:1–10:15 were not originally concerned with any major twelve-tribe onslaught against the Canaanites. These narratives probably originated and circulated independently in Benjaminite circles. The "all Israel" orientation and the role of Joshua, who was apparently an Ephraimite (see Josh 24:30), have been superimposed upon these traditions. It was probably the Deuteronomist who stressed the concept of a massive conquest of Canaan by a unified Israel. (Noth, and others, have argued that the traditions in Josh 1–12 were already brought together by an editor about 900 BCE; see Weippert, 127.)

In Josh 2–10, a number of the narratives appear to be etiologies, that is, stories told to explain some phenomenon by reference to some past event assumed to be the cause of the phenomenon (see above, pp. 134-35, and Priest). Some of these are name etiologies; for example, the place names Gibeath–haaraloth and Gilgal are explained in Josh 5:2-9. Often, as here, etiologies are merely motifs or subsidiary elements in the larger story. Some of the etiologies, however, seem to be the primary purpose of the entire narrative. Josh 7:2–8:29 contains an account of the taking of Ai. Since archaeological excavations at et-tell, the generally accepted site of Ai, have shown that the site was unoccupied from about 2350 to 1220 BCE and that for years after 1220 there was only a small village on the site, this whole story seems to be without a historical basis. Since the name Ai means "the ruin," the narrative is best seen as an unhistorical etiology explaining a prominent ruin. The same is probably the case also with the account of the capture of Jericho (Josh 6) which stresses Yahweh as the giver of the victory, a victory in no way dependent upon human effort (see Josh 24:11). The archaeological evidence from Jericho shows no substantive occupation from about 1350 to about 800 BCE. Again this suggests an etiological origin expressing the need of the people to explain a prominent ruin.

The story of Jericho shows a remarkable religious orientation—in the function of the priests, the role of the ark, the significance of the number seven, and the sacred circumambulation of the city. A similar cultic or religious concern pervades Josh 3-5. The entry into the promised land is depicted as a religious processional. A monument of twelve stories is constructed ("in the midst of the Jordan," 4:9; "in Gilgal," 4:20), the males are circumcised, and the first Passover in the land is observed.

The narrative of the covenant with the Gibeonites (Josh 9) apparently reflects some early treaty agreement between the Israelites (Benjaminites ?) and the inhabitants of Gibeon. This treaty agreement seems to have been later broken by the Benjaminite Saul (see II Sam 4:1-3; 21:1-14). The present form of the story lays the blame for animosity between Israelites and Gibeonites upon the trickery of the latter. The description of the "southern campaign" (Josh 10:29-39) has been seen as historical by some scholars and unhistorical by others. Some of the material in this section differs from other Old Testament references. For example, in Josh 10:36-37, Hebron is taken by all Israel under Joshua; but in Judg 1:9-10 Judah takes Hebron while in Josh 15:13-14 it is Caleb who possesses the city. Similarly, Debir is elsewhere said to have been captured by Calebites (see Judg 1:11-15).

The account in Josh 11 of the battle at the waters of Merom and the burning of Hazor and slaughter of its king presents problems which are difficult to solve. (1) Jabin, king of Hazor, also appears as king of the city at the time of Deborah (see Judg 4:2). (2) The description of the burning of Hazor (Josh 11:10-15) is expressed in very general and highly theologized terminology. (3) The historical episode lying behind this narrative may have been a campaign by some Israelites in their acquisition of territory—perhaps the tribe of Naphtali (see the role of Naphtali in the war with Jabin in Judg 4). It is impossible however to be very specific.

Josh 12 provides a "wrap-up" of the conquest but it is a list (especially 12:7-24) which bears all the marks of artificiality and lateness. Many of the names in this list appear earlier in Joshua; however, several appear only in this summary in regard to the conquest. This list may date from sometime during the period of the monarchy when all these places were under Israelite control.

Josh 1–12 obviously intends to present a picture of the Israelite conquest of Canaan. It is in reality neither a unified presentation nor a historically reliable collection. Independent narratives and lists deriving from various times, reflecting various interests, and embodying various genres have been brought together under the general aegis of the conquest theme and have been impressed into the service of deuteronomistic theology. Perhaps some early, pre–deuteronomistic collection of these traditions once existed, but it would be difficult to reconstruct. The independent traditions frequently seem to preserve recollections of tribal warfare between Israelites and

Canaanites, but it is impossible to reconstruct the outline of a conquest from these traditions. (On the problems associated with the occupation of Canaan, both literary and archaeological, see J. M. Miller, *IJH*, 213-84.)

The second main block of material in the book of Joshua consists primarily of the so-called "apportionment of the land" (Josh 13-22). This section opens with a reference to Joshua's age ("now Joshua was old and advanced in years"; Josh 13:1a), a description which is repeated in 23:1b in the introduction to the deuteronomistic version of Joshua's farewell address. Between these two passages, diverse material has been collected, all of which deals in one way or another with the issue of land occupation by the various tribes. Josh 13:2-13 refers to the land which remained to be possessed; Josh 13:15-32 reviews the territory east of the Jordan allotted by Moses to the tribes of Reuben, Gad, and half of Manasseh; Josh 14-19 describes Joshua's assignment of land to the tribes west of the Jordan; Josh 20 notes the designation of six cities as places of refuge so "that any one who killed a person without intent could flee there, so that he might not die by the hand of the avenger of blood" (20:9; see also Ex 21:13; Deut 4:41-43; 19:1-13; Num 35:9-34); Josh 21 describes the assignment of cities to the three priestly (Levite) families of Kohath, Gershon, and Merari (see Num 35:1-8; I Chron 6:54-81); and Josh 22 reports the dismissal of the east Jordanian tribes and a subsequent dispute over an altar constructed by the eastern tribes on the west bank of Jordan.

Within the description of the tribal allotments (Josh 13-19), there are two distinct types of lists: city lists and tribal boundary lists. City lists are most extensive for the tribes of Judah (Josh 15:20-62) and Benjamin (Josh 18:21-28). It is widely assumed that these lists for Judah and Benjamin reflect the actual administrative structure of these districts but probably from late in history, certainly not from the premonarchical period. Of the border lists, the most detailed are those for Judah (Josh

15:1-12) Ephraim (Josh 16:1-8), Manasseh (Josh 17:7-10), Benjamin (Josh 18:12-20), Zebulun (Josh 19:10-14), Asher (Josh 19:24-29), and Naphtali (Josh 19:33-34). Since the work of Alt and Noth, in the 1920s and 30s, it has frequently been assumed that these border lists reflect actual political realities of Israelite geography in the period of the judges (see Aharoni, 227-39). Of these boundary lists, however, only that for Benjamin can be clearly and unequivocally delineated. The theory that these border lists date from the time of the judges has been allied with a view that early Israel existed as a twelve-tribe confederacy (or amphictyony) in premonarchic times, a topic which will be discussed in more detail in the next section on the book of Judges.

The list of cities of refuge (Josh 20) recognizes that the right of asylum was an ancient practice. Asylum was generally sought at sanctuaries or in important sanctuary towns. The list of Levitical cities has frequently been viewed as an idealistic and priestly construct. (Note the priestly oriented passages in Josh 18:1; 19:51; and throughout 22.) Recently, it has been argued that the concept of Levitical cities goes back to the time of David. Such cities and the Levites are assumed to have performed strategic religious and administrative duties in cities located on the frontier of Israel or in areas only nominally under Israelite and Yahwistic control (see I Chron 26:29-32; Aharoni, 269-273). While this theory contains some very attractive features, it remains beyond proof.

The central purpose of the deuteronomistic book of Joshua was to emphasize that the land of Canaan—in its entirety—was promised land and that Israel's occupation of that land was the gift of God shared in by all the tribes. In order to present such a view, this historian utilized and created materials of various sorts. These materials and traditions were in many ways reflective of the actual political realities in Canaan but probably more reflective of conditions under the monarchy than of those prior to the establishment of kingship. The Deuteronomist assumes that the Israelites, when loyal to their God, overcame their enemies by divine intervention and that the conquered territory was then distributed by divinely controlled lots. Such tenets are central to his theology, but these are difficult for the modern historian to integrate into a presentation of history qua history. Fortunately, the historian possesses those materials incorporated by the Deuteronomist into his work. The original shape and content of these have not been totally obliterated and thus make possible a minimal reconstruction of early tribal history and life.

(II) *The Book of Judges.* Within the Deuteronomistic History, the period of the judges opened at Judg 2:6 (or perhaps 2:10), which resumed the story broken off at Josh 23:16, and continued through Samuel's address in I Sam 12 which marks the beginning of the period of the monarchy. The present structure of the book of Judges may be outlined as: (1) prelude (1:1–2:5 [9]), which provides a picture of the settlement; (2) an introduction to the period of the judges (2:6 [10]–3:6); (3) narratives about the judges (3:7–16:31); (4) stories about the origin of the tribal sanctuary and migration of Dan (17–18; the latter story is actually a conquest narrative); and (5) an account of a war against the Benjaminites because of their outrageous act at Gibeah and its subsequent conseqences (19–21).

The materials in Judg 3:7–16:31 form the heart of the book of Judges. Even here, one finds two major types of materials. Judg 10:1-5 and 12:8-15 provide a list of five judges about whom little is told and no exploits narrated. (The number would be six if the reference to Jephthah in Judg 12:7 belongs to this list and is not a summary statement to the Jephthah exploits narrated in Judg 11:1–12:6.) About each of these judges we are told the name of the judge, his home, the number of years he functioned as judge, and the place of his burial. About some of these judges, legendary type statements are made concerning their numerous offspring. The other traditions in Judg 3:7–16:31 are heroic narratives about the exploits of "deliverers" who are also called judges.

Attempts have been made to outline the prehistory of these deliverer traditions in their pre-deuteronomistic form (see Rogers).

(1) At the earliest stage, these traditions circulated as independent narratives or stories (see the poetic parallel in Judg 5 to the narrative in Judg 4). Originally, these stories told about tribal heroes who aided in the military exploits and defense of the tribes. Historically, the deliverers were probably the leaders of only tribal groups, not all Israel, and their activity consisted in leading one tribe or adjacent tribes in their military campaigns, primarily defensive in nature. Many of these deliverers may have existed simultaneously and have therefore been contemporaries and not successors. The descriptions of these leaders suggest that some of them may have been as much strong-armed opportunists as altruistic saviors.

(2) A cycle of these heroic legends may have been edited to form a book about early Israelite deliverers. It has been suggested that this original collection was composed of Judg 3:12–9:55. A framework was provided for these stories which stressed that Israel sinned against Yahweh, who oppressed them by subjugation to their enemies but saved them through the deliverer when the people cried out for aid. This framework can be seen, for example, in Judg 3:12,14,15a,30. In this framework, the nature of the sin is not specified and no significance is given to the people's confession or repentance from sin. Also, in this pre-deuteronomistic work, the deliverers functioned only for a limited time and not for the remainder of their lives.

(3) In the deuteronomistic phase, the deliverer traditions were combined with the list of judges and deuteronomistic materials and interpretations added. For the Deuteronomist, the deliverers were understood as judges who functioned throughout their lives as the

holders of an office. For the Deuteronomist, the primary sin of the people was apostasy from Yahweh and the worship of other gods. Confession and repentance of sin are depicted as basic elements in the scenario of Yahweh's response to the people's plight. The best synopses of the Deuteronomist's perspective are found in Judg 2:11-19; 10:6-16.

If the original deliverer book contained Judg 3:12–9:55 minus the deuteronomistic additions, then the Jephthah and Samson stories may have been incorporated into the hero stories by the Deuteronomist or in the case of the latter by some later hand. The Samson stories (Judg 13–16) differ from the other hero exploits and have not been subjected to the deliverer schematization to the same extent as the other stories. Samson is depicted as primarily a folk hero and attention focuses on his character as an individual rather than as a redeemer figure. There are two concluding statements about Samson (Judg 15:20; 16:31) which might suggest that the Samson stories were handed down in two cycles before being utilized by the Deuteronomist or inserted into the work at a later time. Jephthah may have appeared in the judges list (Judg 12:7) and also in a hero narrative. The Jephthah stories do not show the same amount of deuteronomistic or pre-deuteronomistic editing as the stories in Judg 3:12–9:55. Thus it may have circulated independently. The tradition about Othniel (Judg 3:7-11) appears to be a pure schematic creation of the Deuteronomist unbased on any ancient tradition. The single verse about Shamgar (Judg 3:31) is something of an enigma: it follows neither the deliverer nor judge pattern and may have been an insertion into the text based on Judg 5:4 and perhaps influenced by the Samson stories (see Judg 15:16).

The narratives in Judg 17–18 and 19–21 clearly appear to be insertions of miscellaneous material into the Deuteronomist's work. They interrupt the continuity of the accounts of the judges. If the Shamgar and Samson traditions were not originally part of the Deuteronomistic History, then the Deuteronomist worked with a scheme of twelve judges between Joshua and Saul: Othniel (3:7-11), Ehud(3:12-30), Deborah/Barak (4-5), Gideon/Jerubbaal (6-8), Abimelech (9), Tola (10:1-2), Jair (10:3-5), Jephthah (10:6-12:7), Ibzan (12:8-10), Elon (12:11-12), Abdon (12:13-15), and Samuel. The twelve judges would be a reflection of the twelve tribes.

A number of individual and isolated traditions remain after the various frameworks, schematizations, and deuteronomistic additions have been removed from the material in the book of Judges. These traditions in no way provide a comprehensive or systematic presentation of Israelite tribal life in the premonarchical period. The following may be said about these traditions and the glimpses of tribal life which they present.

(1) The traditions of Ehud, Deborah/Barak, Gideon, Abimelech, and Jephthah reflect conditions and events of tribes settled in the north. Ehud led Benjaminites, with perhaps some assistance from Ephraimites, in their struggles against Moabite encroachment into central Palestine (Judg 3:12-30). Deborah/Barak led the tribes of Naphtali and Zebulun in a war against Canaanite forces (Judg 4). The poetic version of the Deborah war in Judg 5 extends the participating tribes to include Ephraim, Benjamin, Machir (Manasseh?), and Issachar; but the use of this poem as a victory song and perhaps in cultic celebrations would suggest that the original story has undergone extensive elaboration (see Mayes, 87-98). The complicated Gideon story (Judg 6–8) seems to embody a tradition about a local action of Abiezites and Ephraimites led by Gideon against Midianite encroachment into the Jezreel Valley. The tradition about Abimelech (Judg 9) concerns the city-state politics of the city of Shechem and an attempt by Abimelech to establish a city-state type kingship in the area. Jephthah seems to have been a free-floating leader of soldiers of fortune, not unlike the later David (see I Sam 22:1-2), whose services were

available for hire. He is pictured defending Gileadites in East Jordan against the Ammonites (Judg 11) and against Ephraimites (Judg 12:1-6). The tradition about Jephthah's vow in Judg 11:30-31,34-40 appears to be an attempt to associate the ritual weeping for a departed goddess with some historical event.

(2) The traditions about Samson (Judg 13-16) are set in southwestern Palestine where the antagonists are the Philistines. The traditions assume that the tribe of Dan was still settled in this area and had not yet migrated to north central Palestine (see Judg 1:34-35; 18). The general folkloristic character of the Samson stories means that these stories must be interpreted as fine examples of the storyteller's art. Historically, they point to the existence of conflict between southern tribal groups and the Philistines encroaching from the west.

(3) While Judg 17-18 primarily concerns the cult place at Dan, these stories do suggest that tribal activity and acquisition of territory in the premonarchical period were undertaken by single tribes (see Malamat). The Danite conquest of the territory of Laish is, of course, placed quite late in these accounts. In many ways, Judg 17-18 would have been more at home with the traditions in the book of Joshua than with those of the book of Judges.

(4) The traditions in Judg 19-21 have been set within an "all Israel" orientation. Perhaps behind the present shape of the narratives one can see the conflicts between Israelite tribal groups, such as that between Ephraim and Gilead in Judg 12:1-6. Judg 19-21 should probably be related to struggles between Ephraim and Benjamin. These two tribes were closely related (see Judg 3:15-30) although Ephraim seems to have claimed dominance in central Palestine (see Judg 8:1-3; 12:1-6). According to Gen 35:16-18, Benjamin was born in Palestine; that is, the tribe came into being there and perhaps reasonably late. Judg 19-21 may reflect the strife concomitant upon Benjamin's breakaway from Ephraim and its rather unsuccessful assertion of independence. The name

Benjamin means "sons of the south" and suggests a name given to the group from a more dominant group to the north, i.e., Ephraim.

(5) The individual traditions in Judges, like those in Joshua, do not support the biblical view that early Israel was a twelve-tribe confederacy in premonarchical days. Since Martin Noth's influential work on Israel as a twelve-tribe league or amphictyony, published in 1930, this view has frequently been assumed in treatments of Israelite history. The theory of an Israelite amphictyony assumes that the lists of twelve tribes in Gen 49; Num 1; 26; Deut 33; etc. reflect early political realities. The argument presumes that early Israel was a religious confederation, utilized a common faith and a central sanctuary, was ruled over by tribal representatives and judges, took concerted actions against dissident members, came to share a common store of legal and historical traditions and engaged in united military undertakings. As we have seen, the predeuteronomistic traditions in Joshua and Judges simply do not support such sweeping hypotheses about premonarchical times. (For Noth's amphictyonic theory and a critique, see A. D. H. Mayes, *IJH*, 297-308.)

(III) *The Books of Samuel.* The present books of Samuel may be outlined as follows: (1) birth and youth of Samuel (I Sam 1–4:1a); (2) the ark narrative (I Sam 4:1b–7:2); (3) Samuel as judge (I Sam 7:3-17); (4) the rise of the monarchy and the reign of Saul (I Sam 8–14); (5) Saul and David (I Sam 15–31); (6) stories about the rise to power and reign of David (II Samuel).

The most clearly deuteronomistic material in the books of Samuel is found in I Sam 7–12 and II Sam 7. I Sam 12 marks the Deuteronomist's conclusion to the period of the judges and introduces the period of the monarchy. Major deuteronomistic texts are interspersed in I Sam 8–10, which describes the origin of the monarchy. I Sam 7 presents the deuteronomistic version of Samuel as the last judge. The present form of II Sam 7 contains the

Deuteronomist's version of Yahweh's dynastic promise to David. A strong influence of the Deuteronomist can be seen in the manner in which the traditions about Saul, David, and Solomon are presented. The overall narrative structure in all three cases shows the ruler first as under the "blessing" or describes his successes and then as under the "curse" or describes his failures, shortcomings, and troubles (see Carlson). This of course might have some resemblance to this historical course of events but has probably resulted in highly schematized presentations.

Various attempts have been made to analyze the material in Samuel in order to reconstruct its possible predeuteronomistic form. The following sources have been isolated although there are scholarly differences over details: (1) the Samuel birth and youth narratives (I Sam 1–3); (2) the ark stories (I Sam 4–6; II Sam 6); (3) the narrative of David's rise to power (I Sam 15–II Sam 5; sometimes II Sam 6–8 are included here); (4) the throne succession story (II Sam 9–20—I Kings 1–2; sometimes II Sam 6–8 as well as II Sam 21:1–14; 24 are seen as parts of this work). II Sam 21–24 is generally considered to be diverse supplements to the Davidic tradition.

The stories of Samuel's birth and youth (I Sam 1-3) contain many of the features of a folklore tale–the unusual birth of a hero or redeemer figure which has parallels in the birth stories of Isaac, Joseph, Moses, and Samson. The etiological explanation of the name of Samuel in I Sam 1:20 has raised questions about whether or not this birth narrative was originally told about Samuel. The etiology actually explains the name Saul–"the one asked for." Some have assumed that this story once told of the birth of Israel's first king, however, Saul's father was named Kish (I Sam 9:1) not Elkanah. The present form of this material stresses the significance of Samuel and thus prepares the reader for I Sam 7.

The ark stories in I Sam 4–6 had an origin separate from the Samuel stories. Samuel plays no role in the ark stories, and the ark plays no role in the narratives about Samuel (however, see I Sam 14:18; but here the Greek reads "ephod"). The Deuteronomistic History seems to have utilized the already existing stories of I Sam 1–3 to introduce the figure of Samuel, who dominates the narrative from I Sam 7 onwards and thus did not include I Sam 4–6. If the Deuteronomist included the material in his history, certainly no real use was made of the traditions. It has generally been assumed that the ark stories in I Sam 4–6 plus the story of David's bringing the ark to Jerusalem (II Sam 6) formed an independent ark narrative. This story would have had its setting and usage among priestly circles at the temple in Jerusalem.

The traditions about Saul in I Sam 8-12 have been heavily edited by the Deuteronomist (see Mettinger, 80-98). He inherited the traditions about Saul in which Samuel was already depicted as the one who anointed Saul as king. In these traditions, Samuel is portrayed as a prophet with authority to designate Yahweh's choice (see II Kings 9:1-13). The pro-Saul and pro-monarchic traditions about Saul probably already circulated during the time of Saul's reign to explain how he became king and to justify the new institution. Very little about Saul's reign has been preserved (see I Sam 14:47-48). Pro-Samuel prophetic circles have greatly influenced the present shape of the Saul traditions.

The pro-David sentiments overlap the Saul narratives. The story of David's rise to power probably began with a narrative about Yahweh's rejection of Saul, a constant theme in the stories about David in I Samuel. There is almost universal agreement that the narrative of David's rise to power included I Sam 16–II Sam 5, which begins with the story of David's anointment by Samuel as Saul's successor while David was still an innocent and unavaricious lad and concludes with his capture of Jerusalem. As an independent narrative, the rise of David may have included the anti-Saul story in I Sam 15 as well as the story of David's bringing the ark to Jerusalem (II

Sam 6), some form of Nathan's prophecy (II Sam 7), and the account of David's reign in II Sam 8 (see Mettinger, 27-47). The figure of David seems early to have attracted traditions previously ascribed to others (compare the Goliath story in I Sam 17 with II Sam 21:19). Within the traditions about his rise have been preserved memories of David's service as a mercenary in Saul's army (see I Sam 16:14-23; 18:5; 22:14), his leadership of a band of renegade opportunists and knaves (I Sam 22:1-2), his operation of a protection racket (I Sam 25), and his service to Israel's enemy, the Philistines (I Sam 27). In spite of the wealth of Davidic traditions in Samuel, we really know little about the actual reign of David and the course of events during his rule. Only II Sam 8 provides anything like a description of his years in power and this text merely offers a summary of his international achievements. The reason for this paucity of historical knowledge is the fact that the traditions about David were produced for other than purely historiographical reasons. The narrative of David's rise to power appears to have been a work produced, probably after the death of Solomon, in order to stress several factors. (1) David is presented as the divinely chosen to rule over Yahweh's people, both Israel and Judah. (2) David is depicted as Saul's successor.(3) David's fidelity to Saul and Israel is stressed so that he is not presented as a usurper of royal power. (4) David is shown as the true ruler over Israel and her savior. All of these emphases would suggest that the work was produced to justify and support the claims of the Davidic family as the chosen rulers over Israel and Judah at a time when this was challenged, i.e., after the death of Solomon.

The throne succession story, which certainly included II Sam 9–20 and at least parts of I Kings 1–2, has been one of the most studied sections of the books of Samuel (see Mettinger, 27-32; and Whybray). Since the throne succession narrative was isolated and investigated as an independent unit, scholars have extolled its artistic craftsmanship, its secular orientation, and its early date. Speaking of the work, Eduard Meyer wrote:

Thus the golden age of the Hebrew monarchy produced genuinely historical writing. No other civilisation of the ancient East was able to do so. Even the Greeks achieved it only at the height of their development in the fifth century, and then as quickly fell away again. Here, on the contrary, we are dealing with a nation which had only just become civilised. The factors which were conducive to this, including the possession of an easily learned script, came to them as to the Greeks from the former occupants of their land; but this only makes their achivement the more astonishing. Here, as in all historical situations, we have the insoluble problem of innate ability. By virtue of their achievement in historical writing, realised independently and fully-grown from the start, the civilisation of Israel must be ranged alongside that which was achieved on the soil of Greece to a richer and fuller degree some centuries later. (quoted in von Rad, 1966, 197)

Meyer considered it ironical that Judaism and Christianity considered the texts in the throne succession story as scripture since they were out and out secular texts: "Any kind of religious colouring, every thought of supernatural intervention, is wholly excluded. The course of this world, and the nemesis which is fulfilled in the chain of events set in motion by one's own guilt, all are portrayed as matters of plain fact seen by the onlooker." Other scholars have spoken of the work as an eye-witness account and a historical record of the first order. Von Rad has described the succession narrative and the Yahwistic history as the products of a Solomonic enlightenment when the new and more secularized orders of existence begun under David developed their potential to touch every facet of human life and which saw God's activity as a constant and "widely embracing factor concealed in the whole breadth of secular affairs, and pervading every single sphere of human life" (204).

The following seem to be reasonable conclusions about the throne succession story. (1) The work tells us very little about political events of the reign of David and cannot in any way be considered a court history of David's reign. (2) The work appears to be an apologetic document intent on defending and justifying Solomon's claim to the throne and excusing some of the actions associated with his accession. This would suggest a date early in Solomon's reign. (3) The work is highly novelistic, narrating in detail events confined to bedrooms and engaging in the psychological assessment of characters. Thus it could, at best, be called a historical "novel" but not a work of true historiography. (4) The realism and honesty in the presentation of characters, even that of David, are unique and give the work a distinctively modern cast.

(IV) *The Books of Kings.* The present books of Kings begin with the account of Solomon's accession and conclude with the release of Jehoiachin from prison in 561 BCE, covering roughly four centuries of Israelite and Judean history. The following is an outline of the books' contents: (1) the accession of Solomon (I Kings 1–2); (2) the reign of Solomon (I Kings 3–11); (3) the history of Israel and Judah from the death of Solomon to the fall of Samaria (I Kings 12–II Kings 17); (4) the history of Judah until after the destruction of Jerusalem and the deportation to Babylon (II Kings 18-25).

Numerous predeuteronomistic sources and traditions can be seen in the deuteronomistic version of this material although these have been impressed into the service of the deuteronomistic theology. A constant element of this theology in the books of Kings is stress on history as the realization of God's words (see I Kings 8:24), i.e., the theme of prophetic promise and historical fulfillment. In the following list of biblical passages, those in the left column contain predictions and those in the right column refer to the fulfillments:

[II Sam 7:13]	I Kings 8:20
I Kings 11:29-39	I Kings 12:15

I Kings 13:1-3	II Kings 23:16-18
I Kings 14:6-16	II Kings 15:29
I Kings 16:1-4	I Kings 16:12
[Josh 6:26]	I Kings 16:34
I Kings 21:21-24	
(27-29)	
II Kings 9:4-10	II Kings 10
I Kings 22:17	I Kings 22:35-36
II Kings 1:6	II Kings 1:17
II Kings 21:10-15	II Kings 24:2

Among the predeuteronomistic materials utilized in I-II Kings are (1) the conclusion to the throne succession story, (2) various traditions about Solomon's reign, (3) excerpts from the "Chronicles of the Kings of Israel/Judah," and (4) numerous prophetical traditions.

The original conclusion to the throne story in I Kings 1–2 has undergone deuteronomistic editing, especially in I Kings 2:2-4. Perhaps such passages as I Kings 1:41-53 and 2:13-46 represent secondary, but probably predeuteronomistic, expansions (see Mettinger, 27-29). I Kings 2:12 may have originally concluded the throne succession story.

The traditions about Solomon's reign are a variegated collection. Although I Kings 11:41 refers to the Book of Acts of Solomon, efforts to find any continuous sources in the Solomonic materials have not been successful. I Kings 4:7-19, describing the administrative districts, as well as a few other passages including I Kings 4:1-6, may be dependent upon some ancient sources. Much of the material is reflective of deuteronomistic interests—concern with the temple construction (I Kings 6-7), royal piety (I Kings 8), and the issue of royal obedience to the law (I Kings 9:1-9)—while other material suggests anecdotal stories and the desire to glorify the age of Solomon.

The basic sources used by the Deuteronomist for the history of the separate states of Israel and Judah are the "Chronicles of the Kings of Israel/Judah." The exact nature and content of these chronicles are unknown, but two things seem certain: (1) they are not to be identified with the biblical books of I-II Chronicles, and (2) they were not the official court records (daybooks or annals) of the two monarchies. Perhaps these chronicles should be understood as secondary scribal histories written in chronological order similar to such works known from Babylonia (see *ANET*, 301-7). Such writings were no doubt based on archival documents, royal lists, and so on.

The material utilized by the Deuteronomist for Israelite and Judean history has been subjected to a schematic presentation and to theological editing. Theologically, monarchs are judged according to the cultic and legal principles of the book of Deuteronomy and according to their fidelity to and support of the temple in Jerusalem. The application of such criteria meant that no Israelite king was praised and that only two Judean kings—Hezekiah and Josiah—were viewed as completely loyal to the Law. The historical material is presented according to the following general scheme:

Judah	Israel
1. In such and such a year of so-and-so, king of Israel, began so-and-so to reign over Judah.	1. In such and such a year of so-and-so, king of Judah, began so-and-so to reign over Israel.
2. Facts about his age, length of reign, and the queen mother.	2. Statements about the length and place of his reign.
3. Evaluation of his reign in comparison with David.	3. Condemnation of the ruler for his doing evil and walking in the way of Jeroboam and his sin.
4. Events during his reign.	4. Events during his reign.
5. Reference to further	5. Reference to further

material related to the reign in the Book of Chronicles of the Kings of Judah.	material related to the reign in the Book of Chronicles of the Kings of Israel.
6. Concluding statement about his death and successor.	6. Concluding statement about his death and successor.

This scheme was greatly expanded when the topic under consideration concerned Jerusalem and the temple. At the same time, significant political events and developments in Israel were sometimes passed over or treated in a cursory fashion. We know from ancient near eastern texts, for example, that the reign of Omri and his family was far more outstanding and successful than the deuteronomistic account would suggest.

The Deuteronomist incorporated, edited, and perhaps rewrote several prophetical traditions. These include the Elijah stories (I Kings 17-19; 21; II Kings 1-2), the Elisha traditions (II Kings 2; 4-10); the Isaiah narratives (II Kings 18:13-20:19; see Is 36-39), and narratives about various minor prophetical figures (Ahijah of Shiloh, I Kings 11:29-39; 14:1-18; 15:29; Shemaiah, I Kings 12:21-24; an anonymous prophet, I Kings 12:32-13:32). The hand of the Deuteronomist is most clearly evident in the last group of these prophetic traditions.

D. I and II Chronicles

The books of I and II Chronicles form something of a parallel history to the Pentateuch and Former Prophets. Although the work was divided into two volumes in its early Greek form, it originally constituted a continuous work which may be outlined as follows:

Introductory Genealogies	I Chron 1:1-54
Tribal and Davidic Lists	I Chron 2:1-9:1

Inhabitants of Jerusalem	I Chron 9:2-18
List of Levitical Functionaries	I Chron 9:19-34
Inhabitants of Gibeon	I Chron 9:35-44 (see 8:29-38)
The Reign of David	I Chron 10:1-29:30
The Reign of Solomon	II Chron 1:1-9:31
The History of Judah's Kings	II Chron 10:1-36:23

Chapter 1 contains genealogical lists which have counterparts in the book of Genesis. Chapters 2–8 are a heterogeneous assemblage of tribal genealogies, historic notations, city lists, and diverse folk traditions. Noteworthy are the lists of David's sons (I Chron 3:1-9) and the descendants of Solomon (I Chron 3:10-24). This latter list of the Davidic dynasty carries the family line down several generations after Zerubbabel, who was a major figure in the reconstruction of the temple in postexilic Jerusalem. The list of Jerusalem inhabitants in I Chron 9:2-18 parallels a similar list in Neh 11:3-19 while I Chron 9:35-44 repeats material previously presented.

Several factors about these lists in I Chron 1–9 are noteworthy. (1) Although the book of I–II Chronicles begins with Adam and concludes after the fall of Jerusalem, the time span between Adam and Saul is represented solely by the lists found in these first nine chapters. (2) The lists are extremely variegated representing materials of diverse types. (3) They relate to various historical periods some of which have nothing to do with the time between Adam and Saul. (4) Enormous credulity would be required for one to assume that all of this material was produced at a single time or reflects the work of a single editorial hand. Such lists as these are highly susceptible to errors in transmission and to changes and additions. (5) These lists seem to have been employed to provide a broad background for the discussion of the kingdom of David.

Beginning with chapter 10, Chronicles shifts to a general narrative presentation of Israelite history which commences with the monarchy although the reign of Saul is not treated with any independent integrity—his death at the hands of the Philistines merely forms the staging against which David's assumption of power is presented. (I Chron 10:13-14 alludes to the stories found in I Sam 15 and 28 although the chapter as a whole primarily reproduces I Sam 31.) I Chron 11–29 provides a portrait of David and his reign. Although based on, and frequently repeating verbatim, the Davidic traditions found in the books of Samuel, the version in Chronicles contains significant differences and emphases.

The following elements in the Chronicler's depiction of David are worthy of note. (1) Numerous events and large sections about David found in the Samuel materials are omitted in Chronicles. Among these are David's reign in Hebron and his struggles with Saul's family, the Bathsheba affair, the revolts of Absalom his son and Sheba the Benjaminite, and the troubles over succession attendant upon his old age. That is, whatever would show David in a bad light and suggest any problems during his reign are systematically omitted. (2) Substantial additions have been made to the tradition taken over from Samuel. These include descriptions of David's preparations for the construction of the temple, his organization of temple personnel, and administrative structures in both civil and military spheres. (3) Stress is placed on the unity of the people Israel and David's unchallenged and complete sovereignty over this ideal state.

Solomon and his reign are treated in II Chron 1–9 as fundamentally the continuation and fulfillment of David's rule and aspirations. According to the Chronicler, Solomon assumed the kingship according to the careful arrangements made by David and consented to by the leaders of the nation (contrast I Kings 1–2). He constructed the temple according to plans handed over to him by his father. As in the case of David, the description of Solomon eliminates any incidents that might cloud the monarch's glory—his struggle to secure the throne, his elimination of opposition, the "sins" of Solomon near the end of his reign, and so forth. In other words, Solomon is shown standing only under the blessing. Over six of the nine chapters devoted to Solomon concern the construction and dedication of the temple and portray him as the chosen temple builder. However, the Chronicler followed the material in the Former Prophets more closely in the case of Solomon than in that of David.

The treatment of the separate states of Israel and Judah (II Chron 10–36) is not characterized by any desire to present an ideal religious commonwealth without blemish as was the case with David and Solomon. The rulers are presented with many of the same characterizations as those found in the books of Kings. Significant differences between Kings and Chronicles are found, however, in major additions and expansions to the narrative in Chronicles: the fortification of cities by Rehoboam (11:5-12), the wars of kings Asa and Jehoshapat (14:9-15; 20:1-30), the latter's judicial reforms (19:4-11), the activities of Uzziah (26:6-15) and Jotham (27:1-9), Hezekiah's religious activities (29-31) and his military defense exploits (32:2-6), Manasseh's capture and release by the Assyrians (33:10-13) and his defense and religious activities (33:14-16), and the distinctive presentation of the stages in Josiah's reform (34:1-18). Some of these additions and expansions may preserve authentic historical traditions.

Most noteworthy in Chronicles are sermons, prayers, oracles, and other pious additions which provide a more religious and sanctified atmosphere to the traditions and the events than is the case in Samuel and Kings and give the work a very homiletical and edifying character. Many of these additions are similar to later rabbinic midrash (note the use of the word "midrash" in II Chron 13:22; 24:27). That is, they are commentary-type expositions and interpretations of the deuteronomistic traditions.

240

Later midrash performed a number of functions: (1) to explain the text so as to make it understandable; (2) to reconcile and harmonize conflicting and diverging texts and traditions so as to affirm and illustrate the unity of divine revelation and the uniformity of religious beliefs and practices; and (3) to interpret the text and events so as to proclaim the word of God and edify the community. Many of these characteristics can be seen in the Chronicler's work.

In places, the Chronicler seeks to reconcile differing traditions and/or theological perspectives. In I Sam 17, David is depicted as the killer of Goliath whereas II Sam 21:19 ascribes his death to an otherwise unknown Elhanan. In I Chron 20:5, Elhanan is said to have killed Lahmi the brother of Goliath, thus correcting and reconciling the two traditions. In II Sam 24:1, Yahweh incites David to carry out a census. The Chronicler reconciles this with later theology by seeing Satan as the inciter of David (I Chron 21:1).

The writer makes clear that God controls human life and history and recompenses individuals according to their obedience to the precepts of the faith and their devotion to the service of God in the temple. In I Chron 10:13-14, for example, he pronounces unequivocally the reasons why God slew Saul and gave the kingdom to David: "So Saul died for his unfaithfulness; he was unfaithful to Yahweh in that he did not keep the command of Yahweh, and also consulted a medium, seeking guidance, and did not seek guidance from Yahweh." (Note how the text presupposes knowledge of events in the Deuteronomistic History not reported in Chronicles.) When Jehoshaphat goes forth to battle, he offers prayers to Yahweh, listens to the oracles of the Levites, admonishes his men to faith, allows the singers to precede the soldiers, and enjoys triumph beyond imagination (II Chron 20:1-30).

Before battle the Judean Ahijah lectures his Israelite opponent stressing that Judah has preserved the true faith and is served by a true and faithful clergy in a proper manner and in the proper temple whereas Israel's religion and clergy, supported by an illegitimate monarchy, represent the north's departure from God (II Chron 13:1-12). The people of the north, however, are not denied their special status as people of God: "O sons of Israel, do not fight against Yahweh, the God of your fathers" (II Chron 13:12).

Why was the Chronicler's history written when it parallels so much of the Deuteronomistic History? Scholars have provided various answers to this question (see Williamson, 1-4, 132-40). (1) Some interpreters, like Wellhausen, saw the Chronicler's work as an attempt to present the history of Israel viewed through the prism of the source document P with its priestly and cultic interests. Just as the deuteronomistic historian viewed Israelite and Judean history in terms of the Deuteronomic Code so the Chronicler rewrote Judah's history in terms of the Priestly Source. (2) Others have seen the work as primarily an anti-Samaritan treatise intent on refuting the Samaritan claims for their temple and interpretation of the Torah. As such, the work stressed the temple of Jerusalem as the only legitimate place of worship and Judah as the only legitimate community constituting the people of God. (3) Freedman, Cross, and Newsome argue that an early version of the Chronicler's history was written just after the return from exile to support the Davidic family represented by Zerubbabel and the Zadok priesthood represented by the priest Jeshua (see Ezra 3). The history was thus a political-religious document intended to support the political and religious activity of the Judean community in the early days of restoration efforts. (4) Other scholars see the Chronicler's history as a defense of the theocratic life of the postexilic community. According to this view, the Chronicler contended that the purely religious and cultic community was a faithful embodiment and sufficient realization of the divine-human relationship. Thus, the Chronicler opposed certain prophetically and eschatologically oriented groups which expected and hoped for divine intervention into history and the radical transformation of existence. (5) Other scholars, such as Japhet and Williamson, argue that no single purpose or unilateral perspective can explain the work of the Chronicler. Instead, the work must be viewed in a comprehensive perspective in which "sociological realities, religious views, and polemical purposes are intermingled" (Japhet, *EJ*, 529). Ackroyd contends that the Chronicler should be understood "as the first Old Testament theologian, offering a unifying of strands and trends which may otherwise appear separate; his exegesis of the earlier materials provides a harmonization, but it is one that is also an appreciation of the richness and diversity of the Old Testament religious tradition" (1977, 24).

E. Ezra and Nehemiah

For over a century and a half, a majority of Old Testament scholars have assumed that Ezra-Nehemiah along with I–II Chronicles once constituted a single historiographical work covering the history of Israel down to the time of Nehemiah. The Chronicler's History was a phrase used to refer to all four volumes conceived as a single work. The arguments used to support such a view are:

(1) The introductory sentences of the book of Ezra also appear in slightly shortened form as the concluding sentences of II Chronicles and suggest that the works were a continuous composition.
(2) A similar literary style and distinctive vocabulary are assumed to appear throughout the four books.
(3) The same theological outlook and interests appear throughout all these writings.
(4) The Greek book of I Esdras, which parallels some of

243

this material, begins at II Chron 35 and continues without interruption into the book of Ezra, a continuation which could suggest an original unity between Chronicles and Ezra-Nehemiah.

A number of arguments have recently been advanced to support the separation of I-II Chronicles and Ezra-Nehemiah into two independent works (see Japhet and Williamson). In addition to the argument that the words show literary and vocabulary similarities only because they stem from a common historical and linguistic background, other reasons are advanced to deny a common authorship.

(1) In Chronicles, the house of David occupies center stage whereas it plays no significant role in Ezra-Nehemiah, where not even Zerubbabel is given a Davidic pedigree (compare I Chron 3:19).

(2) The Exodus, the wilderness period, and the conquest of Canaan are seldom even noted in Chronicles whereas these themes are fairly prominent in the prayers and historical reviews in Ezra-Nehemiah.

(3) Marriage with foreigners is a major concern in Ezra-Nehemiah whereas I-II Chronicles contains no reference or allusion to this issue.

(4) I-II Chronicles tends to be far more schematic, tendentious in its presentation of data, and prone to exaggeration than Ezra-Nehemiah, where sober descriptions and realistic presentation of data prevail.

(5) The repetition of Cyrus' decree at the end of Chronicles was probably borrowed from the beginning of Ezra in order to provide an optimistic ending to the canon when, in Talmudic times, Chronicles was the final work in the Hebrew Bible.

(6) That in Ezra 2:36-39 there are only four priestly groups whereas there are twenty-four in I Chron 24 suggests that Chronicles reflects a later cultic situation.

244

(7) I–II Chronicles show a much more conciliatory attitude toward Israel or the north than does Ezra-Nehemiah and is therefore much less exclusivistic in outlook.

(8) I–II Chronicles and Ezra-Nehemiah never appear in this order in any Hebrew manuscript tradition. Ezra-Nehemiah precede I-II Chronicles except in a few manuscripts, including the Aleppo Codex, where I-II Chronicles opens the third section of the canon (the Writings) and Ezra-Nehemiah are the final books.

Even the origin of the books Ezra-Nehemiah, however, is a highly complicated matter. There are a number of indications which suggest that they might have originally existed as separate works in spite of early Jewish tradition which considered them to be a single, continuous composition.

(1) The book of Ezra contains no superscription, but the book of Nehemiah is introduced by the caption "the words (or narrative) of Nehemiah the son of a Hacaliah" which suggests that Nehemiah, or at least an early form of the book, was an independent work.

(2) There are duplications in the two books, the most notable being the list of returning exiles which appears in Ezra 2 and Neh 7.

(3) Ezra material appears in the book of Nehemiah (chapters 8-9). In this section, Nehemiah plays no role and is only mentioned once and in a secondary role (see Neh 8:9). This suggests that the books have been rather artificially combined.

(4) The first person "memoirs" of Nehemiah (Neh 1:1-7:73a + 10 + 12:27-43 + 13) appear to have once constituted an independent work perhaps dating from Nehemiah's lifetime.

(5) Many of the historical problems associated with the work of Ezra and Nehemiah might be best solved on the assumption of two different works.

The historical contents of Ezra-Nehemiah are invaluable for any attempt to reconstruct the life of the restored Jewish community; however, there are numerous problems involved. The question of whether the biblical order of their work—Ezra preceding Nehemiah—is correct has been a debated and insoluble issue in twentieth-century research. The biblical text dates the beginning of Ezra's activity to the seventh year of the Persian king Artaxerxes (Ezra 7:7) and that of Nehemiah to the twentieth year of Artaxerxes. Many scholars assume that Nehemiah's mission began in the twentieth year of Artaxerxes I (464-424 BCE) while Ezra's should be dated to the time of Artaxerxes II (404-358 BCE). The arguments for this are the following:

(1) Nehemiah rebuilt the walls of Jerusalem (Neh 7) whereas Ezra seems to have found them already reconstructed (Ezra 9:9).

(2) In the memoirs of Nehemiah and Ezra (for Ezra's memoirs, see Ezra 7:27-9:15), both men are seldom mentioned together and where they are the names appear to be editorial additions.

(3) Each exercises his authority and carries out his activities independently.

(4) Nehemiah was contemporary with the high priest Eliashib (Neh 3:1) whereas Ezra was contemporary with Jehohanan (Ezra 10:6), Eliashib's grandson (Neh 12:22).

(5) The Elephantine Papyri (Jewish-Aramaic documents from Egypt dated to the fifth-fourth centuries BCE) mention a Johanan (= Jehohanan) as high priest in Jerusalem in 408 BCE. If this Johanan was a contemporary of Ezra then the latter must be dated to the time of Artaxerxes II.

Any attempted solutions to the problem of the relationship between the persons Ezra and Nehemiah and between I–II Chronicles and Ezra-Nehemiah remain hypothetical. The best hypothesis seems to be that which assigns priority of origin to the Nehemiah memoirs. These were subsequently supplemented by the Ezra material with Ezra given prominence and historical priority over Nehemiah. I–II Chronicles are probably a later and independent work.

Ezra–Nehemiah supply the historian with a historically reliable version of Cyrus' edict allowing the Jews to return to their homeland (Ezra 1:2-4; 6:2-5), lists of the returnees (Ezra 2; Neh 7), and the rescript of Artaxerxes (Ezra 7:12-16) and provide evidence about the struggling Jewish province of Judea and the attempts by Nehemiah and Ezra to revitalize and restructure the community for life in the great Persian empire.

Chapter 7

Israelite Prophecy

P. L. Berger, "Charisma and Religious Innovation: The Social Location of Israelite Prophecy," *ASR* XXVIII(1963)940-50; R.V. Bergren, *The Prophets and the Law* (Cincinnati: Hebrew Union College/Jewish Institute of Religion, 1974); J. Blenkinsopp, *Prophecy and Canon: A Contribution to the Study of Jewish Origins* (Notre Dame: Notre Dame University, 1977); M. J. Buss, *The Prophetic Word of Hosea: A Morphological Study* (Berlin: Alfred Töpelmann, 1969); *idem*, "Prophecy in Ancient Israel," *IDBS*, 694-97; R.E. Clements, *Prophecy and Tradition* (Oxford/Atlanta: Blackwell/John Knox Press, 1975); *idem*, "Patterns in the Prophetic Canon," *CA*, 42-55; *idem*, "Interpreting the Prophets," *COTS*, 51-75; J.L. Crenshaw, *Prophetic Conflict: Its Effect Upon Israelite Religion* (Berlin/New York: Walter de Gruyter, 1971); *idem*, "Prophecy, False," *IDBS*, 701-2; I.Engnell, "Prophets and Prophetism in the Old Testament," in his *A Rigid Scrutiny* (Nashville: Vanderbilt University, 1969) = *Critical Essays on the Old Testament* (London: SPCK, 1969)123-79; H. Gunkel, "The Secret Experiences of the Prophets," *Expositor* IX/1(1924)356-66, 427-35; 2(1924)23-32; *idem*, "The Israelite Prophecy from the Time of Amos," *Twentieth-Century Theology in the Making*, ed. J. Pelikan (London/New York: Collins/Harper & Row, 1969)48-75; A. Heschel, *The Prophets* (New York: Harper & Row, 1962); J.S. Holladay, Jr., "Assyrian Statecraft and the Prophets of Israel," *HTR* LXIII (1970)29-51; H.B. Huffmon, "The Origins of Prophecy," *MD*, 171-86; *idem*, "Prophecy in the Ancient Near East," *IDBS*, 697-700; A.R. Johnson, *The Cultic Prophet in Ancient Israel* (Cardiff: University of Wales, 1944, [2]1962); K. Koch, "From the Prophetic Writings," *GOBT*, 183-220; J. Lindblom, *Prophecy in Ancient Israel* (Oxford/Philadelphia: Blackwell/Fortress Press, 1962); B.O. Long, "Prophetic Authority as Social Reality," *CA*, 3-20; W.E. March, "Prophecy," *OTFC*, 141-77; W.L. Moran, "New Evidence from Mari on the History of Prophecy," *Biblica* L(1969)15-56; S. Mowinckel, " 'The Spirit' and the

'Word' in the Pre-Exilic Reforming Prophets," *JBL* LIII(1934)199-227; *idem*, "The Prophetic Word in the Psalms and the Prophetic Psalms," in his *The Psalms in Israel's Worship* II (Oxford/Nashville: Blackwell/Abingdon Press, 1962)53-73; J. Muilenburg, "The 'Office' of the Prophet in Ancient Israel," *The Bible in Modern Scholarship*, ed. J.P. Hyatt (Nashville: Abingdon Press, 1965)74-97; E.W. Nicholson, *Preaching to the Exiles: A Study of the Prose Tradition in the Book of Jeremiah* (Oxford: Blackwell, 1970); H.M. Orlinsky, "The Seer-Priest," *WHJP* III(1971)268-79, 338-44; G. von Rad, *The Message of the Prophets* (London/New York: SCM Press/Harper & Row, 1968); T.H. Robinson, *Prophecy and the Prophets in Ancient Israel* (London: Duckworth, 1923, ²1953); H.H. Rowley, "Ritual and the Hebrew Prophets," *JSS* I(1956)338-60 = his *From Moses to Qumran: Studies in the Old Testament* (London: Lutterworth Press, 1963)109-38; *idem*, "The Nature of Old Testament Prophecy in the Light of Recent Study," *HTR* XXXVIII(1945)1-38 = his *Servant of the Lord and Other Essays on the Old Testament* (Oxford: Blackwell, ²1965)95-134; J.A. Sanders, "Hermeneutics in True and False Prophecy," *CA*, 21-41; J. Skinner, *Prophecy and Religion: Studies in the Life of Jeremiah* (London: Cambridge University Press, 1922); G.M. Tucker, "Prophetic Superscriptions and the Growth of a Canon," *CA*, 56-70; M. Weber, "Warfare and War Prophecy," in his *Ancient Judaism* (Glencoe, IL:Free Press, 1952) 90-117; C. Westermann, *Basic Forms of Prophetic Speech* (Philadelphia/London:Westminster Press/Lutterworth Press, 1967); J.G. Williams, "The Social Location of Israelite Prophecy," *JAAR* XXXVII(1969)119-30; W. Zimmerli, *The Law and the Prophets: A Study of the Meaning of the Old Testament* (Oxford/New York: Blackwell/Harper Torchbooks, 1965/1967).

T he historical-critical study of the nineteenth century concluded that "the prophets are older than the law and the psalms are later than both" (Eduard Reuss writing in 1881). This attitude catapulted the prophets into the center of attention in the study of the history of Israelite religion (see Zimmerli, 17-30). The prophets were rediscovered as historical persons and their message was freed from the bondage of certain scholarly and pious shackles. Many late nineteenth-century critics no longer understood the prophets either as predictors of events in the distant future or as expounders of the Mosaic law. For the first time, the way was open to interpret the prophets in light of the internal evidence of the prophetical books unemcumbered by assumed religious ideas and institutions which supposedly formed the background for prophecy.

To speak of the prophets as forthtellers rather than foretellers became fashionable. This sentiment finds expression in such statements as the following, written in 1929 by R. H. Charles: "Prophecy is a declaration, a forthtelling, of the will of God—not a foretelling. Prediction is not in any sense an essential element of prophecy, though it may intervene as an accident—whether it be a justifiable accident is another question." (*Critical and Exegetical Commentary on the Book of Daniel*, xxvi)

Rather than being the products or the expounders of tradition, the classical prophets came to be considered creative individuals or religious geniuses. Julius Wellhausen spoke of them in the following fashion:

The prophets have notoriously no father, their importance rests on the individual. . . . representative men are always single, resting on nothing outside themselves. . . . The element in which the prophets live is the storm of the world's history, which sweeps away human institutions; in which the rubbish of past generations with the houses built on it begins to shake, and that foundation alone remains firm, which needs no support but itself. When the earth trembles and seems to be passing away, then they triumph because Jehovah alone is exalted. They do not preach on set texts; they speak out of the spirit which judges all things and itself is judged of no man. Where do they ever lean on any other authority than the truth of what they say; where do they rest on any other foundation than their own certainty? (*Prolegomena to the History of Israel,* 398)

A third characteristic of the new approach to the prophets stressed the ethical quality in their preaching. Prophecy was seen as the pinnacle of Israelite religion since it was the prophets who were the great reformers seeking to bring about a transformation in Israelite faith. The preaching of the prophets was expounded as an ethical idealism which sought to shift religion from a cultic to an ethical orientation. Prophetic faith transcended the earlier subhistorical, semimagical, demonistic, and popular folk Yahwism and placed the relationship between God and people on a purely moral basis.

The prophets were viewed as innovators and initiators of major new impetuses in the religion of Israel. Addressing their contemporaries with moral earnestness, with ethical principles, with anticultic emphases, and with individualistic perspectives, the prophets proclaimed the ethical over against the cultic, the individual as opposed to the communal, the internal versus the external, the universal in opposition to the national, monotheism instead of polytheism, and the historical in place of the natural. The prophets were often viewed as reforming theologians and brave individualists proclaiming the primacy of morality and the indispensibility of a personal relation with God.

If one had asked these nineteenth-century Old Testament scholars how the prophets came to be the teachers and theologians of true religious and ethical values, most would have pointed to the individual prophets' religious experiences. Heinrich Ewald (1803-1875), Wellhausen's teacher, wrote as follows:

There can be no true prophet of Yahweh who has not first viewed the full majesty and holiness of Yahweh himself, and who has thereby become so completely filled with the true

253

eternal life that it now lives on as a new life firmly established in him. *(The Prophets of the Old Testament,* 26)

In a similar vein, Wellhausen wrote:

It belongs to the notion of prophecy, of true revelation, that Jehovah, overlooking all the mass media of ordinances and institutions, communicates Himself to the *individual,* the called one, in whom that mysterious and irreducible rapport in which the deity stands with man clothes itself with energy. Apart from the prophet, *in abstracto,* there is no revelation; it lives in his divine-human ego. *(Prolegomena,* 398)

A. The Prophets and Ecstatic Experience

Focus on the prophet as a creative, inspired individual naturally led to attempted examinations of the personal experience of the prophet and even to efforts at remote psychoanalysis. If the prophets were conceived as isolated and unique personalities proclaiming a message peculiar to themselves, discovered in their lonely solitude, and contrary to the general faith and practice of their contemporaries, then the personal experiences through which they had received revelation and arrived at their beliefs and convictions must be all important. This issue of the prophets' personal and spiritual religious experience came to dominate prophetical research for over a generation (see Rowley, 1965).

Gunkel was one of the first scholars to raise to prominence the issue of religious experience. His dissertation, published in 1888, dealt with the question of the work of the Holy Spirit in the popular thought of the apostolic age and in the teachings of St. Paul. In this work, Gunkel stressed the priority of the spiritual, pneumatic experience over theological formulation in understanding the life and faith of the early church and thus opposed the rationalistic interpretation of early Christianity widely current at the time. This approach brought the irrational, extraordinary experiences of persons into the picture and these were subsequently used in understanding the prophets. Gunkel's views, which found expression in later writings, show many similarities to the interpretations of inspiration and inspired persons found in Plato (*Timaeus*, xxxii) and Philo (*De Specialibus Legibus* IV 49; *Quis Rerum Divinarum Heres* 53). Since Gunkel originally worked in the area of New Testament and early Christian backgrounds, his familiarity with Plato and Philo is entirely possible.

Along with Gunkel, Bernard Duhm (1847-1928), Gustav Hölscher (1877-1955), and others turned to the concept of ecstasy to understand and explain the unusual experience of the prophets and drew upon the developing science of folk psychology as outlined by Wilhelm Wundt (1832-1920). Gunkel argued "that these strange men must ultimately remain unintelligible to us unless we understand these secret experiences" (1924, 356). The prophets were compared to ecstatics known from the general study of the history of religion.

When such an ecstasy seizes him, the prophet . . . loses command of his limbs: he staggers and stutters like a drunken man; his sensitiveness to pain is diminished or suspended: his ordinary sense of what is decent deserts him; he feels an impulse to do all kinds of strange actions and seems to have become insane: a feeling of infinite strength possesses him—he can run and leap more than an ordinary person can do: strange emotions and ideas come over him and mingle with what was already in his mind or what his surroundings present to his senses: he is seized by that sensation of hovering which we know from our own dreams. . . . (Gunkel, 1924, 428)

The British scholar T. H. Robinson (1881-1964) attempted to reconstruct a typical ecstatic experience undergone by a prophet:

We can now call before our minds a picture of the prophet's activity in public. He might be mingling with the crowd,

255

sometimes on ordinary days, sometimes on special occasions. Suddenly something would happen to him. His eye would become fixed, strange convulsions would seize upon his limbs, the form of his speech would change. Men would recognize that the Spirit had fallen upon him. The fit would pass, and he would tell to those around the things which he had seen and heard. There might have been symbolic action, and this he would explain with a clear memory of all that had befallen him, and of all that he had done under the stress of ecstasy. (50)

Evidence to support the argument that the prophets underwent abnormal experiences during which they perceived visions and heard sounds and voices and that they frequently spoke in mysterious and cryptic words was found in numerous Old Testament passages. Prophets associated with Samuel, and Saul who fell among their company, "prophesied" in ways certainly to be understood as unusual behavior (I Sam 10:1-13; 19:18-24). The prophets of Baal on Mt. Carmel mutilated themselves (I Kings 18:28-29; see Zech 13:6), and Elisha was able to prophesy to the accompaniment of music (II Kings 3:14-15). Many prophetical texts refer to visionary experiences and Ezekiel's career is described with frequent references to uncommon experiences and to "spiritual" transportation from one place to another. The Hebrew verb "to prophesy" sometimes suggests "to behave in an uncontrolled manner" and the prophet could be referred to as a "madman" (II Kings 9:11; Hos 9:7; Jer 29:26).

If some prophets in ancient Israel underwent various phenomena characteristic of ecstatic experiences which were sometimes stimulated by rhythmic dancing, music, and other means (drink, Is 28:7; Mic 2:11; perhaps drugs?), does this hold true of all the prophets, especially the so-called classical, or writing, prophets? As a rule, scholars have hesitated to categorize all Old Testament prophets as ecstatics and thus to place them all under the same umbrella. Various ways have been used to distinguish the classical prophets (from Amos on) from their predecessors and contemporaries with regard to the question of ecstasy and abnormal experiences.

(1) One approach argues that the classical prophets must be sharply differentiated from the others who were primarily diviners and thus craftsmen and technicians. "Both the seer [= diviner] and the prophet experienced the phenomenon of ecstasy; they differed only in that the former practiced several recognized techniques to induce it that the latter did not. Unlike the prophet, the seer employed music, dance, and group participation to work himself up into a state of ecstasy, even frenzy." "In general, both the seer-priest and the prophets received directives from God in much the same way, through dreams, objects, and sounds." "The prophet . . . opposed everything that smacked of the seer as a craftsman" (Orlinsky, 269, 270, 272). This position assumes that ecstatic experience (though perhaps different in intensity) was common to classical and nonclassical "prophets," but in the case of the former it was not the product of any technical craft.

(2) The difference between the classical and other prophets has been viewed not in terms of a radical differentiation but in terms of an evolutionary development. Here Gunkel's 1924 article can serve as an example. He argued that "the fundamental experience of all types of prophecy is 'ecstasy' " (358). Gunkel, however, distinguished various stages in prophetic ecstasy paralleling the historical development of prophecy: (a) "The prophets whom Saul meets coming down from the high place [I Sam 10:5-13] are in ecstasy—nothing more is said. We must not ask what sort of oracles they uttered. Such ecstasy had originally no purpose beyond itself: it was in itself regarded as the work of Jahweh" (25). (b) In the evolution of the prophetic movement, ecstasy ceased to be a phenomenon in and of itself and became the means for receiving oracular messages. "The first onward step was when the nebiim [= prophets] were applied to for oracles and gave them. . . . They now become the counsellors of their nation in all their difficulties, great and small" (25). (c) With the classical prophets, ecstatic

experience had become a subordinate phenomenon. "Out of the ranks of such 'prophets' there arose men of a nobler stamp, men of a loftier flight of thought and greater breadth of view" (26). "But even in the great men themselves the wild element is plainly perceptible, although its violence is somewhat less. In accordance with this we must take it that their speech was more rational than the 'crying' of the prophets of the oldest time" (27). "Even their strange experiences, their phantastic visions and their strange symbols are but externals. There is more in them than that. They proclaimed to their day the thoughts of God. . . . It is in this change of content that we find the reason why the vehement element in the outward form of their experiences subsides (although it never disappears), and is replaced by inward experiences which we can understand" (30-31). A similar perspective is represented in the following quote from the British scholar John Skinner (1851-1925):

When we look at prophecy, . . . as a human medium of revelation, we can trace a progressive emancipation of its spiritual essence from the ecstatic or visionary forms in which its earlier manifestations consist. At the lowest stage of prophecy . . . , inspiration and ecstasy are identified. Revelation was an occasional thing; the prophet or seer was a man endowed with a peculiar psychopathic susceptibility to divine suggestion or influence, who delivered his oracles piecemeal as they came to him. His message consists either of words uttered unconsciously in a state of trance, or of an announcement of what he has seen and heard in vision; his conscious mental powers playing no essential part in the process. . . . On the higher level represented by the great prophets of Israel this crude and fragmentary conception of inspiration is left far behind. Visions and auditions, mysterious inward promptings to speech and action, are still a part of the prophet's experience; but the field of revelation is no longer confined to them alone. The meaning of the vision passes into the prophet's thinking, and becomes the nucleus of a comprehensive view of God and the world, from which spring ever fresh intuitions of truth and calls to duty. That these again may clothe themselves involuntarily in symbolic imagery is an act which does not in the least detract from the essentially spiritual character of the prophet's discernment of the mind of God. He reflects upon what he has seen and heard, and interprets its significance to himself and his hearers; and the substance of his revelation is not the mere vision or audition itself but the truth which it has evoked or symbolised in his mind. Thus his reasoning and moral faculties are actively engaged in the discovery and delivery of his message; and all that comes home to him with immediate certainty as the result of his initiation into the divine purpose is as truly the word of God to him as the content of the vision itself. (220-21)

(3) A third approach for distinguishing different prophets from one another points to the consciousness, inspiration, and endowment of the classical prophets. This has been done by Mowinckel in the following manner:

The pre-exilic reforming prophets [Amos, Hosea, Isaiah, Micah, Jeremiah, Zephaniah, Nahum, Habakkuk] never in reality express a consciousness that their prophetic endowment and powers are due to possession by or any action of *the spirit of Yahweh.* . . . There is, on the contrary, another fundamental religious conception upon which the whole of the consciousness and prophetic message rest, *the word of Yahweh.* (1934, 199)

Whereas the reforming prophets emphatically stress the fact that they have received Yahweh's word, and are furnished with religious, rational and moral criteria for knowing what really is his word, they do not derive their power from or authenticate their prophetic call by the conception of Yahweh's rû^{a}h [Spirit], which, in fact, they have rejected, but by their own consciousness of possessing his word. To them this means a word which is authenticated by expressing Yahweh's moral nature and demands, and the prophet's own knowledge of God and moral sense. Yahweh's word resembles Yahweh's law in being recognizable by its content rather than by its form. The test is religious and moral, an "apprehension" or "knowledge" of God—not the ecstatic rû^{a}h and mystic union of divine possession. (1934, 225)

259

The following conclusions can be safely drawn from the research on the psychology and nature of prophetic experience. (1) Abnormality in experiences and activity was characteristic, to lesser or greater degrees, of all Hebrew prophets. (2) The ecstatic and religious experiences of the Israelite prophets are not unique but are typologically similar to those known from diverse cultures and times (see Lindblom). (3) While there are great differences in what the Bible tells us about the classical prophets and their predecessors, no radical differentiation should be made.

A basic continuity between the early prophets such as Ahijah and Elijah and the later prophets should be made quite clear. The prophets continue in their call and in their experience; they continue to be charismatic messengers who announce "thus says the Lord"; they continue to represent the old Yahwistic traditions; they continue to be "seized upon" from a wide variety of everyday stations and roles; and they continue to demonstrate the innovative capacity of the charismatic. That the innovations in understanding, appropriating, and modifying the tradition lead ultimately to new departures in the message does not separate in type the early and the later prophets. (Huffmon, MD, 181)

(4) The ecstasy and the passion of the prophet means that they must be understood more as poets than as philosophers, and this is reflected in the form of their public address. "It accords with such a condition of excitation that the prophet's words, as soon as they pass from stuttering to actual language, automatically take metrical form" (Gunkel, 1924, 365).

B. The Diversity of Prophets in Ancient Israel

Old Testament prophetism clearly possessed a complex and variegated character both in historical and phenomenological categories. This is evident even in the terminology used in the text when speaking of prophets. Four terms—ḥoze, ro'e, nabi, and ish (ha) Elohim—are frequently applied to prophetic figures (see Orlinsky, 342-43). The first two are generally translated as "seer" while the last simply means "man of God." Nabi is the most commonly used term and is the Hebrew word translated "prophet." The significance of two terms for "seer" can no longer be determined, and the phrase "man of God" probably carries no more special connotation than our phrase "a holy man." The term prophet seems to have meant something like "spokesman" (see Ex 4:16; 7:1) or "one who calls/is called," but the etymology here, as frequently, supplies no real aid to understanding the function or office of prophet. Our English word comes from the Greek prophētēs, which means "declarer, interpreter." Several prophetical figures are designated both seer and prophet, and Samuel is referred to as seer, prophet, and man of God. I Sam 9:9 suggests that seer was an earlier title for the prophet although later texts continue to use both terms (see II Kings 17:13, where seer and prophet seem to be distinguished).

In the narratives about early Israelite history, prophets are shown functioning in diverse contexts, sometimes as individuals and sometimes in groups. They are shown as functionaries in warfare, rallying the troops to battle (Judg 4:4-9), assuring the participants of victory, planning military strategy (I Kings 20:13-15), symbolically or orally announcing the defeat of the enemy (I Kings 22:10-12; see Is 37), and pronouncing curses and judgments upon opponents (I Kings 20:28). Times of crisis and threat often produce "a reallocation of social roles and the development of new roles" (Huffmon, MD, 177) and some scholars have seen the early military crisis of the tribes as the context for early prophecy.

As war prophets the Yahwe Nabiim appeared in Northern Israel with the beginning of the National wars, actually religious wars, above all, in the wars of liberation against the uncircumcised Philistines. Ecstatic prophecy obviously made its appearance then though probably not for the first time, but it appeared in all genuine wars of liberation—of which the first was the Deborah war. This prophecy at first had nothing to do with any sort of "prediction" . . ., but its business was, as with Deborah, the "mother of Israel," the incitement to crusade, promise of victory, and ecstatic victory magic. (Weber, 97)

The connection of some prophets with warfare and strong nationalistic sentiment seems to have continued throughout Israelite and Judean history.

Prophets are also depicted as being closely associated with the royal court where they served as court advisers, assisting in the determination of the will of the deity and providing divine sanction for policies of state. The classical court prophet in the Old Testament is Nathan, whose career overlapped the reigns of David and Solomon. Gad is said to have been both David's seer and prophet (I Sam 22:5; II Sam 24:11; I Chron 21:9; 29:29; II Chron 29:25). The king and prophet often consulted one another (II Sam 12:1-15; I Kings 20:41-42; II Kings 3:11; Is 7:3-9; 38:1-8; Jer 37:16-17; 38:14-16). Groups of prophets are sometimes associated with the court (I Kings 18:19; 22:6).

Some prophets were connected with sanctuaries. I Sam 10:5-8 mentions prophets coming from the "high place with harp, tambourine, flute, and lyre before them, prophesying." Samuel was pictured as a seer presiding over sacrificial meals (I Sam 9:11-14) and prophets could be consulted on special, holy days (II Kings 4:18-25).

Early prophets are shown operating as individuals and as groups. A band of prophets encountered Saul at Gibeah (I Sam 10:5-13) and a similar group was associated with Samuel at Ramah (I Sam 19:18-24). Elijah and Elisha are described as "father" to a company of "sons of the prophets" (II Kings 2:3; 4:38; 6:1-2) which seems to have lived a communal existence centered in various places (Bethel, II Kings 2:3; Jericho, II Kings 2:5; Gilgal, II Kings

4:38). Such groups may have formed guilds with membership denoted by special marks or clothing (I Kings 20:35-43; II Kings 1:8; 2:23-24).

This diversity of prophets is paralleled in references from ancient near eastern texts which speak of "prophetic" figures. The earliest of such references appear in about thirty letters addressed to the king of Mari, located on the upper Euphrates river, dating from the eighteenth century BCE (see Moran, Huffmon, and *ANET*, 623-25, 629-32). The correspondence, written by royal officials to the king Zimri-Lim, report on "prophetic" figures who primarily deliver messages for the king (see II Chron 21:12). Some of these figures bear titles; others were apparently "lay" persons, both males and females (see Judg 4:4; II Kings 22:14) are included, and sometimes groups of such figures are noted. The two most common titles used to designate those figures are *āpilu/āpiltu*, "answerer, respondent," and *muhhu/muhhūtu*, "ecstatic." As a rule, these persons delivered their oracles in cultic services, however, in some cases it seems the message was proclaimed outside the cult. Since the letters preserved are royal correspondence, the prophetic messages are addressed to the king although two contain oracles spoken to the people. Some of the messages are critical of the king for his failure to perform certain duties and some contain commands addressed to the monarch; however, the majority are favorable to the ruler. Some of the messages were clearly unsolicited. Various gods are quoted as the sources of the messages and sometimes the speakers refer to dreams as the means of divine revelation. The prophetic figures frequently refer to the divine commission to make their proclamations and the letters assume that the king was expected to take their messages seriously.

Other texts include one from the Old Babylonian period from Uruk (see *ANET*, 604), a fourteenth-century Hittite text (see *ANET*, 394-96), an Egyptian text noting an eleventh-century Canaanite ecstatic (see *ANET*, 26), the eighth-century Aramaic text from Zakir (see *ANET*,655-

56), and various texts from the Assyrian period (see *ANET*, 605-6; 625-26; and Huffmon, *MD*, 175-76). In these texts, the spokesmen are referred to with titles completely different from the Mari texts. A number of Egyptian texts contain statements of major social critique, denunciations, and exhortations, similar in many ways to Old Testament prophetic preaching; but these are not delivered as the word of any deity or under the sense of any stated special divine commission (see *ANET*, 407-10, 441-46).

The association of prophets with various Israelite institutions, the diversity of Old Testament prophetic figures, and comparative near eastern materials have raised an issue which has been widely discussed in recent research: Were prophets an established part of the cultic personnel in ancient Israel? A secondary problem related to this issue is the question of whether or not any or all of the classical prophets were members of the sanctuary staff (on prophets and the cult, see Berger and Rowley, 1963).

Wellhausen had already argued in the nineteenth century that the prophetic and priestly functions in early Israel were closely related and that prophets and priests were closely associated.

There is . . . a close relation between priests and prophets, *i.e.*, seers; as with other peoples (I Sam vi.2; I Kings xviii.19, compare with 2 Kings x.19), so also with the Hebrews. In the earliest time it was not knowing the technique of worship, which was still very simple and undeveloped, but being a *man of God*, standing on an intimate footing with God, that made a man a priest, that is one who keeps up the communication with heaven for others; and the seer is better qualified than others for the office (I Kings xviii.30 seq.). There is no fixed distinction in early times between the two offices; Samuel is in I Sam i.-iii. an aspirant to the priesthood; in ix.x. he is regarded as a seer.

In later times also, when priests and prophets drew off and separated from each other, they yet remained connected, both in the kingdom of Israel (Hos. iv.5) and in Judah. In the latter this was very markedly the case (2 Kings xxiii.2; Jer. xxvi.7 seq., v.

31; Deut. xviii.1-8, 9-22; Zech. vii.3). What connected them with each other was the revelation of Jehovah which went on and was kept alive in both of them. It is Jehovah from whom the torah of the priest and the word of the prophet proceeds. . . . This explains how both priests and prophets claimed Moses for their order. . . . *(Prolegomena,* 396-97)

As a rule, late nineteenth and early twentieth century scholarship understood the priests and the prophets, priestly and prophetic religion, in strongly antithetical terms. Paul Volz (1871-1941), writing in 1938, declared:

Old Testament religion, the religion of the prophets, is a religion of the Word. Because of this, the religion of the Old Testament prophets stands in sharpest contrast to the religion of the priests, to cult religion. The religion of the priests is a religion of sacrifice. The priest carries the gifts of men up towards God. The religion of the prophets is a religion of the Word. It brings the voice of God down to men, the voice that creates life and that one must obey. While the cultic ritual is rigid, often remains the same for centuries and sometimes smothers new seeds of faith like a firm blanket, the Word is alive, acting, creating. (translated in Berger, 944)

Such a view of prophetism, as the Protestantism of antiquity, would scarcely see prophets and priests as cooperative functionaries working together in the same religious and cultic institution.

The theory of cultic prophets in ancient Israel has been most convincingly argued by Sigmund Mowinckel and A. R. Johnson. The following arguments are advanced by them.

(1) In early Israel, the difference between priest and prophet was not very great since both responded to inquiries, offered instruction, and performed "sacramental" (representing men before God) and "sacrificial" (representing God to men) functions.

The role of the priest was . . . a dual one. He was not only the

265

Yahweh's spokesman. At the same time, . . . such divine knowledge as he possessed was derived either from a form of divination or from his training in the accumulated experience of the past. (Johnson, 8-9)

The early *nabi* or 'prophet' . . . had at least this much in common with the priest (including the Levite) and the seer: he was consulted for the sake of securing oracular guidance. (Johnson, 25)

The intercessory aspect of the prophet's role has been more or less overlooked. Yet it is undoubtedly true that the . . . 'prophet,' as a professional figure was as much the representative of the people as the spokesman of Yahweh; it was part of his function to offer prayer as well as to give the divine response or oracle. (Johnson, 60)

The role of the prophet as intercessor is suggested by a number of passages (Gen 20:3,7; I Kings 18:41-46; II Kings 6:17; Jer 37:3; 42:1-4; Amos 7:1-6; see Mowinckel, 1962, 62-63).

(2) Prophets are frequently closely related to the priests and the temple, especially in Jerusalem. Elijah, like the prophets of Baal, offers sacrifices (I Kings 18:20-40). That priests and prophets are frequently mentioned together suggests that at least some prophets were cultic personnel (Jer 23:11; 26:7,16; 27:16; 29:26; Lam 2:20; Zech 7:1-3). Prophets associated with the sanctuary served under the supervision and jurisdiction of the priests (Mowinckel, 56; see Jer 29:26) or with a status "at least as high as, if not actually higher than, that of the priests" (Johnson, 63; see Jer 5:30-31).

(3) The cultic prophets were later absorbed into a subordinate order of the Levites as temple singers but still possessed the power of prophecy (compare II Kings 23:2 with II Chron 34:30; see I Chron 25:1-6; II Chron 20:13-19; 29:30; 35:5). According to Johnson, the cultic prophets lost their prestige and status because they continued to proclaim peace and good times in face of the Babylonian threat and were thus proved false (according to the rule of

Deut 18:22) when foreign armies overran Jerusalem and the people were subjected to exile. The cultic prophets were then "brought into definite subjection to the priesthood—and so disappeared" (75; see 66-76).

(4) Mowinckel pointed to the divine speeches and oracles in the psalms as further evidence of prophetic functions within the cult.

> It is very possible that the ritual . . . would provide that at a certain point the prophet was to announce Yahweh's answer to the prayer, and that the substance of the answer was prescribed by the ritual, whereas wording and composition were left to the free and instantaneous inspiration of the prophet. But it is just possible that even the wording of the promise would be prescribed by the ritual, as is the case with, for instance, the formula of absolution in present-day divine services. (1962, 57)

Mowinckel argued that prophetic oracles were spoken to the worshiper(s) during rituals of national and personal lament (see Pss 12:6; 60:8-10; 108:8-10; 91:14-16) and the coronation of Davidic rulers and other royal occasions (Pss 2; 20; 21; 45; 89; 110; 132). Others were used during the great festivals (Pss 50; 81; 95).

The concept of cultic prophets has been subsequently expanded by some scholars to argue that even the canonical prophets were actually cultic prophets and thus members of prophetic guilds. The Swedish scholar, Alfred Haldar, has argued that in Mesopotamian cultures there were two classes of diviners, the bārū and mahhū. The former, which corresponds to the Hebrew "seer," divined through technical means while the latter, which corresponds to the Hebrew "prophet," received oracles in a state of ecstasy. These groups in Israel as in Mesopotamia were organized into corporations centered around the sanctuaries. Going even farther, one scholar has recently argued that Amos was a hepatoscoper, one skilled in using livers to divine oracles (see Rowley, 163, 122-23).

Haldar and others have utilized a comparative approach to the question of prophecy and cult (see Berger and Williams). A different method has been followed by some scholars who interpret the prophets against the background of an annual or periodic renewal of the Sinai covenant in the Israelite cult (see Clements, 1975, 8-23). In the original making of the covenant at Sinai, Moses fulfilled the role of covenant mediator. In the festival of covenant renewal, it is assumed that the role of Moses was taken by the prophetic spokesman—the covenant mediator—who proclaimed, interpreted, and applied the covenant law to the community and announced judgments against the people in the form of covenant lawsuits. This assumes that the prophets occupied an "office" like that of other regular offices in Israel. Some scholars even speak of a succession of prophets who filled the office of covenant mediator. A moderate position on the issue is reflected by Muilenburg.

It does not seem to me to be out-running the evidence to say that there were indeed prophets like Moses [see Deut 18:18]; Yahweh's messengers, his covenant mediators, intercessors for the people, speakers for God. They are sent from the divine King [Yahweh], the suzerain of the treaties, to reprove and to pronounce judgment upon Israel for breach of covenant. . . . So today we no longer speak of Moses or the prophets, or of the law or prophecy, but rather of Moses and the prophets. (97; see also Bergren)

Those who advocate a close relationship between prophets and priests break with one of the central pillars of older prophetical research: the assumption that the prophets totally condemned cultic religion (see Amos 5:21-24; Hos 6:6; Is 1:10-17; Mic 6:6-8; Jer 6:20; 7:21-26).

The denunciation of public worship as practised in the sanctuaries of their time had always been a prominent feature in the preaching of the pre-exilic prophets. . . . Ancient worship culminated in animal sacrifice, and apart from sacrificial worship religion could not exist. . . . The bond uniting the deity and his worshippers was conceived as a physical one, and nothing was needed to keep it intact save the due observance of the stated ritual. Morality might be important, and transgressions of the divinely appointed order might be punished by judgments more or less severe; but the threatened breach could always be healed, and the anger of the god appeased, by enhanced zeal in the performance of sacrificial rites. . . . [For the prophets] not only is sacrifice of no avail as a substitute for religious conduct, but a perfect religious relationship is possible without sacrifice at all. . . . Sacrifice, therefore, is no necessary term of communion between Yahwe and Israel: it does not belong to the essence of religion. And that the principle extends to the cultus in general . . . is strongly suggested by the fact that they never demand a purified ritual, but always and exclusively the fulfillment of the ethical commands of Yahwe. (Skinner, 178-81)

How radically interpretations have changed can be seen in the following statement of Engnell:

No fundamental declarations of anti-cultic principle are to be found in the prophets, no matter how diligently scholars persist in their attempts to find them. In an unprejudiced, true exegesis, which takes the context of the sayings into consideration, it is evident that, in reality, these so-called anti-cultic sayings refer to special cases: they are directed either against certain definite forms of the cult (foreign types, or types which claim to be Yahwistic but are not acknowledged as such by the prophet in question—which first of all is true of all North Israelite cults without exception), or against a cult whose advocates are incriminated in one way or other, especially in their inferior ethical and social practices. The polemical sayings which have been interpreted as essentially anti-cultic (for example, Amos 5:21ff.; Hos. 6:6; Isa. 1:11ff.; Jer 7:21ff.) fall into one of these categories. (139)

Many passages within the prophetical books and regulations in Deuteronomy testify to controversy and conflict among various prophets in ancient Israel. The first appearance of such conflict is found in the narrative of I Kings 22 where the prophet Micaiah prophesies differently from four hundred prophets and attributes their message to an evil spirit sent from Yahweh (I Kings 22:19-23; see Ez 14:9). Many of the canonical prophets denounce other prophets, accusing them of leading the people astray: by prophesying for money (Mic 3:5-6,11; Ez 13:19), by lying (Is 9:15; Jer 8:10; 14:14; and elsewhere), by proclaiming visions of their hearts (Ez 13:2; 22:28), by preaching peace when there is no peace (Ez 13:10; Jer 6:14; and elsewhere), by not having "stood" in Yahweh's council (Jer 23:18), by having no divine commission (Jer 29:8-9; 14:14; and elsewhere), by prophesying in the name of Baal (Jer 2:8; 5:31; 23:13; 32:32-35), by practicing sorcery (Ez 13:1-7), and so on (see Crenshaw, 1971, 1-4). In several passages, where the canonical prophets speak against their prophetic opponents, the Greek translators used *pseudoprophētēs* to render the Hebrew *nabi*. This has led to speaking of these opponents of the classical prophets as "false prophets."

The canonical prophets and Deuteronomy sought to lay down certain criteria by which one could know which prophet spoke the genuine word of Yahweh (see Crenshaw, 49-61). Some criteria focused on the message and its mode of receipt: it must come from Yahweh and not other gods (Deut 13:1-5), the word must be fulfilled (Deut 18:22; Jer 28:9) it must not be the result of dreams or visions (Jer 23:25-28), and the message must not delude the people (Jer 13:10; 28:8). Other criteria focused on the character and person of the prophet: the prophet must not be immoral (Jer 23:14; Is 28:7), must not prophesy for money (Mic 3:5-6; Ez 13:19), and must have experienced genuine revelation and been privy to Yahweh's council (Jer 23:18, 21-22).

Various attempts have been made to identify and/or to characterize the antagonists of the classical prophets (see Crenshaw and Sanders). They have been seen as ecstatics, as professional *nebiim*, as Zionist and nationalistic spokesmen, as cultic personnel, as sounding boards of popular opinion, as pro-establishment propagandists, and as persons who failed to meet any or all of the above noted criteria. More recent study has suggested the following about these prophets. (1) An evaluation of them as false prophets is based on the designation of the canonical prophets as true prophets. (2) Those prophets who preached peace and nationalism in the final days of Judah, for example Jeremiah's opponents, were proven wrong and unrealistic by the course of historical events. (3) The opponents of the classical prophets were probably perceived by their contemporaries as having the same (or better) credentials as the canonical prophets, perhaps drew upon the same theological traditions, and used similar forms of address.

What constituted the difference between the classical prophets and their opponents? Obviously the difference was one of degree rather than kind: the classical prophets employed a radically different hermeneutic from their opponents—they "read" the earlier traditions (texts) and the contemporary situations (contexts) and perceived a radically distinct understanding of God and his relationship to his people.

> What seems quite clear is that the so-called false prophets did not refer, in times of threat, to God as God also of the enemy. Such an affirmation of God the creator of all peoples is a part of the canonical monotheizing process . . . to which, apparently, the so-called false prophets did not, like the true prophets, consciously contribute. (Sanders, 40)

The most dramatic of the prophetical conflicts is narrated in Jeremiah 28. In this chapter, Jeremiah and Hananiah are shown debating the issue of the length of the exile. Sanders comments on the difference between the two prophets:

> If the message of Hananiah as prophet can be viewed also as applying authoritative tradition to the context that he and Jeremiah both faced, the debate takes on a dimension beyond

271

what has so far been suggested in studies on it. If he used the traditions of "form" in delivering his message, as has often been noted, might he not also have used the traditions of "text"? Those who transmitted the record of the debate to the literary form we inherit in Jeremiah 28 do not suggest reference to authoritative "text" tradition. But with the constitutive hermeneutic of God as redeemer and sustainer with emphasis on his grace, he might well have preached in the following manner: "Thus says the Lord of hosts, the God of Israel [who brought Israel up out of Egypt, guided it in the wilderness, and brought it into this land]: I have broken the yoke of the king of Babylon. Within two years I will bring back to this place all the . . . " (Jer 28:2-3 with insertion). He might have said, in the debate, "Jeremiah, it is a question of having faith in God that he is powerful enough to keep his promises. He is not whimsical. He who brought us out of Egypt and into this land is strong enough to keep us here. It is a matter of firm belief in his providence and sustaining power." And Jeremiah, upon returning with the iron yoke, might have said, "Hananiah, he who brought us out of Egypt and into this land is strong enough *and free enough* to take us out of here. It is a matter of belief in God not only as redeemer and sustainer, but also as creator of all." (38-39)

That major distinctions must be drawn between the judgmental and classical prophets from the eighth century onward and their opponents and contemporaries seems clear. To determine the basis upon which such distinctions rested is difficult if not impossible. Some interpreters have pointed to the experiences of the prophets which gave them an empathic identity with God (so Heschel). Sanders has spoken of the classical prophets' participation in the monotheizing process and reliance upon a view of God as creator. Von Rad viewed the prophets as engaging in a dialogue with older Israelite traditions in light of the new events which they saw already on the horizon. Gunkel, Mowinckel, and others have pointed to the more reflective and penetrating character of the content of the classical prophets' preaching. Holladay has seen the shift in Assyrian statecraft—from a policy of dealing with subordinate rulers to dealing with the populace as a whole—as the basis for the rise of a class of prophets that condemned the entire nation. Perhaps not one but several of these factors were influential in the rise of the classical prophets with their messages of radical divine judgment. They certainly appeared on the scene when Israel and Judah were confronted with major stress and were at the point of being sucked into the maelstrom of international affairs. Years ago, Wellhausen wrote:

There had subsisted in Palestine and Syria a number of petty kingdoms and nationalities, which had their friendships and enmities with one another, but paid no heed to anything outside their own immediate environment, and revolved, each on its own axis, careless of the outside world, until suddenly the Assyrians burst in upon them. These commenced the work which was carried on by the Babylonians, Persians, and Greeks, and completed by the Romans. They introduced a new factor, the conception of the world—the world of course in the historical sense of that expression. In presence of that conception the petty nationalities lost their centre of gravity, brute force dispelled their illusions, they flung their gods to the moles and to the bats (Isa. ii). The prophets of Israel alone did not allow themselves to be taken by surprise by what had occurred, or to be plunged in despair; they solved by anticipation the grim problem which history set before them. They absorbed into their religion that conception of the world which was destroying the religions of the nations, even before it had been fully grasped by the secular consciousness. Where others saw only the ruin of everything that is holiest, they saw the triumph of Jehovah over delusion and error. Whatever else might be overthrown, the really worthy remained unshaken. (*Prolegomena*, 472-73)

C. The Forms of Prophetic Speech

Although the classical prophets are referred to as the writing prophets, it has been widely recognized that they were primarily speakers and not authors. Gunkel was one of the first scholars to attempt a systematic analysis of the forms of prophetic address (see above, chapter four, section D). He argued that the basic prophetic speech consisted of a threat, which proclaimed a coming act of judgment, and a reproach, which explicated the reason for the judgment.

Gunkel's analysis has been criticized, especially his choice of terminology (Westermann, 64-70, and Koch, 191-94), and attempts have been made to outline more definitely the basic prophetic forms of address. Developing the concept of the prophet as divine messenger, a point already stressed by Gunkel, Westermann has outlined the basic judgment speech as follows (using Amos 7:16-17 as example):

A. The reason for the judgment
   or Accusation: You say, "Do not prophesy against Israel, and do not preach against the house of Isaac."

B. Messenger Formula: Therefore thus says the Lord:

C. Announcement
   of Judgment: "Your wife shall be a harlot in the city, and your sons and your daughters shall fall by the sword, and your land shall be parceled out by line; you, yourself shall die in an unclean land, and Israel shall surely go into exile from its land."

According to Westermann, this form could be expanded in various ways. The following illustrates its more complex development (using Micah 2:1-4 as an example):

A. Reason for the Judgment
   1. Accusation   Woe to those who devise wickedness and work evil

		upon their beds! When the morning dawns, they perform it, because it is in the power of their hand.
2.	Development of the Accusation	They covet fields, and seize them; and houses and take them away; they oppress a man and his house, a man and his inheritance.

B. Messenger Formula: Therefore thus says the Lord

C. Announcement of Judgment

1.	Intervention of God	Behold, against this family I am devising evil, from which you cannot remove your necks; and you shall not walk haughtily, for it will be an evil time.
2.	Results of the Intervention	In that day they shall take up a taunt song against you, and wail with bitter lamentation, and say, "We are utterly ruined; he changes the portion of my people; how he removed it from me! Among our captors he divides our fields."

Westermann assumes that the simpler form was characteristic of the prophetic judgment-speech addressed to individuals (see his discussion, 129-63). The more complex form was a later development of the announcement of judgment against the individual and was addressed to the nation or major groups within the nation (169-89).

Westermann offers an alternative to Gunkel's terminology because he feels that Gunkel's term "threat" does not adequately characterize what the prophet said since a "threat" suggests a conditional speech or should contain conditional elements. These conditional elements do not appear, and therefore "threat" does not reflect the nonconditional prophetic address with its note of finality. Likewise, the term "reproach" is considered too weak to represent the judgmental charge with which the prophet accuses his audience.

Koch has criticized Westermann's interpretation of the prophets as messengers of God since they are never so designated and because the general messenger speech which consists of (1) the messenger formula, (2) an indication of a pressing situation, (3) the wish of the sender, and (4) a concluding characterization does not parallel what Westermann outlines as the prophetic speech of judgment. Instead, Koch proposes to speak of the prediction of disaster which has the following structure:

A. *An indication* of the situation (or diatribe/reproach): "Here the religious, social or political situation is set out, and also the relationship between God and those for whom the prophecy is intended" (211). See II Kings 1:16; Jer 29:25,31.

B. *Prediction of disaster (or threat):* This "comprises the real substance of the prophecy" and speaks of the coming disaster, the intervention of God, and the consequences of the intervention (211-12). See II Kings 1:4; Jer 36:30; 28:16; and so on.

C. *Concluding characterization:* This "is the shortest part of the saying, rounding off the prophecy" (212). See II Kings 1:4, Jer 28:4.

For Koch, the prophecy of salvation has a similar structure (213-15): (1) indication of the present situation (which may be an exhortation: Jer 33:3; I Kings 11:31; II Kings 3:16; 4:43), (2) prediction of salvation or promise (Jer 28:3; 32:37; 33:6; 34:4-5), and (3) concluding characterization (Jer 28:4; 32:44; 34:5; 39:18).

The work of Gunkel and the criticisms and alternatives offered by Westermann and Koch point to a basic quandary of form-critical research on prophetic speech: there is no consistent, clearly definable structure to prophetical address which can be applied in a majority of cases. Those units of speech which conform to the patterns of Westermann and Koch are the exception more than the rule. Gunkel felt that the threat was proclaimed as the word of Yahweh, while the reproach was the prophet's word giving the reasons for the judgment. Even such a general scheme as this falls to the ground since frequently "reproaches" are presented as the word of God and sometimes the threat speaks of Yahweh in the third person. Even to distinguish between divine and human word in the prophets as separate genres is impossible (see Buss, 1969, 65).

The following generalizations may be made about prophetic speech. (1) The prophets addressed their contemporaries with words which spoke about the future. (2) The word about the future was generally proclaimed as a word of God and was announced in the first person. (3) The word about the future might be either negative—announcing judgment, disaster, or punishment—or positive—announcing hope and salvation. (4) The negative word about the future was generally grounded in wrongs related to the sinful condition of the individual, the group, or the nation: God's future negative action was proclaimed as divine reaction to a human predicament. (5) The positive word about the future was not grounded in or anchored to human activity: "The prospect presented therein is not the future arising from man but an occurrence based in God" (Buss, 1969, 126).

D. The Origin of Prophetical Books

The prophetical books of the Old Testament claim to present us with the words of Yahweh which came to the prophets and which they addressed to ancient Israel and Judah (see the superscriptions to the books and the discussion of these by Tucker). The process by which the prophecies, delivered in oral form, came to be written down as well as the final composition of the prophetical books are matters on which only very tentative and hypothetical observations can be given.

The prophetical books contain a variety of literary materials: reports, speeches, and prayers. The reports may be subdivided into several types of material: (1) superscriptions which provide the opening verse or verses to the books, (2) brief notations which sometime specify the time and place of a prophetic experience or address (for example, Is 2:1; 13:1; Jer 21:1; Zech 7:1), and (3) various forms of narratives. The narratives may be stories about the prophets (Amos 7:10-17; Jer 26), sometimes reporting symbolic acts which they performed (Is 20; Jer 19), or first person accounts about prophetic activity (Hosea 3; Amos 7:1-9; 8:1-3). Many of these narratives also contain speeches by the prophets as part of the accounts. Other narratives report what has been designated the "call to the prophetic vocation" (Is 6; Jer 1:4-10; Ez 1-3). The prayers designate those prophetical words addressed directly to the deity such as Amos 7:2,5; Is 6:11; Hab 3; and the so-called complaints of Jeremiah (11:8-23; 12:1-6; 15:10-21; 17:12-18; 18:18-23; 20:7-18).

This vast array of material in the prophetical books, plus the fact that the books frequently do not appear to be structured in either a chronological or logical order, raises the question of how the books came into being. Older scholarship sought to analyze this problem along literary critical lines similar to those involved in pentateuchal studies (see Robinson, 50-59). Generally three stages were postulated for the process. (1) There was initially the preaching of the prophet in short, oral sayings which were handed down by his hearers or followers and combined into small collections and written down. During this phase of development, autobiographical material may have been written down or dictated by the prophet himself while biographical material was transmitted by the disciples or close followers of the prophet. This material about the prophet was put in writing and sometimes combined with written speech material to comprise small collections or booklets. Stage one therefore saw material move from an oral form to written collections. (2) The second phase witnessed the combining of the individual small collections. Units were combined on the bases of various principles: similarity of subject matter, catchwords, and theological outlook. At this stage, original sayings were sometimes given a new application or twist due to the editorial process or contemporary needs and interests. At this stage, additional material was added which frequently spoke of a restored people and a good future to come. (3) The final phase in the process saw the collections viewed and treated as books by editorial redactors at which time further materials may have been added from diverse sources. It has been generally assumed that the process reflected in these three stages may have involved a time span of decades or even centuries.

A frontal assault on this "literary" approach to the origin of the prophetical books was launched, especially by several Scandanavian scholars (see Knight, RTI, 215-59). Several arguments underlie this traditio-historical (or history of tradition) approach. (1) Literary criticism subjects the prophetical writings to a "modern anachronistic book-view, coupled with a doctrinaire evolutionistic outlook, and the literary analytical method, with its essentially negative attitude toward the distrust of the tradition" (Engnell, 169). (2) The prophetic traditions like most near eastern literature were originally transmitted orally among circles of traditionalists whose origins go back to the prophets themselves. (3) "Essentially, this oral transmission does not endanger the stability and 'intactness' of the tradition. On the whole, in the ancient Near East, oral tradition is not an inferior form of tradition involving great risks for the tradition material. Actually, the situation is just the opposite. And this is true very *especially of the literature of the Old Testament, . . . "* (Engnell, 168-69). (4) The fidelity of the oral tradition process, however, can assume "that a certain living transformation of the tradition . . . is inescapable and self-evident. But we must assume that this transformation did not affect fundamental matters and that it was not of any radical nature whatsoever, although, during the period of transmission, the material may have been gradually expanded in different contexts" (Engnell, 169). (5) Since the original words of the prophets and the minor contributions of the traditionalists have been interwoven, "it is also fundamentally incorrect to make the systematic separation of the *ipsissima verba* of the prophet—the words from the master's own mouth—from the secondary material *the basis of the critical scientific approach*, or to evaluate the material according to this standard" (Engnell, 169). (6) As a rule, many advocates of the traditio-historical approach agree that the fixation of the material in written form was a late—perhaps exilic and later—phenomenon. Some scholars, like Engnell (163-69), assume that this oral process was not operative with all the prophetical materials. For example, he considers some prophetical writings, such as Joel, Habakkuk, Nahum, and Second-Isaiah, to have been artistic works originally produced in written form.

Obviously, the origin of the prophetical books is a major problem which can perhaps never be completely illuminated or reconstructed (see Lindblom, 220-91 and Blenkinsopp, 96-123). The following points about the process seem noteworthy. (1) No single pattern of development which eventuated in the prophetical books can be applied to all the prophetical traditions. Some works, such as Isaiah and Micah, seem to have been the products of a much longer and more complex process than others. (2) The collection and writing down of prophetic traditions probably already began, in some cases, during the lifetime of the prophet (see Is 8:16-17; 30:8; Jer 36). (3) Some prophetical works, such as Nahum and Joel, may have existed in written form from the beginning. (4) The inclusion of narrative material and vocation reports in the prophetic books was one way of claiming authority for the prophet and the status of revelation for his words by appeal to divine commission (which may have already been a factor during the prophet's ministry), by appeal to patterns of prophetic behavior, and by appeal to the criterion of fulfillment (see Long). (5) The prophetical traditions were understood as a living word of God which could be reapplied and reinterpreted to address new and changing situations. Sometimes this reinterpretation was achieved through the additions of words which expanded the application of the text—for example, the addition of Judah to oracles originally addressed to Israel. Sometimes, entire pericopes were incorporated—for example, the Judah oracle in Amos 2:4-5. Especially in the case of Jeremiah, "the book represents subtantially the final literary expression and deposit of a tradition which grew and developed at the hands of a body of people who sought not only to transmit the prophet's sayings but to present an interpretation of his prophetic ministry and preaching on the basis of theological concerns and interests which were of vital importance for them in the age in which they lived. Such a tradition would have emerged and evolved not at the hands of individual authors and editors, but within the context of an active preaching and teaching ministry which addressed itself to a listening audience . . . . " (Nicholson, 4) (6) The inclusion and editing of prophetical traditions frequently reflect the understanding of prophecy which came to characterize Hebrew thought especially in the so-called deuteronomistic circles (see Clements, 1977). This understanding of prophecy finds expression in the deuteronomic criterion of fulfillment (see Deut 18:22) as well as the deuteronomistic assessment of the prophetic function and evaluation of the people's fatal history:

Yet Yahweh warned Israel and Judah by every prophet and every seer, saying, "Turn from your evil ways and keep my commandments and my statutes, in accordance with all the law which I commanded your fathers, and which I sent to you by my servants the prophets." But they would not listen, but were stubborn, as their fathers had been, who did not believe in Yahweh their God. They despised his statutes, and his covenant that he made with their fathers, and the warnings which he gave them . . . . (II Kings 17;13-15)

This theological perspective was not dominated by a pessimistic view of the past but was motivated by an optimistic hope for the future (see Deut 30:1-10). Even the judgmental prophets and their warnings could be seen as contributing to this hope. The classical prophets, in this light, were seen not just as spokesmen of judgment but as harbingers of hope: they not only "revealed what was to occur at the end of time, and the hidden things before they came to pass" (Sirach 48:25) but they also "comforted those who mourned in Zion" (48:24); "they comforted the people of Jacob and delivered them with confident hope" (49:10). Thus most of the prophetical books are edited so as to have the prophet's last word be a word of hope.

E. Summary Remarks on Prophecy

In concluding this rather brief discussion of basic issues and problems in understanding the prophets, a few general statements seem in order (see Buss, 1969, 116-29). (1) Prophecy must be understood as one element among others in the larger whole of the religious and social culture of the ancient Hebrews. Prophecy functioned as a complement to priestly tradition and wisdom (Jer 18:18) and is not fully understandable when isolated from the other components of Israelite life. (2) Prophecy is closely related to priestly functions and tradition in that both place emphasis on divine revelation. Thus prophetic speech and thought are closely related to priests and cult, and prophecy as a phenomenon no doubt had roots in and close ties to the cult.

Prophecy shares with priestly tradition a heavy emphasis on divine revelation, expressed stylistically by Yahweh's speaking in the first person. It differs from priestly word in that the priest presents above all the traditions of the sacred past which are believed to have general significance for Israelite life, while the prophet responds basically to particular situations. Since the priestly tradition is foundational, it forms the framework within which the prophet operates; in this sense, the content of the priest's word stands normally above the prophet's. (Buss, *IDBS*, 694)

Priestly functions dealt with human existence in light of a sacral understanding of existence based on past revelation, sacred practice, and routine conditions, and sought to provide salvation and peace through routine and regularized ritual. Prophecy, addressed to unique situations, demanded radical decision and action in light of a crisis assessment of existence. The classical prophets "saw present evil active in such a way that it culminates in doom still to come; in other words, they see an operation of evil even without being required to do so by circumstances" (Buss, 1969, 119). (3) Although the prophets could present their message infused with the rhetoric of persuasion, as in the case of Deutero-Isaiah, their address was generally in the form of divine or dogmatic announcements. Even this form of proclamation, with its strong denunciatory style and fate-creating intent, should be seen against the general principle that "the prophetic message by nature intends to awaken and arouse, to call the people of God back from their perverse ways" (Westermann, 11).

CHAPTER 8

THE PSALMS

B. W. Anderson, *Out of the Depths: The Psalms Speak for Us Today* (Philadelphia: Westminster Press, 1974); C. Barth, *Introduction to the Psalms* (Oxford/New York: Blackwell/Scribner's, 1966); H. Birkeland, *The Evildoers in the Book of Psalms* (Oslo: Jacob Dybwad, 1955); W. Brueggemann, "From Hurt to Joy, From Death to Life," *Int* XXVIII (1974)3-19; M. Buttenweiser, *The Psalms: Chronologically Treated with a New Translation* (Chicago: University of Chicago, 1938; reissued with a "Prolegomenon" by N. M. Sarna, New York: KTAV, 1969); B. W. Childs, "Psalms Titles and Midrashic Exegesis," *JSS* XVI(1971)131-50; *idem*, "Reflections on the Modern Study of the Psalms," *MD*, 377-88; R. E. Clements, "Interpreting the Psalms," *COTS*, 76-98; D. J. A. Clines, "Psalm Research Since 1955," *TB* XVIII(1967)103-26; XX(1969)105-25; P. Drijvers, *The Psalms: Their Structure and Meaning* (New York: Herder & Herder, 1965); J. H. Eaton, *Kingship and the Psalms* (London: SCM Press, 1976); I. Engnell, "The Book of Psalms," in his *A Rigid Scrutiny* (Nashville: Vanderbilt University, 1969) = *Critical Essays on the Old Testament* (London: SPCK, 1970)68-122; E. Gerstenberger, "Psalms," *OTFC*, 179-223; H. Gunkel, *The Psalms: A Form-Critical Introduction* (Philadelphia: Fortress Press, 1967); A. R. Johnson, "The Psalms," *OTMS*, 162-209; *idem*, *Sacral Kingship in Ancient Israel* (Cardiff: University of Wales, 1955, ²1967); R. H. Kennett, "The Historical Background of the Psalms," in his *Old Testament Essays* (London: Cambridge University Press, 1928)119-218; H.-J. Kraus, *Worship in Israel: A Cultic History of the Old Testament* (Oxford/Atlanta: Blackwell/John Knox Press, 1966); S. Mowinckel, *The Psalms in Israel's Worship*, 2 volumes (Oxford/Nashville: Blackwell/Abingdon Press, 1962); L. Sabourin, *The Psalms: Their Origin and Meaning* (Staten Island: Alba House, 1969); S. Terrien, *The Psalms and Their Meaning for Today* (Indianapolis: Bobbs-Merrill, 1952); C. Westermann, *The Praise of God in the Psalms* (Atlanta: John Knox Press, 1965); *idem*, "Psalms, Book of," *IDBS*, 705-10.

Twentieth-century research on the Psalms has worked under the shadow of Gunkel's form-critical approach (see above, pp. 139-43) which sought to establish the typical aspects of various psalms genres. Typical experiences in human life were then related to and used in understanding the various genres. Since the typicality of the experiences reflected in the psalms pointed to the cult, it was assumed that the psalms were either employed in or influenced by the cult and by the rituals used in worship.

A. Approaches to Psalms Study

Gunkel's analysis of the psalms was developed as an alternative to other methods of interpreting the Psalter which had existed prior to and have continued to be utilized alongside or as alternatives to the form-critical approach. One such approach emphasizes the psalms as religious and poetic compositions expressive of individual piety. This manner of interpretation is reflected, for example, in A. F. Kirkpatrick's commentary published in 1902. He wrote:

The Psalter is a collection of religious lyrics. Lyric poetry is defined as "that which directly expressed the individual emotions of the poet"; and religious lyric poetry is the expression of those emotions and feelings as they are stirred by the thought of God and directed God-wards. This is the common characteristic of the Psalms in all their manifold variety. The Psalms alone gives us a glimpse into the inner religion of the best spirits in the nation, and bear witness to the faith, the love, the devotion of pious souls, even under the limitations of the Old Covenant. (x-xi)

Kirkpatrick gave a lengthy quotation as a preface to his volume which apparently was intended to serve as an illustration of his interpretive attitude, although the quote is far more pious than his commentary as a whole. This quotation, nonetheless, can serve as an example of the pious and poetic individualistic approach to the psalms:

In the Psalms the soul turns inward on itself, and their great feature is that they are the expression of a large spiritual experience. They come straight from "the heart within the heart," and the secret depths of the spirit. Where, in those rough cruel days, did they come from, those piercing, lightning-like gleams of strange spiritual truth, those magnificent outlooks over the kingdom of God, those pure outpourings of the love of God? . . . In that wild time there must have been men sheltered and hidden amid the tumult around them, humble and faithful and true, to whom the Holy Ghost could open by degrees the "wondrous things of His law," whom He taught, and whose mouths he opened, to teach their brethren by their own experience, and to do each their part in the great preparation. (v)

This approach has scrutinized the psalms in search of the piety and genius of individual poets who sought to give expression to their inward feelings and emotional experiences so others might learn from and share them.

Another method of treating the psalms has focused on historical concerns and sought to assign each psalm to its proper chronological niche and to dissect each in quest of the reflections of historical events. How did the supposed authors respond to the historical environment in which they lived? How did they express their psychological and theological reactions to the impact of historical events? What contours of Israelite history and what streams of religious development can be traced beneath these pious and poetic lives? These were the types of questions explored in attempts to use the book of Psalms to elucidate Jewish history and Jewish history to elucidate the psalms.

The quest for at least a broad historical context for use in interpreting the psalms can be illustrated by C. A. Briggs' discussion of the date of Ps 23:

The language and syntax of the Ps. and all its ideals are early. There is not the slightest trace of anything that is post-deuteronomic. The historical circumstances of the poet must have been peaceful and prosperous. We cannot go down so late as the prosperous times of the Greek period, or the late Persian period. We cannot think of the Exile, or early Restoration, for the literature of those times is full of trial and sorrow. Absence from the temple is indicated by the Hebrew text, but that is due to a textual error. The temple was the habitual resort of the poet. He was a guest there. We cannot, therefore, think of the Exile, or of the time of David, the traditional author of the Ps. . . . The three figures, shepherd, guide, host, are all simple, natural, and characteristic of the life in Jerusalem and its vicinity at any period in Biblical history. A short walk from Jerusalem at any time would lead to gloomy wadys and the pastures of the shepherds. We cannot think of the period of conflict with the Assyrians and Babylonians. We must, therefore, go back to an earlier and simpler period, the days of the early monarchy, not earlier than Solomon, or later than Jehoshaphat. *(The Book of Psalms,* 207-8)

The most ambitious attempt to relate the psalms to historical events and circumstances is represented in the study of Moses Buttenweiser. For him, the psalms display "a continuous development extending from the time of Joshua, when the oldest datable psalm was composed, down to about the middle of the third century B.C., when the psalter was completed" (xxix). Attempting to date each psalm precisely, many to the exact year and event, Buttenweiser distributed the psalms over the various periods of Israelite history, dating 115 psalms to the postexilic period. For Buttenweiser, not only was it imperative to interpret the psalms against the background of their assumed historical context but it was also necessary to consider the psalms an invaluable source of historical data.

The Psalms are a mirror of the spiritual growth of Israel . . . [and a] chronological study would afford a truer insight into the evolutionary process of Israel's religious life and thought than all the other biblical writings. . . . The Psalms are an equally valuable source of information concerning the political history of Israel from the earliest pre-Exilic times down to 300 B.C. What they reveal with regard to events and conditions often differs widely, if not altogether, from the current presentation. Especially is this true in the case of the post-Exilic psalms. These are indeed the most important source for post-Exilic history, and the data they present enable us to emend the sketchy and inaccurate account of the pre-Maccabaean post-Exilic centuries which has hitherto been based solely upon the scanty source material supplied by historical records, in the narrower sense of the term, and which has utterly ignored the testimony of the Psalms. (xxxix)

Such an interpretation assumes not only that the psalms provide incidental references which can be used to augment historical records but also that the psalms may be used to reconstruct the course of history and to correct and emend the accounts found in the historical records themselves.

The quest for historical circumstances which could be used in understanding the psalms has frequently led scholars to date the psalms very late. At the turn of the century, a majority of critical scholars placed the origin of many psalms within the postexilic period. Many sought to date the psalms during the Maccabean period and thus as late as the second century BCE (see Kennett). In supporting such late dating, scholars pointed to the developed ethical monotheism, the concern for the individual, the piety, the interest in the law and temple worship, and the general theological outlook found in the psalms as more reflective of early Judaism than ancient Israel. The frequent references to enemies within the psalms were related to the internal struggles among Jewish parties. The following quote illustrates the main arguments of this form of approach.

Personal religion finds classical expression in the Psalter. After the downfall of the state in 586, beginning with Jeremiah, religion ceased to be for the Jews a natural concomitant of nationality and gradually became an ideal of righteousness to be attained through unremitting personal effort and the help of the merciful God who has made known his will in his Law and listens to the prayers of the faithful. This new conception of religion as a personal life impregnated with the thought of God and his requirements divided the Jews into two mutually hostile camps: the Pious, or righteous, zealous in their single-minded observance of the Law and frequently poor in worldly goods; and the ungodly, or wicked, more concerned with success in the affairs of this world than with the attainment of righteousness and divine approval, which to them bore no relation to earthly prosperity. Pious and wicked were sharply divided on the question of a divine retribution for human deeds, and the wicked stoutly denied that piety inevitably brought tangible rewards. The Psalter is the book of the Pious; the wicked, whose voice is heard in parts of Job, Proverbs, and Ecclesiastes are denounced and cursed therein with passionate zeal. (R. H. Pfeiffer, *Introduction to the Old Testament*, 637-38)

Pfeiffer described the Psalter as a "Hebrew handbook of personal religion" (634) intentionally created "for the edification of the laity, particularly the lower middle class" (620). He denied any real association of the psalms with temple worship:

The Psalter reflects far more the religion of the synagogue than that of the Temple: it expresses the religious emotions of the laity rather than the rituals performed in the sanctuary by the clergy. Even the doxologies, liturgies, and hymns sung in the Temple service, which are included in the Psalter, were selected because they were suitable for private devotion. The Psalter, in its first edition, cannot truly be understood except as a religious anthology for the reverent Jew, prepared for the purpose of stimulating that personal piety which became characteristic of the Pharisees. (620)

B. Issues in the Form-Critical Study of the Psalms

Gunkel's form-critical approach to the Psalms has become the most widely utilized approach in twentieth-century research. The most creative and controversial impulse emanating from this form-critical study of the

Psalter has not been the division of the psalms into various types but rather the problems associated with the issue of their *Sitz im Leben*. Prior to Gunkel, W. T. Davison, for example, offered a classification of the Psalms very similar to that of Gunkel, but he was incapable of utilizing this classification as an interpretive tool:

The Psalms have sometimes been classified according to their subject-matter [by Bleek, Driver, Hupfeld], but any such an arrangement is open to obvious objections. The subdivisions necessarily overlap, and many psalms refuse to be classified. . . . The analysis might run somewhat as follows: i. Songs of Praise to Jehovah; (a) as God of nature, Ps 8. 19:1-16. 29. 65. 104; (b) in relation to man, as God of Providence, 103. 107. 113. 145; ii. Didactic Psalms, on the moral government of the world, etc. Ps 1. 34. 37. 49. 73. 77; and of a more directly ethical character, 15. 24:1-6. 32. 40. 50. iii. National Psalms, including (a) prayers in disaster, e.g. 44. 60. 74. 79. 80, etc., and (b) thanksgivings for deliverance, e.g. 46. 47. 48. 66. 68. 76, etc. iv. Purely historical Psalms, 78. 81. 105. 106. 114. v. Royal Psalms, 2. 18. 20. 21. 45. 72. 101, etc. vi. The more directly personal Psalms are of very various character: sometimes (a) they contain prayers for forgiveness or recovery from sickness, 3. 4. 6. 7. 22; sometimes (b) thanksgiving predominates, as in 30. 40. 116; or (c) the prevailing strain is one of faith or resignation, e.g. 16. 23. 27. 42. 121. 139; or the law is praised, as in 1. 19:7-14. 119, or the house of God, as in 84. 122. 132. Such a classification, however can hardly be considered to be of use, except in a very general and superficial way. (*HDB* IV [1902] 161)

Along with many others, Davison divided the psalms into groups, primarily on the basis of content, and came out with a typology not far from that of Gunkel. The close similarity in typological analysis by such different scholars as Gunkel and Davison at the turn of the century intimated one factor which was to characterize twentieth-century research on the psalms: the classification of the psalms into various types was not to be the most heated issue of debate (see Clines, 1969, and Westermann). As a rule, scholars have also agreed with Gunkel in his suggestion that the various types of psalms originally had their setting in worship services in the cult (see Clines, 1967, 105-10).

Two main issues have embroiled form-critical scholars in controversy and debate in their attempts to understand when and how the psalms were employed in ancient Israelite life. (1) The first is the question of the identity of the "I" and the enemies which appear in so many psalms. (2) The second involves the problem of the psalms' relationship to the cult and the nature of the primary cultic activities.

(1) Numerous psalms contain first person references. This is especially true of what Gunkel called the "individual psalms of lament." Who is the "I" that speaks in the psalms? Who is praying to God? Numerous answers have been given to this question.

(a) Gunkel argued that the "I" who speaks in many psalms, especially in laments was the individual sufferer who poured out his grief often in private, away from public view, and thus outside the cult. On the relationship of some of those psalms to the cult, Gunkel wrote:

Very many of the psalms which have come down to us do not belong to the poetry of the cult. They presuppose no particular cultic acts. They were not intended to be sung only on specific occasions but could be sung or prayed anywhere. Accordingly, out of the Cult Songs have grown Spiritual Poems. Here a kind of piety which has freed itself of all ceremonies expresses itself, a religion of the heart. Religion has cast off the shell of sacred usage, in which, until now, it has been protected and nurtured: it has come of age. (26)

The Spiritual Laments of the Individual constitute the largest group of songs in the Psalter. Here, and in the Wisdom Literature, is the place where individuality is expressed in the Old Testament. These songs, above all, are the prototypes of Protestant hymnody. From the standpoint of poetry, they are not always outstanding; but from the standpoint of religion, they are the imperishable treasure in the Psalter. (33)

Gunkel concluded that these psalms reflect the actual

feelings and pleas of particular people who were the pious sufferers bowed by the weight of their troubles.

Pure and authentic religion is to be found only where tremendous struggles have been experienced. The man whose ways are prospering can perhaps do without the divine helper; but the sufferer, who despairs of humanity and of the world, will lift up his hands, out of the depths of his distress, to the God who dwells on high.

But how is it that there were at that time so many sufferers that their prayers constitute the material of a special literary type in the Psalter? The answer to this we learn from the descriptions which the psalmists themselves paint: they speak of themselves as the poor, the distressed, the humble, and the silent faithful. They complain of oppression by the rich, the mighty, the proud, and the insolent. Everywhere it is assumed that these poor very frequently are identical with the pious, while most of the evildoers care nothing about God. Thus the poor and the rich stand opposed to each other, not only as two social strata but, at the same time, as two religious groups. We know that such conditions existed during early Christian times, as well as during the Greek period, when the nobles and the wealthy identified with the Hellenistic rules and Hellenistic culture, while humble folk remained true to the old religion. The same was doubtless true in the Persian period, when Ezra and Nehemiah had to battle against mixed marriages and betrayal of the fatherland—by the nobles and the high priests! (33)

Thus, for Gunkel, the "I" who speaks in many of the psalms is the weak, the poor, the oppressed, the humble, the faithful. Their enemies are the strong, the rich, the mighty, the proud, the insolent. Both those who prayed and their enemies were Israelites.

(b) A second approach to the identity of the "I" offering prayer has denied that the personal references were spoken by an individual worshiper and has argued that the "I" is a personification of the community. This view, which was first proposed in a thoroughgoing fashion by Rudolf Smend (1851-1913) in 1888, maintains that it is the congregation or community groups or the entire nation which describes its affliction and prays for help (see Ps 129:1-3, where this is clearly the case).

If it is the nation who speaks as "I" in many psalms, then the enemies described as inflicting suffering and oppressing the community must be political powers as well. This view has been argued by the Scandanavian scholar Birkeland. He concludes: "The evildoers in the Book of Psalms are gentiles in all cases when a definite collective body or its representatives are meant. Israelite groups are included as far as co-operation with foreigners is concerned. Evildoers in a general sense do occur, but even so the application to gentiles seems probable" (93). Birkeland argued that the same enemies appear in "I" psalms as in psalms where it is clearly Israel who is praying. He concluded, however, that frequently in the psalms it is the king as the representative of the people who speaks and the enemies are national enemies. A consequence of his approach is the denial of any individual psalms in the proper sense of the word. The psalms in which first person references occur were all either national or royal psalms and none were ever originally intended for the use of the ordinary Israelite. Even the enemies in psalms which speak of illness, such as Pss 6; 30; 38; 41; 102, are interpreted with reference to foreign powers: the enemies were foreign political leaders who had taken the opportunity of the monarch's illness to attack Israel.

(c) A third approach to the problem of the speaker in the psalms containing first person references has identified the speaker with the king. Gunkel recognized a group of ten psalms as royal psalms which were employed in ritual services in which the king was the central figure. In subsequent studies, many scholars have argued that the king was the central actor in Israelite worship and therefore have assigned a far greater number of psalms to the category of royal psalms (see Clines, 1967, 118-26, and Eaton, 1-26). The most radical form of this approach assumes that the king functioned in worship not only as the high priest but as the representative or incarnation of God whose death and resurrection were annually celebrated on the autumnal new year's day. A more moderate view is represented by such scholars as Johnson and Eaton who nonetheless stress the significant role of the king in the Jerusalem cult. Johnson has argued that an indispensible role was "played by the Messiah of the House of David [i.e. the reigning king] in the ritual and mythology of the Jerusalem cultus during the period of the Israelite monarchy . . . " (134). According to Johnson, the most significant worship service in the Jerusalem temple was centered around a major festival in which the king was the central performer.

The leading actor in this drama is the Davidic king, in whom the life of the nation as a corporate whole finds its focus. This work of 'salvation' . . . , as it is called, is portrayed by means of some kind of mime in which the kings (i.e. the nations) of the earth, representing the forces of darkness and 'Death' as opposed to light and 'Life' and commonly designated the 'wicked' . . . , unite in an attempt to overthrow Yahweh's covenanted followers, i.e. His 'votaries' . . . or the 'righteous' . . . , under the leadership of the Messiah. The latter, who is also described as the Servant of Yahweh, suffers an initial humiliation; but this issues in his salvation and that of his people, for it involves the recognition of an ultimate dependence upon Yahweh rather than 'the arm of flesh', and thus sets the seal upon the basic plea of 'fidelity' . . . , 'devotion' . . . , and 'righteousness' . . . on the part of the Messiah and his subjects. As a result victory (or salvation) is eventually secured through the dramatic intervention of Yahweh Himself in the person of the 'Most High', who makes His presence felt at the dawn of this fateful day, and delivers the Messiah and *ipso facto* the nation from the forces of darkness and 'Death.' In this way Yahweh revals His own 'fidelity' . . . , 'devotion' . . . , and 'righteousness' . . . in relation to His covenant people. Further, this deliverance from

'Death' marks the renewal of life or the rebirth of the king in question. It is the sign that in virtue of his faithfulness and basically by reason of his faith this suffering Servant and humble Messiah has been adopted as 'Son' of Yahweh or, to express this mediatory office in another way, has become an everlasting Priest 'after the order of Melchizedek'; and, as such, he is enthroned on Mount Zion as Yahweh's unmistakable viceregent upon earth. This is not all, however, for Yahweh's earthly victory has its counterpart in the heavenly places. The rebellion of the kings of the earth is but a reflection of the rebellious misrule of the lesser gods in the divine assembly, to whom the 'Most High' had granted the jurisdiction over those territories which were occupied by the other nations of the earth. Accordingly the overthrow of these rebellious gods, who, having shown their unfitness to rule, are condemned to die like any earthly princes. Thus Yahweh proves to be what has been aptly called 'the enduring power, not ourselves, which makes for righteousness'; and the helpless, the poor, and the humble, not merely in Israel but throughout the world, may look foward to an era of universal righteousness and peace, as the one omnipotent God comes with judicial power to destroy the wicked, to justify His Messiah and His Messiah's people in their responsible mission to the world, and to enforce His beneficent rule upon the earth. (135-36)

According to Johnson, the king in the annual festival was ritually (1) subjected to humiliation and suffering, (2) attacked by enemies and the powers of darkness and of death, (3) delivered by the intervention of God, (4) triumphant over his enemies, and (5) reinstated to reign as Yahweh's viceregent on earth.

Accepting Johnson's reconstruction of the role of the king in the Jerusalem cultus, Eaton has extended, like many scholars, the number of psalms which should be classified as royal. In addition to the ten royal psalms isolated by Gunkel, Eaton adds over fifty more to this class, distinguishing between those psalms utilized in the ritual outlined by Johnson and others which were utilized in concrete historical circumstances. He categorizes these psalms as follows:

A distinction may be attempted between those psalms which seem to have been created purely for regular rituals, and those which, whether rendered in festivals or not, were designated to seek help or give thanks for some historical event. The former are the minority: 51 (and perhaps 102), which may belong to the annual day of atonement; 91 and 121, which convey God's assurances to his king; 75, where the king warns of judgment; 22, which shows him in rites of suffering succeeded by restoration, and 23, his subsequent testimony; 118, where he looks back on the rites of chastisement and deliverance as he proceeds into the temple. These could well be from the major ritual sequences of the autumn festival. To them might be added 36, where the king prays for the destruction of the wicked, and 92, where he testifies to the triumph of God in which he participates.

Psalms occasioned by some particular event are most clearly 41 (the king sick and insecure) and 71 (the king old and insecure); then many that reflect warfare: 7; 11; 17; 27; 31; 35; 40; 42-3; 44; 54; 55; 56; 59; 60; 62; 63; 66; 69; 70; 108; 109; 140; 141; in several others the military aspect is not brought out but can reasonably be asumed: 5; 16; 28; 142; 143; in several the enemy seems to exert a lasting domination: 9-10; 73; 77; 80; 94; in Psalm 4 the crisis seems to include a dearth.

There are a few others which should probably be included in the preceding paragraph, but which, on account of their more schematic character, could otherwise be added to the ritual group, though this seems less likely. In some, warfare is prominent: 3; 57; 120; in some, just 'enemies': 52; 86; 139; and still vaguer, 61; 116; 138. (130-31)

(2) Gunkel contended that many of the psalms were used in worship services in the Jerusalem cult. The question of the nature and content of the cultic context has been one of the most debated issues in twentieth-century Old Testament study. Gunkel argued that the great hymns in the Psalter were employed during the great national festivals and celebrations (Feast of Unleavened Bread-Passover, Feast of Weeks, and Feast of Tabernacles). Community laments were employed during times of national distress. Thanksgiving psalms were employed in conjunction with offering thanksgiving sacrifices, and

so on. Gunkel's comments on the cultic context within which the psalms were employed have been felt to be unsatisfactory and attempts have been made to define more fully the nature of this cultic activity. To a large extent, the debate has centered on the character and content of the major festival(s) in ancient Israel.

(a) The Norwegian scholar Sigmund Mowinckel (1884-1966) proposed that many of the psalms—over forty—should be understood as having been employed in a ritual enthronement of Yahweh as king during the fall festival (Feast of Tabernacles). Since his first volume on the subject was published in 1922, Mowinckel's theory has been second only to Gunkel's work in its stimulation of discussion.

Beginning from Pss 47; 93; 95-100, Mowinckel argued that many psalms suggest that Yahweh was annually enthroned as king in Jerusalem in a great religious drama. According to him, the basic elements in this drama were (1) a sacred procession around the temple by worshipers and priests carrying the ark-throne of Yahweh, (2) the dramatization of the triumph of Yahweh over the mythological and historical enemies of creation and Israel, presented as a repetition and renewal of the original, primeval creation and as judgment over the nations of the earth, and (3) the proclamation and celebration of Yahweh's assumption and reign as king over creation, the world, and Israel.

It is plain that a 'feast of Yahweh's enthronement' must have existed, the main foci of which must have been Yahweh's enthronement and his kingship, based on his victory over the powers of chaos and the primeval ocean, and the creation, repetition and re-experience of these 'facts of salvation' in and through the festival, and further, the renewal of the historical 'salvation': the election, the deliverance from Egypt, and the making of the covenant. The most prominent act of this festival was the great procession with its dramatic and symbolic character, the personal presence of Yahweh being symbolized by the ark.

This feast was originally one aspect of the old agricultural feast of harvest and new year, probably characteristic of a certain day in the festal complex, possibly the seventh; later on, great parts of its complex of ideas were passed on to the new special new year's day, the 1st of Tishri. The enthronement aspect of the feast of new year and Tabernacles can be traced back to the monarchic period.

Another aspect of the festal complex of harvest and new year was its nature as a repeated festival for the consecration of the Temple, commemorating the inauguration of the cult of Yahweh in Jerusalem; to the feast for the consecration of the Temple was attached an annual purification of the same.

The feast for the consecration of the Temple also had the character of a renewal of the covenant with David and the royal house; this idea is naturally linked up with the idea of a renewal of the covenant on Mount Sinai, completed by the covenant with David. Therefore the offspring of David, the king of Israel, would also play an important role in the rites and conceptions of the festal complex. (I, 129-30)

Mowinckel built his case around the group of psalms (47; 93; 95-100) which Gunkel and others had designated "Enthronement Songs." Generally, scholars, including Gunkel, had assumed that these psalms either proclaimed the eternal kingship of Yahweh or should be understood as psalms influenced by prophetic preaching (especially that of Second Isaiah) and were thus eschatological hymns. Gunkel wrote about these eschatological hymns:

Prophetic influence has many times left its imprint on the Hymns, . . . especially in a characteristic variety of Hymns, the Eschatological Hymns. The prophets, looking retrospectively in spirit to a great turning point, which [to them] had already taken place, composed the hymn of jubilation which the final generation would one day sing. This marvelous literary form, which never fails to make an impact, the psalmists had learned from the prophets. Thus, the lyric poetry which the prophets had learned from the psalmists is given back to them in a new form. These Eschatological Hymns in the Psalms, which have often been misinterpreted by commentators and made to refer to this or that historical event, sing of the end-time, when the nations will assemble in tumult and the mountains fall into the heart of the seas—until the city of God, wonderfully transformed into a paradise, appears, and Yahweh with one final mighty blow brings all wars to an end. . . . (31)

Mowinckel argued that these psalms did not reflect any historical events nor were they composed in anticipation of the coming kingdom and reign of God. They referred instead to the actual realization of Yahweh's kingship dramatized and actualized in the celebrations of the autumn festival. He proposed that the Hebrew expression *Yahweh malak* found as the opening words of some of the enthronement hymns (see Pss 93:1; 97:1) should be translated "Yahweh has become king" and not "Yahweh reigns." Thus, for Mowinckel, year by year, Yahweh reassumed kingship and was reenthroned as king in the Jerusalem ritual drama.

Mowinckel was influenced by several factors, in addition to the biblical texts, in his reconstruction of the elements in the autumn festival. (1) The anthropological studies of primitive societies, especially by some Scandanavian scholars such as Johannes Pedersen and Vilhem Grønbech, had stressed the great importance of the cult in such societies. Mowinckel shared an understanding of the comprehensive importance of the cult and its dynamic and dramatic quality: "Cult or ritual may be defined as the socially established and regulated holy acts and words in which the encounter and communion of the Deity with the congregation is established, developed, and brought to its ultimate goal. In other words: a relation in which a religion becomes a vitalizing function as a communion with God and congregation, and of the members of the congregation amongst themselves" (I, 15). For Mowinckel, the cult was the place where the revitalizing relationship with God was established, nurtured, and re-created. In the cult, acts (ritual) and words (myth and poetry) belong together; the words belong to the acts as complement and interpretation. The psalms are thus a deposit of the spoken word of the cult which accompanied the ritual acts of the ancient Jerusalem cult. Mowinckel was one of the first Protestant scholars to break with the anticultic, antipriestly, antisacramental attitude which had its roots in the Reformation and had blossomed into full flower in nineteenth-century Old Testament scholarship. (2) Research on the importance of religious festivals and the nature of cultic activities in other ancient near eastern societies was also utilized by Mowinckel as comparative data (see Johnson, *OTMS*, 186-96; Gerstenberger, 188-92).

A. R. Johnson, among English language scholars, has been most sympathetic to Mowinckel's views. Johnson has reconstructed the elements of the autumn ritual drama in the following manner:

The following features are to be recognized in the festival under discussion as celebrated in Solomon's Temple between the tenth and sixth centuries B.C. In the first place we have (a) the celebration of Yahweh's original triumph, as leader of the forces of light, over the forces of darkness as represented by the monstrous chaos of waters or primeval ocean; (b) His subjection of this cosmic sea and His enthronement as King in the assembly of the gods; and (c) the further demonstration of His might and power in the creation of the habitable world. Cosmogony, however, gives place to eschatology; for all this is the prelude to the thought of His re-creative work, which is expressed in the form of a ritual drama, and, as such, is wholly in line with what we are told about prophetic symbolism. . . . In this ritual drama the worshippers are given (a) an assurance of final victory over 'Death', i.e. all that obstructs the fullness of life for mankind which was Yahweh's design in the creation of the habitable world; (b) a summons to a renewal of their faith in Yahweh and His plans for them and for the world; and (c) a challenge to a renewed endeavour to be faithful to Him and His demands, so that the day may indeed dawn when this vision of a universal realm of righteousness and peace will be realized, and His Kingdom will be seen in all its power and glory. Moreover, the summons and the challenge are directed first and foremost towards the ruling member of the House of David, in whom rest the hopes of Yahweh and His people; for we now know that, humanly speaking, the leading actor in this drama is the Davidic king, in whom the life of the nation as a corporate whole finds its focus. (134-35)

Johnson differed from Mowinckel in his reconstruction of the major fall festival and the employment of the psalms in the ritual in the following ways: (1) Johnson assigned a far greater role to the annual ritual humiliation and exaltation of the Davidic king than Mowinckel; (2) fewer psalms were associated with the enthronement of Yahweh ritual; and (3) Johnson argued that the overall orientation of the festival was toward the realization of a completely new era and therefore possessed an eschatological perspective while Mowinckel placed the emphasis on the festival's orientation to the coming year and the revival and revitalization of the social unit.

(b) An alternative to Mowinckel's theory of an annual enthronement festival has been proposed by Artur Weiser, who interprets the psalms in light of a reconstructed Israelite covenant festival. Weiser assumes that the dominant theology in ancient Israel was covenantal. For Weiser, this festival was a time of national renewal and commitment when the entire community recalled and relived the making of the original covenant at Sinai. As reconstructed by Weiser, the following elements were components of the covenant festival: (1) the theophany of God's self-revelation, (2) the proclamation of his name, (3) the revelation of his nature in the form of a recapitulation of the salvation history (*Heilsgeschichte*), (4) the proclamation of the divine will and judgment, (5) the people's profession of loyalty to Yahweh and his commandments, and (6) the renunciation of foreign gods. The reflection of these elements in the psalms allows Weiser to relate practically the entire Psalter to this covenant renewal festival. Psalms about Zion and the king reflect an extension of the *Heilsgeschichte*; psalms about Yahweh's kingship were integrated into the festival as a secondary

303

development; and even psalms focusing on the individual and wisdom were related to the covenant festival since the individual could only participate in the blessings of Yahweh as a member of the covenant community. (For Weiser's views, see the introduction to his commentary, 35-52.)

(c) As an alternative to Mowinckel's all important festival of Yahweh's enthronement and Weiser's all-encompassing festival of covenant renewal, H.-J. Kraus has proposed the idea of a royal Zion festival focusing upon the establishment of the Yahwistic cult in Jerusalem and the founding of the Davidic dynasty (179-218). Kraus strongly opposes any mythological or naturalistic interpretation of worship in the Jerusalem temple and stresses instead the historical traditions of the placement of the ark in Jerusalem, the role of the temple as the house of Yahweh, the choice of Zion as God's dwelling, and the establisment of the house of David as the chosen and elect dynasty. The events narrated in II Sam 6–7 were commemorated in the annual Zion festival. Following Gunkel, Kraus argues that the psalms which speak of the kingship and enthronement of Yahweh are eschatological in perspective and dependent upon the prophetic preaching of Deutero-Isaiah.

C. The Psalms and the Cult

Gunkel's form-critical analysis of the psalms was given definitive expression in his *Einleitung in die Psalmen* (1933), a work completed after his death by his student Joachim Begrich (1900-1945). His description and division of the psalms still remain basic to practically all research on the subject. His insights, however, must be modified in light of the more thoroughgoing cultic interpretation as exemplified in the studies of Mowinckel. The following general considerations seem valid in any interpretation of the Psalter based on the work of Gunkel and Mowinckel.

(1) There are various ways in which many of the psalms may be categorized or grouped: communal, individual, and royal; praise and petition; lament and thanksgiving; psalms for the celebrative and festive times of life and psalms for the crises in human existence (both communal and individual); psalms for use of laity and those for use by the professional clergy; and so on. What this means is that the cult in Israelite life was intended to serve the totality of life and the total community and not merely the nation as a whole or royalty alone. (It should be noted, however, that the routine rites of passage associated with birth, puberty, marriage, and death were only indirectly, if at all, related to cultic occasions in ancient Israel.)

Westermann has recently argued that what have traditionally been called thanksgiving psalms are actually a form of praise which he calls "declarative praise." He distinguishes this type of praise from hymnic praise in the following manner: "Declarative praise [thanksgiving] is the recounting in praise of God's saving acts for his people and for individuals. Descriptive praise [hymns] is the praise of God in his being and his activity as a whole" (*IDBS*, 707). On this point, Westermann, like Gunkel, ends up with two classifications and the differences are primarily the labels which one attaches to groups of psalms.

(2) The psalms, in their original usage, should be understood against the actual realities of cultic worship; that is, they must not be read through pious or eschatological spectacles which blind the interpreter to the actual life situations reflected in and the affirmations contained in the psalms. Such things as the realization of salvation and the enthronement of God which are noted in the psalms must be understood in terms of cultic actualities and not as eschatological hopes and promises. Form criticism is as much concerned with sociological and cultic contexts as it is with literary types. One cannot agree with Westermann, who writes: "The 'categories' of the Psalms are not first of all literary or cultic in nature.

They are this of course, but it is not the essential element. They designate the basic modes of that which occurs when man turns to God with words: plea and praise" (1965, 153). Such a position theologizes away the importance of the sociological and cultic contexts out of which the psalms developed.

(3) The psalms were no doubt employed within the context of diverse and complex cultic activities. The old adage that "the book of Psalms and the book of Leviticus should be read in parallel columns" contains a great measure of truth. "Psalm and sacrifice belong together" is another way of saying the same thing. It is, of course, often difficult to reconstruct much of the supposed cultic context involved. Ritual and festival texts in the Old Testament and later Jewish tradition often provide aids. References within the psalms themselves may be used to ascertain the broad cultic activities of which the psalms themselves were a part.

(4) The book of Psalms should not be made to fit within any limited definition of its contents. One frequently sees the book referred to as "the prayer book of ancient Israel" or "the hymn book of the Second Temple." All such categorization is misleading and prejudices interpretation. The Psalter actually contains prayers and petitions (generally addressed directly to God), praise (which generally speaks of God in the third person), thanksgiving (addressed basically to Yahweh), divine speech (addressed to the worshiper and/or congregation), and proclamation (addressed to a human audience) as well as texts which appear to reflect ritual activity. This variegated and complex character of the Psalter must always be borne in mind.

(5) The Psalter as we now possess it, and therefore the individual psalms, have lost their association with their original *Sitz im Leben*. The psalms passed through various stages of usage and interpretation and eventually ended up as sacred scripture with a sanctity unto itself. Radical reinterpretations and new understandings of

306

many psalms must have taken place when Israel no longer possessed a king (after 586 BCE), when many of the psalms came to be interpreted eschatologically (as is reflected for example in the Qumran scrolls and New Testament), when the psalms were utilized in synagogue services where the original cultic context was exchanged for another cultic context (perhaps such psalms as 1 and 119 were composed during this period), when David came to be understood as the author of most of the psalms which were then searched for psychological insight into his religious psyche and devotion, and when the book became a part of sacred scripture (see Childs, 1971). This complex process cannot be reconstructed in detail (see Childs, *MD*, 379-82), and what will be said in the next section will be concerned with what can be deduced about the earliest phase of usage.

D. Psalms Types and Cultic Ritual

Basic to any attempt to understand the psalms is the recognition that the Psalter contains psalms originally employed in services within which three groups were prominent: individual worshipers, royalty, and the community at large. Within each category, there exists a polarity of sentiment and expression: celebration and sorrow.

(1) *Psalms of the Individual Worshiper.* Old Testament texts speak of five occasions in which cultic activities were performed which centered on the individual.

(a) When the individual fulfilled religious obligations—such as offering the first fruits (see Deut 26:1-11) or presenting tithes (Deut 26:12-15)—rituals were involved in which the worshiper (and his family) were the center of activity. Deut 26 does not spell out in detail the procedures involved although the Mishnah (*Bikkurim* 3:1-7) presents the ritual of first fruits which included recitation of Deut 26:5-11 and the "singing" of Ps 30. These rituals were no doubt characterized by celebration and thanksgiving, especially when harvest and business had been productive.

(b) When the individual was ill or diseased was a special time of worship (see Sirach 38:9-12, which outlines four steps for the sick: prayer, confession of sin and repentance, offering of sacrifice, and consultation of the physician). Lev 13-15 outlines some of the procedures followed at the time of illness but unfortunately provides information only about those cases in which possible contagion was suspected.

(c) When special legal procedures were carried out, the individual could be brought into a special relationship to the cult. One such occasion was when the person sought asylum in the sanctuary (see Ex 21:12-14; Deut 19:1-13; I Kings 1:49-53; 2:28-35). Another occasion was when special appeal was made to God and sanctuary personnel, after ordinary legal processes could reach no verdict or could not operate (see Ex 22:7-8; Deut 17:8-13; 19:15-21; I Kings 8:31-32). The texts do not tell us how verdicts were arrived at although ordeal (Num 5:5-31) and casting of lots (Josh 7; I Sam 14:41-42) were certainly known. Notice that the priest(s) plays an important role in the stipulations of Deut 17:8-13.

(d) When the sinner needed to find atonement for his sin, special cultic conditions prevailed. Lev 4:1–6: 7 discusses some of these and the procedures involved confession, restitution, and sacrifice.

(e) Special times of worship for the individual were associated with the fulfillment of vows (see Gen 28:18-22; II Sam 15:7-9) or the presentation of special or freewill sacrifices (see Lev 7:16).

In addition to these five stipulated times of worship, ancient Israelites certainly presented their distress before Yahweh over various and sundry manners (see I Sam 1, where the failure to have a child is the occasion of distress).

Individual psalms of distress comprise the largest group within the Psalter. (On their general structure, see

above, pp. 139-140.) The use of stereotyped and metaphorical language made it possible to describe the distress
in pictographic form which gave full vent to the
worshiper's emotional state. This characteristic, however, frequently makes it difficult for the interpreter to place
the psalm within specific cultic contexts. Laments of the
sick (see Pss 6; 13; 31; 38; 39; 88; 102), the accused (see Pss
7; 17; 26; 27), the penitent (see Pss 25; 51; and
38:3-4,17-20; 39:8-11; 41:4), and the oppressed (see Pss 3;
9; 10; 13; 35; 52; 55; 56; 57; 62; 69; 70; 86; 109; 120; 139;
140; 141; 143) are clearly evident although the psalms of
the oppressed with their frequent references to enemies
may not be so clearly distinguishable from laments of the
sick and accused since even the sick had enemies—those
who avoided his company (see Job 19:13-22), the powers
(demons?) of evil and death, and perhaps even "sor-
cerers" (see Ezek 13:17-23). Frequently, these laments
appear to contain words spoken by sanctuary personnel
to the worshiper offering encouragement and direction
(see Pss 4:5; 27:14; 31:23-24; 55:22; and the whole of Ps
37).

When the sick possessed some disease that rendered
them unclean, it is possible that prayers and pleas were
offered in their name by proxy—by an intercessor. Job
33:19-28 seems to take this practice into consideration:
verses 19-25 speak of the prayer of the intercessor (the
angel or messenger) followed by the healed one offering
the prayer of thanksgiving (verses 26-28; see also Job
19:23-27 and Pss 42-43). Eccl 5:4-6 refers to the
"messenger" who comes from God to remind the one who
has vowed to keep his vow.

In several of the individual laments, there is a shift from
lament to praise, from mourning to joy, from distress to
celebration. Various attempts have been made to explain
this shift (see Brueggemann, 8-10): (1) some cultic official,
in the name of God, may have spoken a word of assurance
or forgiveness or proclaimed the worshiper righteous (see
I Sam 1; Hos 14:1-7, which assumes the use of such

oracles in worship as do Pss 12:5; 60:6-8; 91:14-16; 108:7-9) as a response to the plea; (2) the ritual involved may have itself incorporated elements in which the worshiper could affirm his own self-confidence in the outcome of his petition (see Ps 26:6-7); and (3) the offering of petition and thanksgiving may have itself assured and been assuring to the worshiper of divine intervention. However the divine response and reaction to the petition were communicated, and the role of the sanctuary personnel as spokesmen of God appears most likely, the Israelite worshiper could frequently leave the temple assured that God had (or had not) responded to his plea (see Ps 6:8-9).

A counterpart to the lament, which looks out of the distress and petitions for redemption, is the thanksgiving psalm, which looks back upon the alleviated distress and praises God for the experience or assurance of redemption (see Pss 30; 32; 34; 73; 103; 111; 116; and above, p. 140). The thanksgiving psalm was no doubt part of a thanksgiving service when the individual, among other activities, fulfilled the vows made in the lament ritual. The vows made were generally promises to praise God, to bear testimony to his deliverance, to teach others, and to offer sacrifice (see Pss 7:17; 9:14; 22:22; 35:28; 51:13; 52:9; 54:6; 56:12; 71:15; see also Pss 66:13-15; 116:12-14, 17-19). Sacrificial meals and joyous celebrations probably with small groups—family members, friends, and neighbors—were no doubt part of the thanksgiving rituals (see Ps 30:11-12).

Many of the thanksgiving psalms contain both proclamation to a human audience and thanks to God. The first is the fulfillment of the vow to teach others and to offer testimony while the latter, probably offered at the time of sacrifice, is the genuine thanksgiving. That many of these psalms contain instructional material and that what is called "wisdom" or "didactic" psalms appear in the Psalter should not be surprising since instruction and testimony were elements in the thanksgiving ritual.

(Instruction by the priests—what we might loosely term "preaching" or priestly wisdom—seems to have been an element in the lament ritual.)

Individual thanksgiving, of course, was not limited to those times following distress. The ordinary flow of life with the gifts of family, field, and flock offered occasions for thanksgiving and celebration. The thanksgiving ritual after serious distress such as unclean disease, sin, or legal accusation served as the ritual reintegrating the person into society at large, the cultic community, and renewed fellowship with God. It was thus a rite of passage, a celebration of personal rehabilitation, social reinstatement, and divine atonement.

(2) *Royal Psalms.* Since Gunkel, the importance of the king in the life and cult of ancient Israel has been stressed more and more (see Eaton, 1-26, for a survey of research). This greater emphasis has been the result of three factors: (1) form criticism has sought for appropriate cultic contexts within which psalms can be properly understood, and this has pointed more and more to royal rituals; (2) scholarship has tended to date many psalms earlier, before the exile, and therefore at a time when the king in Jerusalem was still a dominant influence; and (3) comparative near eastern studies have made clear how dominant the monarchy was in the life and cult of Israel's neighbors (on royal rituals outside Israel, see Eaton, 87-102). Some scholars, such as Engnell, have seen the king and royal theology as the clue to not only the psalms but much of the rest of the Old Testament as well, while others still follow the minimalist approach represented by Gunkel.

There were certainly a number of occasions in Israelite life in which the king was the central character and which provided opportunity for the use of royal psalms: the coronation, departure to and return from battles, royal weddings, illness or other calamities, times of personal and national triumphs. The story of Sennacherib's invasion of Judah, Hezekiah's reactions, and his subsequent illness, narrated in Is 36–39, provide insights into the typical occasions in which the king was threatened, worshiped, was saved from distress, and again worshiped. I Kings 1 and II Kings 11 incidentally provide information on features of the royal coronation. The king, however, is seldom mentioned in Old Testament law codes; and the historical and prophetic books, as a rule, are critical of the institution and its occupants. Thus, much of the royal theology must be deduced from the psalms and royal rituals reconstructed on the basis of hypotheses and assumed comparative parallels.

There are basically two problems related to the issue of royal psalms. (1) How many of the psalms should be considered in the category of royal psalms? It is widely assumed that Pss 2; 72; 101; and 110 comprised part of the royal coronation. Pss 22; 28; 61; 63; 71; 89; and 144 have generally been seen as royal laments, while Pss 18; 118; and 138 are understood as royal thanksgivings. Pss 20; 21; and 45 are certainly to be seen as royal. Debate centers over how many of the remaining psalms, especially individual psalms of laments, were actually royal in usage. As noted earlier, Eaton assigns about sixty psalms to such a usage. A good case seems to have been built for the view that many of the individual psalms in which the "I" is opposed by enemies are actually royal psalms in origin, although these may have also been "democratized" and used in rituals for commoners (for a contrary view, see Gerstenberger, 205-6). The number of psalms which are to be categorized as royal depends upon how one approaches the second problem associated with royal psalms.

(2) Was there in Israel, as in other cultures, an annual royal ritual in which the earthly king was subjected to humiliation and exaltation as assumed by scholars such as Johnson, Engnell, and Eaton? Mowinckel spoke of this position as "a theory . . . to the effect that in the royal psalms of lamentation we do not have real dangers and sufferings, which have befallen the king; and that the king

is not really suffering, but only 'suffering in the cult,' that is to say he is taking part in a cultic 'play' or drama, where he suffers, only to be later exalted" (I, 242-43). Mowinckel, in spite of his emphasis on the mythical aspects of the Jerusalem cult, refused to accept such a theory and argued that what the royal psalms reflect "are real human historical conditions, and real historical distress and affliction and suffering, and no ritual sham suffering" (II, 255).

It is entirely possible that threats to and opposition against the Jerusalem king and his subsequent symbolic victory over them were acted out and proclaimed in an annual celebration of the monarch's enthronement. The evidence for this is the following: (1) In the coronation ritual triumph over enemies was celebrated (see Pss 2;110). (2) The coronation of the new king coincided with the new year festival at which time Yahweh's triumph over the historical and chaotic powers was celebrated (see below). (3) Symbolic triumph over enemies by the king is clearly illustrated in Old Testament texts (see II Kings 13:14-19). (4) The Hezekiah story in Is 36–39 (with parallels in II Kings 18-20) demonstrates that in response to the king's lament in the cult (Is 37:15-20) oracles announcing salvation and victory were spoken to the king (Is 37:21-29). Since it is highly unlikely that this episode ever happened in the manner presented in Is 37, the passage may reflect typical and therefore annual cultic practices.

There are a number of factors, however, which suggest that too much should not be made of the king's ritual humiliation and exaltation. (1) A central element in the Mesopotamian ritual, which is utilized in reconstructing the Hebrew ritual, was the monarch's negative confession about his rule as part of his humiliation (see Eaton, 92). No counterpart to this appears in the psalms. (2) The king in the Old Testament is never presented as acting the part of the deity in the cult as did the king in other cultures. (3) The highly dramatized character of the king's humiliation and victory that is assumed by Johnson and others is not supported by Old Testament texts where the "victory" is symbolized in rather simple form and primarily by the proclaimed word of victory rather than in highly ritualized sham fights (see I Kings 22; II Kings 13:14-19; Is 37). (4) There is no concrete, textual evidence that the annual celebration of the king's coronation comprised a part of any Israelite festival. (It must be remembered, however, that the Old Testament traditions were given their final formulation after the end of the state of Judah—"when there was no king in Israel.")

(3) *Communal Psalms.* Primary worship services in ancient Israel were community affairs. Cultic services were observed in the temple daily, the three national festivals were centered there, and times of crisis and triumph were celebrated there. Psalms of various types have been associated with this temple worship.

According to the Mishnah (*Tamid* 7:4), Pss 24; 48; 82; 94; 81; 93; and 92 were successively sung, one per day, at the daily services in the temple. How early this practice was cannot be determined but it certainly points to the use of psalms even in daily, routine worship.

The basic festivals of early Israel were the Feast of Unleavened Bread (later combined with Passover), Harvest (Feast of Weeks or Pentecost), and Ingathering (Feast of Booths or Tabernacles). These festivals were agriculturally oriented (see Ex 23:14-17; 34:18-26).The first celebrated the end of the old cereal-harvest year and the beginning of the new with the reaping of the first ripe barley. For a week, the new grain was eaten unleavened and the old grain was not mixed with the new (which prohibited the transference of an old yeast starter to the new dough!). The Feast of Harvest concluded the spring harvest of cereal crops. The Feast of Ingathering in the early fall celebrated the harvest of grapes, olives, and fruits (what one gathers rather than harvests) and the beginning of the new agricultural year. At the earliest stage, these festivals were tied to the agricultural cycle and the ripening of the crops, although they generally fell near or at the time of the vernal equinox, the summer solstice, and the autumnal equinox. The spring festival also fell near the time of the last spring rains and the autumn festival fell near the beginning of the rainy season after a rainless summer.

The festivals in Israel were therefore oriented to the concerns of nature, cosmic order, and the fertility and well-being of flock, field, and family. In a limited fashion, these festivals were overlaid with historical concerns. This was especially the case with the spring celebrations—Unleavened Bread (Ex 23:15) and Passover (Ex 12). In later Judaism, for example in the book of Jubilees and at Qumran, the Feast of Weeks in the third month was understood as the time when the Law was revealed (see Ex 19:1).

Numerous hymns and psalms were probably employed at the festival celebrations. The Mishnah describes how Pss 113–118 (the so-called Hallel psalms) were sung in the temple when the Passover lambs were being slaughtered and again during the Passover meal. Pss 135; 136; and 147 would have also been appropriate for the occasion.

The fall festival celebrated the close of the old agricultural year and the beginning of the new year. Thus it was both past and future oriented. The only Old Testament passage which refers to the basic content of this festival stresses the festival as a celebration of the kingship of Yahweh (see Zech 14:16-21). The following considerations seem to be valid in understanding the fall festival in early Israel. (1) The central orientation of the festival must be understood in terms laid down by Mowinckel; namely, the festival celebrated Yahweh's "kingship over the whole created cosmos, comprising control of the forces of nature, the regulation of the season, the giving of fertility in field and herds and the stability and order of human society" (Clements, 85). (2) If the fall festival was at all oriented to the renewal of the Sinai covenant (as assumed by Weiser and others), this was a subordinate element and pobably one introduced late. (Very few of the psalms reflect Sinai covenant theology.) (3) The fall festival in early Israel was probably a three-day affair (see Ex 19:10-15; Hos 5:15–6:3; Amos 4:4 [but taking the Hebrew text in is literal sense: "bring your sacrifices for the morning, your tithes for the third day"]). Two days of this festival were probably spent in rituals of purgation, purification, and penitence; and the third day was the day of joyous celebration, the cultic "day of Yahweh." In the Deuteronomic reform, the celebration became a seven-day festival (see Deut 16:13) and was further elaborated in the post-exilic period into three distinct observances (Rosh Hashanah, Yom Kippur, and Succoth; Lev 23:23-43). (4) The Zion theology was given special proclamation in the festival since it was from here that God ruled as king. (5) The Davidic theology must have been an important element since the king as God's Messiah was the earthly vassal and representative of Yahweh.

The following features and psalms appear to have been part of the fall festival. (1) The ritual of atonement and purification for the people, the priests, and the temple (see Lev 16) was conducted during the first days of the festival. Psalms of divine judgment and communal confessions and laments were offered (see Pss 50; 81; 85; 90; 91; 94). Thus the humiliation and penitence were national in scope and not limited to the monarch. (2) The ark was removed from the temple. This annual removal of the ark, symbolizing the temporary departure of Yahweh, probably lies behind the novelistic features of II Sam 15:24-30 (see II Chron 35:3). (3) The ark was returned to Jerusalem in solemn procession (Ps 132). (4) Pilgrims and the ark reentered Jeruselem and the temple precincts early on the morning of the major day of the festival perhaps after a circumambulation of the holy city (Pss 68; 24; see Ps 48:12-14). (5) The ark was reinstalled in the holy of holies symbolizing Yahweh's reassumption of his reign as king (Ps 47). (6) Yahweh's kingship, his judgment of the world, and his reign in the assembly of the gods were celebrated with joy, sacrifice, and acclamation (Pss 82; 93; 95-100) as was his election of Zion as his dwelling place (Pss 46; 48; 78; 87; 125).

In addition to set seasons, other times of divine worship were occasions when psalms were employed. After victory, hymns and thanksgiving were offered (see Ex 15; Judg 5; I Macc 4:24; 5:54; 13:51; II Macc 10:7,38). Other spontaneous celebrations were occasions for praise. When the nation was threatened (see I Kings 8:33-37), national laments were offered as one part of the supplication ritual. Psalms reflecting such threats and crises to community life are 12; 44; 58; 60; 74; 79; 80; 83; and 137. After the alleviation of the distress, thanksgiving was in order although few communal thanksgivings have been preserved in the Psalter (see Pss 65; 66; 67; 75; 100; 105; 106; 107; 124). Probably hymns of praise served the community on such occasions. Pss 75 and 106 suggest that in ancient Israel even confession of sin and acceptance of judgment were means of giving thanks to God.

CHAPTER 9

ISRAELITE WISDOM LITERATURE

P. L. Berger and T. Luckmann, *The Social Construction of Reality: A Treatise in the Sociology of Knowledge* (Garden City: Doubleday, 1966); W. Brueggemann, *In Man We Trust: The Neglected Side of Biblical Faith* (Atlanta: John Knox Press, 1972); R. E. Clements, "Interpreting the Wisdom Literature," *COTS*, 99-117; J. J. Collins, "The Biblical Precedent for Natural Theology," *JAAR Supplement* XLV(1977)35-67; J. L. Crenshaw, "Method in Determining Wisdom Influence upon 'Historical' Literature," *JBL* LXXXVIII (1969)129-42 = *SAIW*, 481-94; *idem*, "Wisdom," in *OTFC*, 225-64; *idem*, "Wisdom in the OT," *IDBS*, 952-56; *idem*, "Studies in Ancient Israelite Wisdom: Prolegomenon," *SAIW*, 1-60; E. Gerstenberger, "Covenant and Commandment," *JBL* LXXXIV(1965)38-51; M. Hengel, *Judaism and Hellenism: Studies in their Encounter in Palestine during the Early Hellenistic Period* (London/Philadelphia:SCM Press/Fortress Press, 1974); L. Köhler, "Justice in the Gate," in his *Hebrew Man* (London/Nashville: SCM Press/Abingdon Press, 1956) 127-50; B. W. Kovacs, "Is There a Class-Ethic in Proverbs?" in *Essays in Old Testament Ethics*, ed. J. L. Crenshaw and J. T. Willis (New York: KTAV, 1974)171-89; W. G. Lambert, *Babylonian Wisdom Literature* (Oxford: Clarendon Press, 1960); W. McKane, *Prophets and Wise Men* (London: SCM Press, 1965); *idem*, *Proverbs: A New Approach* (London/Philadelphia: SCM Press/Westminster Press, 1970); R. E. Murphy, "Form Criticism and Wisdom Literature," *CBQ* XXXI(1969)475-83; *idem*, "The Interpretation of Old Testament Wisdom Literature," *Int* XXIII(1969) 289-301; L. G. Perdue, *Wisdom and Cult; A Critical Analysis of the Views of Cult in the Wisdom Literatures of Israel and the Ancient Near East* (Missoula: Scholars Press, 1977); J. F. Priest, "Where is Wisdom to be Placed?" *JBR* XXXI(1963)275-82 = *SAIW*, 281-88; *idem*, "Humanism, Skepticism, and Pessimism in Israel," *JAAR* XXXVI(1968)311-26; G. von Rad, "Job XXXVIII and Ancient Egyptian Wisdom," in his *The Problem of the*

Hexateuch and Other Essays (Edinburgh/New York: Oliver & Boyd/McGraw-Hill, 1966)281-91 = SAIW, 267-77; idem, "The Joseph Narrative and Ancient Wisdom," in his Problem of the Hexateuch, 292-300 = SAIW, 439-47; idem, Wisdom in Israel (London/Nashville: SCM Press/Abingdon Press, 1972); H. H. Rowley, "The Book of Job and its Meaning," BJRUL XLI(1958-59)167-207 = his From Moses to Qumran: Studies in the Old Testament (London: Lutterworth Press, 1963)141-83; J. C. Rylaarsdam, Revelation in Jewish Wisdom Literature (Chicago: University of Chicago Press, 1946); R. B. Y. Scott, "Solomon and the Beginnings of Wisdom in Israel," VTS III(1960)262-79 = SAIW, 84-101; idem, Proverbs, Ecclesiastes (Garden City: Doubleday, 1965); idem, "The Study of the Wisdom Literature," Int XXIV(1970)20-45; idem, The Way of Wisdom in the Old Testament (New York/London: Macmillan/Collier-Macmillan, 1971); M. Smith, Palestinian Parties and Politics That Shaped the Old Testament (New York: Columbia University Press, 1971); S. Talmon, " 'Wisdom' in the Book of Esther," VT XIII(1963)419-55; M. Weinfeld, "The Origin of Humanism in Deuteronomy," JBL LXXX(1961)241-47; idem, "Deuteronomic Literature and Wisdom Literature," in his Deuteronomy and the Deuteronomic School (Oxford: Clarendon Press, 1972) 244-319; R. N. Whybray, Wisdom in Proverbs (London: SCM Press, 1965); idem, The Succession Narrative: A Study of II Samuel 9–20; I Kings 1 and 2 (London: SCM Press, 1968); idem, The Intellectual Tradition in the Old Testament (Berlin/New York: Walter de Gruyter, 1974); R. J. Williams, "Wisdom in the Ancient Near East," IDBS, 949-52; W. Zimmerli, "The Place and Limit of the Wisdom in the Framework of the Old Testament Theology," SJT XVII(1964)146-58 = SAIW, 314-26; idem, "Concerning the Structure of Old Testament Wisdom," SAIW, 175-99.

The author of the Wisdom of Solomon, writing probably in the first century BCE, commented on the various fields of human learning which he had mastered. He declares:

> For it is he (God) who gave me unerring knowledge of what exists,
>   to know the structure of the world and the activity of the elements;
> the beginning and end and middle of times,
>   the alternations of the solstices and the changes of the seasons,
> the cycles of the year and the constellations of the stars,
>   the natures of animals and the tempers of wild beasts,
> the powers of spirits and the reasonings of men,
>   the varieties of plants and the virtues of roots;
> I learned both what is secret and what is manifest,
>   for wisdom,the fashioner of all things, taught me.
>
> (Wisdom of Solomon 7:17-22)

If the claims of this text about "universal knowledge" could be transposed into contemporary idiom, the author would speak of his knowledge of earth sciences, meterology, astronomy, zoology, demonology, psychology, botany, and pharmacy.

Writing a century or so earlier, Jesus ben Sirach described how wisdom had come to dwell in a special way in Israel.

> "I came forth from the mouth of the Most High,
>   And covered the earth like a mist. . . .
> In the waves of the sea, in the whole earth,
>   and in every people and nation I have gotten a possession.
> Among all these I sought a resting place;
>   I sought in whose territory I might lodge.
> Then the Creator of all things gave me a commandment,
>   and the one who created me assigned a place for my tent.
> And he said, 'Make your dwelling in Jacob,
>   and in Israel receive your inheritance.' . . .
> So I took root in an honored people,
>   in the portion of the Lord, who is their inheritance.
> I grew tall like a cedar in Lebanon,

and like a cypress on the heights of Hermon.
I grew tall like a palm tree in Engedi,
   and like rose plants in Jericho;
like a beautiful olive tree in the field,
   and like a plane tree I grew tall. . . .
Come to me, you who desire me,
   and eat your fill of my produce.
For the remembrance of me is sweeter than honey,
   and my inheritance sweeter than the honeycomb.
Those who eat me will hunger for more,
   and those who drink me will thirst for more.
Whoever obeys me will not be put to shame,
   and those who work with my help will not sin."
All this is the book of the covenant of the Most High God,
   the law which Moses commanded us as an inheritance for
the congregations of Jacob. (Sirach 24:3,6-8,12-14,19-23)

Both of these quotes about wisdom come from books written late in Jewish life and from works that did not find their way into the Hebrew canon. A number of features in these passages are noteworthy and reflective of the role of wisdom and learning in maturing Judaism. (1) Wisdom or knowledge is understood as an entity in itself which pervades the whole of creation. (2) Wisdom exists as a special creation of God. (3) Wisdom encompasses not only scientific knowledge of the world and human existence but also the commandments embodied in Mosaic legislation, i.e., the contents of both rational reflection and revelatory activity fall under the purview of wisdom. (4) In a special way, Israel has been granted a unique relationship to wisdom and has offered wisdom a fertile field in which to flourish and flower. (5) Although wisdom is something to be acquired, it is also the gift of God and the product of wisdom's self-giving nature. (6) Wisdom's enticing invitation promises a life without shame, existence without sin, and knowledge without end.

This elevated assessment of intellectual concerns found in the Wisdom of Solomon and the book of Sirach represents a late and highly developed understanding of the role of knowledge in human life. Lying behind such an evaluation is a long tradition of rational reflection about human experience and conduct in the multifaceted orders of creation. Some of this reflection and its products are embodied in the so-called wisdom books of the Hebrew scriptures—Proverbs, Job, and Ecclesiastes. Unfortunately, only the shadows and contours of this reflection on life in Israelite culture can be traced by modern scholarship. The strictly wisdom books in the canon are all post-exilic in their final form, but the intellectual tradition which is represented therein was no doubt as ancient as the nation itself, as complex as the course of Israel's historical existence, as multifarious as her institutional structures, and as diverse as her experience and understanding of the world.

A. Wisdom in Israel

The Old Testament term translated "wisdom," ḥokmāh, is used with a diversity of meanings and in a variety of contexts. Passages which speak of intellectual and moralistic concerns frequently employ not only the word ḥokmāh but also a number of apparently synonymous equivalents (see Prov 1:1-5). This multiplicity of meanings and terminology produces imprecision in scholarly attempts to grasp exactly what the ancients meant when they spoke of "wisdom."

The designation of certain Old Testament books and sections of material as "wisdom" is, of course, a modern and scholarly labeling and has no roots in the Jewish division of the canon. No canonical collection of books was titled "wisdom" in the Hebrew Bible. Scholars differ widely not only in their understanding of the nature of "wisdom" in ancient Israel but also in what books and literary works should be placed in this classification.

In Israel, a person's knowledge and ability could be

spoken of as wisdom in a spectrum that encompassed cunning shrewdness, technical expertise, moral discipline, and scholarly erudition. King Solomon, the paradigmatic representative of the Israelite wise man, is depicted as possessing a wide variety of wisdom.

The famous wisdom of Solomon is presented in the narratives of that king's reign in I Kings 1–11 [as]: (1) the cunning required for Solomon to settle David's old grudge against Joab (2:1-2, 5-6); (2) the moral discernment necessary for the establishment of true justice (3:9, 12); (3) the intellectual brilliance and encyclopedic knowledge that found expression in Solomon's thousands of proverbs and songs (4:29-34); (4) the special competence of a ruler and administrator (5:7,12). (Scott, 1971, 6)

If wisdom could embrace such a broad spectrum of skills and attitudes, what constituted its content and how was it acquired? Certainly not everyone in Israel was expected to be the equal of Solomon, and surely the average person did not possess the monarch's unlimited opportunities and options.

The acquisition of wisdom—in both its technical-vocational and general senses—constitutes part of that process known as socialization. Berger and Luckmann have described this process in terms of the sociology of knowledge. "The individual . . . , is not born a member of society. He is born with a predisposition toward sociality, and he becomes a member of society" (129). Socialization involves the process by which the individual becomes a member of society, "taking over the world in which others already live" apprehending "the world as a meaningful and social reality" (130). The basic or primary socialization is undergone in childhood.

Every individual is born into an objective social structure within which he encounters the significant others who are in charge of his socialization. These significant others are imposed upon him. Their definitions of his situation are posited for him as objective reality. He is thus born into not only an objective

325

social structure but also an objective social world. The significant others who mediate this world to him modify it in the course of mediating it. They select aspects of it in accordance with their own location in the social structure, and also by virtue of their individual, biographically rooted idiosyncrasies. The social world is "filtered" to the individual through this double selectivity.

. . . Primary socialization involves more than purely cognitive learning. It takes place under circumstances that are highly charged emotionally. (131)

In the primary socialization, the person achieves or is given a self-identity within a given social structure which is understood as the objective world. The external world with its significant figures and view of reality is internalized. This internalization of society, social mores and values, and reality is never a once-for-all process. Self-understanding, self-identity, and self-consciousness as well as one's appropriation of society and all that accompanies it may develop in new ways and involve dialectic tension between the self and its context. Persons may be inducted into new internalization of social realities, new approaches to life, and new values which may deepen, challenge, or destroy some components in the primary socialization.

The older and parenting generation serves as the socializing agent and context for the young being socialized. It is the older generation that transfers to the new not only an understanding of the world but also the skills and dispositions for living in that world. This transference, whether the skills of a trade or an approach to the art of living, occurs in a communal context.

Every individual always possesses a family, a tribe or a town, that is some specific form of community life. This community life has its ethical atmosphere; it compels the individual to live up to specific expectations which people have of him, it provides him with long established examples and values. As a rule the individual conforms unthinkingly to these community-determined factors; but *vice versa,* the rules of behaviour are also, in turn, conformed to these factors. It would, therefore, be unrealistic to try to understand the behavioural rules of a community as a more or less direct expression of specific, absolute, ethical convictions of principle. The role which a man has to play in the community into which he is born is to a great extent conditional and determined by community considerations. (von Rad, 1972, 75)

The knowledge and values of a community are transferred through the total life of the community. All its institutions—family, cult, economics, politics—contribute, some more directly than others, to the socialization process.

All communities demand that its members submit to certain standards and patterns of behavior. Certain actions are required while others are prohibited. These requirements and prohibitions are regulated by laws supervised and enforced by legal institutions. Such regulations and prohibitions function to protect and preserve basic human institutions and relationships and to order society toward certain goals. At the same time, society or elements in a community can advocate and encourage patterns of behavior and attitudes toward existence which do not and cannot enjoy legal sanction. Thus a society can establish regulations which prohibit the violation of a person's well-being, life, or property and can take action against offenders. However, a society can only encourage caring and considerate attitudes and actions of a self-sacrificial nature by its members. Both of these elements—the regulated and the recommended—are factors in the socialization process. (To a limited extent, these elements overlap since each seeks to support and sustain social structures. This partially explains the parallels and similarities between certain proverbs and legal traditions; compare Prov 22:22, 28 with Ex 23:6 and Deut 19:14.)

Very little is known from the Old Testament about the

socialization process in ancient Israel. Since Israelite life was structured around the extended family, it must be assumed that this kinship group constituted the primary context of the socialization process. The extended family, in a patrilineal society like that of Israel, consisted of the patriarch, his wife or wives and concubines, the sons and their wives, and the children. The extended family included members down to the third and fourth generation (see Ex 20:5). The extended family was part of larger kinship groups which included clans and tribes (see I Sam 10:21). The primary obligations for preparing the children for life in the world fell upon the father. The Talmud noted the minimum requirements that were the responsibility of the father to the son: "He must circumcise him, redeem him, teach him Torah, teach him a trade, and find a wife for him" (Kiddushin 29a). A literary and somewhat idealized portrait of the father as teacher is found in Proverbs:

When I was a son with my father,
   tender, the only one in the sight of my mother,
he taught me, and said to me,
   "Let your heart hold fast my words;
   keep my commandments, and live;
do not forget, and do not turn away from the words of my mouth.
   Get wisdom; get insight.
Do not forsake her, and she will keep you;
   love her, and she will guard you." (Prov 4:3-6)

In spite of the patriarchal orientation of Israelite society, the Old Testament also stresses the importance of the mother's instruction (see Prov 1:8; 6:20; 31:1,26).

On the analogy of other cultures, the existence of schools has been postulated for Israelite culture. The first direct reference to a school in Hebrew literature, however, is no earlier than the book of Sirach (51:23). Schools or formal educational structures, once they become an integrated part of a culture, play an important role in the socialization process. Schools demand a special class, namely teachers and scholars, and also create the opportunity for the academic pursuit of knowledge. With the development of cultural complexity and the elaboration of institutional structures, special education becomes a necessity. If schools existed in ancient Israel, then one might find the *Sitz im Leben* of much Israelite wisdom, especially that found in the book of Proverbs, in such institutions.

If Israelite "wisdom" and sages played important roles in their culture, as there seems no reason to doubt, and their functions contributed to the complex socialization process, how can these roles and functions be understood and subsequently related to the Old Testament wisdom traditions? Although there is enormous diversity of opinion among scholars on these matters, at least the following considerations seem valid about the sociological contexts of wisdom.

(1) The primary socializing unit throughout Jewish history was the family. In the family, the elder generation represented the depository of wisdom. The older members of the family passed on the learned wisdom of the past, inducted new members into the customs, mores, and traditional beliefs of the family and its community context, and sought to instill an approach to life aimed at well-being and success. This tradition of wisdom was transmitted primarily through the actions and life-style of the older generation and was absorbed in osmotic fashion by the younger generation. Without doubt, wisdom based on the experiences of living was encapsulated in the form of wise sayings, admonitions, stories, and commandments and was taught directly to the young. Much of this wisdom may have been formulated as proverbs or maxims which appealed to the memory and challenged the will. This type of family or clan wisdom was not based on any systematically conceived and expressed philosophy of life rooted in clearly formulated principles of existence and ethical norms. It was instead pragmatic and experiential, based on lessons learned from life. The goal

of such instruction was competency in living which included but also greatly transcended what later came to be called morality.

There are no Old Testament narratives which present scenes of family life that might make possible a reconstruction of how this family education was transmitted. Such episodes were too common and ordinary to warrant the attention and consideration which literary depiction would have required. At the same time, it is impossible to determine how much of the Old Testament wisdom traditions, say in the book of Proverbs, stems from and was utilized in the family context.

(2) Next to the family and clan, the village or town was the most important communal context for the socialization of persons. Throughout Israelite history, the vast majority of the people lived in fortified agricultural villages. Most of these were quite small. Jerusalem, at the time of David, for example, was less than ten acres in size. Inside the fortifications, villages were densely populated and space was scarce. Those who lived in the village went out daily to labor in the surrounding fields.

The main gate to the town, through which the daily "coming and going" took place, constituted the hub of village life. It served as a market place where produce and products were sold and traded, as the place of justice where civil and criminal cases were tried, as the "civic center" where gatherings of all sorts were possible, and as the social and intellectual center of the community where the elders and the leisured could sit, socialize, and converse. The suffering Job is pictured, nostalgically recalling "when I went out to the gate of the city, when I prepared my seat in the square" (in front of the gate; Job 29:7). Without doubt, much of the popular folk wisdom originated and was utilized in the village gate. Here the village "intellectuals" and homespun philosophers gave vent to their understanding of life and its problems, dialogued about the great issues of human existence—life and death, love and hate, sorrow and joy, wealth and poverty, right and wrong, wisdom and foolishness—and sharpened their ability to describe, distill, and encapsulate their wisdom and understanding. Some persons no doubt were known and revered for their wisdom (see II Sam 14:1-24; 20:14-22, where the wise ones are women). In describing his reputation in the gate, Job declared:

Men listened to me, and waited,
  and kept silence for my counsel.
After I spoke they did not speak again,
  and my word dropped upon them.
They waited for me as for the rain;
  and they opened their mouths as for the spring rain.

(Job 29:21-23)

A good reputation in the gate was a highly desired goal in life (see Prov 31:23,31). "Wisdom is too high for a fool; in the gate he does not open his mouth" (Prov 24:7). When the poet chose to describe where wisdom calls to men, he spoke of "beside the gates in front of the town, at the entrance of the portals" (Prov 8:3).

Although we are fairly well informed (see Köhler) about the process of "justice in the gate"—the nature and function of the village legal assembly—we know very little about "wisdom in the gate." In spite of this, there are sufficient indications to suggest its great importance in the life of Israel and in the history of the biblical wisdom traditions.

(3) Ancient Israel certainly possessed teachers and thus some form of educational structures and traditions. Whether one should speak of schools is a debated issue (see Whybray, 1974, 33-43). Writing was certainly known and employed in Israel and simple instruction in handwriting to produce competency requires, as every schoolchild knows, long hours of work and instruction. That writing in the ancient world seems to have always been taught through the use of existing texts, which were memorized, transcribed, and copied, would suggest the existence of school texts. The administration of Israelite

government would have required the keeping of diverse records as well as foreign correspondence. This would have necessitated the training of at least a small cadre of educated elite as well as members of a bureaucratic support system. The rather complex administrative structures in Israel are reflected in the lists of administrators under David and Solomon (II Sam 8:15-18; 20:23-25; I Kings 4:1-6). The employment of official documents and records for the general public also required an educated scribal activity (see Jer 32:9-12; 36:4). The very existence of the Hebrew scriptures, many from an early period, as well as numerous Hebrew inscriptions unearthed at Israelite sites testify to the reality of an educated class in Israel.

Some scholars have assumed that the age of David and Solomon was a period of great enlightenment in Israel (see above, pp. 191-193; Brueggemann; and Crenshaw, *SAIW*, 16-20). According to this view, primarily advocated by von Rad, the earlier life and culture of Israel had always viewed the world and history and interpreted experiences and events in a direct relationship to the divine and sacral concepts. With David and Solomon, Israel underwent a radical intellectual revolution which resulted in a strong secularization of life. This secularization produced new perspectives on the world and a certain worldliness in thought.

Old wisdom [i.e., folk and family wisdom] in Israel was influenced by that enlightened intellectuality. To the obvious question as to the way in which this new conception finds characteristically theological expression, one must unhesitatingly reply that it does so in the recognition of a relative determinism inherent in events and also in the recognition of a relative value inherent in worldly things (life, property, honour, etc.). One must again qualify this by saying that it cannot precisely have been a matter of 'discovery' for, to be precise, a life without at least a tacit consideration of these factors would be unthinkable. And yet there is a great difference. (von Rad, 59)

The enlightenment of the Solomonic period, it is assumed, produced a great interest in education and in the wisdom and literature of other cultures (for a contrary view, see Scott, *SAIW*, 84-101). The internationalism and economic prosperity led to the emergence of a class of wise men at the court. From these circles came the earliest historical writing in Israel, encyclopedic lists of natural phenomena, court schools, educated royal advisors, and a class ethic for the prosperous upperclass. The wise men at the court, of whom the advisor Ahithopel represents one example (see II Sam 16:23), made a significant impact upon all aspects of Israelite life but especially in the area of foreign affairs (see McKane, 1965).

Von Rad's portrayal of the Solomonic enlightenment and its educational impact has probably gone beyond the evidence. The following developments, however, can be seen as direct influences emanating from the Davidic-Solomonic epoch. (a) This period was the first in Israelite history where it is possible to speak of Israel as possessing the channels and associations which would have opened the culture to major influences from non-Palestinian civilizations, especially Egyptian. The assumption that Israel—the court and officialdom—was the recipient of such influences, including the impact of wisdom literature, does not seem unwarranted. (b) The development of education must have been fostered by the political and economic conditions and requirements of the day. (c) Schools or educational structures would seem to have been a natural development. The elaborate developments associated with the temple and its personnel could have produced the need for what might be called a "temple school." The training of persons for service at the court and in royal and military administration would seem to have required some continuing form of education and therefore professional teachers. (d) A class of educated personnel would have been associated with the court, and to this extent the court could be seen as the patron and promoter of wisdom. Perhaps it was this association which led to the idealistic picture of Solomon's wisdom (see I Kings 4:29-34). (e) The stratification of classes in society, a product of administrative and economic processes, must have become more characteristic of society with the development of a national state. This could have led to the encouragement of a class ethic, that is, an ethic or wisdom for the upperclass or professionals (see Kovacs). (f) The extended family continued to function as the primary context for education and to perform its role as the basic socializing unit although its perspectives may have been considerably broadened through contact with the larger world.

(4) By the time of Ben Sirach (about 180 BCE), scribes and scholars had developed as a professional class in Jewish culture. Their profession, he wrote, "depends on the opportunity of leisure; and he who has little business may become wise" (38:24). He describes the preoccupation of certain groups with physical labor which prevented their concern with "intellectual affairs."

All these [farmers, craftsmen, smiths, potters] rely upon their
    hands,
    and each is skillful in his own work.
Without them a city cannot be established,
    and men can neither sojourn nor live there.
Yet they [unlike the scribes] are not sought out for the council
    of the people,
    nor do they attain eminence in the public assembly.
They do not sit in the judge's seat,
    nor do they understand the sentence of judgment;
they cannot expound discipline or judgment,
    and they are not found using proverbs.
But they keep stable the fabric of the world,
    and their prayer is in the practice of their trade. (Sir 38:31-34)

Although Ben Sirach considered the study of the Torah to be a primary concern of the scribe he also points to the diverse source of the scribe's knowledge.

He will seek out the wisdom of all the ancients,
  and will be concerned with prophecies;
he will preserve the discourse of notable men
  and penetrate the subtleties of parables;
he will seek out the hidden meanings of proverbs
  and be at home with the obscurities of parables.
He will serve among great men and appear before rulers,
  he will travel through the lands of foreign nations,
  for he tests the good and the evil among men. (39:1b-4)

When he described the activities of the scribe, Ben Sirach declared:

He will be filled with the spirit of understanding;
  he will pour fourth words of wisdom
  and give thanks to the Lord in prayer.
He will direct his counsel and knowledge aright,
  and meditate on his secrets.
He will reveal instruction in his teaching,
  and will glory in the law of the Lord's covenant.
Many will praise his understanding,
  and it will never be blotted out;
his memory will not disappear,
  and his name will live through all generations.
Nations will declare his wisdom,
  and the congregation will proclaim his praise;
if he lives long, he will leave a name greater than a thousand,
  and if he goes to rest, it is enough for him. (39:6b-11)

Thus, by the end of the third century, there had developed a scribal tradition and approach in Judaism which felt free to draw upon all available sources of knowledge, including the Mosaic tradition, and which saw itself as the bearer of a teaching responsibility (see the quote from the Wisdom of Solomon at the beginning of this chapter).

The exact course which led to this development can no longer be detailed. Only a few hints can be gathered from the Old Testament itself. The term "scribe" (sophēr), in texts describing pre-exilic conditions, is used of persons who exercised administrative powers and possessed secretarial capabilities. A *sophēr* ("secretary") was an official in the royal administration (II Sam 8:17; I Kings 4:2; II Kings 12:10; 22:3) and possessed a special chamber in the royal palace (Jer 36:12). The term was also applied to persons outside governmental service who functioned as recorders and secretaries (Jer 36:4, 26).

A new use, or the first attestation of such usage, of the term appears in the description of Ezra as a "the priest, the scribe, learned in matters of the commandments of the Lord and his statutes" or a "scribe of the law of the God of heaven" (Ezra 7:11-12). Ezra was thus a "doctor of the law," a member of a professional class which may have developed under exilic conditions. As a priest, Ezra was both a student/interpreter and a teacher of the law (Ezra 7:10). The Chronicler offers witness to the existence of scribes among Levitical and priestly circles (I Chron 2:55; II Chron 34:13). One may assume that part of the function of these scribes was the training of students and teachers of the law. Their interests and concerns, however, may have exceeded a concern with the law and have incorporated learning borrowed from many quarters. During the Maccabean struggles, for example, the Jerusalem priesthood was more open to the practices and thought of Hellenistic culture than other segments of the society (see Hengel, I, 78-83).

On the basis of evidence supplied by Ben Sirach and the references to "wisemen" (maskîlîm; see below, p. 389) in the book of Daniel (11:33, 35; 12:3), it is safe to assume that in post-exilic times there were also professional scribes/teachers whose intellectual pursuits and instruction drew upon the broadest areas of human learning. Their instruction and services, unlike the priestly scribes, were performed alongside the religious institutions. Some of these scribes may have had some connection with the synagogue, a lay institution, but nothing certain can be said on this since the origin of the synagogue is shrouded in mystery.

A contemporary scholar has summarized the varied

roots of the near eastern wisdom traditions in a manner that is reasonably descriptive of the process in Israel:

Three roots of the international Wisdom movement can be distinguished: (a) the universal practice of instruction by parents and teachers in the knowledge and skills as well as in the moral standards that have proved advantageous for success in living; (b) the giving of counsel by those men (or women) who have gained a reputation for unusual intelligence, knowledge, and good judgment; and (c) the special skills and intellectual powers associated with literacy in a generally illiterate society. The key figures were thus the parent or teacher, the counselor, and the scribe. The first of these is as old as the family, the second as old as the larger society. Both are logically and chronologically prior to the third; and they retained their importance after the invention of writing had created the scribal profession and eventually produced the thinker and literary artist. (Scott, 1965, XLII)

B. The Character of Israelite Wisdom

A number of genres are employed in Old Testament wisdom literature (see above, pp. 151-54; Crenshaw, 1974; and von Rad, 1972, 24-50). Although scholars are in general agreement about the analysis into literary types, there is a great difference of opinion about the socio-logical context and function of the various genres.

(1) The basic form of wisdom expression is the sentence, proverb, or saying. The old description of a proverb as a "short saying based on long experience" is apropos ancient Israel's proverbs. Such sayings seek to state a general truth or insight in a succinct, interest-catching, sometimes witty, and frequently assonant form.

Many biblical proverbs are comprised of two parallel lines. The second line in some way develops the first. This represents a type of "rhyming" in which the thoughts of the two lines are rhymed. One form of this type of parallelism is synonymous parallelism in which the second line gives expression to the thought of the first line but in different words and from a different perspective. The following are examples:

It is not good to be partial to a wicked man,
    or to deprive a righteous man of justice. (Prov 18:5)
A false witness will not go unpunished.
    and he who utters lies will not escape. (Prov 19:5)
Slothfulness casts into a deep sleep,
    and an idle person will suffer hunger. (Prov 19:15)
The rich rules over the poor,
    and the borrower is the slave of the lender. (Prov 22:7)

Far more frequent are proverbs stated in antithetic parallelism where the second line offers an antithesis to the first. Practically all the proverbs in Prov 10–15 fit into this classification. Examples are:

A wise son makes a father glad,
    but a foolish son is a sorrow to his mother. (Prov 10:1)
A son who gathers in summer is prudent,
    but a son who sleeps in harvest brings shame. (Prov 10:5)
Hatred stirs up strife,
    but love covers all offenses. (Prov 10:12)
A good wife is the crown of her husband,
    but she who brings shame is like rottenness in his bones. (Prov 12:4)
Hope deferred makes the heart sick,
    but a desire fulfilled is a tree of life. (Prov 13:12)
A tranquil mind gives life to the flesh,
    but passion makes the bones rot. (Prov 14:30)

A third form of parallelism is called synthetic, in which the second line is a further development of the initial statement. Sometimes the secondary statement completes or intensifies the primary; sometimes it makes the specific more general or *vice versa*. Examples are:

The mind of the wise makes his speech judicious,
    and adds persuasiveness to his lips.
Pleasant words are like a honeycomb,

sweetness to the soul and health to the body. (Prov 16:23-24)
A hoary head is a crown of glory;
  it is gained in a righteous life. (Prov 16:31)
Wine is a mocker, strong drink a brawler;
  and whoever is led astray by it is not wise. (Prov 20:1)
He who states his case first seems right,
  until the other comes and examines him.
The lot puts an end to disputes
  and decides between powerful contenders. (Prov 18:17-18)
Death and life are in the power of the tongue,
  and those who love it will eat its fruits. (Prov 18:21)

Some simple proverbs are built around comparisons which might be called parabolic parallelism. These constructions are reflected in English translation in several ways: "better . . . than . . . ," "as . . . so," "like . . . is . . . ." Examples are:

Better is a little with righteousness,
  than great revenues with injustice. (Prov 16:8)
Better is a dry morsel with quiet
  than a house full of feasting with strife. (Prov 17:1)
It is better to live in the corner of a housetop
  than in a house shared with a contentious woman. (Prov 25:24)
Better is open rebuke than hidden love. (Prov 27:5)

As the heavens for height, and the earth for depth,
  so the mind of kings is unsearchable. (Prov 25:3)
As a door turns on its hinges,
  so does a sluggard on his bed. (Prov 26:14)
As in water face answers to face,
  so the mind of man reflects the man. (Prov 27:19)

Like vinegar to the teeth, and smoke to the eyes,
  so is the sluggard to those who send him. (Prov 10:26)
Like clouds and wind without rain
  is a man who boasts of a gift he does not give. (Prov 25:14)
Like a lame man's legs, which hang useless,
  is a proverb in the mouth of fools. (Prov 26:7)
Like a dog that returns to his vomit
  is a fool that repeats his folly. (Prov 26:11)

Within the book of Proverbs, there also appear numerous short sentences which can only be described as admonitions, exhortations, and prohibitions. These forms, instead of stating a fact or perception in an impersonal fashion, appeal directly to the listener. Examples of admonitions and exhortations are:

Leave the presence of a fool,
    for there you do not meet words of knowledge. (Prov 14:7)
Train up a child in the way he should go,
    and when he is old he will not depart from it. (Prov 22:6)
Hearken to your father who begot you,
    and do not despise your mother when she is old. (Prov 23:22)
Discipline your son, and he will give you rest;
    he will give delight to your heart. (Prov 29:17)

Examples of prohibitions are:

Do not rob the poor, because he is poor,
    or crush the afflicted at the gate;
for Yahweh will plead their cause
    and despoil of life those who despoil them.
Make no friendship with a man given to anger,
    nor go with a wrathful man,
lest you learn his ways
    and entangle yourself in a snare.
Be not one of those who give pledges,
    who become surety for debts.
If you have nothing with which to pay
    why should your bed be taken from under you?
Remove not the ancient landmark
    which your fathers have set. (Prov 22:22-28)

Many of these admonitory commands and prohibitions have parallels in Old Testment laws. Like the laws, "they have been preserved and transmitted within the society which they sought to protect. Not priests or prophets but fathers, tribal heads, wise men, and, secondarily, court officials, . . . are the earliest guardians of the precepts. Basically, it is the father, who addresses his son directly, counseling him for his life. The father speaks from experience and with authority, and thus the peculiarly persuasive tone of the commandments, which does not need the threat of legal punishment, becomes explainable" (Gerstenberger, 50-51).

The exhortations and prohibitions frequently occur with motivation clauses which offer the supporting evidence or reasons for a particular course of behavior.

Let your foot be seldom in your neighbor's house,
   lest he become weary of you and hate you. (Prov 25:17)
If your enemy is hungry, give him bread to eat,
   and if he is thirsty, give him water to drink;
for you will heap coals of fire on his head,
   and Yahweh will reward you. (Prov 25:21-22)
Do not boast about tomorrow,
   for you do not know what a day may bring forth. (Prov 27:1)

(2) Numerical sayings bring together lists of phenomena possessing similar characteristics. The number in the lists vary from one to two up to nine to ten. As a rule, the similarity becomes apparent, and in a surprising fashion, only when the diverse phenomena are viewed from a particular perspective. Examples are:

Three things are never satisfied;
   four never say, "Enough":
Sheol, the barren womb,
   the earth ever thirsty for water,
   and the fire which never says, "Enough." (Prov 30:15b-16)

Three things are stately in their tread;
   four are stately in their stride:
the lion, which is mightiest among beasts
   and does not turn back before any;
the strutting cock, the he-goat,
   and a king striding before his people. (Prov 30:29-31)

Four things on earth are small,
   but they are exceedingly wise:

the ants are a people not strong,
   yet they provide their food in summer;
the badgers are a people not mighty,
   yet they make their homes in the rocks;
the locusts have no king,
   yet all of them march in rank;
the lizard you can take in your hands,
    yet it is in kings' palaces. (Prov 30:24-28)

There are six things which the Lord hates,
   seven which are an abomination to him:
haughty eyes, a lying tongue,
   and hands that shed innocent blood,
a heart that devises wicked plans,
   feet that make haste to run to evil,
a false witness who breathes out lies,
   and a man who sows discord among brothers. (Prov 6:16-19)

(3) Although there are no genuine riddles in the Old Testament wisdom literature, biblical references to riddles appear (Ps 49:5; Hab 2:6; Sir 39:3) and Prov 1:6 suggests that riddles were a stock-in-trade of the wise man's repertoire. The Queen of Sheba is supposed to have "jousted" with Solomon about riddles (I Kings 10:1-5; II Chron 9:1-4). The only true riddle in the Old Testament occurs in the Samson stories (Judg 14:10-18; see Prov 23:29-30; Sir 22:14). The riddle reflects a playful attitude in which the question conceals the answer and the truth is discovered by participation in a game.

(4) Like the riddle and numerical proverbs, the fable and allegory convey truth or a viewpoint through the use of cipher and metaphor and require a double reading to recognize the inner meaning of what is being conveyed. The fable, in which various nonhuman antagonists engage in verbal combat, was widespread in ancient cultures. Plants, animals, minerals, seasons, tool implements, parts of the body, and so forth were endowed with speech and extolled their greatness and importance (see Williams; ANET,592-93; Lambert, 150-212). The most

full-blown fable in the Old Testament is Jotham's fable (Judg 9:7-15) which is a political satirization of the monarchy as a form of government (see II Kings 14:9). The fable is very similar to the allegory in that the hearer is required to provide an identification of the elements in order to reach an appropriate interpretation. Fables or historical allegories appear in Ezek 17 and 19 and were widespread in apocalyptic literature (see Dan 7).

Two allegorical passages appear in wisdom literature: Prov 5:15-23 and Eccl 12:1-6. In the former, the wife is described as a cistern and a well. The allegory serves as an admonishment to beware of other women and to remain true to one's own wife. In the latter, growing old is depicted in metaphorical language as the gradual deterioration and demise of a flourishing household.

Although some of the metaphors are difficult, the following appear to be self-evident: the keepers of the house are the arms, the strong men are the legs, the grinders are the teeth, those that look through the windows are the eyes, the doors on the street are the ears, the daughters of song is the voice, the almond tree is the gray hair, the grasshopper is the creaking bone or sluggish movement, the snapped silver cord, broken golden bowl, shattered pitcher and broken wheel are death. (Crenshaw, 1974, 246-47)

(5) Many exmples of ancient near eastern wisdom literature are presented in autobiographical form. In such texts, the aged sage offers his readers/hearers the learning drawn from long and varied experience. The autobiographical form probably reflects a literary genre or stereotypical approach rather than actual experience. Frequently such forms are presented as the final testimony of the departing (see, for example, the Testaments of the Twelve Patriarchs in the Pseudepigrapha). The book of Ecclesiastes adopts this form of presentation (see especially 1:12–2:26) although the autobiographical scheme is not characteristic of its entire contents.

Several passages in Proverbs are presented in autobiographical form (Prov 4:3-9; 7:6-27; 24:30-34; see also Ps 37:25; 73; Job 4:8; 5:3; Sir 34:11-12).

I passed by the field of a sluggard,
  by the vineyard of a man without sense;
and lo, it was all overgrown with thorns;
  the ground was covered with nettles,
  and its stone wall was broken down.
Then I saw and considered it;
  I looked and received instruction.
A little sleep, a little slumber,
  a little folding of the hands to rest,
and poverty will come upon you like a robber,
  and want like an armed man. (Prov 24:30-34)

This stylistic form, no doubt, was one means the instructor employed to attract the listener's attention; but it also enlivened the presentation, laid claim to the teacher's personal experience and authority as authentication, and encouraged the listener to reflect upon his own experience.

(6) A genre which gave full potential for the examination of multifaceted problems was the dialogue. This type of disputation literature enjoyed widespread popularity throughout the Near East (see *ANET*,405-7;600-604). Diverse protagonists appear in the texts: tamarisk tree and date palm, master and slave, a man and his soul, a man and his friend(s). Generally under discussion is the relative worth of certain professions, items, or courses of action. Within the Old Testament, only the book of Job is written in dialogue form.

(7) A class of texts found in Egypt, Mesopotamia, and Israel was the list or onomasticon which catalogued the names of natural phenomena, places, trades, flora and fauna, minerals, cities, and so forth. In addition to 3000 proverbs and 1005 songs attributed to Solomon, such lists appear to be ascribed to him: "He spoke of trees, from the cedar that is in Lebanon to the hyssop that grows out of the wall; he spoke also of beasts, and of birds, and of reptiles, and of fish" (I Kings 4:33).

Utilization of such lists appears in Job 38–39 (see also Ps 148; Sir 43). In these texts one finds descriptions and enumerations of phenomena which move from the heavens to heavenly bodies to meteorological elements to things on earth. The descriptive enumeration in the form of a rhetorical interrogation which characterizes the speech of Yahweh in Job 38–39 also appears in Egyptian texts. The latter texts, like their biblical counterparts, are frequently characterized by the movement from cosmological to meteorological to terrestial phenomena (see von Rad, 1966).

Such onomastica reflect an early "scientific" approach to the world that sought to organize data in a comprehensive fashion. With such knowledge, one possessed a handle on the universe of phenomena which aided in the understanding of existence and provided a framework for the incorporation of new data. Such data and lists no doubt constituted a component in such an educational curriculum of the wise as is noted in Wisdom of Solomon 7:17-22. The priestly writer's description of creation in Gen 1, with its ordered and scientific presentation of creation, probably relied upon the type of learning which formed the basis of the onomastica.

(8) The wise in Israel also produced what can only be described as polished literary poems. An example, although not a literary gem, is the poem on the ideal wife in Prov 31:10-31. This text is composed in an acrostic pattern; that is, the first line begins with the first letter of the alphabet, the second with the second letter, and so on through the entire twenty-two letters of the alphabet. One of the best-known literary creations is found in the book of Ecclesiastes.

For everything there is a season,
and a time for every matter under heaven:
a time to be born, and a time to die;
a time to plant, and a time to pluck up what is planted;
a time to kill, and a time to heal;
a time to break down, and a time to build up;

a time to weep, and a time to laugh;
a time to mourn, and a time to dance;
a time to cast away stones, and a time to gather stones together;
a time to embrace, and a time to refrain from embracing;
a time to seek, and a time to lose;
a time to keep, and a time to cast away;
a time to rend, and a time to sew;
a time to keep silence, and a time to speak;
a time to love, and a time to hate;
a time for war, and a time for peace. (3:1-8)

The book of Job contains numerous didactic poems which are complete in themselves as is Prov 1—9. For example, poems describe the fate of wicked men (see Job 15:17-35; 20:2-29; 27:13-23) as well as the one whom God chastens (Job 5:17-27). Some poems in Job manifest a hymnic style (on hymnic style, see above, p. 141).

(God) removes mountains, and they know it not,
    when he overturns them in his anger;
who shakes the earth out of its place,
    and its pillars tremble;
who commands the sun, and it does not rise;
    who seals up the stars;
who alone stretched out the heavens,
    and trampled the waves of the sea;
who made the Bear and Orion,
    the Pleiades and the chambers of the south;
who does great things beyond understanding,
    and marvelous things without number. (Job 9:5-10)

Of the above genres, and the list is not exhaustive, only very general comments may be made about their original sociological settings in Israelite culture. The forms most likely deriving from and used in the family and clan contexts are the single proverb and admonition/prohibition. Many of the single proverbs, sentences, riddles, and numerical proverbs may have been related to the popular folk culture—the wisdom in the gate. The more developed forms of wisdom—onomastica, dialogues, and

didactic poems—seem to presuppose a structured educational context and a professional teaching or scribal
class. What role should be assigned to court wisdom and
the training of a learned officialdom remains uncertain.
Such material as is found in Prov 16:10-15; 23:1-3; 25:1-7
seems to presuppose the world of the royal court; but this
is an exception rather than the rule and little, even in
Proverbs, possesses the character of career advice for
officials.

The character and content of Old Testament wisdom
have created problems for certain biblical, especially
Protestant, theologians. Proverbs, Job, and Ecclesiastes
are distinctly different from the remainder of the Old
Testament. Stated in rather radical form, the following
may be noted as the distinctive traits of Old Testament
wisdom in comparison with the other main specimens of
literature. (1) Unlike the law, wisdom literature neither
appeals to nor propounds commandments understood as
the revealed and timeless will of God granted to man and
whose obedience is the means to the blessings of God and
a righteous life. The majority of the genres of wisdom are
content to give expression to the way things are, to facts
drawn from observation and experience, or else they
appeal to the hearer with an exhorting admonition
offering practical advice which, if observed, promises to
enhance one's self-interest. The goals of wisdom were the
ability to understand one's environment, the capacity to
choose and pursue the proper course of action and at the
proper time, and the skill to act so as to ensure one's
survival and success. (2) Unlike the narrative literature,
wisdom shows little or no concern with the distinctive
history of Israel, its political and historical vicissitudes,
or with an understanding of the divine as a God who acts
in history to direct its course and to reveal his will.
Neither miracles nor supernatural interventions fall
within its purview. Instead, wisdom is concerned with
the issues confronting humanity in general, with man as
man, and with the typical and ever-recurring aspects of

life. (3) Unlike the prophets, the teachings of the wise are not presented as the word of God and are not substantiated with a "Thus says Yahweh." The speech of God in Job 38–41 is an exception, but it is a questioning of Job, not a proclamation. Wisdom's claim for authority rests on the appeal to tradition, to the person of the wise, to the rationality of the teaching, and to its compatability with experience. Unlike the prophets, the wise men did not address the human situation from a divine perspective, laying the world under judgment and demanding radical alteration in the structure and course of human life. Wisdom accepts the world as it is and does not advocate the stance of a crusading reformer or social critic. "Its statements try to grasp life from the aspect of that which always remains the same; they are open not to daily social problems but to that which is generally valid and which survives no matter what the social circumstances" (von Rad, 1972, 76). (4) Unlike the psalms, wisdom (although Job is an exception) does not focus on the divine-human relationship. Matters of sin and forgiveness, guilt and judgment, where they appear at all, lie at the periphery of concern. Wisdom focuses on interpersonal relations, the individual's relationship to social customs and institutions, and the problems of success and failure.

These characteristics have led many biblical scholars to declare that the wisdom literature is an alien body in the Old Testament, at best, a first cousin to paganism, or a secular instrusion into an otherwise religious and spiritual literature. At times, the wisdom literature, especially Ecclesiastes, has been declared to be nonbiblical, a position similar to declaring part of the U.S. Constitution to be unconstitutional!

Since Old Testament wisdom does not present itself as the product of divine inspiration or lay claim to the status of special divine revelation, it may be said to represent a horizontal rather than a vertical approach to truth and reality (see Rylaarsdam, 55). Or it may be understood as one example of what the church has traditionally designated "natural theology," that is, "the attempt to articulate the religious dimension of common human experience independently of special revelation" (Collins, 35).

Although much of wisdom dealt with matters of everyday life which could be understood as having no special relationship to the deity or sacred history, wisdom was not without its theological perspectives. This theological aspect can be seen in the four following ways.

(1) Throughout the wisdom traditions there is a stress on the limits which knowledge and wisdom encounter in the world.

Confidently, (the wise men) evaluate what has been experienced and bring every didactic aid into service in order to bring the pupil, too, to the point of trusting the experience of the teaching in question. But his freedom in the utilization of experiences, this ability to shape life, is not their only or even their last word. Occasionally even the wise men seem to exercise a degree of self-restraint in talking, as if they were anxious to go in the opposite direction, of limits which are imposed on wisdom and on the mastery of life, even, indeed, of situations where all human ingenuity is rendered ineffective. (von Rad, 1972, 99)

The limits to the human mastery of life recognized the presence of an incalculable dimension to existence. This meant that there was no infallible and predictable movement leading from human plan to execution, from human act to desirable consequence. Beneath the deeds and consequences of human actions there was frequently seen the depth of divine mystery.

A man's mind plans his way,
 but Yahweh directs his steps. (Prov 16:9)
Many are the plans in the mind of a man,
 but it is the purpose of Yahweh that will be established (Prov 19:21)
No wisdom, no understanding, no counsel,
 can avail against Yahweh.

349

The horse is made ready for the day of battle,
  but the victory belongs to Yahweh. (Prov 21:30-31)

(2) A frequently appearing emphasis in wisdom literature is laid on the "fear of Yahweh" as a basic principle.

The fear of Yahweh is the beginning of knowledge;
  fools despise wisdom and instruction. (Prov 1:7)
The fear of Yahweh is the beginning of wisdom,
  and the knowledge of the Holy One is insight. (Prov 9:10)
The fear of Yahweh is instruction in wisdom,
  and humility goes before honor. (Prov 15:33)
Behold, the fear of Yahweh, that is wisdom;
  and to depart from evil is understanding. (Job 28:28)

Two things should be said about this association of the "fear of Yahweh" and wisdom. (a) Fear of Yahweh appears in the Old Testament with a wide range of meanings (see von Rad, 1972, 66). These range from awe before Yahweh to obedience to the will of Yahweh to commitment to Yahweh. The expression should never be understood as mere psychic fright before God. (b) The idea of the fear of Yahweh as the first principle of knowledge and wisdom already reflects an attempt to think systematically about the relationship between wisdom and Yahwism.

(3) A further, and apparently chronologically later, development in wisdom thought was the personification of wisdom. The classical text presenting this view is Prov 8. In this text, the following elements are noteworthy: (a) Wisdom is understood as a female figure. (b) She calls out to man from the midst of life beckoning man to turn to and love her. (c) Dame Wisdom promises blessings and benefits for those who heed her invitation. (d) Wisdom is described as having been created in the beginning before the world was established and its features set. (e) She is presented as a "darling child" (perhaps a better translation than "master workman" in Prov 8:30) who is not only Yahweh's joy and delight but

350

also one who delights and rejoices in Yahweh and his creation.

This figure of personified wisdom seems dependent upon some of the near eastern imagery used in describing divine goddesses. The closest parallel is the figure of the Egyptian goddess Maat who, as the young daughter of the sun-god, is embraced in frolicking fashion by her father. Maat in Egyptian wisdom was also a central concept embracing the ideas of cosmic order, truth, right, justice, and law. More importantly, in such a personification, wisdom is given a special status with Yahweh. If Yahweh created the world through wisdom (Prov 3:19-20) and wisdom was present before all things (Prov 8), then there could be no gulf between wisdom and Yahwism. The discovery of the orders and principles of creation and all its manifestations is a discovery of the work and will of Yahweh.

(4) A further theologizing stage in wisdom thought is reflected in those texts which identify the whole of man's "scientific" knowledge with wisdom understood as a gift from God and which associate wisdom in a special way with the Torah given through Moses. (See the quotes from Wisdom of Solomon and Sirach given at the beginning of this chapter.)

C. Proverbs, Job, and Ecclesiastes

Within the development of wisdom literature in Israel, as within that of Egypt and Mesopotamia, there arose two widely differing strands of tradition. One line of approach, characteristic of the book of Proverbs, represents a confident and trusting attitude toward man's ability satisfactorily to understand and master life and reflects a positive assessment of man's capacity to comprehend the ways and will of God in the world. This tenor of the material holds true in spite of the proverbial recognition of wisdom's limitations. Many proverbs reflect this assurance and extol trust in Yahweh.

In the fear of Yahweh one has strong confidence,
    and his children will have a refuge. (Prov 14:26)
Commit your work to Yahweh,
    and your plans will be established. (Prov 16:3)
He who gives heed to the word will prosper,
    and happy is he who trusts in Yahweh. (Prov 16:20)
The name of Yahweh is a strong tower;
    the righteous man runs into it and is safe. (Prov 18:10)
The fear of man lays a snare,
    but he who trusts in Yahweh is safe. (Prov 29:25)

On the other hand, there developed a strand of skeptical wisdom literature which not only questioned many traditional assumptions and cherished beliefs but also laid seige to many of the time-honored religious claims, and in the process gave expression to the anguish of human existence and to the torment of living with unanswered questions. The books of Job and Ecclesiastes fall into this category.

The book of Proverbs actually constitutes a small library of wisdom traditions. Nine individual collections are present, some clearly denoted by superscriptions: 1–9; 10:1–22:16; 22:17–24:22; 24:23-34; 25–29; 30:1-14; 30:15-33; 31:1-9; 31:10-31. This thesaurus of material, probably edited late in Israelite history (fourth century BCE?), gathers up wisdom traditions deriving from all periods of Israelite history. It is impossible to arrange these collections in any clear chronological relationship. Although general scholarly opinion has assumed that such collections of isolated proverbs as found in Prov 10:1–22:16 are early while the instructional poems like Prov 1–9 are late, even these generalities are open to doubt. In Egyptian culture, didactic treatises (like Prov 1–9) were produced as early as the third millennium BCE, whereas collections of aphorisms of the proverbial type developed very late. In Mesopotamian culture, on the other hand, anthologies of proverbial wisdom (similar to Prov 10:1–22:16) date from the earliest times. (For a discussion of various forms and documents of nonbiblical near eastern wisdom parallel to Proverbs, see Williams and McKane, 1970, 51-208.) Such evidence would caution against any dogmatism about dating. Nonetheless, the extended discourses in Prov 1–9, both in form and content, seem to be the latest material in the book.

The literary dependence of Israelite wisdom found in Proverbs upon its near eastern counterparts was placed in a new light with the publication of the "Instruction of Amen-em-opet" (see *ANET*, 421-25) in 1923. This document, probably to be dated before 1000 BCE, contains such striking parallels to Prov 22:17–24:22 that some form of literary dependence is almost certain. Israelite borrowing from Egyptian sources seems undeniable. The instructional speeches in Prov 1–9 show striking parallels in form to Egyptian didactic discourses which use a conventional "father-son" address style (see Whybray, 1965). Such interrelatedness illustrates the international character of certain forms of wisdom and the universality of the issues with which wisdom dealt and of the insights into life which it offered.

The book of Job has been described as "the supreme literary masterpiece in the Old Testament and one of the greatest creations of the world's literature" (Rowley,141). In spite of almost universal appreciation for the book and the excellence of commentaries written on it (see especially those by E. Dhorme, R. Gordis, M. H. Pope, and N. H. Tur-Sinai), the work possesses characteristics which remain enigmatic. As a literary work, it is *sui generis*, and yet no other Old Testament book has such close parallels in the literature of Egypt and especially Mesopotamia (see *ANET*,589-91,596-604). At the same time, the book shares many characteristics with other Old Testament genres and reflects traits which can be related to actual life-situations in ancient Israelite culture and life.

The problem of the genre classification can best be seen in light of an outline of the book.

The prologue and the epilogue may have once circulated in Israel as a folk narrative which told of a pious, wealthy person who, in the face of great loss and personal suffering, continued to express his selfless piety and was restored to his former position as a reward. If so, this narrative was edited to form the setting for the creative poet who produced the dialogues and speeches in 3:1– 42:6.

Various attempts have been made to discover the model employed by the poet in his reworking of the old tale. One model has been sought in the secular lawsuit: (a) Job's statement of his case (3); (b) the presentation of the arguments in the case (4–27); (c) Job's final statement and oath (29–31); (d) the verdict of God as judge (38–41); and (e) Job's acceptance of the verdict (42:1-6). Another model may be seen in the lament ritual and prayers of the accused when an appeal was made to Yahweh in the sanctuary (see Ex 22:7-8; I Kings 8:31-32; Deut 17:8-13; 19:15-21; and above, p. 308). According to this model,the following would be the structural scheme: (a) the statement of the accused (3); (b) the presentation of the argumentation of the accusers and accused (4–27; see Ps 55:12-14); (c) the statement and oath of innocence (29–31; see Pss 17:3-5; 26:4-11); (d) the divine verdict (38–41); and (e) Job's acceptance of the verdict (42:1-6; see Deut 17:8-13). The existence of Mesopotamian texts which deal with the problem of the innocent sufferer or with the problems of social injustice, sometimes involving dialogues between friends (see *ANET*,601-4), might suggest that Job was modeled on an international literary genre but no comparative specimen equals its grandeur.

To define the central issue in the book of Job as the "problem of human suffering" places the work in too broad a context. The central issues are the questions of divine justice, of whether the fortune one encounters in life is the consequence of his doing, and of how the righteous sufferer can understand his status before God. Interpreters have consistently felt that the divine answer and Job's response do not fully resolve the issues raised in the speeches. Job, who has continually affirmed his innocence, is not really answered by the divine—he is not vindicated or made to understand his suffering. God does not defend his justice or provide a self-interpretation. Job is simply presented with a God and a world whose ways and wonders are beyond the rational comprehension of man and cannot be judged by human standards. Before such, one can only yield himself, in faith, with a heroic submission; but the author allows Job in even this to find the serenity of a divine-human relationship.

The book of Ecclesiastes, cast in the form of a royal testament, is even more skeptical about life and religion and what they offer than the book of Job. Writing as an intellectual of great individuality, the author of Ecclesiastes challenged the fundamental presuppositions underlying any approach to life which would affirm its ultimate value and offer a rational understanding in either transcendental or humanistic perspectives. "Vanity of vanities! All is vanity," is the slogan and theme which runs throughout the book.

Writing as if Solomon, who was understood to have tasted life at the "highest" level with wealth and power sufficient to indulge his whims and to explore every avenue of curiosity yet who was noted for his wisdom and learning, the author claims that human experiences, analytic observation, and rational reflection all lead to the same critical conclusion—life does not make sense. One by one, but in no clearly organized or philosophically integrated fashion, Ecclesiastes denies the tenets upon which religion and wisdom rested. Neither creation nor history allows man to comprehend the ways and will of God or the goal of human existence (1:4-11; 4:13-16; 6:10-12; 9:13-15). Historical events are ephemeral, life is without real movement, and there is an opaque barrier between human comprehension and the divine (3:10-15; 11:3-8). The correlation between action and consequence is denied; there is no immutable operation which brings rewards to the good and punishments to the bad (7:15; 8:10-11,14) since time and chance determine the shape of life (9:11-12). The meaning of life cannot be found in pleasure (2:1-8), one's work (5:18-20), one's reputation and memory (2:12-17; 9:13-16), or religion (5:1-6; 9:1-3); and there is no time beyond death when matters will be rectified, questions answered, and final judgment given (3:16-21). Even wisdom itself, though better than folly (1:13), could provide no ultimate answer (2:14-16; 7:23-25; 8:16-17; 9:1-6) and could contribute to one's vexation (1:12-18). Everything in life is transitory; old age and death await all (12:1-7), and at times death seems preferable to life (4:1-3; 6:3-6).

In spite of his pessimism, the author did not counsel suicide. Instead he recomends that one find as much enjoyment in life as possible by seeking tranquility and living quietly (2:24-26; 5:18-20; 8:15; 9:4-10; 11:8, 10), especially while one still enjoys youth (11:9) before the pains and rigors of old age (12:1-7).

Ecclesiastes' prescription for life was not new. As early

as the Gilgamesh Epic, the hero searching for immortality is counseled by a barmaid, in a form somewhat more hedonistic than that offered by Ecclesiastes.

Gilgamesh, whither rovest thou?
The life thou pursuest thou shalt not find.
When the gods created mankind,
Death for mankind they set aside,
Life in their own hands retaining.
Thou, Gilgamesh, let full be thy belly,
Make thou merry by day and by night.
Of each day make thou a feast of rejoicing,
Day and night dance thou and play!
Let thy garments be sparkling fresh,
Thy head be washed; bathe thou in water.
Pay heed to the little one that holds on to thy hand,
Let thy spouse delight in thy bosom!
For this is the task of mankind! (*ANET*, 90)

D. Other Wisdom Literature?

Traditionally, only Proverbs, Ecclesiastes, and Job have been considered wisdom books in the Old Testment. (Sirach and Wisdom of Solomon are representatives in the Apocrypha or deutero-canon.) Recently, many scholars have argued that other books or portions thereof are products of wisdom or else have been strongly influenced by wisdom concerns (see Crenshaw, *SAIW*, 9-13, 481-94, for a survey and bibliography).

Von Rad has argued that the Joseph story (Gen 37; 39–50) is so unlike the other patriarchal narratives that this dissimilarity demands explanation. Thus he argues that the story has a different origin and intent. He sees the narrative as a product of the royal court under Solomon, written when there was a great interest in producing a competent body of trained administrators. The figure of Joseph would have illustrated the ideal educated man who possessed the twin virtues of outspokenness and good counsel. As such, Joseph was an example of the wise men's ideal personality: "a man who by his upbringing, his modesty, his learning, his courtesy and his self-discipline has acquired true nobility of character" (SAIW, 441). Like the Egyptian Tale of Two Brothers (ANET, 23-25), which bears striking similarities to the Joseph story, this narrative could be seen as a product of wisdom circles illustrating in narrative form what the proverbs extolled in aphoristic form.

> It displays no historico-political interests, nor any cultic, aetiological motive. It is equally devoid of any specifically theological interest in redemptive history. We can only say that the Joseph story, with its strong didactic motive, belongs to the category of early wisdom writing. (SAIW, 445-46).

Weinfeld has sought to demonstrate that the Deuteronomic literature found in the book of Deuteronomy, the Deuteronomistic History, and the prose sermons in Jeremiah were "the creation of scribal circles which began their literary project some time prior to the reign of Josiah [639–609 BCE] and were still at work after the fall of Judah" (1972, 9). His reasons for relating Deuteronomy to wisdom and scribal circles are: (1) its interest in the moral and humanistic aspects of Hebrew law; (2) the rhetorical character of the material with its strong homiletical and exhorting style; (3) its didactic stress on instruction and teaching; (4) the emphasis in Deuteronomy on material benefits understood as rewards which parallels a similar perspective in wisdom literature; and (5) the appearance in Deuteronomy of prescriptions and commands which appear in the wisdom books but in less developed form.

Within the Former Prophets, the so-called Throne Succession Story (see above, pp. 232-35) has been compared to political novels found in Egyptian culture and understood to have been strongly influenced, if not produced by, wisdom circles (Whybray, 1968). Whybray writes:

> We may therefore suggest with some confidence that the Succession Narrative was written during the early years of

Solomon's reign, soon after the events described in I Kings 2, and while the régime was still threatened by disaffected parties: it is primarily a political document intended to support the régime by demonstrating its legitimacy and justifying its policies. At the same time it is a work of great literary distinction and independence, far from being a political hack-work commissioned by the king. It was written by a member of a sophisticated court circle, who combined literary skill and great psychological insight with a new understanding of the working of Yahweh in history and with a deep devotion to the honor of David as the principal instrument through which he guided the destinies of his Chosen People. (54-55)

. . . There is sufficiently close resemblance between Proverbs and the incidents and situations of the Succession Narrative to show that the author of the latter was not merely a man who shared the general outlook of the wisdom teachers, but was himself a wisdom teacher in the sense that he set out deliberately to illustrate specific proverbial teaching for the benefit of the pupils and ex-pupils of the schools. (95)

Talmon has argued that the book of Esther should be considered a historicized wisdom-tale similar to the Joseph story. "It may be described as an *enactment* of standard 'Wisdom' motifs which are present also in other biblical narratives of a similar nature, and which biblical literature has in common with ancient near eastern wisdom literature, as defined by the literary-type analysis" (426). Interest in court life, the absence of specifically Jewish history and religiosity, the generalized concept of the deity, the anthropocentric interest of the work, and the stress on human wisdom appearing in the book are all seen as supporting his contention.

Discussing the biblical traditions and books in a broad cutural context and in terms of their party politics (whether hostile or conciliatory toward non-Jewish peoples and influences), Morton Smith has attributed several biblical works to an educated gentry in post-exilic times and thus to what might be broadly called wisdom circles.

All this material—Proverbs, Job, Ecclesiastes, Ruth, Jonah, Judith, Tobit, Esther, and the Song of Songs—is essentially belletristic and as such is sharply distinguished from the national legend and history, laws and prophecies, preserved by the earlier Yahweh-alone tradition. This belletristic material testifies to the continued existence from the sixth to the second century of a lay circle enjoying wealth, leisure, and considerable culture (and of lay scribes and teachers who copied this material and perpetuated it as part of a humane literary education). This circle cared little for the old Israelite literature which had been preserved by the Yahweh-alone party. . . . On the whole the most remarkable characteristic of this upper-class material, vis-a-vis the earlier Israelite literature, is its independence and originality, the reflection of a social clique which . . . was in close touch with the changes of international fashion: gnomic verses in the sixth century [Proverbs], poetic drama in the fifth [Job], philosophic reflection in the fourth [Ecclesiastes], romances and erotic poetry in the third and later [Ruth, Jonah, Judith, Tobit, Esther, and Song of Song] . . . . Thus the Judean aristocracy, for which this literature was produced, kept in touch with the intellectual and artistic developments of the hellenistic world. (159-60)

What is to be said about this tendency to see strong wisdom influence in, if not authorship of, many Old Testament books? Have scholars "thrown caution to the wind in assessing wisdom influence within the Bible itself" (Crenshaw, *SAIW*, 9)? A number of points should be noted. (1) The scholarly tendency to divide Old Testament books into various literary classes has frequently led to the assumption that such sharp divisions also existed in the life and culture of ancient Israel and that each was little related to the other. (2) Within ancient Israel, there were certainly different groups and strata in society with different orientations and interests. Some of these must have been far more secular or nonreligious than others. (The assumption that few in the ancient world were "secularized" is probably a modern romantic construct.) Approaches to similar issues among these groups would have differed considerably. (3) The literature which originated in different groups would reflect the orientation and assumptions of that circle. (4) The goals for which the literature was produced would greatly influence the content and character of the material. (5) The subject matter discussed in the literature determined, to some extent, the manner in which it was presented. (6) All literature in the ancient world was produced and transmitted by educated persons and, to this extent, by wise men. (7) Most educated persons were acquainted with and drew upon all elements of the culture but were more dependent upon that stratum of culture into which they were socialized. Thus one would be surprised if "wisdom" concerns and elements did not make themselves felt across a broad spectrum of Old Testament literature which falls outside the "wisdom corpus" per se.

CHAPTER 10

DANIEL AND JEWISH APOCALYPTIC

J. Barr, "Jewish Apocalyptic in Recent Scholarly Study,"
BJRUL LVIII(1975) 9-35; M. Buss, *The Prophetic Word of
Hosea* (Berlin: Alfred Töpelmann, 1969); R. J. Clifford,
"History and Myth in Daniel 10–12," *BASOR*
CCXX(1975)23-26; J. J. Collins, "Jewish Apocalyptic
against its Hellenistic Near Eastern Environment,"
BASOR CCXX(1975)27-36; *idem*, "Apocalypse: Towards
the Morphology of a Genre," *SBLSP*(1977)359-70; *idem*,
The Apocalyptic Vision of the Book of Daniel (Missoula:
Scholars Press for Harvard Semitic Museum, 1977); G. R.
Driver, "Sacred Numbers and Round Figures," in
Promise and Fulfilment, ed. F. F. Bruce (Edinburgh: T. &
T. Clark, 1963)62-90; J. Ferguson, *Utopias of the Classical
World* (London: Thames and Hudson, 1975); D. Flusser,
"The Four Empires in the Fourth Sibyl and in the Book of
Daniel," *IOS* II(1972)148-75; J. G. Gammie, "The Clas-
sification, Stages of Growth and Changing Intentions in
the Book of Daniel," *JBL* XCV(1976)191-204; H. L.
Ginsberg, "Daniel, Book of," *EJ* V, 1277-89; A. K. Grayson,
Babylonian Historical-Literary Texts (Toronto: Universi-
ty of Toronto, 1975); P. D. Hanson, "Jewish Apocalyptic
against its Near Eastern Environment," *RB*
LXXVIII(1971)31-58; *idem*, *The Dawn of Apocalyptic*
(Philadelphia: Fortress Press, 1975); *idem*, "Old Testa-
ment Apocalyptic Reexamined," *Int* XXV(1971)454-79;
idem, "Apocalypse, Genre." "Apocalypticism," *IDBS*
(1976)27-34; *idem*, "Prolegomena to the Study of Jewish
Apocalyptic," *MD*, 389-413; W. L. Humphreys, "A
Life-Style for the Diaspora: A Study of the Tales of Esther
and Daniel," *JBL* XCII(1973)211-23; K. Koch, *The
Rediscovery of Apocalyptic* (London: SCM Press, 1972);
S. Niditch and R. Doran, "The Success Story of the Wise
Courtier: A Formal Approach," *JBL* XCVI(1977)179-93; R.
North, "Prophecy to Apocalyptic via Zechariah," *VTS*
XXII(1972)47-71; H. H. Rowley, *The Relevance of
Apocalyptic* (London/New York: Lutterworth/Associa-
tion Press, 1944, ³1963); *idem*, "The Unity of the Book of
Daniel," in his *The Servant of the Lord and other Essays*

on the *Old Testment* (2d and rev. ed.; Oxford: Blackwell, 1965)247-80; D. S. Russell, *The Method and Message of Jewish Apocalyptic* (London/Philadelphia: SCM Press/Westminster Press, 1964); W. Schmithal, *The Apocalyptic Movement: Introduction and Interpretation* (Nashville: Abingdon Press, 1975); M. E. Stone, "Lists of Revealed Things in the Apocalyptic Literature," *MD*, 414-52; J. W. Swain, "The Theory of the Four Monarchies: Opposition History under the Roman Empire," *CP* XXXV(1940)1-21; G. Vermes, *The Dead Sea Scrolls in English* (Hammondsworth/Baltimore: Penguin Books, 1962, ²1975).

The book of Daniel occupies a unique position in the Old Testament: it is the only work which belongs to the category of apocalyptic literature. The term "apocalypse" is a Greek word meaning "revelation" which appears as the first word in a New Testament book—The Revelation to John. From its appearance there, the term has been employed to designate "literary compositions which resemble the book of Revelation, i.e., secret disclosures about the end of the world and the heavenly state" (Koch, 18). In addition to the Christian book of Revelation and the Old Testament book of Daniel, several nonbiblical works from antiquity fall into this category. Among these are such Jewish works as I Enoch, II Baruch, and II Esdras (IV Ezra). The latter was accepted as Christian scripture for centuries but no longer forms part of the Catholic canon.

What, however, is an "apocalypse"? For generations, scholars have attempted to define "apocalyptic" literature and thought by pointing to certain particular characteristics and elements in the materials (see Koch, 23-22; Russell, 104-39) or various levels of form and content.

On the level of simple *language* use we could list features like the following: repetitiveness in language, the use of long discourses, the prevalence of counting and listing, the symbolism of numbers, the imagery of birds and beasts and dragons. A second (and perhaps "higher") level belongs to the *structure* of apocalypses: commonly the writer's name is not mentioned (the Book of Revelation is here one exception, perhaps), and the matter is put into the mouth of a person of primeval times, like Noah, or Lamech, or Enoch, or at least one of late biblical or exilic times, like Baruch, Daniel or Ezra; this person of ancient times is represented as having received a vision, being taken up into a heavenly world, and shown mysterious things which then have to be explained to him. The explanation often comes from an angel, and angels are part of the mechanism of much apocalyptic. The experiences of the visionary cause violent inner disturbances, fainting, falling down and so on. Yet a third level is *the sort of thing that is told*: often we have the retelling of long historical sequences, usually in hidden symbolic forms, where conflicts between animals—bulls, sheep, lions, eagles—are used to symbolize historical human conflicts. We have the description of the heavens, of winds, of the tree of life, of strange mountains. On a fourth level we have something that could be taken more as *doctrine*: for instance, ideas of resurrection, or of the dawning of a new age, the coming of a crises in world history. (Barr, 16)

Recently, an attempt has been made both to clarify and to simplify what is meant by "apocalyptic" while simultaneously stressing the "common core of constant elements" found in all forms of the literature. As a literary genre, an apocalypse is defined as "a genre of revelatory literature with a narrative framework, in which a revelation is mediated by an otherworldly being to a human recipient, disclosing a transcendent reality which is both temporal, in so far as it envisages eschatological salvation, and spatial, in so far as it involves another, supernatural world" (Collins, *SBLSP*, 364). That is to say, an apocalypse is a type of literature in which a person has revealed and interpreted to him mysteries about things and conditions in the other world(s) and/or about developments which are to occur in the future.

A. The Nature of the Book of Daniel

Even a cursory reading of Daniel is sufficient to recognize that there are two basic sections in the book.

366

The first part (Dan 1–6) contains tales about Daniel and his companions which speak of Daniel in the third person. In these narratives, Daniel is depicted as a pious and loyal Yahwist who possesses the power to interpret dreams and visions. In the second half of the book (Dan 7–12), Daniel has dreams and experiences visions which are interpreted to him by angelic figures, and the material is narrated in the first person. Obviously, therefore, only Dan 7–12 falls within the category of apocalyptic as defined above.

In addition to this division between the two halves of the book, a further complicating matter is the fact that the book is composed in two languages: Dan 1:1–2:4a and 8:1–12:13 in Hebrew, Dan 2:4b–7:28 in Aramaic. The division of the book into tales (Dan 1–6) and visions (Dan 7–12) does not coincide with the division into two languages. Both of these issues raise questions about the unity and purpose of the book, but before these can be further examined, it is necessary to explore the question of the figure of Daniel and the traditions about him.

According to the book, Daniel was taken, as a young lad, into Babylonian exile in 606/5 BCE (see Dan 1:1) where he remained active until after the capture of Babylon in 538 BCE (see Dan 6:28). Attempts to identify and to place the hero of the book in some general context have usually sought for reference to him elsewhere in the scriptures. Ezra 8:2 and Neh 10:6 mention a Daniel, but no significant information is provided which would suggest identification. Further, that both of these references place the person called Daniel in the second half of the fifth century or later creates insurmountable chronological problems. A second approach associates the figure in the book of Daniel with a legendary character alluded to in other biblical passages. Ez 28:3 contains a taunt hurled at the prince of Tyre which asks if he is "indeed wiser than Daniel." In Ez 14:14, Daniel appears alongside Noah and Job as a person of great righteousness. Outside the biblical texts, references are made to a Daniel. The fourteenth century Ugaritic texts contain legends about a king Danel who judges equitably and defends the widow and the fatherless. In the pseudepigraphic book of Jubilees, a Danel appears as the great-great-grandfather of Noah and is related to the legendary figure of Enoch, a person noted for his wisdom and predictive powers (Jubilees 4:20). These references suggest that Daniel was a name attached to a legendary person common to the folklore of several cultures and historical periods who was especially noted for his wisdom and righteousness. The passages in Ezekiel demonstrate that at the time of the exile a righteous and wise but legendary figure was associated with the name Daniel. This association could explain why tales and visions could be affixed to this name in the post-exilic period.

Jewish stories about Daniel were more extensive than those which have been preserved in the Hebrew Bible. The Greek version of the book of Daniel contains the story of Susanna, in which Daniel functions as a wise judge who rescues the Jewish maid from her detractors, as well as the narrative called Bel and the Dragon, in which Daniel again is the hero. In addition, fragments of Aramaic texts discovered at Qumran speak of a Daniel who is shown presenting a summary of world history before the ministers of a king. Another fragment contains a story very similar to Dan 4 although the Jewish hero is not named and the "mad king" is Nabonidus, not Nebuchadnezzar. (For a translation of this so-called "Prayer of Nabonidus," see Vermes, 229.)

In light of these traditions and references to Daniel from such widely diverse literary and chronological circumstances, two conclusions seem obvious. (1) The central figure in the book of Daniel probably does not reflect any historical personage but instead is to be associated with the legendary wise and righteous man Daniel. (2) Numerous traditions about this figure were in circulation in post-exilic Judaism of which those in the book of Daniel represent only a selection.

In Dan 1, Daniel and his friends are described being

educated for service at the court of Nebuchadnezzar. With exemplary zeal, they adhered to the Jewish dietary laws, refusing to eat from the king's table for fear of consuming unkosher food. At the end of a set period, they are shown to have prospered physically and mentally on a diet of vegetables and water.

Dan 2 narrates how Daniel interpreted Nebuchadnezzar's dream which had baffled the wise men of the royal court. In the king's dream, an image of various metals was smashed by a stone uncut by human hands. Daniel reveals that the parts of the statue, composed of various metals, represent successive kingdoms which will finally be destroyed to be replaced by a "kingdom which shall never be destroyed" (Dan 2:44). The multiple metals—gold, silver, bronze, iron, iron mixed with clay—of which the image was composed show a progressive diminution in quality, but little is made of this in the story since the statue is totally destroyed all at once. Daniel is lavishly rewarded by the king for his interpretive powers.

Chapter 3 relates an episode in which Shadrach, Meshach, and Abednego refused to bow down and worship before an image set up by Nebuchadnezzar. Affirming a willingness to suffer martyrdom rather than worship pagan gods, the three are thrown into a fiery furnace but are miraculously saved to the astonishment of the king, who proclaims the greatness of the Hebrew god and promotes the three.

In chapter 4, the king dreams again. Daniel interprets the dream to mean that the king will become temporarily "mad" and live like a beast until he acknowledges that the god of Israel "rules the kingdom of men, and gives it to whom he will" (Dan 4:25). The dream subsequently becomes "historical" reality which is climaxed by Nebuchadnezzar's confession.

The feast of Belshazzar, the handwriting on the wall, and the accurate prediction of Daniel that the Medes and Persians would take over from Babylon comprise the elements in Dan 5.

In chapter 6, Daniel is cast into a lion's den for failure to obey a law of Darius the Mede, under whom Daniel was serving as a superior officer. After Daniel's miraculous rescue from the lions, Darius wrote to all his kingdom that people must "tremble and fear before the God of Daniel" (Dan 6:26).

In the second half of the book, Daniel is provided revelations about future events to take place on earth as well as revelations about developments in the heavenly sphere which eventually determine the course of history on earth. These revelations will be further discussed in the following sections. At this point, one factor needs to be noted: the revelations to Daniel spell out the course which history will take from the time of the Persians until the time of the "little horn" who will persecute the faithful and whose demise will usher in the final days, i.e., from the time of the Babylonian empire until the days of Antiochus IV Epiphanes.

If the second part of Daniel, chapters 7–12, clearly relates to the period of Antiochus' oppression of the Jews, as is widely accepted, the question of the relationship between the two parts of the book arises anew. As was noted earlier in this section, stylistic variations as well as differences in the portrayal of Daniel set the two parts off from one another. Does the first part of the book have the same historical frame of reference as the second part? If so, how do these traditions about the legendary Daniel relate to the particular emphases of the apocalyptic section of the book and to the specific context of the conflict between Antiochus and the Jews?

One approach to this issue would be to argue that the book of Daniel is a unit and that the work was composed by the author to address the persecuted community suffering under Antiochus (see Rowley). I Maccabees 1 and II Maccabees 1–7 report his desecration of the Jerusalem temple, the sanctuary's dedication to Zeus Olympius, and the ruler's harsh actions against the Jews. Rowley argues that it is possible to relate every story of the

370

first part of the book to the troubles and issues confronting the Jewish community during the reign of Antiochus (175-164 BCE).

The first chapter is the story of Jews who refused to eat unclean foods. In the time of the Maccabaean crisis, when Antiochus sought to compel the Jews to eat swine's flesh that had been sacrificed to idols, many chose to die rather than defile themselves with unclean foods [I Macc 1:47,62-63; II Macc 6:8, 18-20; 7:1], and Judas the Maccabee is said to have lived on herbs for fear of pollution [II Macc 5:27]. So far as the second chapter is concerned, it is linked by its climax to chapter 7 and the later chapters of the book, and its hope of the imminent establishment of the everlasting kingdom of righteousness is one that was certainly cherished in Maccabaean days. The third chapter is the story of Jews who refused to worship the great image which Nebuchadnezzar set up. Antiochus Epiphanes turned the Temple into a heathen shrine and set up there an idol or idols. Since the Temple was dedicated to Zeus Olympius [II Macc 6:2], an image of Zeus would be expected, and since the king claimed to be Zeus manifest in the flesh, it is likely that it would take the form of a statue of the king. Jerome tells us, indeed, that an image of Zeus and statues of the king were placed in the Temple. While these may not have been colossal in size, they were monstrous in significance in the eyes of faithful Jews, and this chapter would well stimulate men to resistance to the king's commands. The fourth chapter is the story of a king whose overweening pride is punished by madness. It is known that Antichus who fancied himself a god incarnate, was called by his people Epimanes, madman. [Polybius, *Histories*, XXVI.10] This chapter, then, might well be understood in that day as a reference to Antiochus, and bring its promise of humiliation at the hands of God. The fifth chapter tells of a king who profaned the Temple vessels, upon whom the judgment of heaven fell. Antiochus is stated to have removed the sacred vessels of the Temple with his own hands [I Macc 1:21-24], and to people who were filled with horror at such sacrilege this chapter could bring the hope of the outpouring of divine wrath upon him. The sixth chapter tells of the minions of a king, who both encouraged him to suppress religious freedom and treacherously spied on the loyal and denounced them to the king, only to find their plots recoil upon themselves. In the days of Antiochus there was a section of the Jews who fawned on the king for their own advancement, who encouraged him in all his attacks on the liberties of the loyal, and who were traitors to their own people [I Macc 1:11-15; II Macc 3:4-8; 5:23]. This chapter brought its promise that upon them, too, would fall the vengeance of God. At the same time it encouraged the faithful to continue in their faithfulness, and to be unmoved by the threats of a king, or by the malice of his servants. (Rowley, 276-78)

The name Nebuchadnezzar possibly contained a veiled reference to Antiochus Epiphanes for those who were "informed" about how to read the text and thus would have helped relate these tales to Seleucid times. In Hebrew, the letters of the alphabet were used to indicate numerical value, with the first letter having the value of 1, and the second 2, and so on. In cuneiform, Nebuchad-nezzar's name was *nabu-kudduri-usur* and should have been transliterated into Hebrew as Nabuchadrezzar, a form which appears frequently in Jeremiah. Written Nebuchadnezzar, the name has the same numerical value as Antiochus Epiphanes:

$$n + b + w + k + d + n + ' + \d{s} + r$$
$$50 + 2 + 6 + 20 + 4 + 50 + 1 + 90 + 200 \qquad = 423$$

$$' + n + \d{t} + y + w + k + w + s + ' + p + y + p + n + s$$
$$1 + 50 + 9 + 10 + 6 + 20 + 6 + 60 + 1 + 70 + 10 + 70 + 50 + 60 \qquad = 423$$

Such use of numerology is well known as a feature of much apocalyptic thought (see Rev 13:18).

A number of factors, however, suggest that the author of the book of Daniel did not compose the tales found in chapters 1-6 but borrowed these from the general traditions told about the legendary wise man Daniel. (1) The tales in Dan 1-6, with the possible exception of chapter 2, are not apocalyptic in orientation and do not as clearly reflect the crisis situation of a suffering communi-ty. Instead, they reflect a more positive assessment of the political situation and perhaps were suggestive of a particular life-style for Jews living under foreign and sometimes difficult rulers (see Humphreys). As such, they tend to utilize the common folklore plot of the success of the unpromising or the rise of the wise courtier (see Niditch-Doran). (2) No explicit, unambiguous reference to the persecution of Antiochus appears in chapters 1-6. (3) Even in Dan 2, the weakness of the final kingdom (iron mixed with clay = the Hellenistic successors to Alexander the Great) is related to the inability of intermarriage to hold together the iron and clay (Dan 2:43) and not to the kingdom's arrogance against the divine and persecution of his chosen. (For the view that the book of Daniel emerged in three stages, see Gammie.)

Although the issue is beyond the matter of certainty, the evidence would suggest that the author of the book inherited traditional tales about Daniel and his associates and then used the figure of Daniel as a vehicle for the apocalyptic material addressed to the situation produced by the crisis and persecution during the time of Antiochus. Nonetheless, the tales in Dan 1–6 would have contained a message for those who lived under oppressive foreign government and use of tales about Daniel which were apropos to the time of Antiochus could explain why such Danielic stories as Susanna and Bel and the Dragon, if one assumes they were in existence, were omitted from the second–century version of the book.

The problem of the use of two languages in the book and the relationship of this issue to the questions of the unity and purpose of the work have received no completely satisfying solution although numerous proposals have been made (see Ginsberg; also Collins, *Apocalyptic Vision*, 15-19). It is possible to assume that the entire book was originally written in either Hebrew and Aramaic and portions translated, or that the shift to Aramaic in Dan 2:4 was modeled on Ezra, where 4:8–6:18 are in Aramaic, or that the traditions in different languages had different origins, and so on. Collins has proposed a plausible and simple explanation: The author, who like many other

Jews of the time was bilingual, inherited a collection of court-tales in Aramaic (Dan 1–6) to which he associated Dan 7–12. Dan 7 was written in Aramaic to interlock what follows with the earlier chapters and to overlap the two halves. Dan 1:1–2:4b was translated into Hebrew so that the Aramaic would be enclosed by Hebrew, as in the book of Ezra, and thus served to bind the book into a unity.

B. The Nature of Apocalyptic Writings

The author of the book of Daniel, and the traditions upon which he drew, utilized a scheme of various ages or kingdoms to characterize the general development of stages in history. In addition, the author wrote much of his material in the form of what might be called pseudo-prophecy, that is, in the form of predictions after the event (*vaticinia ex eventu*). This employment of pseudo-prophecy does not mean that there are no genuine predictions in the book, for there are, and these will be discussed in the next section.

In Dan 2, the successive kingdoms are represented by the four metals which comprise the statue. In Dan 7, the imagery is that of four beasts—lion, bear, leopard, and "a fourth beast, terrible and dreadful and exceedingly strong"—which seem to parallel the metal imagery in chapter 2 (for beasts as devourers, see Hos 13:7-8; Jer 5:6). The four kingdoms which these symbols represent are the Babylonian (represented in the book by the gold, the lion, and Nebuchadnezzar and Belshazzar), the Median (represented by the silver, the bear, and Darius the Mede), the Persian (represented by the bronze, the leopard, the ram, and Cyrus), and the Macedonian or Greek (represented by the iron, the "fourth beast," and the he-goat). The latter kingdom is shown as a divided kingdom out of which the little horn will arise whose reign will be the last before the final end of earthly controlled kingdoms.

The characterization of ages or kingdoms with references to metals had a widespread usage in antiquity—both geographically and chronologically. The Greek author Hesiod in the eighth century described human history in terms of ages—the heroic followed by the golden, silver, bronze, and iron ages (*Works and Days*, 106-201). For Hesiod, this scheme expressed the view that history is characterized by a progressive decline although he wistfully expressed some hope of a latter, better age. A similar scheme based on distinctions according to metals is found in the late (Hellenistic Age) Persian document, Zand-ī Vohūman Yasn, an expansion of a lost text of the Avesta (see Collins, 1975, 29). In this account, Zarathustra dreams about a tree containing branches composed of four different metals ranging from gold to mixed iron, apparently referring to the Greeks, which represents the final reign before the millennium.

The description of successive reigns or four kingdoms without the metal imagery was widely used in the Hellenistic Age and later (see Swain; Flusser; and Collins, *Apocalyptic Vision*, 37-40). The Roman chronicler, Aemilius Sura, probably in the early second century BCE, wrote:

The Assyrians were the first of all races to hold power, then the Medes, after them the Persians and then the Macedonians. Then, when the two kings Philip and Antiochus of Macedonian origin had been completely conquered, soon after the overthrow of Carthage, the supreme command passed to the Roman people.

The so-called fourth Sibylline Oracle, which again appears to be Hellenistic, also works with the four-monarchies concept—Assyria, Media, Persia, and Macedonia. The scheme of successive world monarchies was apparently already known to the historians Herodotus and Ctesias. (The priestly stratum in the Pentateuch seems also to have worked with a four-age scheme—from Adam to Noah, from Noah to Abraham, from Abraham to Moses, and from Moses onward.)

The appearance of Media in the scheme—and in the

book of Daniel—is noteworthy since Media never ruled over any great empire especially not in the western area of the Near East. This has led to the assumption that the scheme—Assyria, Media, Persia, Macedonia—originated in Persia or Media, where some familiarity with the Medes could be assumed, and during the Hellenistic Age, when there was hostility to the Seleucids who were Macedonian successors to Alexander the Great. To begin with, the Assyrians was apparently based on the fact that they were the first truly international empire. Several passages in the Old Testament point to the role and significance of the Medes (Is 13:17; 21:2; Jer 25:25; 51:11,28) and may have greatly influenced the conceptualization of the traditions in Daniel. Why Babylonia is omitted from some of the schemes remains problematic.

The prediction about the existence of the various kingdoms in Daniel is clearly pseudo-prophecy since the author of Daniel was obviously living in the age of the "little horn," Antiochus IV Epiphanes. (Dan 11:2-39 contains a reasonably accurate account of historical developments down to about 164 BCE.) Why did the author resort to such pseudo-prophecy and refer only obliquely, without names, to the kingdoms and rulers? Numerous suggestions have been proposed to explain why the author wrote pseudepigraphically under the name Daniel: (1) to disguise his identity and thus avoid retaliation from the authorities; (2) because the age of prophecy was assumed to have ended earlier, in the time of Ezra, and thus for authentication some pre-Ezra origin had to be claimed; (3) to attribute the work to a great name and thus enhance the work's prestige; (4) to enforce a deterministic view of history by claiming that events follow a course determined and predicted long before their occurrence; (5) to enhance the work's claim as prediction by showing that predicted events yet to come are certain since they are part of a scheme which involves predictions that have already been fulfilled, and so on. The exact reasons for such pseudepigraphic and pseudo-prophetic works like Daniel were probably manifold. Obviously, if the author wished to claim reliability for his truly "predictive" statements, one way was to include predictions of past events which an audience would clearly recognize as having already been fulfilled. The only way to achieve this was to write as if one stood at one point in history whereas in reality the true historical context was years later.

The practice of writing predictions about past events in order to justify the status quo or to establish credibility for predictions about the future was a very old custom in the Near East. Comparative material can be found in Egyptian literature, some written centuries before Daniel (the so-called admonitions of Ipu-Wer and the prophecy of Neferti; see *ANET*, 441-46, 676). One of the examples closest to Daniel is a cuneiform text from the early Hellenistic Age recenty published by Grayson. The text is broken at the beginning but preserved portions clearly indicate that the opening section speaks of the downfall of Assyria. The dominance of Babylon is noted and the reign of its kings commented on although without the rulers being named. The following is clearly a description of Nabonidus (text from Grayson, 30–37, partially restored):

A rebel prince will arise. . . .
The dynasty of Harran he will establish.
For seventeen years he will exercise sovereignty.
He will oppress the land and the festival of Esagil he will cancel.
A fortress in Babylon he will build.
He will plot against Akkad.

The text then proceeds to discuss Cyrus but refers to him as king of Elam:

A king of Elam will arise, the sceptre. . . .
He will remove him from his throne. . . .
He will take the throne and the king who arose from the throne. . . .
The king of Elam will change his place. . . .

He will settle him in another land. . . .
That king will oppress the land and. . . .
All the lands will bring to him tribute.
During his reign Akkad will not enjoy a peaceful abode.

Futher Persian rulers are mentioned and then the text speaks of the coming of the army of the Hanaeans (from *hanu*, a cunieform term sometimes used to refer to the inhabitants of Thrace, therefore "westerners"). The Hanaeans are obviously the Greeks. At this point the text is very fragmentary but appears to refer to rulers down to Seleucus I. Fragmentary readings have been preserved of the ending which suggests that the content was a secret of the great gods (see Dan 12:4) to be shown only to the initiated. "Statements of this kind are attested on many Babylonian tablets of the late period" (Grayson, 27).

A secret/taboo of the great gods.
You may show it to the initiated but to the uninitiated you must
    not show it.
It is a secret/taboo of Marduk, lord of the lands.
. . . first, tablet
. . . Munnabtum
. . . written, collated

A number of factors about this text are noteworthy and several comparable to features in the book of Daniel. (1) The work clearly comes from the Hellenistic Age and apparently from early in the reign of the Seleucid kings. Thus it appears to predate much in Daniel. (2) The text probably reflects an anti-Seleucid sentiment. (3) The various kings reflect the Assyrian, Babylonian, Elamite (Persian), and Macedonian kingdoms, that is, a four-kingdom scheme. (4) The rulers are not mentioned by name but sufficient information is provided about each to make identification obvious to the initiated or informed. The rulers are not represented as beasts as in Daniel; such representation allowed the latter to appear even more mysterious and to caricature international powers in a more bizarre fashion than would be otherwise possible. (5) The work appears to be revelatory material and is certainly written as pseudo-prophecy. (6) The text was written down as a secret document only for those who possessed understanding.

In the use of world ages or successive kindoms, the employment of pseudo-prophecy, the utilization of indirect references to rulers, and the principle of pseudepigraphy, the book of Daniel clearly stands within a general tradition of Hellenistic Age literature (see Collins, 1975).

C. The Apocalyptic Vision of Daniel

The book of Daniel proclaims that universal history—symbolized by the four kingdoms (Dan 2) and the four beasts (Dan 7)—will run its course to be succeeded by the kingdom of God or the rule over the earthly world by the heavenly world. This is expressed in rather general and imprecise terms in Dan 2 in the imagery of the composite statue's destruction by a rock uncut by human hands. The fact that the stone was untouched by human hands stresses that the destruction of the evil powers of this world and the establishment of God's kingdom are not the product of human activity or the outgrowth of historical developments but are the work of divine intervention and the otherworldly shattering of the historical process. The intervention of God has both its negative and positive aspects:

Then the iron, the clay, the bronze, the silver, and the gold, all together were broken in pieces, and became like the chaff of the summer threshing floors; and the wind carried them away, so that not a trace of them could be found. But the stone that struck the image became a great mountain and filled the whole earth.

And in the days of those kings [of the divided kingdom] the God of heaven will set up a kingdom that shall never be destroyed,

379

nor shall its sovereignty be left to another people. It shall break in pieces all these kingdoms and bring them to an end, and it shall stand for ever. (Dan 2:35, 44)

In the second half of the book, the predictions are more specific regarding the exact time of God's intervention and more descriptive of the heavenly events accompanying the establishment of the divine kingdom on earth. Chapters 7–12 consist of four basic units (7; 8; 9; 10:1–12:12 [12:13 or perhaps 12:5-13 appear to be additions]). In each of these, there is the promise of the judgment and destruction of the ruler who represents the final manifestation of the earthly kingdom and its overt and arrogant hostility toward the true god. These units are not composed to suggest a sequence in the visions; rather, they are individual recapitulations of the same feature.

In Dan 7, the judgment of the fourth kingdom and "the little horn," its last ruler, is depicted as taking place in the heavenly tribunal where God the Ancient of Days presides surrounded by the heavenly hosts. The reign of the little horn is viewed as a time of warfare between the earthly ruler and the heavenly hosts, the saints of the Most High, which comes to an end after the ruler's dominance for "a time, two times, and half a time." The little horn's judgment brings his dominion to an end. In Dan 7:13-14, the dominion over the entire world is given over to "one like a son of man." Enormous scholarly debate and discussion have taken place in an effort to identify this figure (see Collins, *Apocalyptic Vision*, 123-52). Being like a son of man (= human being), the figure is human-like and humane over against the beastly and arrogant character of the earthly kingdoms. The writer is obviously referring to an angelic being, probably the angel Michael, since the figure is present at the heavenly tribunal and comes to the Ancient of Days "with the clouds of heaven." In Dan 7:18, it is the saints (holy ones) of the Most High who receive the kingdom; that is, God gives dominion over earth to the angelic powers. In Dan 7:27, the dominion over the earth is given to the "people

380

of the saints of the Most High" who are clearly to be understood as Israel or the loyal faithful among the Jews (see 8:24). In all three cases, the eschatological and final charcter of the new dominion is stressed (7:14,18,27). These three descriptions of the exercise of sovereignty in the coming kindom of God are mutually complimentary: in the new and final age shortly to dawn at the judgment of the little horn, the loyal Jews ("the people of the saints") shall have dominion along with the heavenly angelic powers ("the saints of the Most High") who are led by Michael, the guardian angel of Israel ("the one like a son of man"; see Dan 10:21; 12:1) and Prince of princes (see 8:25).

Chapter 8 recapitulates Dan 7 in slightly different imagery. The period of warfare between the ram (Media-Persia) and the he-goat (Greece) will be followed by the rise and rule of the little horn (Antiochus IV Epiphanes) who will desolate the temple and take away the burnt offering in the sanctuary (see I Macc 1:54-59; II Macc 6:1-2). Such desolation was to last for 1,150 days (8:14 = "a time, two times, and half a time" [7:25] = 3½ years) after which the little horn shall be broken "but, by no human hand" (8:25).

The apocalyptic interpretation of an earlier prophecy is the central thrust of Dan 9. In Jer 25:11-12 and 29:10, seventy years, the time of a full life span (see Ps 90:10; Is 23:13-18), is conceived of as the length of Jerusalem's desolation following the city's destruction by the Babylonians. The seventy years are interpreted by the author of Daniel as seventy sabbath years (70 x 7 = 490 years; see II Chron 36:21) and are understood as the time between Jeremiah's prophecy (587/6 BCE) and when the "decreed end is poured out on the desolator" (9:27). If the author wrote without knowledge of the death of Antiochus (see Dan 11:45), which occured in late 164 BCE, but after the rededication of the temple in December, 164 BCE (see Dan 8:14), then he must have been coordinating the end of the 490-year period with the expected course of events which would coincide with the death of the wicked king. That is, the seventy weeks were expected to run their course about 164 BCE and the end be ushered in. The historical allusions in Dan 9:24-27 can be reasonably well-identified: (1) the destruction of Jerusalem and Jeremiah's prediction (587/6 BCE), (2) the coming of an anointed one (perhaps Joshua, the high priest, who played a role in the return to Jerusalem in 538 BCE); (3) the cutting off of a further anointed one (the murder of the high priest Onias III in 171 BCE; see II Macc 4:32-34); (4) the period of Jewish collaboration with Antiochus (171-167 BCE); and (5) the time of the cessation of offering in the temple (167-164 BCE). The only way to correlate the writer's calculations and historical references, other than assuming that he possessed faulty chronological knowledge (so Driver), is by assuming that he utilized two fixed points in calculating the weeks. One week of years passed between the destruction of Jerusalem and the coming of the first anointed:

587 BCE—49 years (7 weeks) = 538 BCE (the time of return from exile).

In Dan 1:1, reference is made to the siege of Jerusalem in 605 BCE, an event otherwise unknown. If this fixed point was used for the calculation of the second period of 42 weeks, the following results:

605 BCE—434 years (62 weeks) = 171 BCE (the time of Onias III's death).

One-half week (3½ years) passed before the desecration of the temple in 167 BCE, and a further half week was to pass before the end of the desolator in 164 BCE.

In the fourth vision (Dan 10:1–12:12), the seer, in pseudo-prophetic fashion, presents a rather detailed history from the era of the Greco-Persian wars to his own day (see Clifford). His cryptic presentation avoids referring to any ruler by name but he supplies sufficient information to allow the informal reader to see that history has been accurately "predicted" (compare the Babylonian cuneiform text discussed above). At Dan 11:40, the apocalypticist begins his authentic predictions. Three stages are predicated in the final apocalyptic drama. (1) After a period of warfare between the king of the south (Egypt) and the king of the north (Syria), the king of the north (Antiochus IV Epiphanes) is to be destroyed encamped "between the sea (the Mediterranean) and the glorious holy mountain (Jerusalem)." (2) Michael will intervene in the subsequent chaos to redeem the faithful "whose name shall be found written in the book" (12:1). (3) Some individuals, probably the loyal faithful and the unusually bad, will be resurrected from the dead, "some to everlasting life, and some to shame and everlasting contempt" (12:2). "Those who are wise shall shine like the brightness of the firmament; and those who turn many to righteousness, like the stars for ever and ever," that is, the saved or the wise shall be transformed to an angelic state to share the life of the heavenly hosts (see Collins, *Apocalyptic Vision*, 170-79). (The continued existence and transformation of the world are not discussed by the author but seem to be assumed in some passages [see Dan 7:13-14,18,22,27; 9:24; 12:2].) Death as the ultimate enemy is overcome.

D. The General Background of Jewish Apocalyptic

In the book of Daniel, one encounters a cacophony of concepts orchestrated in a fashion that is unique in the Old Testament. (1) The correct understanding of life and reality is not conceived in terms of ritual sacramentalism to be entered and experienced, as in priestly tradition, or as a message to be proclaimed, as in prophetic tradition; instead, it is wisdom and knowledge to be taught and learned; information to be transmitted. (2) Reality is presented in terms of extreme polarization: earthly rule—the kingdom of God, beastly rulers—the angelic hosts, the present—the time to come, martyrdom and suffering—resurrection and heavenly reward, and human striving—divine intervention. (3) History is presented as a predetermined continuum, unfolding like the tune of a player piano whose score has been written on a heavenly roll, which moves toward its end rather than its fulfillment. (4) Reward for faithfulness and the fulfillment of life, at least for the wise, are located beyond the chasm separating historical and trans-historical conditions. (5) The realization of divine purpose is not achieved through divine actions which direct history but through divine intervention which overwhelms and annihilates history. (6) Those of understanding are challenged to live in passive resistance to earthly rulers, in noncompliance with their beastly schemes, and in suffering and martyrdom to await the sure hope of divine intervention (thus the author's use of the older legends in chapters 1-6).

The general Hellenistic Age context of the book of Daniel and its similarity to literary materials from that period have been noted above in section B. Jewish apocalyptic literature, however, differs from its Hellenistic counterparts in two basic ways. (1) The historical struggle is conceived in radically transcendental perspectives. The conflict is perceived as not merely or even primarily between human, national, or international powers but between "powers and principalities" transcending historical reality. Dan 10 speaks of the princes of Greece and Persia (10:13,20) as angelic powers similar to Michael, "your prince" (10:21). The beasts arise from the sea, the mythical source of chaos and evil; and their conflict is with God and the heavenly hosts. (2) The ultimate resolution of the struggle does not eventuate in nationalistic revival, in anti-Seleucid triumph, or in messianic earthly realizations but in something far more radical—in the establishment of the kingdom of God, an everlasting dominion.

How are the theological developments evident in Daniel in particular and in Jewish apocalyptic literature in general to be understood and explained? Two broad answers to this question have been widely advocated (see Hanson, *MD*, and Collins, 1975, 33-34). (1) One approach argues that the development of apocalyptic within post-exilic Judaism was due to the influence of foreign culture and thought. Generally, Persian thought, with its stress on ethical and cosmic dualism as well as historical determinism, has been seen as the primary influence by supporters of this position. (2) A second approach sees apocalyptic thought as a product of the development and growth of Israelite life and faith. Supporters of the view that apocalyptic was a genuine development within Judaism are divided over whether its roots are to be found in prophetic thought or in wisdom speculation.

A central concern underlying apocalyptic thought, which was shared by the classical prophets, is the radical tension between life and history as they are experienced and life and history as they ideally should be. Eschatology, apocalyptic, and utopian thought are means by which a culture or community expresses this tension and speaks of "a solution of the contradiction between what is (history) and what ought to be (the mythological order)" (Buss, 137; on utopian thought in the ancient world, see Ferguson).

Several of the early prophets, such as Hosea, gave expression to this tension and contradiction in existence and spoke of the eschatological time to come when, after Israel's downfall and reconstitution, the problematics of the human situation would be overcome.

His [Hosea's] message is thoroughly eschatological in the sense that it envisions a mythological order beyond statehood or human making. The new life indeed will be collective and dedicated to natural welfare; but it will be one thoroughly dominated by Yahweh—just as the mythological order of paradise at creation is centered in the action of deity. The ordinary political function of the prophet is thus transcended.

Not relative guidance within the imperfect historical order but a direction toward ultimate reality is given. The fact that the new order is conceived in earthly terms should not hide the fact that its paradisiacal form goes beyond anything known to experience and points to a divine kingdom. (Buss, 132-33)

The eschatological visions of the classical prophets, as exemplified in Hosea, are still far from the later apocalyptic visions. For example, in prophetic eschatology, the source of the national predicament—evil—is primarily located in the life of the nation itself, proclamation of the good time to come beyond the judgment is tied to the call for repentance and change, implying that human actions are still considered decisive in the course of history, the envisioned utopian conditions are still this-worldly, and hope centers on the reconstitution of the nation Israel and the re-creation of its early history. These features are missing or have been radically transformed in the book of Daniel.

Between eschatological visions of the classical prophets and the apocalyptic visions of the later seers, many developments had taken place in and left their impact on Jewish life. (1) The people had lost their national independence, witnessed the demise of their national monarchy, and been forced to stifle their nationalistic drives. (2) The Jewish community, like many other peoples during the Persian and Hellenistic periods, was dominated by powers distant and beyond its control. Self-determination was limited and always precarious. The Jews were awash in international waters. This condition intensified in the Hellenistic Age when Palestine functioned as a major near eastern battleground. Between Alexander's death and Antiochus IV Epiphanes, Jerusalem was captured by foreign armies on at least ten occasions. During the same period, scores of military campaigns were fought in and across the country. Economic exploitation, deportation, enslavement, and bureaucratic oppression were characteristic rather than exceptional. It is no wonder that many Jews felt a helplessness in the historical process and an alienation in their own land and assumed a certain passivity toward historical events. Endurance in the present and ultimate hope in God must have frequently seemed the only sensible postures when confronted with evil so broad and diffuse, so embodied in powers before whom men of faith were powerless. "Decisive individual or collective eschatologies develop in connection with a sense of the problematics of the human situation. The more desperate and distrubed the human order appears—especially sharply felt in the more developed religions—the stronger is an expectation of an End" (Buss, 136). (3) In the Hellenistic Age, the prophetic works, frequently with proclamation and promises of coming redemption, were given and exercised authority in the community. In addition, the older theology and mythology associated with the state, kingship, and Jerusalem (see above, pp. 298-304) had to be reinterpreted as divine word and promise but in a radically new situation. To understand the future, one had to exegete and interpret the sacred traditions and texts of the past (see Dan 9; and already, Is 45:21; 48:6, Ez 38:17).

Attempts have been made to trace the development of Israel's speculation about the future—eschatology—from the classical prophets to the apocalypticists in light of such developments as those noted in the preceding paragraph. Hanson, for example, speaks of various stages in the development—from prophetic eschatology to apocalyptic eschatology to apocalyptic proper (see his article in *IDBS*, 28-34, and North).

The transformation of prophetic eschatology into apocalyptic eschatology was the gradual result of community crisis and national disintegration, circumstances which led prophets like Jeremiah and Ezekiel to envision redemption increasingly on a cosmic level through the use of motifs drawn from myth (Jer. 4:23-28; Ezek. 47). The full force of the alienation resulting from the disintegration of the pre-exilic social system and its supporting symbolic universe was experienced by Second Isaiah [Is 40-55], in whose writings we witness an early, vivid expression of apocalyptic eschatology. (Hanson, *IDBS*, 32)

Hanson thus argues that apocalyptic eschatology developed as a reaction to the alienation and disintegration engendered by the fall of Jerusalem, the destruction of the temple, and the collapse of Judean statehood. After the exile, further apocalyptic movements came into being (see Haggai and Zech 1-8). He concludes that subsequent apocalyptic groups came into existence and that several specimens of their writings which span the time from the exile to the latter half of the fourth century are found in the Old Testament (Is 34-35; 24-27; 56-66; Malachi; Zech 9-14; and possibly Joel). Second–century apocalyptic, to which Daniel belongs, was a response similar to earlier movements but at a time when the "Jewish community [was] engulfed by shattering events of a magnitude matched previously only by the Babylonian decimation of the sixth century" (*IDBS*, 33).

Hanson is certainly correct when he points to the influence upon apocalyptic of prophetic eschatology and the older theology and mythology associated with the royalty and cult in Jerusalem. However, there are dimensions in apocalyptic's desire to make known the secrets of the cosmos that go far beyond either prophetic eschatology or the older Israelite theology. This interest in esoteric knowledge, more noticeable in such works as I Enoch than Daniel, points to circles concerned with cosmology and "science," that is, to what might be called "wisdom" (not, however, the "practical" wisdom noted in chapter 9 above, but what might be more adequately described as "mantic wisdom"). As Dan 11 especially illustrates, the authors of apocalyptic were learned men conversant with a thorough knowledge of history. They were able to exegete the signs of the times in light of a radical eschatological perspective. The stress in apocalyptic lies more, therefore, on the role of the wise interpreter than on the prophetic identity with the divine. The apocalypticist may have shared the interest in learned "sciences," prognosis of the future, and interpretation of the divine will, but without identity with the divine, characteristics which one sees in the ancient Mesopotamian *barus*, and perhaps the Old Testament "seers." After the seventh century BCE, Mesopotamian cultures possessed persons trained in interpreting future events and fate through astronomical consideration. From Mesopotamia, astrology spread throughout much of the ancient world. (The beasts in Daniel may reflect zodiacal concerns.)

The descriptions of Daniel and his friends in chapters 1–6 present them as model wise men *(maskîlîm)*. It is the *maskîlîm* who lead others to understanding (Dan 11:33-35) and who "shall shine like the brightness of the firmament" (Dan 12:3) after the resurrection. No doubt, the author of Daniel should be seen as one of these *maskîlîm*, having "learning and skill in all letters and wisdom; and . . . understanding in all visions and dreams" (Dan 1:17).

In summary, so far as the origins and roots of apocalyptic are concerned, one must conclude that apocalyptic was a complex but unique phenomenon.

Apocalyptic was not a "borrowing" from any source whatever, but is a phenomenon in its own right, with complex sources . . . there is indeed continuity with Old Testament tradition . . . Continuity, however, implies development, and therefore change. The manner in which apocalyptic developed Israelite traditions is closely paralleled by developments in other traditions in the Hellenistic Near East. Therefore, continuity with the past, with Israelite tradition, is complemented by continuity with its contemporary environment. (Collins, 1975, 34)

389

iNdEX OF MOdERN AUThORS

Ackroyd, P. R., 200, 243
Aharoni, Y., 200, 223
Albright, W. F., 46, 79, 122
Allen, D. C., 84, 106, 108
Alt, A., 122, 149-51, 223
Anderson, B. W., 286
Ap-Thomas, D. R., 46
Auld, A. G., 200, 206
Austruc, J., 116

Barr, J., 46, 51, 364, 366
Barth, C., 286
Barthélemy, D., 46, 51
Begrich, J., 304
Beidelman, T. O., 84, 120
Berger, P. L., 250, 264-65, 268, 320, 325-26
Bergren, R. V., 250, 268, 320
Birkeland, H., 286, 295
Blau, L., 46, 52
Bleek, F., 292
Blenkinsopp. J., 250, 280
Bornkamm, H., 84
Braun, R. L., 200
Briggs, C. A., 84, 106, 120, 288
Brueggemann, W., 156, 191, 193-94, 196, 200-201, 286, 309, 320, 332
Budde, K., 125
Buss, M. J., 122, 124, 250, 277, 282-83, 364, 385-87
Buttenweiser, M., 286, 289-90

von Campenhausen, H. F., 16
Carlson, R. A., 200
Carpenter, J. E., 84, 106
Casey, P. M., 84, 90
Cassuto, U., 156, 172-73
Charles, R. H., 252
Cheyne, T. K., 84, 115, 117-18
Childs, B. S., 84, 87, 286, 307
Clark, W. M., 122
Clements, R. E., 250, 268, 281, 286, 315, 320
Clifford, R. J., 364, 382
Clines, D. J. A., 286, 292-93, 296
Colenso, J. W., 119
Collins, J. J., 320, 349, 364, 366, 373, 375, 379-80, 383, 385, 389
Coppens, J., 84, 120
Crenshaw, J. L., 122, 151-52, 250, 270, 320, 332, 337, 343, 357, 360

Cross, F. M., 46, 79, 156, 194-95, 200, 215, 217-18, 242

Davison, W. T., 293
DeVries, S. J., 84, 120
Dhorme, E., 353
Doran, R., 364, 373
Drijvers, P., 286
Driver, G. R., 364, 382
Driver, S. R., 120, 292
Duff, A., 84
Duhm, B., 255
Durham, J. I., 156, 195

Eaton, J. H., 286, 296-98, 311-13
Eichhorn, J. G., 115
Eissfeldt, O., 175-76
Engnell, I., 156, 173, 197, 250, 269, 279-80, 286, 311-12
Ewald, H., 118, 253

Farrar, F. W., 84
Ferguson, J., 364, 385
Fitzmyer, J. A., 46, 57
Flusser, D., 364, 375
Fohrer, G., 122, 152, 175-76
Frankena, R., 156, 196
Frazer, J., 125
Freedman, D. N., 200, 242
Frei, H. W., 84, 114
Fretheim, T. E., 156, 193
Furnish, V., 84, 104-5

Gammie, J. G., 364, 373
Geddes, A., 117
George, J. F. L., 119
Gerstenberger, E., 286, 302, 312, 320, 341
Ginsburg, C. D., 46
Ginsberg, H. L., 364, 373
Gordis, R., 353
Graf, K. H., 119
Grant, R. M., 84, 90-93, 97
Gray, E. M., 84, 90, 106, 108, 115-17
Gray, J., 200, 218
Grayson, A. K., 364, 377-78
Gressmann, H., 123, 181
Grønbech, V., 301
Gunkel, H., 121-49, 152-54, 180-81, 184, 191, 250, 254-60, 272-77, 286-305, 311

Hadas, M., 46, 62
Hailperin, H., 85, 98-100

Haldar, A., 267
Hamann, J. G., 125
Hanson, P. D., 364, 385, 387-88
Harford, G., 84, 106
Hegel, G. W. F., 170
Hengel, M., 320, 336
Herder, J. G., 125
Heschel, A., 250, 272
Holladay, J. S., Jr., 250, 272
Hölscher, G., 255
Huffmon, H. B., 249, 260-61, 263-64
Humphreys, W. L., 364, 373
Hupfeld, H., 118, 292

Ilgen, K. D., 117

Japhet, S., 200, 243-44
Jellicoe, S., 46, 62-65
Jenks, A. W., 156, 193
Johnson, A. R., 122, 141, 250, 265-66, 286, 296-98, 302-3, 312-13

Kahle, P., 63
Kaufmann, Y., 194
Kennett, R. H., 286, 290
Kennicott, B. F., 48
Kirkpatrick, A. F., 287-88
Kithcen, K. A., 156, 174
Kittel, R., 49
Klein, R. W., 46, 79, 200
Knierim, R., 122, 152
Knight, D. A., 122, 152, 279
Koch, K., 122, 250, 274, 276-77, 364-65
Köhler, L., 122, 150, 320, 331
Kovacs, B. W., 320, 334
Kraeling, E. G., 85
Kraft, R. A., 46, 67
Kraus, H.-J., 286, 304
Krentz, E., 85
Kuenen, A., 120

de Lagarde, P., 63
Lambert, W. G., 320, 342
Leiman, S. Z., 16, 20, 24, 30, 33-35, 38
Lenin, N., 124
Levine, B. A., 156, 194
Lewis, J. P., 16, 34
Lindblom, J., 250, 260, 280
Lindsell, H., 156, 169
Loewe, R., 85, 95
Lohfink, N., 200, 207
Long, B. O., 250, 281
Lowth, R., 125
Luckmann, T., 320, 325-36

390

McCarthy, D. J., 156, 195
McKane, W., 46, 320, 333, 353
McKenzie, J. L., 200
Maier, G., 156, 169
Malamat, A., 200, 228
March, W. E., 122, 250
Marx, K., 124
Mayes, A. D. H., 195, 200, 227, 229
Mettinger, T. N. D., 201, 231-32, 235
Metzger, B. M., 46, 68
Meyer, E., 181, 233
Meyer, R., 16
Michaelis, J. D., 115
Miller, J. M., 222
Momigliano, A., 16, 22
Moore, G. F., 156, 177
Moran, W. L., 250, 263
Morgenstern, J., 176
Mowinckel, S., 183, 250, 259, 265-67, 272, 286, 299-304, 312-13
Muilenburg, J., 122, 127, 251, 268
Murphy, R. E., 320

Newsome, J. D., 201, 242
Nicholson, E. W., 156, 179, 201, 214, 251, 281
Niditch, S., 364, 373
Nineham, D. E., 85
North, R., 201, 364, 387
Noth, M., 156, 181, 187-90, 193, 195, 207, 215, 219, 223, 229

Oepke, A., 16, 34
Olrik, A., 122, 131-33
Orlinsky, H. M., 16, 27, 30, 33, 46, 51, 251, 257, 261

Pedersen, J., 301
Perdue, L. G., 320
Pfeiffer, R. H., 175-76, 292
Polzin, R. M., 156, 197
Pope, M. H., 353

Preus, J. S., 85, 93, 97-98, 102
Priest, J. F., 201, 219, 320
Purvis, J. D., 16, 27, 46, 61

von Rad, G., 156, 174, 181-87, 190-91, 195-96, 201, 214-15, 218, 233, 251, 272, 320, 327, 332-33, 337, 345, 348-50, 357
Rauschenbusch, W., 124
Reimarus, H. S., 115
Rendtorff, R., 156, 180, 197
Reuss, E., 119, 125, 131, 252
Richardson, A., 85
Roberts, B. J., 46, 48, 50, 68
Robertson, D., 156, 197
Robinson, T. H., 251, 255, 278
Rogers, M. G., 201, 225
de Rossi, J. B., 48
Rowley, H. H., 251, 254, 264, 267, 321, 353, 364, 370-72
Russell, D. S., 365
Rylaardsdam, J. C., 321, 348

Sabourin, L., 286
Sanders, J. A., 16, 18-19, 26, 251, 270-72
Sandmel, S., 157, 196
Schmid, H. H., 157, 197
Schmithals, W., 365
Scott, R. B. Y, 321, 333, 337
Semler, J. S., 115
Skinner, J. A., 251, 258, 269
Smalley, B., 85, 98
Smend, R., 295
Smith, M., 201, 321, 359-60
Smith, W. R., 120, 159
Stone, M. E., 365
Sundberg, A. C., Jr., 16, 18, 34, 36-39, 43-45
Swain, J. W., 365, 375

Talmon, S., 47, 56, 58, 70, 79, 201, 321, 359
Terrien, S., 286
Thompson, J. A., 47
Thompson, R. J., 157, 168

Tigay, J. H., 157, 177
Tov, E., 47
Tucker, G. M., 122, 251, 278
Tur-Sanai, N. H., 353

Van Seters, J., 157, 194, 196-97
Vater, J. S., 117
Vatke, W., 119
Vermes, G., 16, 26, 47, 57-58, 365, 368
Vink, G., 157, 194
Volz, P., 265

Wacholder, B. Z., 16, 23
Wagner, N. E., 157, 196
Weber, M., 251, 262
de Wette, W. M. L., 117, 160
Weil, G. E., 47, 54
Weinfeld, M., 157, 179, 201, 207, 321, 358
Weippert, M., 201, 219
Weiser, A., 303-4, 315
Wellhausen, J., 120, 125, 129, 131, 157, 159-68, 170, 178, 189, 191, 204, 206, 242, 252-54, 264, 273
Westermann, C., 251, 274-77, 283, 286, 292, 305
Whybray, R. N., 201, 232, 321, 331, 353, 358-59
Wilcoxen, J. A., 122, 130
Williamson, H. G. M., 201, 242-44
Williams, J. G., 251, 268
Williams, R. J., 321, 342, 353
Willis, J. T., 320
Winnett, F. V., 157, 196
Witter, H. B., 116
Wolff, H. W., 156, 191, 193-94, 196, 201, 215
Wundt, W., 255
Würthwein, E., 47

Young, E. J., 156, 170-72
Zeitlin, S., 16, 30-32
Zimmerli, W., 251-52, 321

iNDEX OF SUBJECTS

Admonitions, 340
Akiba, 33
Allegorical Interpretation, 92-93
Allegory, 155, 342-43
Amen-em-opet, 353
Amphictyony, 190-91, 195, 223, 229
Apelles, 90
Apocrypha, 42-44

Aquila, 65
Aristeas, 61-63
Aristobulus, 89, 92
Asylum, 223
Athanasius, 38-39
Augustine, 39-41, 62, 94
Autobiographical Sayings, 155, 343-44

Bacon, Francis, 105-6

Bodenstein, Andreas, 42

Cassian, John, 93
Celsus, 89, 91
Chronology, 24-25
le Clerc, Jean, 107, 112
Codexes,
  Greek,37
  Hebrew, 49, 245
Council of Carthage, 41

iNDEX OF bibLicAL pAssAGES